ASPECTS OF THE BELFAST AGREEMENT

Aspects of the Belfast Agreement

Edited by

RICK WILFORD

OXFORD
UNIVERSITY PRESS

OXFORD

UNIVERSITY PRESS

Great Clarendon Street, Oxford OX2 6DP

Oxford University Press is a department of the University of Oxford.
It furthers the University's objective of excellence in research, scholarship,
and education by publishing worldwide in

Oxford New York

Athens Auckland Bangkok Bogotá Buenos Aires Calcutta
Cape Town Chennai Dar es Salaam Delhi Florence Hong Kong Istanbul
Karachi Kuala Lumpur Madrid Melbourne Mexico City Mumbai
Nairobi Paris São Paulo Shanghai Singapore Taipei Tokyo Toronto Warsaw

and associated companies in Berlin Ibadan

Oxford is a registered trade mark of Oxford University Press
in the UK and in certain other countries

Published in the United States
by Oxford University Press Inc., New York

British Library Cataloguing in Publication Data

Data available

Library of Congress Cataloging in Publication Data

Data available

ISBN 0–19–924262–3 (hbk)
ISBN 0–19–924404–9 (pbk)

1 3 5 7 9 10 8 6 4 2

Typeset by Hope Services (Abingdon) Ltd.
Printed in Great Britain
on acid-free paper by
Biddles Ltd
Guildford and King's Lynn

Preface

On 10 April 1998 the lengthy pursuit of a political settlement for Northern Ireland seemed to have been concluded when eight political parties and the UK and Irish governments signed up to the Belfast Agreement. After almost two years of fitful negotiations orchestrated by former US Senator George Mitchell, the demanding schedule of the final week of the talks yielded an intricate political bargain that encompassed something for (almost) everyone. Its subsequent endorsement by the electorates, north and south, at the referendums of 22 May and the substantial pro-Agreement majority which emerged from the Assembly elections in Northern Ireland a month later, suggested that—unlike in 1974— the bargain could and would stick. However, the existence of an electorally strong anti-Agreement unionist bloc within the new Assembly cautioned against complacency, as did the determination of republican dissidents committed to the prosecution of the 'long-war': a commitment enacted with terrible force in Omagh on 15 August 1998.

The considerable difficulties involved in negotiating the Agreement were equalled by those encountered during the process of its implementation. The particular problem of achieving a start to the decommissioning of paramilitary weapons caused a delay of more than eighteen months in restoring devolved institutions to Northern Ireland and was the operative cause of the return to direct rule in February 2000. The suspension of devolution, the least worst option in the view of the British Government, thereby breached the promise of Good Friday 1998.

While the future remains uncertain, notwithstanding the restoration of devolution at midnight on 29 May 2000, this edited collection reflects on aspects of both the design of the Belfast Agreement and its implementation. Its provenance was a round-table discussion held at the 1998 conference of the Irish Political Studies Association held in Newry, Co. Armagh. The four panel members, Arthur Aughey, John Coakley, Anthony McIntyre, and Henry Patterson, led a lively debate on various aspects of the Agreement and I would like to thank them for inspiring the project and, together with the other contributors, for their commitment to its fruition.

Editing a volume such as this requires a great deal of give and take—not quite to the extent of the suppleness displayed by the parties to the Agreement perhaps, but nevertheless I am extremely grateful for the patience displayed by the authors. I would also like to thank Ruth Dilly at Queen's for her technical help in preparing the manuscript. Dominic Byatt at OUP also deserves my thanks for displaying George Mitchell-like fortitude in awaiting the text. Finally, I would like to acknowledge the support of my wife, Chris, and our sons, Huw and Mael, for putting up with an all too often absent husband and father.

RW

Contents

List of Tables

Abbreviations

AIA   Anglo-Irish Agreement (1985)
ANIA   Americans for a New Irish Agenda
APNI   Alliance Party of Northern Ireland
BIC   British-Irish Council
BIIC   British-Irish Intergovernmental Conference
DFM   Deputy First Minister
DUP   Democratic Unionist Party
ECHR   European Convention on Human Rights
FM   First Minister
IICD   Independent International Commission on Decommissioning
INC   Irish National Caucus
IRA   Irish Republican Army
JMC   Joint Ministerial Committee
LVF   Loyalist Volunteer Force
MLA   Member of the Legislative Assembly
NILP   Northern Ireland Labour Party
NIO   Northern Ireland Office
NIWC   Northern Ireland Women's Coalition
NSMC   North-South Ministerial Council
PR   Proportional Representation
PUP   Progressive Unionist Party
RUC   Royal Ulster Constabulary
SDLP   Social Democratic and Labour Party
SF   Sinn Féin
STV   Single Transferable Vote
UDA   Ulster Defence Association
UDR   Ulster Defence Regiment
UDP   Ulster Democratic Party
UKUP   United Kingdom Unionist Party
UUC   Ulster Unionist Council
UUP   Ulster Unionist Party
UUUC   United Ulster Unionist Council
UVF   Ulster Volunteer Force
UWC   Ulster Workers Council

Notes on Contributors

ARTHUR AUGHEY, *University of Ulster*
Arthur Aughey is Senior Lecturer in Politics at the University of Ulster. He is the author of *Under Siege: Ulster Unionism and the Anglo-Irish Agreement* (1989) and co-editor of *Northern Ireland Politics* (1996).

JOHN COAKLEY, *University College Dublin*
John Coakley is Lecturer in Politics at University College, Dublin and Director of its Institute for British-Irish Studies. He edited *The Social Origins of Nationalist Movements* (1992) and is co-author of *The Rise of the Irish Presidency* (2000).

ADRIAN GUELKE, *Queen's University, Belfast*
Adrian Guelke is Professor of Comparative Politics at Queen's University. He is the author of *Northern Ireland: The International Perspective* (1988), *The Age of Terrorism and the International System* (1995), and editor of *New Perspectives on the Northern Ireland Conflict* (1994).

BRIGID HADFIELD, *University of Essex*
Brigid Hadfield is Professor of Law at the University of Essex and was formerly Professor of Public Law at Queen's University. An expert on constitutional law, her more recent publications include 'The Belfast Agreement: Sovereignty and the State of the Union', *Public Law* (1998) and 'The Nature of Devolution in Scotland and Northern Ireland: Key Issues of Responsibility and Control', *Edinburgh Law Review* (1999).

ANTHONY McINTYRE
Anthony McIntyre is a former IRA volunteer and former republican prisoner. He completed his doctoral thesis, a study of Irish republicanism between 1969 and 1973, at Queen's University in 1999. Currently he is co-editor of *Fourthwrite*, the journal of the Irish Republican Writers Group and chairperson of the Monaghan-based Ex-Prisoners Assistance Committee.

PAUL MITCHELL, *London School of Economics and Political Science*
Paul Mitchell is Lecturer in Politics at the LSE. He is the co-editor of both *How Ireland Voted 1997* (1999) and *Politics in Northern Ireland* (1999), and is co-editor of the journal *Irish Political Studies*.

BRENDAN O'LEARY, *London School of Economics and Political Science*
Brendan O'Leary is Professor of Political Science and current Head of the

Department of Government at the LSE. He is the author, co-author and editor of twelve books including (with John McGarry), *The Future of Northern Ireland* (1990), *Explaining Northern Ireland: Broken Images* (1995), and *The Politics of Antagonism: Understanding Northern Ireland* (1996 2nd edn).

HENRY PATTERSON, *University of Ulster*
Henry Patterson is Professor of Politics at the University of Ulster. He is the author of *The Politics of Illusion* (1989) and co-author of *Northern Ireland 1921–1996: Political Forces and Social Classes* (1996).

CLIVE WALKER, *University of Leeds*
Clive Walker is Professor of the Faculty of Law and Director of the Centre for Criminal Justice Studies, University of Leeds. He is the author of *Political Violence and the Law in Ireland* (1989), *The Prevention of Terrorism in British Law* (1992, 2nd edn), and *Miscarriages of Justice* (1999).

GRAHAM WALKER, *Queen's University of Belfast*
Graham Walker is Reader in Politics at Queen's University Belfast. He is the author of *Intimate Strangers: Political and Cultural Interaction between Scotland and Ulster in Modern Times* (1995) and co-editor of *Unionism in Modern Ireland* (1996).

RICK WILFORD, *Queen's University of Belfast*
Rick Wilford is Reader in Politics at Queen's University. He is the co-editor of both *Politics in Northern Ireland* (1999) and *Contesting Politics: Women in Ireland, North and South* (1999).

STEFAN WOLFF, *University of Bath*
Stefan Wolff is Lecturer in European Studies at the University of Bath. He is the editor of two forthcoming volumes, *German Minorities in Europe* forthcoming and *The Integration of Ethnic Germans in the Federal Republic of Germany* forthcoming.

Aspects of the Belfast Agreement

INTRODUCTION

RICK WILFORD

On 30 November 1999, in moving the Order to devolve powers to Northern Ireland, Peter Mandelson remarked: 'After a quarter of a century the curtain is finally coming down on Direct Rule'.[1] It was a suitably theatrical phrase for a moment of constitutional drama, both within and beyond Parliament, yet subsequent events were to rob it of prophetic value. Three days earlier, the Ulster Unionist Council (UUC) had endorsed the decision of the Ulster Unionist Party (UUP) leader, David Trimble, to 'jump first' by participating in the creation of the power-sharing Executive—on the understanding that the process of decommissioning paramilitary weapons by the Irish Republican Army (IRA) would begin at the end of January 2000. This understanding, involving a reversal of the 'no guns, no government' policy earlier adopted by the UUP, was based on the perception among the party's leadership of the outcome of the Mitchell review that was concluded in mid-November. However, the UUP's new stance was not unconditional. To gain the support of the Council, Trimble deemed it necessary to lodge a post-dated resignation letter with its President, Josias Cunningham, which would take effect in the event of the failure by the IRA to begin decommissioning.

There was considerable uncertainty about the date that the resignation of David Trimble and his three prospective ministerial colleagues might be 'triggered': 31 January 2000, when John de Chastelain, the chair of the Independent International Commission on Decommissioning (IICD), was due to publish his first progress report; or 12 February 2000, when the UUC was to reconvene to review progress on decommissioning. In the event, Trimble's yellowing letter remained unopened in Cunningham's pocket, stayed by Mandelson's decision to suspend devolution on 11 February 2000. The exact circumstances surrounding the Secretary of State's decision remain uncertain, and contested, especially when he was aware of the tone and content of the second report from the IICD concerning the IRA's attitude towards decommissioning.[2] Amid spin, counter-spin, and a volley of mutual recriminations, the curtain on direct rule was again raised. To mix metaphors, after just 72 days devolution was placed in cool storage. By way of its response, the IRA withdrew its interlocutor to the IICD.

Following intense Anglo-Irish efforts to resolve the impasse, the likelihood that devolution would be restored was increased following an IRA statement on 6 May 2000. The statement committed the IRA leadership to the initiation of 'a process that will completely and verifiably put IRA arms beyond use' via renewed contact with the IICD in order to agree the modalities of what the IRA termed 'a confidence building measure to confirm that our weapons remain secure'. Although this measure did not entail a public display of decommissioning, but rather the inspection of an unspecified number of arms dumps by two agreed inspectors—the former Finnish President, Martii Ahtisaari and Cyril Ramaphosa, the former general secretary of the African National Congress—the IRA's initiative created sufficient space to enable David Trimble to secure the endorsement of a small majority of the UUC (53 per cent) on 27 May 2000 backing his recommendation that the UUP should re-enter devolved government.

The restoration of devolution on 29 May 2000 meant that any hastily penned obituaries of the Belfast Agreement had to be shelved. This edited collection was not, however, intended as an epitaph to the Agreement. Instead, the inspection of the motives of its framers; the discussion of its consociational design; an assessment of its effects on the electorates, north and south; its legislative implementation; and the outworking of a number of its features were, and remain, the major purposes of this book.

While the precise origins of the Agreement are the subject of some controversy, the source of this collection is undisputed. In the late autumn of 1998 I chaired a panel discussion of the Agreement at the annual conference of the Irish Political Studies Association. The presentations by the panel members—Arthur Aughey, John Coakley, Anthony McIntyre, and Henry Patterson—generated a wide-ranging discussion that sparked both light and not a little heat: thus, the idea for a book was spawned. The panel members were invited to develop their respective papers: Aughey on Trimble's pragmatism; Coakley on differing and competing interpretations of the Agreement among both Ireland's political élites and its electorate; McIntyre on the strains of evolving a revised republican project; and Patterson on the policy continuities between the Major and Blair administrations. In addition, a number of experts were asked to contribute chapters on various facets of the Agreement.

Its constitutional import is the text of Brigid Hadfield's contribution. It focuses upon the legislative implementation of the Agreement within the context of what she terms 'cross-cutting constitutionalism' and the evolution of multilayered democracy within the UK, while Brendan O'Leary and Steffan Wolff each reflect on aspects of the Agreement's design. In O'Leary's case, its novel 'consociational plus' character, and in Wolff's, a comparison with the 1973 Sunningdale Agreement. The 'internal' influences on the Agreement—the chapters by Aughey, Patterson, and McIntyre—are complemented by Adrian

Guelke's discussion of the roles performed by international actors, notably the Clinton Administration in the US, and the new regime in South Africa, and John Coakley's chapter which includes a discussion of the evolving stance—tergiversations, perhaps—of successive Irish governments towards 'the north' and the conflicting perceptions of the Agreement within the Irish electorate. The widespread support for the Agreement expressed at both the May 1998 referendum and the subsequent Assembly election a month later, raised the possibility that a new, cross-cutting political cleavage was emerging in Northern Ireland, one turning on a pro- and anti-Agreement axis. This prospect provides the basis for Paul Mitchell's chapter, analysing the outcomes of the election. Clive Walker addresses one of the most controversial aspects of the Agreement, the reform of the Royal Ulster Constabulary (RUC), in discussing the report of the Patten Commission, reactions to it and the response by the British Government announced in January 2000. Two institutional aspects of the Agreement are also documented, one from Strand One the other from Strand Three. The latter, the British-Irish Council, is discussed by Graham Walker, and the former, the Assembly/Executive interface, by the editor.

The conference took place within an uncertain context. The Assembly had been elected on 25 June 1988, but was still in its shadow, or as one panel member memorably described it, 'shadowy', phase. Inter-party effectively, UUP/Social Democratic and Labour party (SDLP) agreement on the reconfiguration of government departments, and hence the shape and size of the nascent Executive Committee, had not yet been reached. Prisoners were being released on licence, the Commissions on the RUC and the criminal justice system had been established, moves to create the Equality and Human Rights Commissions were underway, but there was no detectable movement on decommissioning. Against this background, for many unionists the implementation of the Agreement had a lopsided character, one not entirely balanced by the prospect of the amendments to Articles 2 and 3 of the Irish Constitution and the acceptance of the consent principle on both sides of the border. Indeed, one of the issues that bulked large at the panel discussion was the motive of the Ulster Unionists in signing up to the Agreement, another the reasons for its endorsement by Sinn Féin, questions that are addressed here by, respectively, Arthur Aughey and Anthony McIntyre.

Variable Geometry

In exploring the principles that underlie the Agreement it is difficult to avoid the conclusion that the 'inertia' of consociationalism had prevailed among its signatories. It is certainly the case that the defining features of the consociational model first elaborated in the Sunningdale Agreement of 1973, are apparent in the new Agreement—see Wolff, in Chapter 2 of this volume. Yet, while recourse to the model is necessary, it is not sufficient to capture the complexity of the Agreement, not least because of its confederal character (see O'Leary, in Chapter 4 of this volume).

To understand the Agreement involves exploring its provenance. One path to enlightenment is to perceive British policy since the imposition of direct rule in 1972 as an exercise in variable geometry. There have been two constant elements in the design of policy, the more obvious of which has been a commitment by successive British *governments*[3] to devolve power to Northern Ireland. The other has been the *ideé fixe* of consociationalism, a kind of off-the-peg model of how divided societies are to be governed, derived from the earlier work of Arend Lijphart.[4] The third element has been rather more mutable, although since the Anglo-Irish Agreement (AIA) of 1985 it has become a cornerstone of the design, namely, the 'Irish dimension'. The AIA was not simply a means of governing Northern Ireland on something akin to a bilateral basis—albeit that Dublin's role was, to borrow Garrett Fitzgerald's phrase, less than executive but more than consultative—it also constrained unionism to accept that the Republic's involvement in the province's affairs was a *sine qua non* of any grand political design, a prospect that unreconstructed loyalists and more die-hard unionists continue to refuse to countenance. Thus, although the Irish dimension did wax and wane, and wax again, between 1972 and 1985, it is an essential part of the 1998 Agreement, albeit in a less muscular form than was expressed in the *Framework Documents* of 1995[5]—and certainly in a less developed and free-standing mode than that preferred by Sinn Féin.

These, then, are the three planes of policy geometry that have converged in the Belfast Agreement.[6] Its consociational plane, whether regarded as contrived or imaginative, describes the politics of accommodation. Its four key characteristics—cross-community power sharing, the proportionality 'rule', segmental autonomy, and the mutual veto—are each designed to effect stable democratic government within a divided society where majority rule is untenable. Each of these features of the model is present in the Agreement, although majoritarianism is provided for in relation to non-'key' decisions within the Assembly, both as a plenary body and also through its statutory committees—see Wilford, in Chapter 6 of this volume.

Lijphart did not intend that consociations were to be ends in themselves, rather that they could provide a means of moving towards a more 'normal' mode of competitive politics in the medium to longer term. In the shorter-run, a heavy premium is placed on mutual trust and confidence, initially among the relevant élites, which, *ceteris paribus*, descend to envelop contending communities. In this respect one may, perhaps, depict consociationalism as 'trickle-down politics'. This begs at least one very large question: whether political leaders can necessarily deliver their followers, as Brian Faulkner and pro-Sunningdale unionists discovered to their cost in 1974—and both David Trimble and Gerry Adams have found since Good Friday 1998.

The 1973 Sunningdale Agreement was the first attempt by a British government to restore devolution to Northern Ireland, see Wolff, Chapter 2 in this volume, and, at first sight, it would seem to have much in common with the Belfast Agreement, including a commitment to power-sharing. Yet, there are several aspects of the 1998 Agreement that distinguish it from its predecessor. Besides the massively changed *context* created by the IRA's, albeit interrupted, 'complete cessation of military operations' and the subsequent cease-fire by loyalist paramilitaries: its political inclusiveness, the mandatory provision for north–south institutions—Brian Faulkner dismissed the Council of Ireland, which proved to be potentially negotiable, as 'necessary nonsense'—and the 'British-Irish Council', underscored its novelty. In addition, the commitment to an equality culture, a new regime of human rights, reform of both the RUC and the criminal justice system, together with the accelerated prisoner release scheme, each contributed to the singularity of the Agreement. Its endorsement on both sides of the border via a referendum also invested it with the resource of popular support that had never existed for the Sunningdale package. Moreover, the referendum in the Republic of Ireland on 22 May 1998 legitimized the proposed changes to Articles 2 and 3 of the Irish Constitution—see Coakley, in Chapter 12 of this volume—replacing the formal claim to the 'six counties' with an aspiration to unite the people of Ireland. This constitutional change, dislodging the irredentist prop that had helped to bolster the 'long war', was one that the Irish Government had refused to implement in 1973.

If one was to conjure up the irreconcilable goals of undiluted unionism and atavistic republicanism, the fact that there was an Agreement in 1998 implies, correctly, that much was ceded by each party. In particular, Sinn Féin's position was altered significantly during the talks process. It began by opposing a local, effectively partitionist, Assembly, the proposition that north–south bodies would be accountable to such an Assembly, and any change to the Irish Constitution that involved removing the formal territorial claim to the north. However, it relinquished each of these negotiating planks during the talks. In turn, a majority of Ulster Unionists accepted the principle of power-sharing with reconstructed, that is, decommissioned, republicans, the integral nature of institutionalized cross-border bodies with executive powers, the review of the RUC—although not all aspects of its outcome—an accelerated prisoner-release scheme, and the contingency of Northern Ireland's place within the UK—the principle of consent having become the constitutional imperative on each side of the border. Of course, to paint Trimble's leadership of the UUP with an undiluted orange brush, or Adams's leadership of Sinn Féin with one steeped in darkest green, would be to miss an essential point. Each demonstrated a capacity for intelligent and flexible leadership, couched in Trimble's case in somewhat pragmatic terms—what Aughey defines as the 'Tancredi option'—and finessed by Adams as a transitional stage in the republican project.

A Difficult Birth

Looking back to the run-up to 10 April 1998, a birthing metaphor seems an apt way of characterizing the delivery of the Agreement, not least because the subsequent delay in its implementation and the later suspension suggests that its arrival may have been premature.

First, and seemingly at odds with the last remark, the Agreement had a lengthy gestation period. If one, rather misleadingly, regards the election of the Northern Ireland Forum in April 1996 as the moment of conception, it was almost two years to the day. According to Seamus Mallon, Deputy Leader of the SDLP and subsequently Deputy First Minister, the Agreement had a longer lineage: 'Sunningdale for slow learners' was his rather wry interpretation of it. But this remark is as misleading as it is diverting, since the Agreement is a much more subtle and inclusive bargain than was reached at Sunningdale—see Wolff, in Chapter 2, and O'Leary, in Chapter 4 of this volume.

Secondly, on several occasions between the Forum election and 10 April 1998, the talks process threatened to miscarry. The chronic Orange Order parade saga at Drumcree, the two temporary exclusions of Sinn Féin and one of the Ulster Democratic Party—the political wing of the largest loyalist paramilitary organization, the Ulster Defence Association (UDA)—the withdrawal of the Democratic Unionist Party (DUP) and the UK Unionists from the process, all threatened to bring the talks to an early demise.

Thirdly, there was the possibility of a false alarm. The initial deadline of midnight 9 April 1998 set by talks Chairman, George Mitchell, passed without issue. Following a further period of arduous labour, shortly before 5pm on the following day a majority of the UUP's negotiating team eventually agreed to the proposals, thereby allaying the risk of a phantom pregnancy or, even worse, a stillbirth.

Fourthly, while safely delivered on Good Friday, there remained a risk of neo-natal mortality, in part because Sinn Féin reserved its position until its wider membership was consulted *via* two specially convened conferences. The second hazard stemmed from within the ranks of the UUP where disaffection with the Agreement grew quickly as several members of their talks team disclaimed parentage. Any threat that the republican movement would orphan the Agreement was averted when the delegates to the second of Sinn Féin's conferences voted overwhelmingly in its favour. However, division with the UUP continued to threaten its well-being. While David Trimble carried a majority of both the party's Executive and Council in favour of the deal prior to the referendum, five of its ten MPs openly opposed the Agreement, while a sixth, Jeffrey Donaldson, maintained a studied silence even though his walkout from the talks late in the afternoon of Good Friday signalled his opposition to its terms—he was to vote against it at the ensuing referendum. The disaffected Ulster

Unionists joined ranks with other members of the unionist 'family' urging voters to reject what they regarded as the misbegotten offspring at the referendum on 22 May 1998.

By July 1999 and despite a mixture of support, encouragement and inducement from London and Dublin and Washington, the infant Agreement failed to take its first faltering steps towards devolution, stumbling over the issue of the decommissioning of paramilitary weapons and occasioning the temporary 'resignation' of Seamus Mallon as Deputy First Minister Designate. The UUP's refusal to participate in the formation of the shadow Executive on 15 July meant that the Agreement suffered a relapse. Thereafter it was placed in an incubator, pending the diagnostic review led by George Mitchell that began on 6 September 1999.

The review, which stretched until 18 November 1999, involved inter-party meetings in Belfast and London, and entailed much shuttle diplomacy by Mitchell. It was based upon the three principles agreed by the parties on 25 June 1999 during negotiations hosted by Tony Blair and Bertie Ahern designed to meet the British Prime Minister's 'absolute deadline' of 30 June 1999. While the deadline—chosen to enable devolution to Northern Ireland to coincide with devolution to Scotland and Wales on the following day—was breached, the principles to which the pro-Agreement parties had committed themselves survived. Namely, an inclusive executive exercising devolved powers, the decommissioning of all paramilitary arms by 22 May 2000, and decommissioning to be carried out in a manner determined by the IICD.

George Mitchell choreographed the steps by which the principles would be realized. That devolution should take effect, the Executive should meet and the paramilitary groups should appoint their representatives to the IICD 'all on the same day, and in that order'.[7] With Trimble's successful negotiation of the UUC meeting on 27 November 1999 and the parliamentary endorsement of the Order three days later, 'devolution-day' became 2 December 1999, though the nomination of the shadow Executive and the chairs and deputy chairs of the Assembly's statutory committees had already taken place on 29 November. The fully empowered Executive met on the morning of the 2 December 1999 minus its two DUP Ministers, and the IRA confirmed its appointment of an interlocutor later that day. The speed with which the institutions of each of the three Strands were established was impressive, buoyed by a not unqualified confidence that within a matter of weeks paramilitary weapons would begin to be decommissioned. Such confidence as there was proved, however, to be misplaced and, in the circumstances, the Secretary of State felt constrained to take what he believed to be the least worst option: suspension. During the parliamentary debate of 8 February 2000 on the emergency legislation paving the way for the reimposition of direct rule, Mandelson stated the position in blunt terms: 'It is not a choice between suspension and carrying on as we are. It is a choice between pause or bust in the institutions'. In his view, the resignation of Trimble and his UUP ministerial colleagues would 'shatter irreversibly' those institutions since the 'cross-community majority would not exist for another ticket',[8] that is, of Trimble and Mallon as First and Deputy First Ministers, respectively.

Whether or not the Secretary of State's decision to suspend was avoidable, or indeed constitutional, is arguable. More immediately, the shift in the balance of view within the UUC has excited much comment about Trimble's grip on the leadership of his party. On 18 April 1998, 72 per cent of the Council (510 votes to 210) had endorsed the Agreement, creating the momentum for a small union-ist majority in its favour at the 22 May referendum. At the Assembly election of 25 June 1998, however, the Ulster Unionist Party suffered its worst ever elect-oral result and the balance of pro- and anti-Agreement unionists returned to the Assembly was finely poised—see Mitchell, in Chapter 3 of this volume. By 27 November 1999, and in the wake of the eleven-week Mitchell review, David Trimble's proposition that the UUP should enter the power-sharing Executive before decommissioning had begun, garnered the support of just 58 per cent of the UUC. Moreover, a leadership challenge by fellow MP, Martin Smyth, the party's chief whip at Westminster, maintained the pressure on the pro-Agreement bloc within the UUP. The outcome of the post-suspension vote— 57 per cent for Trimble, 43 per cent for Smyth—at the UUC's annual general meeting on 25 March 2000, while showing no haemorrhage of support from Trimble since the previous November, did confirm the deep division within the party over the question of a re-entry into the voluntary coalition prior to pal-pable evidence of decommissioning by the IRA. From a pro-Agreement per-spective, this difficult situation was further aggravated when the Council voted to remain outside devolved government unless the British government resiled from its undertaking to change the name of the RUC.

The risk involved in the UUC's endorsement of 'jumping first' into devolved government was underscored by a survey published shortly after the return of direct rule.[9] The survey—undertaken between mid-October 1999 and mid-January 2000, thereby straddling the Mitchell review and the devolution of pow-ers—reported that almost half of the population wanted to see total decommissioning before the formation of the Executive, while a further 36 per cent wanted some advance decommissioning to have occurred. It also disclosed that no one community monopolized concern over the issue: 93 per cent of Protestants wanted at least some prior decommissioning, a view shared by some 75 per cent of Catholics. Although the survey revealed a robust level of overall support for the Agreement—67 per cent of respondents said they would again vote 'Yes', compared to the 71 per cent at the referendum in May 1998— Protestants were sharply divided. If the referendum was to be re-run, 48 per cent said they would vote 'No', and 47 per cent 'Yes', with the remainder unde-cided. Thus, although the ground of Protestant opinion had appeared to shift since the referendum, there was no evidence of a mass exodus into the 'No' camp, while Catholic opinion remained solidly behind the Agreement.

The intricacy of the Agreement's interlocking architecture, including the checks and balances it supplies in both Strands One and Two, is testimony to the care with which it was crafted. Such attention to institutional detail—especially by the UUP and the SDLP who supplied most of the thinking relating to Strand One—was, however, purchased at a cost. While explicable, indeed vital, as a means of contributing to mutual trust and confidence, it did have the effect of marginalizing the discussion of substantive policy issues—that is, what the Executive Committee and the Assembly might actually *do* in terms of its programme for government. The delay in agreeing the shape and size of the Executive during the long shadow phase and the subsequent difficulties encountered in devolving power meant that relatively little effort was directed to the nascent programme. The lag involved in constructing the Executive, whose eventual composition—six unionists/loyalists and six nationalists/republicans— embodied what may be styled 'parity of ministerial esteem', coupled with the continuing impasse over decommissioning, meant that it was accorded only brief attention during the shadow period. It was not until December 1999, after the devolution of powers, that the Executive was in a position to revisit the programme, by which time it had no option other than to adopt the spending plans bequeathed by the direct rule regime for the forthcoming financial year. This in itself created a set of constraints, or at least reined-in the ambitions of ministers. Moreover, the ten weeks of devolution allowed neither the time nor the space for anything other than a hasty re-start to the process of devising a programme, itself a 'key' decision as defined by the Agreement, thus requiring unanimity within the Executive and cross-community support within the Assembly. However, the lack of movement on the programme did not mean that the potential of the Agreement to contribute to the social transformation of Northern Ireland had been forfeited. Its signatories, by endorsing the equality agenda,[10] the creation of the Human Rights Commission, sanctioning the review of the RUC and the reform of the criminal justice system, ensured that the legacy of the Agreement could prove more durable than the devolved institutions themselves. In effect, not all aspects of the Agreement would be lost if the political structures fail to take root.

The title of this collection—'Aspects of the Belfast Agreement'—is a deliberate one. While it does not supply a full survey of the Agreement's many facets, this collection does convey the subtleties and complexities of the Agreement's design, the opportunities and constraints presented by its negotiation, as well as the difficulties entailed by some features of its implementation. The collection begins with the comparison of the Sunningdale and Belfast Agreements and the analysis of the results of the 1998 Assembly elections, by Wolff and Mitchell in Chapters 2 and 3 respectively. These chapters are followed by O'Leary's more focused analysis of the Agreement in Chapter 4, its legislative implementation in Chapter 5 (Hadfield), the implementation of both the Strand One institutions in Chapter 6 (Wilford) and the British-Irish Council (BIC) in Chapter 7

(Graham Walker), as well as a critical analysis of the Patten Report in Chapter 8 (Clive Walker). The final 'section' explores the roles of key actors in the process of reaching the Agreement: Patterson on the Major and Blair governments in Chapter 9; Aughey on the UUP in Chapter 10; McIntyre on the republican movement in Chapter 11; Coakley on competing interpretations of the Agreement within the Republic of Ireland in Chapter 12; and Guelke on the international community in Chapter 13.

Those searching for an editorial 'line' will be disappointed: the collection seeks neither to convert the Agreement's critics, confirm its disciples in their beliefs nor to sway its agnostics in one direction or another. While the contributors navigate the same textual and contextual ground, they do not necessarily arrive at the same destination. Collectively, however, the authors provide analyses of the most recent and hard-crafted bargain that was designed to bring about a political settlement to Northern Ireland: though its robustness remains to be fully tested.

ENDNOTES

1. House of Commons Debates (H. C. Debs), 30 November 1999, col. 253.
2. The British government published the two IICD reports after the suspension was effected. The first due to be disclosed on 31 January 2000 was withheld by the government for 11 days because its gloomy tone was deemed to be unhelpful. For the full text of the reports see the *Irish Times*, 12 February 2000.
3. In opposition, both the Conservatives and the Labour party contemplated alternatives to devolution. In its 1979 general election manifesto, the Conservative party proposed the revitalization of local government in Northern Ireland as an alternative to devolution, while between 1981 and 1994 the Labour party adopted a policy of Irish unity by consent.
4. Lijphart, A., *The Politics of Accommodation: Pluralism and Democracy in the Netherlands*. (Berkeley/Los Angeles, CA: University of California Press, 1968); and 'Consociational Democracy', *World Politics*, 21 (1969): 207–25.
5. There were two *Framework* Documents: *A Framework for Accountable Government in Northern Ireland*, authored by the British Government, and *A New Framework for Agreement*, co-authored by the British and Irish Governments.
6. For the full text of George Mitchell's statement see the *Irish Times* 18 November 1999.
7. Wilford, R., 'Regional Assemblies and Parliament', in P. Mitchell and R. Wilford (eds.), *Politics in Northern Ireland* (Boulder, CO: Westview Press, 1998), 117–41. See also O'Leary, B., 'The British-Irish Agreement: Consociation Plus', *Scottish Affairs*, 26 (1999), 1–22.
8. H. C. Debs, 8 February 2000, cols. 134–5.
9. The *Life and Times Survey* was funded by the Economic and Social Research Council (ESRC) and involved face to face interviews with a representative sample of 2200 adults across Northern Ireland. Initial results were published in the *Belfast Telegraph* on 14 and 15 February 2000.
10. The new Equality Commission was the subject of separate legislative proposals by the British Government and was not contingent upon the implementation of the Agreement. See the White Paper, *Partnership for Equality* (1998), Cm 3890. The Agreement did suggest the creation of an Equality Department, although in the event it was not established as part of the new departmental structure announced in December 1998. See Wilford, in Chapter 6 of this volume.

2

Context and Content: Sunningdale and Belfast Compared

STEFAN WOLFF

Introduction

Since the re-escalation of the Northern Ireland conflict in the 1960s, several attempts have been made to arrive at an inclusive settlement satisfying the conflicting parties in the province as well as the Republic of Ireland and the United Kingdom. At the heart of each of these attempts has been the recognition by the majority of the parties involved in the conflict that there are at least two dimensions to any potentially successful settlement—an internal dimension providing for the more equal political participation of both communities and the protection of their identities; and an external dimension taking account of the relationship between the nationalist community in Northern Ireland and the Republic of Ireland. Since the first introduction of direct rule in 1972 only two initiatives found, at least for some time, sufficient support in both communities to lead to formal agreements and the implementation of negotiated institutional structures. These were the Sunningdale Agreement of 1973 and the Belfast Agreement of 1998.

Both are, in essence, consociational settlements with a strong cross-border dimension—see O'Leary, in Chapter 4 of this volume. However, there are also significant differences between them, both in terms of content and the circumstances surrounding their negotiation, implementation, and operation. These differences are important since they shed light on why the Sunningdale Agreement failed whereas the Belfast Agreement seemed to have a reasonable chance of success. In order to provide a structure for the analysis of these differences, I will initially outline the criteria that determine whether or not a consociational settlement with a strong cross-border dimension can provide long-term stability and peace in situations of intense intergroup conflict. This will be followed by a brief comparison of the content of the two agreements and a more detailed examination of the reasons for the failure of Sunningdale and the apparent initial success of the Belfast Agreement.

The Stability of Consociational Settlements

In the context of ethnic conflict management, consociations are ideally characterized by four features: a grand coalition between parties representing the main ethnic communities, minority veto rights, proportionality in public sector employment and expenditure, and segmental autonomy.[1] While these aspects were all present in the Sunningdale and Belfast Agreements, another had been added to take account of a specific feature of the Northern Ireland conflict. What is at stake in this conflict, to a significant extent, apart from access to resources, equal opportunities, and political participation, is the issue of *national belonging*. This manifests itself in the competing aspirations of the unionist and nationalist communities: to either maintain the constitutional links with the United Kingdom, or to sever them and establish alternative links with the Republic of Ireland. As a consequence, the Northern Ireland conflict, unlike many other ethnic conflicts, not only involves ethnic groups and the institutions of their host-state, but also the kin-state of one of the groups. In this sense, Northern Ireland has not only been a disputed territory between the two communities living there, but also between Great Britain and the Republic of Ireland.

This interstate dimension, as well as the fact that an influential Irish diaspora lives in the United States, and that both the United Kingdom and the Republic of Ireland have actively participated in the European integration process since 1973, adds a fourth dimension to the Northern Ireland conflict; namely the role of international actors—see Guelke, in Chapter 13 of this volume. The stability of any settlement reached in such a conflict will, therefore, always depend on factors that can be found on four levels: the disputed territory, the kin-state, the host-state, and the international context.[2] The individual factors that are associated with each of these levels in the context of the Northern Ireland conflict— including the policy agendas and policies of, and their perception by, each of the conflicting parties; the relationship between the two communities and the political élites representing them, and between them and the British and Irish Governments; the internal and external constraints under which all parties act; and the institutional set-up of the social and political system in Northern Ireland—supply the guidelines for the following analysis.

The Content of Sunningdale and Belfast Compared

Before analysing the breakdown of the Sunningdale Agreement and the relative, if faltering, success of the Belfast Agreement, it is necessary to give a brief overview of the content of each of the agreements. As Table 2.1 reveals, there

TABLE 2.1. *The content of the Sunningdale and Belfast Agreements compared*

	Sunningdale Agreement	Belfast Agreement
Signatories	UK, RoI, UUP, SDLP, APNI	UK, RoI, UUP, UDP, PUP, NIWC, L, APNI, SF, SDLP
Consent principle	X	X
Self-determination	O	X
Reform of the policing system	X	X
Prisoners	X	X
Bill of Rights	X	X
Abandonment of violence	X	X
Security co-operation	X	X
Cross-border co-operation	X	X
Recognition of both identities	O	X
Intergovernmental co-operation	X	X
Institutional role for the RoI	X	X
Power-sharing	(X)	X
Inter-island co-operation	O	X
Devolution of powers	X	X

Notes: X—issue addressed; (X)—issue implicitly addressed; O—issue not addressed
UK—United Kingdom of Great Britain and Northern Ireland, RoI—Republic of Ireland,
UUP—Ulster Unionist Party, UDP—Ulster Democratic Party, PUP—Progressive Unionist
Party, NIWC—Northern Ireland Women's Coalition, L—Labour, APNI—Alliance Party of
Northern Ireland, SF—Sinn Féin, SDLP—Social Democratic and Labour Party

are very few differences in relation to core issues addressed by the agreements reached in 1973 and 1998.

Despite their similarities there are also a number of significant differences, primarily related to contextual factors and procedural regulations. The latter relate to three main issues: d'Hondt-proportionality in the Executive, reflecting the relative strengths of the parties in the Assembly; complex voting procedures in the Assembly ensuring virtual veto rights for each of the two communities; and the fact that the implementation of decisions taken by the North-South Ministerial Council has been made dependent upon their approval by both the Irish Parliament and the Northern Ireland Assembly. This reflects the commitment, in particular by the British and Irish Governments, to assure the unionist community that no decision can be made without their consent. The Belfast Agreement is also distinct from the constitutional arrangements put in place in 1973 in that it does not require a formal grand coalition, although it 'created strong incentives for executive power-sharing'.[3] Moreover, the 1998 Agreement was the outcome of a more inclusive process that involved representatives of paramilitary organizations alongside the mainstream constitutional parties.

The Failure of Sunningdale and the Success of Belfast: A Contextual Analysis

A Short Background to the Sunningdale Agreement

As a result of severe intercommunal violence and the inability of the authorities in Northern Ireland to address this and the underlying problems, the British Government suspended the parliament and government in the province early in 1972. The Conservative Government elected two years earlier relied initially on a policy of economic and social reforms in Northern Ireland that it had inherited from its Labour predecessors. However, the new Government faced new challenges: the fragmentation of the unionist party system[4] and the rise to political prominence and influence of loyalist die-hards like William Craig, the founder of Vanguard, and Ian Paisley, the leader of the Democratic Unionist Party (DUP); a radicalization of sections of the nationalist community; a resurgence of IRA violence and a continuation of loyalist violence; and a worsening of relations between nationalists and the British army.

A first attempt to start an inclusive dialogue among the constitutional parties in the province failed after only three of the seven parties[5] in the Northern Irish Parliament accepted the first Secretary of State, William Whitelaw's, invitation to a three-day conference in September 1972 to discuss the future direction of constitutional reform in Northern Ireland. Despite the fact that no formal agreement was reached between Unionists, the Alliance Party, and the Northern Ireland Labour Party (NILP), Whitelaw presented a Green Paper in October 1972, entitled *The Future of Northern Ireland: A Paper for Discussion*,[6] which also included a policy paper by the Social Democratic and Labour Party (SDLP) reflecting its demands for the creation of power-sharing arrangements as an interim solution on the path to eventual Irish unification.[7] What was crucial in the Government's new approach to the situation in Northern Ireland was its acknowledgement of an 'Irish dimension' and a reaffirmation of the principle of consent in matters regarding Irish unification.[8] After a referendum had been held in Northern Ireland on the constitutional status of the province, the so-called 'border poll', which had shown a clear majority in favour of continuing links with the United Kingdom,[9] the British Government put forward its constitutional proposals in a White Paper, entitled *Northern Ireland Constitutional Proposals*. These proposals became law in the Northern Ireland Constitution Act of 1973 and detailed the legislative powers of the Assembly[10] and the competences and structure of its executive arm,[11] the funding of the new arrangements, the procedures for a Human Rights Bill, and the establishment of a Council of Ireland.

Based on an a Single Transferable Vote (Proportional Representation) (STV PR) electoral system which returned between five and seven candidates in each of the parliamentary constituencies—and on a turnout of 72.5 per cent—the elections on 28 June 1973 returned 78 representatives from eight parties to the new Assembly. The Ulster Unionists won 29.3 per cent of the vote and sent 24 members to the Assembly, followed by the SDLP with 22.1 per cent and 19 successful candidates. Together with the Alliance Party, which won 9.2 per cent of the vote and 8 seats, they formed a coalition government, the Northern Ireland Executive, initially supported by 51 members of the Assembly. Subsequently, representatives of the British and Irish Governments and of the parties involved in the designated executive met at Sunningdale and discussed and agreed the setting up of the Council of Ireland.[12] The conference also agreed on closer co-operation in security-related matters, on inviting the Council of Ireland to draft a human rights bill, and on the possibility of a future devolution of powers from Westminster to the Northern Ireland Assembly and the institutions of the Council of Ireland. As of 1 January 1974 all these new arrangements took effect.

A Short Background to the Belfast Agreement

After almost fifteen years during which the settlement of the Northern Ireland conflict, despite a variety of initiatives, was no nearer to resolution, the situation began to change for the better. In October 1988, the Ulster Unionist Party (UUP), the DUP, the Alliance Party, and the SDLP had met in Duisburg, West Germany, without, however, achieving any breakthrough. Talks had also been held between the SDLP and Sinn Féin in the first half of 1988. These developments, coupled with the public acknowledgement by the then Secretary of State for Northern Ireland, Peter Brooke, that the IRA could not be defeated militarily, that he would not rule out talks between the Government and Sinn Féin should IRA violence cease, and that the British Government had no selfish strategic or economic interests in Northern Ireland, paved the way for the Brooke/Mayhew[13] talks, involving the UUP, the DUP, the Alliance Party, and the SDLP. These talks were held between March 1991 and November 1992 during a break in the operation of the Anglo-Irish intergovernmental conference to ensure the participation of the unionist parties. With no major progress made, and a decreasing willingness to co-operate on the part of the DUP, the talks eventually collapsed when the resumption of the Maryfield secretariat[14] prompted the unionists to withdraw from the talks.

After further talks between John Hume and Gerry Adams, leaders of the SDLP and Sinn Féin respectively, had become public knowledge, they issued two joint statements, in April and September 1993—dubbed collectively as the 'Hume/Adams initiative'—outlining nationalist and republican views of the 'road to peace'. At the end of the year, following a series of meetings, the Irish Prime Minister Albert Reynolds and British Prime Minister John Major issued their *Joint Declaration*. Further confidence-building measures followed early in 1994 when the broadcast ban on Sinn Féin was lifted in the Republic of Ireland,

Gerry Adams was granted a visa to enter the USA, and the Northern Ireland Office issued a statement in which it addressed questions by Sinn Féin concerning the *Joint Declaration*. Although Sinn Féin remained critical of the Declaration, a secret meeting was held between the then Secretary of State for Northern Ireland, Patrick Mayhew, and a Sinn Féin delegation in August, which was followed by the IRA's announcement of the 'complete cessation of all military activities' on 30 August. On 13 October 1994 the Combined Loyalist Military Command announced its cease-fire. At the end of the year the British Government, represented by officials of the Northern Ireland Office, began a series of talks with those political parties affiliated to paramilitary organizations, namely with Sinn Féin on 9 December 1994, and with the Progressive Unionist Party (PUP) and the Ulster Democratic Party (UDP) on 15 December 1994. Thus, within a year of the *Joint Declaration*, cease-fires had been announced by the major paramilitary organizations that, unlike those of the past, seemed, if not permanent, at least longer term. In addition, the British Government had entered into official and formal talks with representatives of the paramilitary organizations of both communities.

The British and Irish Governments then developed *A New Framework for Agreement*, which proposed structures for north-south, that is Northern Ireland–Republic of Ireland and east-west, that is British-Irish, institutions and sought to integrate the earlier suspended three-strand talks with a new effort at peace-making.[15] The British Government also proposed its own ideas for a possible solution of the conflict within Northern Ireland in *A Framework for Accountable Government in Northern Ireland*, in which a separation of powers between legislature, executive, and judiciary was recommended to the political parties of Northern Ireland.

Despite the setback caused by the end of the first IRA cease-fire in February 1996, the British and Irish Governments announced the beginning of all-party talks, following elections in May, for June 1996. Although Sinn Féin polled a record 15.5 per cent of the vote in these elections, the party was not allowed to take its seats at the negotiating table because IRA violence continued and the party did not sign up to the Mitchell principles of non-violence.[16] The subsequent multi-party talks commenced as planned but did not bring about any significant results in their first year. The election of a Labour Government in May 1997, the emphasis Labour put on reaching a settlement in Northern Ireland, and the perception, especially among the nationalist community, that there was a new approach to Northern Ireland, opened up new possibilities. In July 1997, the IRA renewed its cease-fire. After Sinn Féin had signed up to the Mitchell Principles the party was allowed into the talks at Stormont, precipitating a walk-out by the DUP and the UK Unionist Party. After more than six months of intensive negotiations, punctuated by several setbacks, eight political parties in Northern Ireland and the British and Irish Governments reached the Belfast Agreement.

Failure and Success (I): The Conditions in Northern Ireland

The balance of power in the Assembly after the 1973 election seemed to provide a promising and strong basis in favour of the new arrangements, since those who campaigned on an anti-White Paper platform were in an overall minority, despite having secured a majority of first preference votes and seats for unionists.[17] Even before the conference at Sunningdale opposition on the unionist side started to grow. On 5 December 1973, five of the seven Westminster MPs of the Unionist Party allied themselves with Harry West, who had headed the anti-White paper campaign within the Unionist Party. This seriously weakened the stance of its then leader and Chief Executive designate, Brian Faulkner. His grip on the leadership of the party was undermined further when, on 6 December 1973—the first day of the Sunningdale Conference—six hundred representatives of constituency associations of the Unionist Party, Vanguard, the DUP, and the Orange Order joined forces in the United Ulster Unionist Council (UUUC). The UUUC perceived the Sunningdale Agreement as signalling the end of the union with Britain, in particular as there was no adequate assurance by the Irish Government recognizing Northern Ireland as part of the United Kingdom.[18] On 4 January 1974, the Ulster Unionist Council, the governing body of the Unionist party, rejected the proposed Council of Ireland by 427 votes to 374. Faulkner resigned as leader of the party, but remained in place as Chief Executive. West succeeded Faulkner as party leader on 22 January, and the paradoxical situation arose whereby the head of the Executive was opposed by a majority in his own party.

To date, David Trimble has avoided a similar fate by skilful manœuvring and has remained in control of his UUP. The Ulster Unionist Council has until now supported Trimble's course of supporting the Belfast Agreement, but the support figures have become narrower: declining to 58 per cent in the crucial vote on, 27 November 1999, on the compromise reached after the Mitchell Review of the Belfast Agreement, and holding at 57 per cent when he was challenged by Martin Smyth for the leadership of the party on 12 February 2000. At the same time the unionist community as a whole remains similarly divided over whether to support the peace process in its current form or not. Ian Paisley's Democratic Unionists are the main force of opposition, yet even they decided to nominate ministers and committee members for the Northern Ireland Executive, Paisley himself chairing the Agriculture and Rural Development Committee. Prior to devolution, it was not entirely clear whether the DUP would pursue a similar course as in 1974, setting out to 'wreck the assembly', or whether they would form some kind of constructive opposition. In the event, they took their Executive seats while at the same time they sought on three occasions to exclude their erstwhile 'partners' in the voluntary coalition, Sinn Féin from the Assembly—see Wilford, in Chapter 6 of this volume. More important, however, is the fact that the political representatives of loyalist paramilitaries, the PUP, which has two members in the Assembly, and, 'off-stage', the UDP have thus far supported the peace process and distanced themselves from the opponents to the Belfast Agreement. With the 'others'—the Alliance Party and the Women's Coalition, also in support of the Agreement and capable of redesignating themselves as 'unionists' within the Assembly—the political basis for its opponents is far narrower than it was in 1974.

A further aspect of the situation in Northern Ireland that proved to be one of the causes for the failure of Sunningdale was the continuation of IRA violence throughout the brief existence of the power-sharing executive in 1974.[19] In combination with the absence of the hoped-for co-operation of the Irish Government in security matters, the rising death toll diminished the chances of unionists being persuaded by the usefulness of the Sunningdale arrangements—especially since the price they were supposed to pay for an improved security situation was the 'Irish dimension'. Yet, violence did not only originate from republican paramilitary groups but also from their loyalist counterparts. The perceptions and fears among the radical sections in each community found deadly expression in the two major violent incidents of the period during which the Sunningdale Agreement was operated. On 4 February 1974, nine soldiers and three civilians were killed in an IRA bomb attack on a British army coach on the M62 motorway in Yorkshire. On 17 May 1974, thirty-three civilians were killed in car bomb explosions carried out by loyalist paramilitaries in Dublin and Monaghan. The escalation of violence also had a further effect on the prospects for success of the Sunningdale Agreement. The mutual infliction of pain legitimized the radicals in each community, thus further diminishing the ground on which moderates could seek and reach agreement.

By the time the Belfast Agreement was negotiated the situation had fundamentally changed. While the goal of a united Ireland is undiminished among nationalists and republicans, and though unionists and loyalists remain attached to the union with Great Britain, this discord no longer manifests itself in violence to the same degree as it did in 1974. Since the beginning of the final round of the negotiation process in the autumn of 1997, all the major paramilitary organizations have upheld their cessations of military activities. This has created a climate of relative calm and peace, enabling the major parties to the conflict to arrive at an agreement.[20] The apparent sincerity with which the accommodation has been reached has also manifested itself in the constructive participation of political parties representing paramilitaries on either side of the sectarian divide, signalled by their endorsement of the Mitchell Principles of non-violence.[21]

For the unionist community, the primary focal point of opposition to the Sunningdale Agreement was its Irish dimension, that is, the Council of Ireland and the competences that it had been assigned in the agreement. However, the nationalist community also became increasingly disaffected with the Sunningdale process, the more it became clear that some of its concerns were not sufficiently well addressed, especially in the area of social and economic policies.

Although the Northern Ireland Executive had published a policy paper on these issues, entitled *Steps to a Better Tomorrow*, in January 1974, there was neither the time nor the political willingness to implement policies aimed at an improvement of the situation of the minority community.

It was all the more important in these circumstances for nationalists, and for the SDLP as their political representative, to preserve those parts of the Sunningdale Agreement that they considered to be in their favour. This brought the SDLP into opposition with those unionist parties which, although in favour of the power-sharing arrangements in Northern Ireland, argued against the ratification of the Sunningdale Agreement as long as the Republic of Ireland continued to uphold its claims to the whole of the island in Articles 2 and 3 of the Irish Constitution. Such a 'watering down' of the agreement, however, was unacceptable to the SDLP, especially as the all-Ireland institutions, in the words of one leading SDLP member, would 'produce the dynamic that could lead ultimately to an agreed single State for Ireland.'[22]

This rift between the two main parties supporting power-sharing also sheds light on the difficulties each faced within their own communities and even within their parties. After Faulkner had lost the support of the Unionist Party, he also began to face opposition to his course of action from among the unionists within his governing coalition after the Ulster Workers Council (UWC) had called for a general strike.[23] Roy Bradford, Minister of the Environment in the Executive, openly defied Faulkner, Merlyn Rees, the then Secretary of State for Northern Ireland, and British Prime Minister Harold Wilson, by publicly arguing for negotiations with the strike leaders.[24] Within the SDLP, its leader Gerry Fitt faced different problems. Not only was there the dilemma of the continuation of internment, but there was also the issue of the rent and rates strike. Instrumental in starting it, the SDLP was determined to end the strike now it had joined the Executive.

These intra-party problems increased the opportunities for radical elements within each community to outflank the moderates, thus crucially undercutting their support. In the case of the unionists, this became evident in the Westminster elections called for 28 February 1974 which were seized upon by the UUUC and turned into a referendum on the new constitutional status of Northern Ireland. Opponents of any change in the *status quo* won 51 per cent of the vote and eleven of the twelve parliamentary seats in Northern Ireland, the remaining seat going to the SDLP. This was so obvious a difference compared to the results of the Assembly election less than a year earlier that the UUUC interpreted the outcome as a popular mandate to continue and stiffen its opposition.

Whereas the 1973 arrangements were implemented by government decree, electorates endorsed the Belfast Agreement in both the Republic of Ireland and Northern Ireland via referendum, thus giving the people a sense of 'ownership' over the outcome. The wave of support for the Belfast Agreement in both

jurisdictions, and within the communities in Northern Ireland, was unprecedented. Already in 1996, a survey on the attitudes of relevant publics in Northern
Ireland towards negotiations and negotiated settlements concluded that, if a settlement based on the 1995 framework documents was to work, unionists would
have to be persuaded that such an agreement would offer 'them the best long-
term insurance they can get' and that there would be no better alternative.[25] It
seemed that among a small majority of unionists such a consensus existed, but
it was up to the Executive and the Assembly elected in June 1998 to deliver in
order to maintain and increase this majority. The same survey concluded that
nationalists should not be told, nor maintain, 'that they have established all the
necessary stepping stones to achieving a unified Ireland within a decade.' The
extent to which this latter condition has been achieved is more difficult to assess.
While the SDLP's leader, John Hume, has on several occasions expressed his
unqualified satisfaction with the structures of the Belfast Agreement,[26] Sinn
Féin President Gerry Adams has made it equally clear that his party's 'goal
remains the establishment of a united free and independent Ireland. We believe
the Good Friday Agreement is the transitional structure that will allow us to
achieve that legitimate objective.'[27]

However, what distinguishes the situation from that 25 years ago is the fact
that there is a more realistic view among leading republicans who acknowledge
that the Belfast Agreement is a necessary prerequisite for the goal of Irish unification—*cf* McIntyre, in Chapter 11 of this volume. While this entails support
for the implementation process, their interpretation of the Agreement as a mere
stage on the road towards a united Ireland bears the seeds of conflict with the
SDLP as well as with the pro-Agreement unionist parties. The republican project also complicates the relationship between the SDLP and pro-Agreement
unionists. The situation may well arise in which the SDLP has to ethnically out-
bid Sinn Féin at subsequent elections, especially if the new constitutional
arrangements do not deliver quickly and visibly enough the benefits expected by
either community. This would, as in 1974, do little to help encourage compromise over the more fundamental divide between the two communities over the
issue of national belonging.

Failure and Success (II): The Role of Great Britain and the Republic of Ireland

Although the elections to the Northern Ireland Assembly in 1973 seemed to be a
clear vote in favour of the new constitutional arrangements, the reality of the situation in the province betrayed this superficial impression. While the co-operating
élites had a secure two-thirds majority *in* the Assembly, their influence and control over their (former) electorate was far less permanent and stable; this was evidently the case of pro-Sunningdale unionists and the binational Alliance Party.[28]
Apart from this lack of popular support for the settlement, there was also an essen-

tial lack of institutional support and a failure of politicians in London and in Dublin to counteract the increasingly ominous threats to the survival of Sunningdale. In order to work, the constitutional arrangements envisaged for Northern Ireland would have required substantial support from London and from Dublin for the parties forming the Northern Ireland Executive who were vulnerable to pressures from within their own communities. That this support for pro-agreement politicians was not forthcoming was one of the major reasons for the failure of this early attempt to resolve the Northern Ireland conflict.

When a motion against power-sharing and the Council of Ireland was defeated in the Assembly by 44 to 28 votes on 14 May 1974, the UWC called for a general strike. Once the strike was under way, the minority Labour Government, which had come to power only after general elections on 28 February 1974, made a number of serious political errors. Buoyed by the failure of earlier strikes, such as those by the Loyalist Association of Workers in 1973, the Government fundamentally misjudged the nature and potential strength of the UWC. A broad coalition of loyalist trade unionists, politicians, and paramilitaries, the UWC had a single-issue agenda with great mobilization potential— 'wrecking Sunningdale'—and the resources and determination to see the strike through to the end. As a consequence of its miscalculations, the British Government almost completely lacked the resolve to either break the strike in its early days, when many moderate unionists were still undecided, or to take decisive steps to restore essential services and law and order.

This inactivity persisted even after a state of emergency had been declared on 19 May 1974, following, among others, the explosion of four car bombs in the Republic of Ireland two days earlier. The Executive, facing an increasingly desperate situation, realized that only a combined military and political initiative could save the Sunningdale Agreement. Yet, lacking in the resources to deliver on the former,[29] its announcement on 22 May 1974 that the implementation of the Council of Ireland would be postponed proved counterproductive. The strikers interpreted this as a sign of weakness, while tensions between Unionists and Nationalists in the Executive grew.

To complicate the situation even further, Harold Wilson, the Labour Prime Minister, condemned the strike in a TV broadcast as a 'deliberate and calculated attempt to use every undemocratic and unparliamentary means for the purpose of bringing down the whole constitution of Northern Ireland'. He also accused the strikers of 'sponging on Westminster and British democracy',[30] a remark which both broadened and deepened the alienation of the unionist community. Even after this statement on 25 May 1974, no decisive steps were taken to end the strike, either by entering into negotiations with the UWC, as Faulkner demanded, or by deploying and using enough security forces, as the SDLP requested. In these circumstances the Executive as a whole lost its confidence in the willingness and ability of the British Government to preserve the constitutional arrangements put in place at the beginning of the year.

The situation in the Republic of Ireland, too, did little to help ensure the success of Sunningdale. Not only was the Sunningdale Communiqué vague in its wording, in particular it lacked a guarantee by the Irish Government concerning the constitutional status of Northern Ireland. This was further aggravated by a ruling of the Irish Constitutional Court on 16 January 1974 on the compatibility of Article 5 of the Sunningdale Communiqué[31] with Articles 2 and 3 of the Irish Constitution. The Court declared that Article 5 was merely a statement of policy, but that any attempt to implement it might be in violation of the constitution.[32] Realizing the potential dangers for the situation in Northern Ireland, the Dáil rejected Independent Fianna Fáil member for North East Donegal, Neil Blaney's motion against partition on 25 February; and on 13 March, the Taoiseach, Liam Cosgrave gave further assurances stating that 'the factual position of Northern Ireland is that it is within the United Kingdom' and that his 'government accepts this as a fact.'[33] Yet, in the eyes of loyalists, this was too little, too late.

The effects on the situation in Northern Ireland were devastating. As neither the Northern Ireland Executive nor the British Government sought clarification from the Irish Government on this issue, the SDLP's interpretation of the new constitutional arrangements—that they were merely transitional on the road to Irish unity—was significantly strengthened. Correspondingly the fears within the unionist community about the constitutional future of Northern Ireland were compounded.

In addition, Wilson's Government did little to assure loyalists of its genuine desire to find a settlement acceptable to all parties. Instead, British policy statements increased loyalist fears of a sell-out. In a speech in Newcastle-under-Lyme, the then Secretary of State for Defence, Roy Mason, acknowledged the pressure put on the government to set a date for the army to be withdrawn from Northern Ireland in order to increase the leverage on politicians in the province to seek a solution to their differences.[34] Even more difficult to explain was a letter by the Secretary of State for Northern Ireland, Merlyn Rees, which was presented at an IRA press conference on 13 May 1974, in which Rees had stated, 'We have not the faintest interest to stay in Ireland and the quicker we are out the better.'[35]

By the time of the Belfast Agreement, these lessons had been learnt. The Irish Government took a more flexible and conciliatory approach in its attempts to accommodate the unionist community and has thus made a significant and positive contribution to the progress of the peace process. Equally, the British Government consistently argued the case of consent, that is, no change in the constitutional status of Northern Ireland without the consent of a majority of its population. The most significant step, however, was the preparedness of the Irish Government to withdraw its constitutional claim to Northern Ireland, subject to the approval of such a move by a referendum in the Republic—see Coakley, in Chapter 12 of this volume. As anticipated, the Irish electorate voted in favour of the constitutional amendment in 1998. The Irish Prime Minister, Bertie Ahern, signed the amendment, formally repealing Articles 2 and 3 of the Republic's constitution, after the Northern Ireland Secretary, Peter Mandelson, and the Irish Foreign Minister, David Andrews, had signed the new Anglo-Irish Treaty on 2 December 1999. The Treaty put formally in place the North-South Ministerial Council, the British-Irish Intergovernmental Conference, and the British-Irish Council, as constituent elements of Strands Two and Three of the Belfast Agreement. It is also noteworthy that, in sharp contrast with the situation in 1973–4, the British Government has placed Northern Ireland high on its agenda[36] and that Prime Minister Blair has made several personal interventions to prevent a breakdown of the peace process.[37]

Apart from the discrete efforts made by both the British and Irish Governments, it has also been vital that the two have acted in concert, at least up until the suspension in February 2000. The partnership did, though, demonstrate a commonality of purpose, thereby eliminating the possibility that the gap between the parties in Northern Ireland might widen as they sought the patronage of either of the two governments. It was equally important that the joint efforts of the British and Irish Governments were endorsed publicly by leading politicians in the United States, including President Clinton, and that, as British, Irish, and US politicians took responsibility for the success of the Belfast Agreement, they included politicians in Northern Ireland.[38] In contrast to 1973–4, the front of supporters of the new Agreement was not only broader, but seemed less likely to crack under pressures that had their source in political quarrels and difficulties elsewhere, as was the case with the Westminster elections of February 1974.

Finally, the role of Great Britain and the Republic of Ireland is also vital with regard to the question of what alternative arrangements would be put in place should the Belfast Agreement fail. A comparison with the situation that existed after Sunningdale reveals that the incentives for both communities to find a *modus vivendi* within the Agreement structure are more compelling than they were before. The failure of Sunningdale meant the re-introduction of direct rule, an outcome that many in the unionist community preferred to power-sharing. A permanent failure of the devolved institutions created by the Belfast Agreement, which was threatened by their suspension in February 2000, could mean that the United Kingdom and the Republic of Ireland may, in time, move towards joint sovereignty over Northern Ireland, see O'Leary in Chapter 4 of this volume. Clearly, this is not an outcome that unionists would welcome. Nationalists, however, would also lose out. Not only would the influence of both communities on policy- and decision-making in Northern Ireland be immensely diminished, but the British presence in Northern Ireland would be maintained, even extended.

Failure and Success (III): The International Context

The pre-negotiation and negotiation stages of the Belfast Agreement, as well as the period since Good Friday 1998, in which steps towards its implementation have been taken, underline the importance of the international context—see Guelke, in Chapter 13 of this volume. This context, especially the involvement of the United States, has been a critical factor in the success to date of this latest effort to settle the Northern Ireland conflict. In particular, the international mediation of the talks process and the simultaneous and subsequent American pressure on, and incentives for, all parties in the process to come to an agreement and to implement it, has played a significant role in the maintenance of the peace process. The Irish Foreign Minister, David Andrews, acknowledged the vital role of former Senator George Mitchell in brokering the Belfast Agreement in 1998 and in seeming to overcome the decommissioning impasse in 1999, as well as the support of other member states in the European Union at the signing of the new Anglo-Irish Treaty.[39] The early endorsement of the post-Agreement peace process in the form of the award of the Nobel Peace Price to John Hume and David Trimble was similarly important. It assisted in encouraging the pursuit of a long-term and stable peace in Northern Ireland and in putting the spotlight on the developments in the province in which the major protagonists could less and less afford to fail in their efforts to seek accommodation.

Conclusion

Despite the fact that the conditions for success were much more favourable in relation to the Belfast Agreement than they ever were for the Sunningdale Agreement, the current peace process has experienced several setbacks. Most have their sources in three issues: the different expectations and interpretations of the Belfast Agreement by the conflicting parties; the decommissioning of paramilitary weapons; and the reform of the policing system. Each of these, and potentially other, problems had the capacity to bring the implementation of the Belfast Agreement to a standstill. The failure to begin the process of decommissioning accomplished precisely that in February 2000, just 72 days after powers were transferred.

In summary, the resolution of the conflict in Northern Ireland, in all its different aspects and dimensions, and in its dependence on factors that can be influenced only to a limited degree by political actors in Belfast, London, and Dublin, is not certain. However, it is not too unlikely to imagine that it may be resolved within and by the institutional framework set out in the Belfast Agreement. The content of the Agreement is more acceptable to a wider spectrum of political groups in Northern Ireland, and the context in which the supporters of this new accommodation seek to implement it has also greatly improved in comparison with the situation in 1973–4.

Yet, a degree of uncertainty over the eventual success of the current peace process remains. The reason for this uncertainty is that the Belfast Agreement is, as was the agreement reached in 1973, dependent upon the continuing co-operation of two communities that still have fundamentally different political aspirations and identities. These, of course, may alter over time, provided that the opportunities and incentives for such change exist.

ENDNOTES

1. *Cf.*, for example, Lijphart, A., *Democracy in Plural Societies*, (New Haven, CT, and London: Yale University Press, 1977), 25–52; and McGarry, J., and O'Leary, B., 'Introduction. The Macro-Political Regulation of Ethnic Conflict', in J. McGarry and B. O'Leary (eds.), *The Politics of Ethnic Conflict Regulation* (London: Routledge, 1993) 36–8.
2. I have explored these issues more fully in Wolff, S., *Managing External Minorities, Disputed Territories, and the Stability of Conflict Settlements*, Ph.D. thesis (London, 1999).
3. O'Leary, B., 'The Nature of the British-Irish Agreement', *New Left Review* 233 (1999): 66–96, at 73.
4. In 1970, a general process of party realignments took place in Northern Ireland that affected not only the Unionist community. In April 1970, the cross-communal Alliance Party of Northern Ireland (APNI) was founded, and in August of the same year, the Social Democratic and Labour Party (SDLP) was established in an effort to unite nationalist, left-wing, and civil rights activists.
5. The March 1969 elections had returned only four political parties to Stormont: Unionists, Nationalists, the Northern Ireland Labour Party, and Republican Labour. As a consequence of the changes in the party system, three more parties had representatives in Stormont: the Alliance Party, the SDLP, and the DUP—Paisley had won an April 1970 by-election.
6. Northern Ireland Office, *The Future of Northern Ireland: A Paper for Discussion*, (London and Belfast: HMSO, 1972).
7. Social Democratic and Labour Party, *Towards a New Northern Ireland*, (Belfast, 1972), reprinted as Annex 7 in Northern Ireland Office *The Future of Northern Ireland* (1972).
8. Northern Ireland Office, *The Future of Northern Ireland* paragraphs 76–8.
9. Edward Heath had promised the border poll at the suspension of the Stormont system in 1972. Boycotted by the Nationalist community, the turnout was under 60 per cent. Of those participating less than 1 per cent voted in favour of Irish unification, thus leaving approximately 58 per cent of the electorate opposed to a union with the Republic of Ireland.
10. The Northern Ireland Constitution Act created three categories of legislative powers: excepted matters—those matters of 'national importance' exclusively dealt with by the Parliament in Westminster; reserved matters—those normally handled by the Parliament in Westminster, but where the Northern Ireland Assembly could, with consent of the British Government and Parliament, obtain the right to pass legislation on a case by case basis; and transferred matters—all non-excepted and non-reserved matters for which the Assembly enjoyed unrestricted legislative powers. Reserved and excepted matters were detailed in Schedules 2 and 3 of the Northern Ireland Constitution Act of 1973, and it was understood that all matters not listed in either of the two schedules would be considered as transferred.
11. Although not directly demanding a power-sharing executive, Section 2 of the Northern Ireland Constitution Act required that the devolution of legislative powers to the new Assembly be withheld until the Secretary of State for Northern Ireland was satisfied 'that a Northern

Ireland Executive can be formed which, having regard to the support it commands in the Assembly and to the electorate on which that support is based, is likely to be widely accepted throughout the community.' The collective membership of the Executive was composed of the Heads of Departments of Northern Ireland, chaired by a Chief Executive, who, at the same time, were to chair functional committees in their area of responsibility reflecting the party balance in the Assembly.

12. The provisions foresaw a Council of Ministers with executive, harmonizing, and consultative functions, consisting of an equal number of delegates from the Northern Ireland executive and the Irish Government, and a Consultative Assembly of thirty members from each of the parliaments, chosen by proportional representation on the basis of the single transferable vote system within each parliament. The Council, operating on the basis of unanimity, was to have executive functions in the fields of the environment, agriculture, co-operation in trade and industry, electricity, tourism, transport, public health, sport, culture, and the arts. Cf. *Communiqué issued by the British and Irish Governments and the parties involved in the Northern Ireland Executive (designate)* on 9 December 1973.

13. Patrick Mayhew succeeded Brooke in 1992.

14. This was part of the permanent institutional framework set up by the Anglo-Irish Agreement.

15. Cf. O'Leary, B., 'Afterword: What is Framed in the Framework Documents', *Ethnic and Racial Studies*, 18 (1995): 862–72, here 867.

16. Former US Senator George Mitchell who later co-chaired the negotiations process recommended 'that the parties to such negotiations affirm their total and absolute commitment: (a) To democratic and exclusively peaceful means of resolving political issues; (b) To the total disarmament of all paramilitary organisations; (c) To agree that such disarmament must be verifiable to the satisfaction of an independent commission; (d) To renounce for themselves, and to oppose any effort by others, to use force, or threaten to use force, to influence the course or the outcome of all-party negotiations; (e) To agree to abide by the terms of any agreement reached in all-party negotiations and to resort to democratic and exclusively peaceful methods in trying to alter any aspect of that outcome with which they may disagree; and, (f) To urge that "punishment" killings and beatings stop and to take effective steps to prevent such actions.' Cf. George J. Mitchell, John de Chastelain, and Harri Holkeri, *Report of the International Body on Arms Decommissioning*, 22 January 1996.

17. DUP—11 per cent (8 seats); Vanguard—11 per cent (7 seats); West Belfast Loyalists—2 per cent (3 seats); Unionists who had not committed to the White Paper—9 per cent (8 seats).

18. Article 5 of the *Communiqué* reads: 'The Irish Government fully accepted and solemnly declared that there could be no change in the status of Northern Ireland until a majority of the people of Northern Ireland desired a change in that status. The British Government solemnly declared that it was, and would remain, their policy to support the wishes of the majority of the people of Northern Ireland. The present status of Northern Ireland is that it is part of the United Kingdom. If in the future the majority of the people of Northern Ireland should indicate a wish to become part of a united Ireland, the British Government would support that wish.' In terms of the Irish declaration, this was clearly short of the sort of change in the Irish constitution that would be made in 1998/99 in relation to Articles 2 and 3.

19. By the end of May 1974, the death toll among British soldiers in Northern Ireland had increased to 214, with an additional 52 RUC members and 45 UDR men killed—the Ulster Defence Regiment being a reserve unit of the British Army established in 1969 to take over military duties from the RUC. Cf. Coogan, T. P., *The Troubles. Ireland's Ordeal 1966–1995 and the Search for Peace* (London: Hutchinson, 1995), 168.

20. One major exception must be made in this context: on Saturday 15 August 1998, 29 civilians were killed in a bomb attack in Omagh carried out by the republican splinter group 'Real IRA'.

21. Sinn Féin, for example, had voted against standing in the 1973 local council and assembly elections as well against contesting the 1974 Westminster elections. See Bishop, P. and Mallie, E., *The Provisional IRA* (London: Corgi Books, 1987), 265.

22. Paddy Devlin, SDLP member of the Assembly and head of the Department of Health and Social Services of the Executive. Quoted in Bishop and Mallie, *The Provisional IRA*, 266. Without defending the all-Ireland institutions, the SDLP would also have faced a likely decline

in its support with the more committed nationalists turning to the republican movement. Cf. Coogan, *The Troubles*, 175.

23. The UWC was founded earlier in 1973 during a strike that had been called against the internment of loyalists.

24. 'The Secretary of State should be encouraged to open lines of communications with the Ulster Workers Council before the province is allowed to slide into chaos.' Quoted in Coogan, *The Troubles*, 171.

25. Cf. Evans, G. and O'Leary, B., 'Frameworked Futures: Intransigence and Flexibility in the Northern Ireland Elections of May 30 1996', *Irish Political Studies*, 12 (1997): 23–47, here 45f.

26. Hume stated that 'we, alone of all the major parties, were able to welcome the Agreement unreservedly.' Cf. John Hume, 'Address to the 29th SDLP Party Conference', 6 November 1999, source: http://sdlp.ie/. In his address to the SDLP's 28th Annual Conference on 14 November 1998, Hume said: 'Our party needs to make no apology for our aspiration to the unity of our people. But let us consider our definition of unity.' He went on to outline his definition of unity as follows: 'At this point in our history, we have achieved a truly valuable unity: the unity of purpose across all previous boundaries of party and tradition that suffuses, informs and directs the institutions and principles of the Good Friday agreement; the unity of purpose that directs the new politics on behalf of all of the people in this society; the unity of purpose undertaken on behalf of all the people of these islands, north and south, east and west.' John Hume, 'Address to the 28th SDLP Party Conference', 14 November 1999, source: http://sdlp.ie/. Website address correct as at June 2000.

27. Adams, G., 'Address to Assembly', 29 November 1999, source: http://sinnféin.ie/. Website address correct as at June 2000.

28. The votes each received in the 1974 Westminster elections were reduced to one third of those achieved in the 1973 Assembly elections. Part of the explanation lies in the different voting systems applied in both elections—Proportional Representation for the Assembly and plurality rule for the Westminster elections.

29. According to the Northern Ireland Constitution Act 1973, security was one of the matters over which the British Government retained exclusive competence. The Northern Ireland Executive was thus entirely dependent upon Westminster for combating the UWC strike.

30. Quoted in Buckland, P., *A History of Northern Ireland*, (Dublin: Gill and Macmillan, 1981), 172.

31. Cf. note 18.

32. Cf. Boyle, K., and Hadden, T., *Northern Ireland: The Choice* (London: Penguin Books, 1994), 120.

33. William Cosgrave quoted in Coogan, *The Troubles*, 169.

34. Cf. Bowyer Bell, J., *The Irish Troubles. A Generation of Violence, 1967–1992*, (Dublin: Gill and Macmillan, 1993), 409.

35. Quoted in Bowyer Bell, *The Irish Troubles*, 410.

36. The replacement of the first Secretary of State for Northern Ireland, William Whitelaw, was a result of 'domestic' problems of the British Government at the time—Whitelaw was recalled to London to head the Department of Social Security and to 'deal with' the miner's strike. The replacement of Mo Mowlam in 1999 by Peter Mandelson was interpreted as a concession to the UUP.

37. These have come at crucial junctures of the peace process. For example, on the eve of the Belfast Agreement in the form of an eleventh hour personal participation in the negotiations, or during the decommissioning impasse in the form of the *Draft Declaration* issued together with Irish Prime Minister Bertie Ahern at Hillsborough Castle on 1 April 1999.

38. A *Joint Statement* by Bertie Ahern, Tony Blair, and Bill Clinton on 18 March 1999 emphasised: 'The Agreement . . . must be implemented in all its aspects and the remaining difficulties must be resolved. We, as leaders, bear that responsibility and that means all of us whether we live in Northern Ireland, the Republic, Britain or the United States.'

39. 'We have benefited throughout from the support of the international community and in particularly our partners in the European Union and our friends across the Atlantic.' David Andrews, Speech at the signing ceremony of the new Anglo-Irish Treaty on 2 December 1999. See *Irish Times* 3 December 1999.

3

Transcending an Ethnic Party System?
The Impact of Consociational Governance on
Electoral Dynamics and the Party System

PAUL MITCHELL

Introduction

This chapter examines the impact of the new institutional architecture of
Northern Ireland—the 1998 Belfast Agreement—on the party system and electoral behaviour of parties and voters. Previous chapters have detailed the making and meaning of the Agreement and considered its likely impact on
policy-making and the future governance of Northern Ireland. Here we focus
on the electoral consequences of consociational rule. An important question concerning the post-Agreement party system is the extent to which the new political institutions—and the return to the Single Transferable Vote electoral
system—*may* attenuate the previously intense communal cleavage by superimposing a new 'pro-power-sharing *versus* anti-power-sharing division' on the
communal party system. Since the agreement is premised on an informal, but
no less real, coalition among the pro-Agreement parties, their co-operation in
government may encourage, and indeed may ultimately depend upon, electoral
co-operation both within and across the traditional communal party systems.
This chapter examines the election results and transfer patterns at the 1998
Assembly elections, and offers a first exploration of the impact of consociational
governance on Northern Ireland's entrenched ethnic party system.[1]

A Challenge to the Ethnic Party System?

Electoral competition in Northern Ireland is contained within what is best
described as an ethnic dual party system; fierce party competition exists within
the context of an overall bipolar constitutional cleavage.[2] In other words, party
politics has been dominated primarily by ethnic parties, which seek only the

support of the electorate on 'their side' of the constitutional divide. Loyalties have a strongly ascriptive character so that relatively few voters 'float across' the primary political cleavage derived from Northern Ireland's clash of national identities. It is only a mild exaggeration to say that at each election two simultaneous but largely separate contests take place. Each community holds its own election to decide who will represent it in negotiations with ethno-national rivals. Thus, there is essentially a 'unionist party system' and a 'nationalist party system'; the electoral interaction between them is marginal, and the more serious party competition takes place mainly within each segmented community.

Typically, parties within communal blocs compete amongst themselves to emerge as their community's pre-eminent spokesperson only when it is safe to do so; they attempt to attenuate within-bloc competition if such competition is likely to help their rivals within other ethnic groups. Little 'normal' inter-bloc competition occurs. Instead, communities try to out-mobilize each other rather than genuinely appeal for cross-community votes. Since very few voters are not committed to one bloc or the other, there are few electoral reasons to be moderate. Party politics in such systems tends to be characterized by ethnic outbidding among rival parties within each bloc.[3] Often such intra-bloc competition develops a centrifugal dynamic. Parties are encouraged to mobilize 'their' community by engaging in extremist and emotive ethnic appeals that suggest that their group's vital interests are in danger of being 'sold out'. Any co-operative overtures by a moderate party in one bloc to like-minded forces in other blocs immediately renders a party vulnerable to the accusation that it is acting as the handmaiden of a sell-out. In ethnic party systems, a unilateral cross-communal move is all too often the last that a politician gets to make!

However, *if* the Belfast Agreement can survive its re-implementation problems it may provide the first context in decades in which cross-communal co-operation can be electorally rewarding. Although the signing of the Agreement cannot be expected instantly to transform established patterns of electoral competition, it does challenge some of the core logic of competition in ethnic party systems. After all, given that the eight parties who signed the Agreement made risky reciprocal concessions at the end of lengthy and intense negotiations, they clearly have some stake in protecting their political investment. Since the Agreement is based on an informal coalition though without a coalition contract primarily among the UUP, SDLP and Sinn Féin, the successful operation of its institutions, and hence the devolution of power to these parties, hinges on their co-operation.

Does the executive alliance between the UUP and SDLP—the 'dyarchy' of effectively joint first ministers: see O'Leary in Chapter 4 of this volume—and the logic of weighted or double majority voting in the legislature, provide sufficient incentives to induce electoral co-operation among the power-sharing political parties? Alternatively, is the ethnic dual party system likely to be resilient despite the new consociational institutions? After all, the Agreement wisely postpones rather than resolves the sovereignty issue, so that most of the larger parties are likely to remain essentially either 'Unionist' or 'Nationalist',[4] though hopefully in a more co-operative manner. These parties, therefore, may continue to be concerned primarily with the electoral battles within their respective communities: to remain or become the largest voice in 'their' bloc. Thus, *if* the new institutions survive, the UUP and SDLP—and possibly also Sinn Féin—are likely to face an important tension between the imperatives of intra-segmental competition and the legislative and executive coalitions, with some of these same electoral rivals, that are essential to the effective working of consociational governance.

Electoral Validation of the Agreement

One of the many positive aspects of the Agreement is that its popular endorsement in referenda and elections may mean that any failure to deliver its full implementation will be unpopular and costly for the party leaders. If the Agreement is seen to unravel, the parties involved will strenuously endeavour to evade responsibility for its demise, but can expect no electoral rewards if they fail to convince the electorate that they are blameless. The more positive spin on the electorate's desire for a stable settlement is that the 'Yes' parties can anticipate collective electoral rewards if they are seen to deliver on the promise of Spring and Summer 1998. Taking a leap of faith for a moment: a fully functioning set of post-Agreement institutions, with a power-sharing government delivering balanced reforms over many years, would surely squeeze the intransigent 'No's' at succeeding elections. The substantive issues at the heart of 'No-Unionist' politics after the 1998 Agreement, therefore, may ultimately be transcended, in a fashion analogous to the fate of the earlier 'No-Unionist' campaign against the Anglo–Irish Agreement of 1985—and of course, even the 'yes' unionists of 1998 were 'no' unionists in 1985. The DUP *did* take its seats in the executive and although it still denounces the Agreement; many in the party—not least its two ministers—are unlikely to be keen to return to the ultimately fruitless 'Ulster Says No' campaign of the late 1980s.

The Agreement itself secured unprecedented popular legitimation on 22 May 1998 when 85 per cent of those voting on the island of Ireland supported it. Of course the 'Yes' vote in the Republic of Ireland was destined to be overwhelming; it was 94 per cent on a disappointing, but average, turnout.[5] The only vote in which there was really something at stake was the referendum in Northern Ireland. The level of mobilization was reflected in the extraordinary turnout of 81 per cent, the highest ever for a referendum in a domestic UK jurisdiction.[6] The overall result was 71 per cent for the agreement and 29 per cent against. Significantly, two exit polls suggest that there was a small majority for the 'Yes'

camp amongst unionists, although Ian Paisley's Westminster constituency—
Antrim North—maintained an impressive consistency by once again voting
'No'.[7]

In addition to imparting democratic legitimacy to the Agreement, the con-
clusive 'Yes' vote at the referendums allowed elections to be held for the new
Northern Ireland Assembly on 25 June 1998. The election marked a welcome
return for Proportional Representation-Single Transferable Vote (PR-STV)
based on the eighteen Westminster seats returning six members each, after the
unhappy flirtation with a rather bizarre version of a non-preferential list system
in 1996.[8] Overall, the election confirmed the referendum result, with pro-
Agreement candidates attracting 73 per cent of the first preference vote.

Candidate Fortunes

In total 295 candidates contested the 108 Assembly seats, or 2.7 candidates per
seat. As in most elections, a significant proportion of those who stood had little
chance of success. For example, of the 75 'others' in Table 3.1, 72 were unsuccessful—three independent unionists were elected—averaging only 518 votes
each. Table 3.1 confirms what we would expect: candidates' fortunes are
strongly related to their party label. The electoral strength of candidates can best
be assessed by examining the ratio between their first preference votes and the
Droop quota, the 'magic' number that guarantees election.[9] Comparing average

TABLE 3.1. *Fate of candidates at 1998 NI Assembly election*

Party	Number	Average vote	Average Droop quota	Elected %	Unsuccessful %
All	295	2743	0.43	36.6	63.4
SDLP	38	4683	0.73	73.7	26.3
UUP	48	3588	0.56	58.3	41.7
DUP	34	4292	0.67	58.8	41.2
SF	37	3861	0.60	48.6	51.4
APNI	22	2393	0.37	27.3	72.7
UKUP	13	2811	0.44	38.5	61.5
PUP	12	1720	0.27	41.7	58.3
NIWC	8	1627	0.25	25.0	75.0
UDP	8	1081	0.17	0	100.0
Others	75	518	0.08	4.0	96.0
Male	246	2853	0.44	38.2	61.8
Female	49	2191	0.34	28.6	71.4

Note: Parties listed are all those that registered at least 1 per cent of the vote.
Table format adapted from Gallagher 'The Results Analysed', 122.

Droop quotas rather than average votes in effect introduces a control for district magnitude and turnout—for example the quota in 1998 ranged from 7,734 in Newry and Armagh to only 5,088 in Antrim East. Only the candidates of the four largest parties have an approximately 50 per cent or better chance of being elected. In 1998 the most valuable party label for a candidate was 'SDLP': 74 per cent of its candidates were elected on an average Droop quota of 0.73. By contrast UUP candidates were much less successful: only 58 per cent were elected on an average quota of 0.56, reflecting the party's depressed vote and possibly the nomination of a few too many candidates.

Although 23 per cent of those elected exceeded the quota on the first count, first preference votes are not the only important factor for most candidates. Sometimes a very creditable vote on the first count is not enough to secure election. The best supported losers were Jack Allen (UUP) and Patsy McGlone (SDLP), both of whom failed to win a seat despite securing over 4,600 votes each—two-thirds of a quota. The Alliance party's Steve McBride met a similar fate: his 4,086 votes, representing 70 per cent of the quota, were not enough to return him to the Assembly. At the other extreme, two candidates with negligible support on the first count, the DUP's Sammy Wilson (663) and UUP's George Savage (669), made it into the Assembly by virtue of impressive internal party transfer solidarity. For example, Wilson received 3,853 votes from Peter Robinson's large surplus on the second count in Belfast East and, once the third DUP candidate was eliminated, subsequently received 76 per cent of his transfers, leaving him only 125 votes short of a quota—UUP transfers put Wilson over the top on the next count.

Party Fortunes and the Electoral System

The most dramatic electoral outcome in 1998 was that for the first time a nationalist party placed first in first preference votes (see Table 3.2). The SDLP increased its vote slightly—+0.6 per cent compared to 1996—and Sinn Féin more significantly (+2.3 per cent), so that the nationalist bloc as a whole expanded to 39.7 per cent—up 2.8 per cent on the most appropriate reference point, the 1996 Forum election. This was the nationalist bloc's best ever result in a PR election—surpassed only by the 1997 Westminster poll—and confirms a modest but clearly significant trend that points to steady growth in the nationalist vote, both relatively and absolutely.[10]

Certain electoral systems, especially those that encourage the transfer of votes from one party to another—such as the French double-ballot system and, most obviously, STV in Ireland—provide incentives to engage in implicit or even explicit coalition formation *before as well as after* elections.[11] STV, by encouraging voters to rank order the candidates and thus parties, rewards co-operative

TABLE 3.2. *Votes and Seats at the 1998 Assembly Election*

	Votes (%)	Change since 1996 (%)	% of two party vote (SDLP-SF;UUP-DUP)	Seats (N)	Seats (%)	Seat 'bonus' (S–V)
SDLP	22.0	0.6	56	24	22.2	0.2
UUP	21.3	-2.9	54	28	25.9	4.6
DUP	18	-0.8	46	20	18.5	0.4
SF	17.7	2.3	44	18	16.7	-0.9
APNI	6.5	0.0	—	6	5.6	-0.9
UKU	4.5	0.8	—	5	4.6	0.1
PUP	2.5	-0.9	—	2	1.9	-0.6
NIWC	1.6	0.6	—	2	1.9	0.3
UDP	1.1	-1.1	—	—	—	—
Ind unionists	1.3	1.1	—	3	2.8	1.5
Others	4.5	1.5	—	0	0	-4.5
Total	100			108	100	

Assembly 'Yes'–'No' Cleavage		
	Seats (N)	Seats (%)	Votes(%)
Nationalists	42	38.8	39.8
'Yes' Unionists	30	27.7	25.0
'No' Unionists	28	25.9	25.5
Others	8	7.4	9.4

Notes: Turnout 69.9%; Disproportionality (LSq. Index): 3.4; Effective Number of Parties (votes): 6.1. — indicates 'none', or 'no seats'.

electoral strategies. STV is an especially appropriate electoral system for ethno-nationally divided multi-party systems because its logic encourages pre-electoral co-operation and potentially even accommodation. While the adoption of STV—or any other electoral system—cannot in itself do much to end protracted conflicts, it does provide electoral rewards to those who engage in accommod-ative behaviour. Parties with electoral partners, other things being equal, win more seats.[12] In addition, in order for parties to attract a greater number of lower preferences, they need to appeal to voters identified with other parties, and hence STV can exert a moderating dynamic.[13] STV should perform this function better than list systems:

Under list systems with preferential voting, deputies would need to concern themselves only with the support of those who will, or might, vote for their party, whereas under STV even the fifth or sixth preference of a supporter of another party could be import-ant, so that deputies need to be concerned about their reputation in every voter's eyes. Gallagher, M., 'Does Ireland Need a New Electoral System?', *Irish Political Studies*, 2 (1987): 27–48, here 41.

Sinn Féin has been electorally rewarded in this manner as a direct conse-quence of moderating its stance and becoming a leading participant in the peace process. Previously, the party was in an isolated electoral position often failing to win seats even with an impressive first preference vote, as other parties moved past it due to transfers in subsequent counts.[14] The moderation of Sinn Féin's stance has boosted its first preference vote and its votes from transfers—see dis-cussion in Terminal Transfers later in this chapter. More SDLP terminal trans-fers now go to Sinn Féin than to the Alliance Party, a clear reversal of earlier voting behaviour.[15] In electoral terms, Sinn Féin has made disproportionate gains from the peace process and in 1998 accounted for 44 per cent of the nationalist vote—see the third column of Table 3.2—to the SDLP's 56 per cent.[16] This is a consequence of the peace process 'legitimating' Sinn Féin's democratic credentials, rather than an aberration.[17] Sinn Féin growth is not directly hurting the SDLP. Rather, the overall expansion of the nationalist bloc has meant that both nationalist parties have experienced growth, albeit at a faster rate in Sinn Féin's case.

1998 was a poor election for unionists and for the two main parties in particu-lar. Given the general popularity of the Belfast Agreement, validated at the sub-sequent referendum, and having made a bold move for peace, the UUP expected or at least hoped for some electoral reward. Indeed, two opinion polls held dur-ing the campaign were reassuring: at the beginning of the campaign the UUP registered 33 per cent support excluding a large number of undecided voters, and a lower but still respectable 27 per cent in the second poll taken ten days before the election.[18] The first tangible evidence of how far the UUP vote had sunk was provided by a much larger exit poll which suggested that its first pref-erence vote could be as low as 20 per cent, just ahead of the DUP with 18 per cent.[19] UUP 'sources' insisted that they 'fully expected to get about 24 per cent' of first preference votes, and to do well from subsequent preferences. They were correct only about the second projection.

In the only poll that mattered the UUP's 21.3 per cent in the 1998 Assembly election was not only down 2.9 per cent on 1996, but was the party's worst ever performance in a Northern Ireland election. Undoubtedly part of the explanation lies in the increased fragmentation within the unionist bloc. Unionist candidates outside the two established parties—UUP and DUP—secured 11.5 per cent of the vote, the highest since the extreme fragmentation of the mid–1970s. The slight fall in the DUP vote of 0.7 per cent was compensated by gains for other 'No' unionists which were collectively up by 2.4 per cent. The Alliance Party remained stalled at 6.5 per cent: its vote share in three of the last four elections. Consistent with unionist fragmentation, the party system as a whole has been growing: the Laakso/Taagepera index of the effective number of political parties (by votes) was 6.15 in 1998, the highest ever in Northern Ireland.[20] Overall proportionality was good, measuring 3.4 on the least squares (or Gallagher) index,[21] making it one of the most proportional elections ever held in Northern Ireland, and a little better than the 1996 Forum elections (3.9).[22]

TABLE 3.3. *Average turnout by constituency type*

	'Unionist'	'Nationalist'	'Balanced'
Number	10	6	2
Average Turnout (%)	64.6	74.9	72.5

Note: 'Unionist' constituencies for the purposes of this table are those in which at least four of the elected assembly members self-identify as unionists—UUP, DUP, PUP, UKUP or independent unionist. Similarly 'nationalist' constituencies are those in which at least four of the elected members belonged to either the SDLP or Sinn Féin. This leaves two 'balanced' constituencies: Fermanagh South-Tyrone elected 3 nationalists (2 SF, 1 SDLP) and 3 unionists (2 UUP, 1 DUP); Belfast South elected 3 unionists (2 UUP, 1 DUP), 2 nationalists (2 SDLP) and one 'other' (NIWC).

Some commentators, especially those sympathetic to the UUP, have suggested that greater abstention by UUP voters accounts for some of the party's losses. While this is indeed plausible there is no direct information on differential turnout by the unionist and nationalist communities, and one should note that turnout overall was up by 5.5 per cent compared to 1996. Nevertheless, I can report some indirect confirmation of this proposition. In an admittedly rough approximation of differential turnout, Table 3.3 reports the average turnout for 'unionist', 'nationalist', and 'balanced' or mixed constituencies. Of course all constituencies are 'mixed' to varying degrees, but for the purposes of Table 3.3 a predominantly 'unionist constituency' is defined as one in which at least four of the six elected assembly members self-identify as unionists—that is, belong to the UUP, DUP, PUP, UKUP or independent unionist. Similarly, a predominantly 'nationalist constituency' is one in which at least four nationalists—SDLP or Sinn Féin—were elected.[23] In total, sixteen of the eighteen constituencies can be distinguished on this basis. The results are clear and quite dramatic: the average turnout in 'unionist constituencies' at 64.6 per cent was just over 10 per cent *lower* than in 'nationalist constituencies' (Table 3.3). Indeed there was only one 'unionist constituency', Upper Bann, in which the turnout of 71.3 per cent was higher than even the lowest turnout among 'nationalist constituencies'—West Belfast, 69 per cent.[24]

Thus, despite the unquestioned absolute and relative growth in the nationalist vote, it does seem plausible that the unionist vote has been depressed by the differential turnout of unionist and nationalist voters. Nevertheless, differential turnout is itself an important competitive dynamic in ethnic party systems.[25] One lesson for the leaders of the unionist parties is that they need to re-evaluate the efforts they are making to mobilize their voters.

Incentives towards Cross-Communal Co-operation

A Consociational Executive Coalition

Coalition cabinets govern most parliamentary democracies. Coalitions are either formed before, but mostly after, elections, when a set of parties negotiate a coalition deal that is usually underwritten by a more or less comprehensive coalition policy document.[26] While the prospect of joining a governing coalition may cause considerable intra-party dissent, 'parties do in practice tend to go into and come out of government as single actors'[27]. For the most part the coalition strategies of Northern Ireland's parties correspond to this unitary actor status, despite the obvious divisions this causes within the UUP. What is unusual is the posture of the DUP. Although the party is largely united behind its leadership, its tactic in a sense is to be 'partly in, and partly out' of the executive and legislative coalitions induced by the institutional rules established by the Agreement. In other words a party, in this case the DUP, can join an executive coalition without joining the legislative coalition that supports it. It can do this because membership in the executive is not based on the mutual consent and mutual veto that is normally the outcome of voluntary coalition negotiations.[28] As such no initial policy coherence can be assumed.[29] Rather, membership in this version of a consociational 'grand coalition' is an automatic entitlement of electoral strength, determined merely by the application of the mechanical d'Hondt divisor. Thus, the party—the DUP—is 'entitled' to posts in the executive although opposed to its very existence.

It is analytically useful to distinguish between executive coalitions and their supporting electoral/legislative coalition. Although these are often coterminous, the frequency of minority governments tells us that executive coalitions often rely on electoral coalitions larger than themselves, by attracting external support from parties or individuals in the legislature who do not join the government. However, it is *highly* exceptional for the executive coalition—normally defined as only those parties holding cabinet ministries—to be larger than its supporting legislative coalition![30] To be sure coalition parties do many unexpected things, but voting against their own government is not normally one of them! Yet this is precisely the situation in Northern Ireland. The DUP has taken its entitlement of two ministries in the twelve-person executive but is not part of the executive's legislative coalition in the Assembly. Indeed, given the chance it will vote against the Trimble-Mallon dyarchy, and is selectively attempting to immobilize the institutions of the Agreement through the special voting procedures.[31]

The explanation of course is that the consociational executive formed in December 1999 is not designed to be a coalition like any other in parliamentary democracies. Indeed, under the Strand One institutions established by the Belfast Agreement, Northern Ireland is not really a parliamentary democracy at all. The usual minimal definition of a parliamentary democracy is that the executive is directly responsible to the legislature via confidence procedures; or more colourfully that, at any moment—at least while parliament is in session!—a parliamentary majority can 'rise up and strike the government dead'.[32] Neither the quasi-presidential joint first ministers nor the Executive as a whole can be dismissed easily by the Assembly. Individual ministers can be removed by a no-confidence vote, but the relevant party can then nominate a replacement.[33] Thus, by institutional design the Agreement provides incentives toward power-sharing by not requiring policy agreement in advance. The Executive once formed is intended to be 'stable' *vis-à-vis* the Assembly in that it cannot be easily dismissed. Of course it is still a 'voluntary' grand coalition rather than a labour sentence; parties can decline to take their ministerial seats although this would result in a disproportionate re-allocation to their rivals, and/or they can resign. In particular the resignation from the Executive of either the UUP or SDLP, for well-known reasons associated with other aspects of the Agreement, effectively terminates the coalition.

Could a 'Yes-No' Institutional Cleavage Emerge in the Assembly?

Given the consociational rules on which the internal aspects of the Belfast Agreement are premised, devolution can only progress by means of concurrent consent within the nationalist and unionists blocs in the Assembly. The 'higher' threshold—'parallel consent'—requires absolute majorities within both blocs. Assuming all 108 members vote, this means that a minimum of 22 nationalists and 29 unionists are required to pass 'key decisions'. The less onerous 'weighted majority' rule—requiring at least 40 per cent of both blocs, plus 60 per cent overall—means for example, that if all 42 nationalists voted for a measure, the minimum number of unionists required would be 24.

To date the practical political focus has been on competitive dynamics within unionism, not least because all 48 nationalist members of the legislative assembly (MLAs) are ostensibly 'Yes' voters. David Trimble's party has 28 members, although one, Peter Weir, resigned the party whip and now sits alongside the DUP in the Assembly. Thus, assuming for the moment that only Weir is a lost cause, Trimble has 27 votes plus the two provided by the PUP, giving him 29 'Yes-unionist' MLAs, the bare minimum needed to win a parallel consent division in the Assembly. Clearly the UUP leader can not afford any further defections if the Assembly is to be workable. The other side of this sharp division within unionism is that the 'No' unionists are within striking distance of reaching the *de facto* 'minority veto' provision of the consociational architecture—the 'petition of concern'—which requires the signatures of 30 members to trigger the special voting procedures. They currently have 28 votes, plus most probably Peter Weir, placing them only one defection short of the ability to trigger the procedures.[34]

A key question is the extent to which the new political institutions may ameliorate the previously intense communal cleavage by superimposing a new 'pro-power-sharing versus anti-power-sharing division'. Part of the explanation is that the Agreement cannot work without an informal coalition government among at least the UUP, SDLP, and Sinn Féin, and that this mutual reliance may foster some implicit electoral co-operation as these parties transfer to other 'Yes' candidates. Preferential electoral systems such as STV allow what Horowitz[35] has called 'vote pooling', an incentive towards some inter-ethnic accommodation, facilitated by making parties to some extent dependent on other ethnic groups for vital transfers.[36] Evans and O'Leary,[37] using survey evidence, found some limited but significant evidence of such effects—see also O'Leary, in Chapter 4 of this volume. They found that about 9 per cent of voters did transfer from nationalist to unionist and vice versa, and not surprisingly the willingness to cross the communal divide was greatest within the 'Yes' camp. This is significant given that the 1998 contest was the first election after the Agreement and because there were no explicit transfer pacts among the 'Yes' parties.[38] If the Assembly survives long enough for a second election—a feat no NI regional parliament has managed since the old Stormont regime—these intercommunal co-operative electoral practises can be expected to become more important.

Finally, the UUP's failure to top the first preference vote was mitigated and somewhat masked by its emergence as the largest Assembly party. The UUP enjoyed a very significant seat bonus of 4.6 per cent, due to transfers made possible by the return to STV.[39] As noted above, some of these transfers came from the SDLP. However Evans and O'Leary[40] found that many of the transfers to

'Yes' unionists were from 'No' unionist candidates. This suggests an interesting tension between two forms of electoral rationality: voting 'sincerely' according to one's communal preference—'No' unionists preferring to transfer to other unionists, even 'Yes' unionists, than to anybody else; and tactical rational voting dictated by the institutional rules of the Assembly for 'No' unionists seeking to immobilize the Assembly, more 'Yes' nationalists are better if this means fewer 'Yes' unionists.[41] It seems likely given the history of communal polarization that 'No' unionist voters 'used their preference schedules to say they preferred "yes but sceptical" unionist candidates to nationalist candidates of whatever kind'.[42] When faced with situations in which there are no other 'No' unionist candidates available, a DUP voter for example, would need to 'transcend' powerful communal loyalties in order to 'rationally' transfer to a nationalist candidate rather than to a 'Yes' unionist in order to help immobilize the Assembly. The next section examines actual transfer patterns.

STV Transfer Patterns in 1998

Transferring the votes of eliminated candidates and the surpluses of elected candidates is the feature that makes STV distinctive. It provides us with potentially rich information concerning voters' entire preference schedules and it accomplishes this in an economical fashion in a single round of voting. It provides some solid evidence of the extent of intra-party solidarity, and some insight into how voters of a particular party feel about the other parties. STV facilitates but in no sense requires pre-electoral coalition formation. On occasion sets of parties present themselves as a 'government in waiting' during an election campaign. Analysis of inter-party transfers allows us to estimate how the voters of these parties feel about their leaders' coalition signals. Also, in the absence of such cues, voters through the pattern of their transfers may suggest—and help make viable—certain combinations of parties in post-election bargaining. As we have seen, the consociational coalition format prescribed by the Belfast Agreement contains no post-election negotiations over coalition formation. Nevertheless, since cross-communal voting is essential to the operation of these institutions, emerging transfer co-operation among the 'pro-system' parties in particular will be important to the executive's viability, and provides an indication of changing relationships among the parties. Thus, this section will examine two types of transfers: those *within* and *among* parties.[43]

The 1998 elections were the first since the negotiation of the Agreement only eight weeks earlier, so it would be idle to expect a wholesale transformation of the party system. To help evaluate the transfer pattern in 1998, consider the pre-Agreement party system. The transfer patterns in the 1989 local government elections, for example, illustrate a recurring theme. In 1989 the five largest parties were able to deliver around 80 per cent of transfers to their other party candidates.[44] Inter-party transfers in 1989 show that the UUP and DUP received only 1.4 per cent and 0.5 per cent respectively from nationalist parties. The SDLP received 8.8 per cent and Sinn Féin 1.1 per cent from unionist parties.[45] In sum, prior to the 'peace process' leading to the Belfast Agreement, internal transfer solidarity within the main parties was extremely high, while cross-communal party transfers were negligible. Vote pooling was virtually non-existent.

TABLE 3.4. *Internal party transfer solidarity*

Party	Average Transfer Solidarity (%)	SD
SDLP (10)	70.4	8.9
UUP (27)	70.9	11.7
SF (15)	87.3	8.5
DUP (13)	70.9	10.7
APNI (4)	67.8	7.1

Note: Figures in brackets indicate the number of cases of within-party transfers. The other parties field multiple candidates too rarely to make a calculation meaningful.

Table 3.4, showing internal party transfer solidarity for the five largest parties in 1998, demonstrates that the parties' transfer discipline, while not quite as high as in 1989, is nevertheless most impressive, especially within Sinn Féin which retained 87 per cent of its transfers. The average transfer solidarity for these five parties in 1998 was 73.5 per cent, better for example than Fianna Fáil in the 1990s, a party noted for its cohesiveness.[46]

Terminal Transfers

The destination of terminal transfers is analysed in Table 3.5 and quite strongly suggests that the Belfast Agreement and wider peace process has induced changes in how party voters feel about or perceive each other. Before considering this in detail it is necessary to note a general limitation of the data. For most parties the number of cases of terminal transfer situations is modest or small (see second column of Table 3.5). For example, there were only two cases of SDLP terminal transfers. Inferring general trends from only two cases is obviously tentative since an 'unusual' transfer—perhaps caused by geographical proximity of two candidates rather than inter-party relations—may be unduly weighted in data of too few cases.

Let us begin with the nationalist parties. Evans and O'Leary,[47] citing preliminary findings by Sinnott[48] released just after the results were announced,

TABLE 3.5. *Destination of terminal transfers in 1998*

Transfers from	Parties available in each case to receive transfers[a]	SDLP	UUP	DUP	SF	AP	UKUP	WC	Pro-Agreement	Anti-Agreement
SDLP	SF, UUP (2)		18.8		52.0					
SF	SDLP (7)	74.2								
SF	UUP, DUP, UKUP (1)[b]		36.7	2.6			3.6			
UUP	SDLP (5)	34.4								
UUP	SDLP, DUP, UKU (2)	18.5		28.6			33.1			
UUP	Pro-A, Anti-A (2)								26.1	61.6
PUP	UUP, DUP, APNI (5)		28.1	26.6		14.9				
PUP	Pro-A, Anti-A (5)								50.5	31.0
DUP	UUP (8)		42.1							
DUP	UUP,UKUP (2)		20.8				72.7			
DUP	Pro-A, Anti-A (4)								25.9	64.4
UKUP	UUP, DUP (4)		15.8	53.3						
UKUP	Pro-A, Anti-A (4)								21.5	70.1
APNI	UUP, SDLP (6)	33.5	34.0							
APNI	UUP, SDLP, NIWC (2)	22.1	30.4					39.9		
APNI	Pro-A, Anti-A (7)								80.3	3.6
NIWC	SDLP (4)	38.1								
NIWC	SDLP, UUP, APNI (2)	22.9	18.5			37.9				

[a] 'Parties available in each case to receive transfers' means *at least* these parties are always available; in most cases, other candidates were also still in the count.

[b] In this case three unionists were the only candidates still in the count. SF transfers helped elect the UUP rather than the UKUP candidate.

Notes: Figures in parentheses indicate the number of cases where these transfer situations arose.
Table format adapted from Gallagher 'The Results Analysed', 139.

report that there is no direct measure of SDLP to UUP transfers. There were very few cases of SDLP terminal transfers because in most cases an SDLP candidate was either elected or eliminated in the final count. There were, however, two SDLP terminal transfers in the Foyle and Fermanagh South-Tyrone constituencies, which were split principally between the UUP and Sinn Féin. Averaging these two cases, the UUP received 19 per cent of SDLP transfers. While modest, this is significantly more than typically occurred prior to the Agreement. Before the peace process Sinn Féin was an isolated party in that it received very few transfers from any source, including the SDLP; however, in these cases it received 52 per cent. In both constituencies SDLP transfers put the Sinn Féin candidate over the quota, although they would both have been elected even without these transfers. Nevertheless, this limited but tangible evidence suggests that SDLP voters may now be much more willing to transfer to Sinn Féin, and that the latter party is clearly reaping some rewards from its more moderate stance. The evidence more strongly, and with more confidence, suggests that Sinn Féin voters are more than willing to reciprocate. Sinn Féin terminal transfers to the SDLP, averaged across seven cases, was 74 per cent, higher than the internal transfer solidarity rates all of the other parties!

There were, however, a few disappointing transfer rates between nationalists. Count 11 in Belfast North is one of the more interesting and involved the distribution of Gerry Kelly's (Sinn Féin) 2,917 surplus votes. Only 43 per cent of these transferred to the SDLP candidate Martin Morgan with 56 per cent becoming non-transferable. A slightly improved transfer rate of 290 votes, or +9.4 per cent would have been enough to deliver the final seat to Morgan rather than an independent 'No' unionist candidate. In other words, a Sinn Féin to SDLP transfer rate of only 52 per cent—well below their average—would have secured the final seat for the 'Yes' camp. It can be reasonably projected that an explicit transfer pact between the nationalist parties would secure the final seat in these types of situations.[49]

UUP terminal transfers reveal more significant evidence of emerging cross-communal electoral co-operation among the pro-Agreement parties. Table 3.5 shows five cases of terminal transfers to the SDLP averaging 34 per cent, a clear departure from the almost total isolation of the communal blocs in the traditional party system. In the East Antrim constituency the penultimate Count 12 left the DUP candidate Jack McKee ahead of the SDLP's Danny O'Connor by only 8 votes. The final count involved the distribution of a UUP candidate's 1,187 surplus votes. The modest but higher UUP transfer rate to the SDLP of 25 per cent, compared to 20 per cent to the DUP was decisive in giving the last seat to a nationalist 'Yes' candidate by 49 votes. A few close results such as this one helped keep the 'No' unionists just short of the 30 Assembly members needed to invoke the special voting procedures. Nevertheless, in a smaller number of cases UUP ballots transferred to 'No' unionists in higher proportions than pro-Agreement candidates (see Table 3.5). Transfers from the PUP, an enthusiastic supporter of the peace process, went mostly to other Pro-Agreement candidates, mainly to the UUP and Alliance party. Also, and not surprisingly, terminal transfers from the two non-confessional parties—the Alliance party and Women's Coalition—went almost exclusively to other pro-Agreement candidates, and in fairly even divisions between the UUP and SDLP (Table 3.5).

Whenever possible the two main 'No' unionist parties transferred heavily to each other. In situations in which a UUP candidate was always available, DUP voters preferred to transfer to the UKUP—at a rate of 73 per cent—and in turn UKUP ballots transferred to the DUP at a rate of 53 per cent. Nevertheless, despite this understandable preference for other 'No' unionists, and consistent with Evans and O'Leary's survey findings, a large number of their ballots ultimately transferred to the UUP. For example, the average DUP to UUP transfer rate across eight cases was 42 per cent, an essential factor in making the new consociational institutions minimally viable. The explanation of course is that many of the UKUP and independent 'No' unionist candidates were eliminated early and thus were not available to receive DUP terminal transfers. In these situations, DUP voters could choose to give their next preference to the 'Yes, but unionist' UUP or could indicate no further preference. Given that ballots with no 'next available preference' become non-transferable and thus played no further part in the count, many not surprisingly gave lower preferences to the UUP.

TABLE 3.6. *Terminal transfers to pro-Agreement candidates*

Transfers from	Pro-Agreement[a]
SDLP (2)	70.8
SF (8)	75.4
UUP (5)	40.4
DUP (9)	49.0

[a] In the cases of the SDLP, SF, and UUP the transfers are to 'other pro-Agreement parties'.

Table 3.6, summarizes terminal transfers from the four main ethno-national parties to pro-Agreement candidates. Not surprisingly nationalist transfers are overwhelmingly made to other pro-Agreement candidates. However, Table 3.6 reveals the apparently anomalous result that DUP voters transferred more heavily to pro-Agreement candidates than UUP voters did! The explanation is that almost all of these DUP transfers to pro-Agreement candidates were to 'Yes' unionists, mainly the UUP. By contrast, in order to vote for a fellow pro-Agreement candidate, UUP voters in most terminal situations had to cross the communal divide. As we have seen, in five cases they did so in significant numbers in favour of the SDLP. But they also transferred more traditionally to other unionist candidates, most of whom opposed the Belfast Agreement. This *may* suggest that, at least on 25 June 1998, crossing the traditional communal threshold was still more difficult for unionist voters than crossing the newer 'Yes-No' institutional division.

Conclusion

I began this article by recalling the nature and dynamics of ethnic party systems and by outlining the virtually mutually exclusive electoral strategies that have long prevailed. The electorate is highly segmented in ethno-national terms, so that party competition has been largely 'catch-self' rather than 'catch-all'. The Belfast Agreement, through its combination of internal consociationalism and 'external' confederalism, is the most imaginative and positive response to the conflict to date. Since the elections to the 1998 Assembly provide the first electoral information since the breakthrough in negotiations, the interesting question that arises is whether this new context and the prospect of consociational governance exerted any impact on electoral dynamics and the party system.

TABLE 3.7. *Terminal cross-communal transfers*

Transfers from	Pro-Agreement unionist	Pro-Agreement nationalist
Pro-Agreement nationalist (3)	24.9	—
Pro-Agreement unionist (11)	—	17.1

While the traditional ethnic party system was certainly not instantly transcended—leaving aside whether or not this would even be desirable, given that both sides have conflicting, but legitimate long-term constitutional aspirations—there is evidence of significant changes in voting behaviour, particularly those revealed by inter-party transfer patterns. Some of the voters of pro-Agreement candidates displayed a new-found willingness to cross the communal divide in order to support each other with lower preferences. Most dramatically, UUP voters transferred to the SDLP at a rate of 34 per cent. Table 3.7, which summarizes the data by including only genuinely cross-communal terminal transfers within the pro-Agreement camp, reveals that nationalists transferred to pro-Agreement unionists at a rate of 25 per cent, while the transfer flow in the opposite direction was 17 per cent.

These transfers suggest at least the beginning of a thaw in Northern Ireland's long-frozen political alignments. In short, although an intriguing 'Yes-No' institutional division now overlies Northern Ireland's traditional ethnic party system, the evidence from June 1998 suggests that obituaries for the communal party system are premature.

ENDNOTES

1. On the very day that a first draft of this paper was completed the British Government indicated its intention to reclaim executive power (3 February 2000). Subsequently, a lack of progress on decommissioning combined with the UK government's decision to prioritize protecting David Trimble's position within his party, led to the suspension of the power-sharing executive and to the return of direct rule from London after only two months of devolution. Nevertheless, the logic of the argument can still be assessed since something like the Agreement must eventually be implemented, given that it is the only real alternative to permanent direct rule. Indeed, the restoration of devolution in May 2000 indicates that for the foreseeable future the Agreement, as Peter Mandelson has put it, is 'the only show in town'.

2. Mitchell, P., 'Conflict Regulation and Party Competition in Northern Ireland', *European Journal of Political Research*, 20 (1991): 67–92; Mitchell, P., 'Party Competition in an Ethnic Dual party System', *Ethnic and Racial Studies* 18 (1995): 773–93; Mitchell, P., 'The Party System and Party Competition', in P. Mitchell and R. Wilford (eds.), *Politics in Northern Ireland* (Boulder, CO: Westview Press, 1999a), 91- 116.

3. See Mitchell (1995), *ibid.*; Rabushka A., and Shepsle, K. *Politics in Plural Societies: A Theory of Democratic Instability* (Columbus, OH: Charles E. Merrill, 1972); Horowitz, D., *Ethnic Groups in Conflict* (Berkeley, CA: University of California Press, 1985).

4. Not least because members of the Assembly are required to pre-designate themselves in ethnic terms: 'At their first meeting, members of the Assembly will register a designation of identity—nationalist, unionist or other—for the purposes of measuring cross-community support in Assembly votes'. This is somewhat contrary to Lijphart's prescription that wherever possible communities should be self-determined rather than pre-determined. See Lijphart, A., 'Self-Determination versus Pre-Determination of Ethnic Minorities in Power Sharing Systems', in W. Kymlicka (ed.), *The Rights of Minority Cultures* (Oxford: Oxford University Press, 1995), 275–87. It is also a focal point for some well-intentioned local critics of the Agreement who see it as a 'sectarian carve-up'. This well-known criticism, that consociational practices institutionalize divisions, is based on the wishful assumption that long-held ethno-national identities could easily be superseded. While pre-designation poses genuine dilemmas for the small cross-communal parties—principally APNI and NIWC—it is much less problematic for the larger parties, and of course helps ensure that 'key decisions' have authentic cross-community support.

5. Wilford, R., 'Epilogue', in P. Mitchell and R. Wilford (eds.), *Politics in Northern Ireland* (Boulder, CO: Westview Press, 1999), 285–303.

6. The comparison with the previous 1973 referendum in Northern Ireland is instructive. Faced with two important constitutional questions, the turnout was only 59 per cent. 99 per cent voted to stay in the UK because nationalists boycotted the poll. As an estimate of opinion the referendum thus served no useful purpose. The contrast with 1998 could not be more dramatic.

7. See Wilford, 'Epilogue'; also Sinnott, R., 'Historic Day Blemished by Low Poll', *Irish Times*, 26 June 1998. The RTE/Landsdowne exit poll reported that 55 per cent of those who described themselves as unionists supported the Agreement at the referendum.

8. Mitchell, P. and Gillespie, G., 'The Electoral Systems' in P. Mitchell and R. Wilford (eds.), *Politics in Northern Ireland* (1999), 66–90.

9. Gallagher, M., 'The Results Analysed', in M. Marsh and P. Mitchell (eds.), *How Ireland Voted 1997* (Boulder, CO: Westview Press, 1999), 121–50. The Droop quota used in STV is $V/(N + 1) + 1$, where V = Total Valid Votes, and N = Number of Assembly members to be elected.

10. See Mitchell, 'The Party System and Party Competition'.

11. See Laver, M., and Schofield, N., *Multiparty Government: The Politics of Coalition in Europe* (Oxford: Oxford University Press, 1990); also Mitchell, P., (1999), 'Government Formation: A Tale of Two Coalitions', in M. Marsh and P. Mitchell (eds.), *How Ireland Voted 1997*, 243–63.

12. The 1997 elections to Dáil Éireann provided a dramatic example of the advantages of electoral alliances. The largest party, Fianna Fáil, would often fail to win the final seat in many

constituencies because of its isolated non-coalition strategy. Transfers among the other parties would determine the destination of the final seat. However, in 1997 Fianna Fáil for the first time had a friendly party with which to form an electoral alliance. The pre-ballot electoral coalition with the Progressive Democrats resulted in Fianna Fáil winning seven extra seats on virtually the same share of the first preference vote. In a parliament in which the arithmetic is usually tight, this was enough to be decisive and ensured an alternation in power. While the Republic of Ireland is of course not an ethno-nationally divided polity, the electoral logic holds.

13. This does depend on the ideological distribution of the electorate. If many voters are located in extreme positions, then it may be possible to adopt co-operative—but not cross-communally accommodative—strategies by appealing to more extremist voters beyond one's party; in this case there are clearly no centripetal benefits.

14. See B. O'Leary, in Chapter 4 of this volume, and 'The British-Irish Agreement of 1998: Results and Prospects', Paper presented at University of Notre Dame, December 1999. See also O'Leary, 'The Nature of the British-Irish Agreement', *New Left Review*, 1999, 66–96.

15. See Whyte, J., *Interpreting Northern Ireland* (Oxford: Clarendon Press, 1990).

16. For example, in the 1989 local government elections SDLP terminal transfers split 47 per cent to Alliance and 33 per cent to Sinn Féin. See Elliott, S. and Smith, F. J., *Northern Ireland: The District Council Elections of 1989* (Belfast: The Queen's University of Belfast, 1992), 37.

17. For example Sinn Féin's average share of the nationalist (two party) vote since the peace process—four elections after the cease-fires—is 43 per cent, compared with just under 30 per cent in the immediately preceding four elections.

18. The first poll was conducted on 1–2 June and the second on 15–16 June, directed by MRBI and carried out by Harris Research Centre. They were both quota controlled samples of 1,000 voters across all 18 constituencies. For details see the *Irish Times* 18 June 1998. As is well known, some aspects of Northern Ireland politics pose insurmountable problems for polling companies. In particular the Sinn Féin vote is usually underestimated—by 8 and 10 per cent in the 1–2 and 15–16 June polls respectively—and not as many voters are as moderate as they claim to pollsters—APNI overestimated at 10 and 9 per cent respectively.

19. An Irish Times/RTE Prime Time exit poll conducted by Ulster Marketing Surveys amongst a sample of 2,000 voters. Accuracy level stated as ±3 per cent (*Irish Times*, 26 June 1998).

20. For the index, see Laakso, M. and Taagepera, R., 'Effective number of parties: a measure with application to West Europe', *Comparative Political Studies*, 12 (1979): 3–27. The 'effective number of parties' is a measure that takes into account the number of political parties and their relative weights. The calculation here is based on vote shares according to the formula: $N_v =$ the sum of $1/p$. See Taagepera, R. and Soberg Shugart, M., *Seats and Votes: The Effects and Determinants of Electoral Systems* (New Haven, CT: Yale University Press, 1989). Stated in words, N is 'the effective number of hypothetical equal-sized parties that would have the same effect on fractionalization of the party system as have the actual parties of varying sizes' (Taagepera and Shugart 79). In the figures reported above independents have been excluded.

21. The measure of disproportionality used is the least squares index (LSq) devised by Gallagher, M., 'Proportionality, disproportionality and electoral systems', *Electoral Studies*, 10 (1991): 33–51. Disproportionality $= \sqrt{1/2\Sigma(vi - Si)^2}$. While there are a variety of different indexes for this purpose, Lijphart regards the least squares method as 'the most sensitive and faithful reflection of the disproportionality of election results'. See Lijphart, A., *Electoral Systems and Party Systems: A Study of Twenty-Seven Democracies, 1945–1990* (New York, NY: Oxford University Press, 1994), 62. 'Others' and independents have been excluded from the calculations.

22. See Mitchell and Gillespie, 'The Electoral Systems'.

23. In many cases more than four of the assembly members elected represented one bloc or the other. The constituencies of North Antrim, East Belfast, and Strangford elected five unionist members, while Foyle and West Belfast returned five and six nationalists, respectively.

24. Once again the highest turnout was in the highly mobilized Mid Ulster constituency (83.2 per cent); the lowest was in North Down (59.2 per cent).

25. See Mitchell, 'The Party System and Party Competition'.

26. See Muller, W. and Strøm, K., *Coalition Governments in Western Europe* (Oxford: Oxford University Press, 2000).

27. See Laver and Schofield *Multiparty Government*, 15.
28. Of course this is neither accidental nor in itself a bad thing. O'Leary has correctly argued that: 'The special skill of the designers/negotiators is that they have created strong incentives towards executive power-sharing and power-division, but without requiring parties to have any prior formal coalition agreement—other than the institutional agreement—and without requiring any party to renounce its long-run aspirations' (O'Leary, 'The British-Irish Agreement of 1998', 7).
29. The offices of the joint first ministers elected on a cross-communal basis are intended to provide policy co-ordination and coherence. However, not only was there no agreed coalition policy document prior to formation—this is common practice, for example, in Italy and France—but even more unusually there were no inter-party negotiations to determine portfolio allocations. Instead parties simply picked ministries in rotation according to d'Hondt.
30. Even if the APNI, PUP, and NIWC are counted as 'external support' parties for the Executive, their ten votes in the Assembly (combined) are not enough to compensate for loss of the DUP's twenty votes in a polarizing vote.
31. To date, the DUP's participation in executive functions has been partial. In the initial phase of devolution, the party focused on its line ministries and committee work. It avoided direct contact with Sinn Féin's two ministers, boycotted all meetings of the Executive Committee and did not participate in North-South co-operation. The difficulties this caused at Executive Committee level were compounded when devolution was restored in May 2000. Confronted with the alternative of reassuming its two ministerial posts or of relinquishing them and going into opposition within the Assembly, they chose the former course but on the basis that they would rotate the ministries among their Assembly members. This enabled the DUP to maintain its presence within the Executive and, though subject to periodic bouts of ministerial musical chairs, to demonstrate that their Ministers were able and effective custodians of office. In that respect, while not acting as 'all-out wreckers' of the Strand One institutions, their action has made the task of realizing joined-up government at Executive level that much more elusive.
32. Laver, M. and Shepsle, K., *Making and Breaking Governments: Cabinets and Legislatures in Parliamentary Democracies* (New York, NY: Cambridge University Press, 1996), 280. However, the Executive is in no sense omnipotent. Its decisions are subject to cross-community voting procedures in the Assembly and to a form of committee oversight that is much more powerful than anything in the British or Irish parliamentary tradition.
33. Strand One, point 25 reads: 'An individual may be removed from office following a decision of the Assembly taken on a cross-community basis, if (s)he loses the confidence of the Assembly, voting on a cross-community basis, for failure to meet his or her responsibilities including, inter alia, those set out in the Pledge of Office. Those who hold office should use only democratic, non-violent means, and those who do not should be excluded or removed from office under these provisions'. *(The Agreement: Agreement Reached in the Multi-Party Negotiations*, no date, no place).
34. Two other tactical matters are relevant. First, while abstentions in parliament may be symbolically meaningful, they are not, as is often suggested, 'neutral'. Many abstentions—for example Sinn Féin's on the nomination of Trimble and Mallon as first ministers—are strategically equivalent to 'Yes' votes. Secondly, the cross-community voting arrangements depend upon ethnic self-designation. Under Assembly Standing Orders a party can change its designation only once during any given Assembly's life. Thus, a not unrealistic scenario that has been floated is that some of the 'others'—for example the Women's Coalition—could redesignate as 'unionist', thus increasing the proportion of 'Yes' unionists. A legal, though politically unrealistic, Machiavellian power manoeuvre would be for the SDLP to redesignate as 'Yes unionists'! In this scenario the cost of building a decisive winning coalition would most likely be electoral annihilation.
35. See Horowitz, *Ethnic Groups in Conflict*; and his, *A Democratic South Africa? Constitutional Engineering in a Divided Society* (Berkeley, CA: University of California Press, 1991).
36. Horowitz however makes a strong case for adopting the Alternative Vote (AV) rather than STV in ethnic party systems largely because the higher effective threshold under AV than STV induces a greater incentive towards vote-pooling. For a variety of reasons, but especially

because AV is a majoritarian and disproportional system, it would not be at all appropriate for Northern Ireland's polarized multi-party system. As we have already seen in relation to elect-oral turnout, the distribution of voters is such that many constituencies are predominantly unionist or nationalist. The imposition of a majority threshold by introducing AV would thus be highly unlikely to induce the vote pooling desired by Horowitz. Indeed, there are good rea-sons to believe that AV would reinforce communal polarization, so that the representation of minority communities would be reduced or even eliminated in many more constituencies than is the case under STV—in 1998 only West Belfast returned six members that were all from the same bloc.

37. Evans, G. and O'Leary, B., 'Northern Irish Voters and the British-Irish Agreement: Foundations of a Stable Consociational Settlement?', *The Political Quarterly*, 71 (2000): 78–101.

38. The SDLP informally recommended that their supporters transfer to pro-Agreement parties, though there was no formal transfer agreement with Sinn Féin despite Gerry Adams's call for one. Perhaps not surprisingly given the sharp competition with the DUP—and in the context of a first post-Agreement election—UUP leader Trimble did not recommend transfers to the SDLP. In these circumstances he probably did as much as he could by saying that UUP vot-ers should make up their own minds on transfers on the basis of local circumstances (*Irish Times*, 24 June 1998).

39. However, note that the UUP has received significant to very dramatic seat bonuses in all Northern Ireland elections under a variety of electoral systems. The bonuses are of course larger with the plurality system (see Mitchell and Gillespie, 'The Electoral Systems', Table 4.4).

40. Evans and O'Leary, 'Northern Irish Voters and the British-Irish Agreement'.

41. *Ibid.*, 89–91.

42. *Ibid.*, 90.

43. Michael Gallagher has noted that due to a recent change of the electoral law in the Republic of Ireland, transfers are not always as informative as they used to be because returning offi-cers are now permitted to perform multiple eliminations of candidates if their combined vote total is less than that of the next lowest placed candidate (Gallagher, 'The Results Analysed', 137). The consequence is that the origin of some transfers is indeterminate. Unfortunately, multiple eliminations are also permitted in Northern Ireland, though they were not all that frequent in 1998. The following results refer only to determinate cases.

44. Elliott and Smith, *Northern Ireland: The District Council Elections of 1989*, 36.

45. See *ibid.*, 35. The figures cited are determinate aggregate transfers—that is, transfers at any stage of the count—rather than terminal transfers when the party of the candidate making the transfer has no other party candidates remaining in the count.

46. In earlier decades Fianna Fáil on average retained around 82 per cent of its transfers (Gallagher, M., 'The Election of the 27th Dáil', in M. Gallagher and M. Laver (eds.) *How Ireland Voted 1992* (Dublin: Folens and PSAI Press, 1993), 57–78; Gallagher, 'The Results Analysed').

47. Evans and O'Leary, 'Northern Irish Voters and the British-Irish Agreement'.

48. Sinnott, 'Historic Day Blemished by Low Poll'.

49. We can also note the one case of a Sinn Féin terminal transfer in which the three candidates remaining in the count were unionists (Fermanagh South-Tyrone). 37 per cent transferred to the UUP candidate and only 6.2 per cent to the two 'No' unionists combined. Irrespective of whether one thinks this should be a pre-condition it is clearly a reality given political dynam-ics within the UUP.

4

The Character of the 1998 Agreement: Results and Prospects

BRENDAN O'LEARY*

Introduction

The 1998 Agreement was a major achievement, both for its negotiators and for the peoples of Ireland and Britain, emerging from a political desert whose only landmarks were failed 'initiatives'. The Agreement's proposed model of devolution was consociational, meeting the criteria specified by Arend Lijphart *namely*, cross-community executive power-sharing; proportionality rules throughout the governmental and public sectors; community self-government or autonomy and equality in cultural life; and veto rights for minorities.[1] A consociation is an association of communities, in this case British unionist, Irish nationalist, and others,[2] that is the outcome of formal or informal bargains or pacts between the political leaders of ethnic or religious groups. The Agreement was the product of both tacit and explicit consociational thought,[3] and of 'pacting' by most of the leaders of the key ethno-national groups and their respective patron-states.

But the Agreement was not just consociational, and departed from Lijphart's prescriptions in important respects. It had important external dimensions; it was made with the leaders of *national*, and not just ethnic or religious communities— unlike most previously existing consociations—and it was endorsed by (most of) the leaders and (most of) the led in referendums across a sovereign border. It was the first consociational settlement endorsed by a referendum that required concurrent majorities in jurisdictions in different states. The Agreement foresaw an internal consociation within overarching confederal and federalizing institutions; it had elements of co-sovereignty in the arrangements agreed between its patron-states; it promised a novel model of 'double protection'; and it rested on a bargain derived from diametrically conflicting hopes about its likely long-run outcome. One supplement must be added: the Agreement's implementation was vulnerable to attempted renegotiation, and to legalism. When this chapter was composed these difficulties were manifest in the UK's unilateral decision in February 2000 to suspend (some of) the institutions of the Agreement.

The Internal Settlement: A Distinctive Consociation

The Agreement established a single chamber Assembly, and an Executive for Northern Ireland. The Assembly and Executive were to have full legislative and executive competence for economic development, education, health and social services, agriculture, environment, and finance (including the local civil service). Through 'cross-community agreement' the Assembly was entitled to expand these competencies; and, again through such agreement, and with the consent of the UK Secretary of State and the Westminster Parliament, the Assembly was entitled to legislate for any non-devolved reserved function. Maximum feasible devolved self-government[4] was therefore within the scope of the local decision-makers—and a convention might have developed in which the Secretary of State and Westminster 'rubber stamped' any measures of the Assembly.[5] Indeed it was conceivable that much public policy in Ireland, North and South, would eventually be made without direct British ministerial involvement—though the British budgetary allocation would be pivotal as long as Northern Ireland remains in the UK.

Elected Assembly members were obliged to designate themselves as 'nationalist', 'unionist' or 'other'—in this respect Lijphart's injunctions in favour of full self-determination rather than pre-determination were violated. After the Assembly was elected in June 1998 this requirement posed difficult questions for the Alliance and other 'cross-community' parties, such as the Women's Coalition. Through standard majority rule the Assembly was entitled to pass 'normal laws' within its competencies, though there was provision for a minority of 30 of the 108 Assembly members, to trigger special procedures that required special majorities—see Wilford, in Chapter 6 of this volume. 'Key decisions', the passage of controversial legislation, including the budget, automatically have these special procedures that require 'cross-community' support. Two rules were designed for this purpose. The first was *'parallel consent'*, a majority that encompasses a strict concurrent majority of the nationalists and unionists. It required that a law be endorsed, amongst those present and voting, both by an overall majority of Assembly members, and by a majority of both its unionist and nationalist members respectively. Table 4.1, which records the numbers in each bloc returned in the June 1998 election, shows that parallel consent with all members present, required the support of 22 nationalists, and 30 unionists, as well as an overall majority in the Assembly. With all present a majority of the Assembly is 55 members—which means that measures may pass under parallel consent procedures that are dependent upon the support of the 'others'—22 nationalists, 30 unionists and 3 others enable the passage of a key decision—so this rule did not automatically render the 'others' unimportant.

The second rule was that of *'weighted majority'*. This required, amongst those present and voting, that a measure have the support of 60 per cent of members,

TABLE 4.1. *The shares of blocs in the 1998 Assembly*

Bloc	Seats won (N)	First preference vote (%)	Seats won (%)
Nationalists	42	39.8	38.8
'Yes' Unionists	30	25.0	27.7
'No' Unionists	28	25.5	25.9
Others	8	9.4	7.4
Total(s)	108	100	100

Key: 'Nationalists' include the SDLP (nationalist) and Sinn Féin (republican). 'Yes Unionists' supported the Agreement, and included the Ulster Unionist Party (UUP) and the Progressive Unionist Party (PUP). 'No Unionists' opposed the Agreement, and included the Democratic Unionist Party (DUP), the United Kingdom Unionist Party (UKUP) which has since split, and independent unionists. 'Others' include the Alliance party and the Women's Coalition.
Note: The voting system was the Single Transferable Vote in 18 six-member constituencies. Percentages do not add to 100 because of rounding.

that is, 65 members when all members vote, or 64 excluding the Speaker (Presiding Officer). And it required the support of 40 per cent of both nationalist and unionist members, that is, in the 1998–2000 Assembly at least 17 nationalists had to consent under this procedure, and at least 24 unionists. All nationalists (42) and the minimum necessary number of unionists (24) had the required combined support for any measure to pass in this way—without support from the 'others'. By contrast, all the others (8), and the minimum number of nationalists (17) and the minimum number of unionists (24), could not deliver a majority, let alone a weighted majority.

The election outcome suggested that pro-Agreement unionists (30) would be vulnerable to pressure from anti-Agreement unionists (28)—indeed one of the UUP's members (Peter Weir) subsequently resigned the party whip and from then on counted as a 'No Unionist'. Even without this resignation, just one UUP Assembly member could have refused to be part of the unionist majority necessary to work the parallel consent rule. But there was a little room for manœuvre. The UUP could have delivered a workable portion of a cross-community majority under the weighted majority rule, even with six dissidents—providing David Trimble, its leader, could be certain of the support of the two Progressive Unionist Party (PUP) Assembly members—which was likely—and providing that he could live with support from Sinn Féin—a much more uncomfortable prospect.

The cross-community consent rules were vital to the design of the internal consociation, but not entirely predictable. The UK legislation implied that the parallel consent procedure must be attempted first, and then the weighted majority procedure could be followed. The operation of the cross-community rules would have depended not just on how parties registered, but on how disciplined they would be—justified fears about disunity within the UUP acknowledged this fact.

There was, lastly, one super-majority rule that was not explicitly concurrent, cross-community, or consociational in nature. Post-Agreement it was decided that the Assembly might, by a two-thirds resolution of its membership, call an extraordinary general election before its statutory four-year term expired. This was agreed in preference to a proposal that the Secretary of State should have the power to dissolve the Assembly—a sign of the local parties' commitment to increasing their self-government rather than accepting continuing arbitration from Westminster. Subsequently, to suspend the Assembly the Secretary of State had to pass new primary UK legislation outside the remit of the Agreement—which is why Irish nationalists regarded the suspension as a breach of the Agreement.

Executive Power-Sharing

The Agreement established two quasi-presidential figures, a novel dyarchy, a First Minister and a deputy First Minister, elected together by the parallel consent procedure. This procedure was intended to supply very strong incentives to unionists and nationalists to nominate a candidate for one of these positions that was acceptable to a majority of the other bloc's Assembly members. In the first elections for these posts, in *designate* form, pro-Agreement unionists in the UUP and the Progressive Unionist Party, who then had a majority of registered unionists, voted solidly for the combination of David Trimble of the UUP and Seamus Mallon of the SDLP. Naturally so did the SDLP, which enjoyed a majority among registered nationalists. The 'No unionists' voted against this combination, while Sinn Féin abstained.

The rule ensured that a unionist and a nationalist shared the top two posts. The Agreement and its UK legislative enactment, the *Northern Ireland Act* (1998) made clear that both posts had identical symbolic and external representation functions. Indeed both had identical powers. The sole difference was in their titles: both were to preside over the 'Executive Committee' of Ministers, and have a role in co-ordinating its work.[6] This dual premiership critically depended upon the personal co-operation of the two holders of these posts, and upon the co-operation of their respective majorities—or pluralities. The *Northern Ireland Act* (1998) reinforced their interdependence by requiring that 'if either the First Minister or the deputy First Minister ceases to hold office, whether by resignation or otherwise, the other shall also cease to hold office' (Article 14 (6)). This latter rule underscored the delicacy of the dual premiership. Indeed the proximate cause of the suspension of the Agreement in February 2000 was the fear that the threatened resignation of the First Minister, David Trimble, would have produced an unworkable Assembly. Given that there were now twenty-nine 'No Unionists' with a blocking veto, the UK

Government feared that Trimble would not have had sufficient support to return to office under the parallel consent rule. In fact the Assembly could have proposed, under its existing procedures, by weighted majority, an amendment to the procedures for electing the First and Deputy First Ministers—which Westminster could have ratified under the mechanisms discussed above—but this possibility was neglected.

This dyarchy, forged in the heat of inter-party negotiations, would have been a novel quasi-presidential development because, unlike executive presidencies, and unlike most prime ministers, neither the First nor the Deputy First Minister formally appointed the other ministers to the Executive Committee. Instead posts in the Executive Committee were to be allocated to parties in proportion to their strength in the Assembly, according to the d'Hondt rule. The premiers did, however, have implicit and explicit co-ordinating functions, as approved by the shadow Assembly in February 1999—see Wilford, in Chapter 6 of this volume.

The d'Hondt rule was fairly clear in its consequences: any party that wins a significant share of seats and is willing to abide by the new institutional rules has a reasonable chance of access to the Executive, a subtle form of Lijphart's 'grand coalition government'. It was a *voluntary* grand coalition because parties were free to exclude themselves from the Executive Committee, and because no programme of government had to be negotiated before executive formation. The initial design created strong incentives for parties to take their entitlement to seats in the executive because if they did not, their entitlement would go either to their ethno-national rivals, or to their rivals in their own bloc. The rules did not, however, formally require any specific proportion of nationalists and unionists. That was temporarily changed: in the course of the crisis over executive formation in the summer of 1999, the Secretary of State introduced a new rule requiring that a well-formed executive consist of at least three designated nationalists and three designated unionists.[7]

The d'Hondt rule meant that parties had the right to nominate ministers according to their respective strength in seats—no vote of confidence was required by the Assembly—and to choose, in order of their strength, their preferred ministries. An individual minister could be deposed from office, by cross-community rules, but the party that held the relevant ministry would have been able to appoint his or her successor from amongst its ranks—see Wilford, in Chapter 6 of this volume.

Crisis over executive formation was the first sign that the Agreement might falter. The crisis arose for political and constitutional reasons. Politically, because David Trimble insisted that Sinn Féin deliver some IRA decommissioning before its members would take their seats in the Executive Committee: 'no government before guns' became his party's slogan. Under the text of the Agreement Trimble had no constitutional warrant to exercise this veto:

1. No party was entitled to veto another party's membership of the Executive—
   though the Assembly as a whole, through cross-community consent, was free
   to deem a party unfit for office.
2. The Agreement did not require decommissioning before executive formation
   on the part of any paramilitaries or of any parties connected to them—though
   it did require parties to use their best endeavours to achieve the completion
   of decommissioning within two years, that is, by 22 May 2000. Indeed it was
   precisely this fact that prompted Jeffrey Donaldson to leave the UUP's negotiating team the day the Agreement was made.
3. Any 'natural' reading of the Agreement mandated executive formation as the
   first step necessary to bring all of the Agreement's institutions 'on line'.

Trimble rested his (flimsy) case on a communication he had received from the
UK premier on the morning of the Agreement, indicating that it was Tony
Blair's view that decommissioning 'should begin straight away'. Communications from UK premiers do not, of course, have the force of law—outside the
ranks of New Labour! Trimble's concern was to appease critics of the
Agreement within his own party, and amongst his voters. His negotiating team
split in the making of the Agreement, a majority of his party's Westminster
members opposed the Agreement, and his new Assembly party contained critics of aspects of the Agreement. So he felt obliged to play for time before implementing the Agreement.

Trimble was initially facilitated in exercising his veto by UK and Irish
Governments sympathetic to his exposed position. He also took advantage of the
fact that the SDLP did not make the formation of the rest of the executive a
pre-condition of its support for the Trimble/Mallon ticket for First and Deputy
First Minister. The SDLP wished to shore up Trimble's political position. One
flexible provision in the Agreement gave Trimble further room for manœuvre.
The Agreement stated that there must be at least six 'Other Ministers', but that
there could be 'up to' ten. The number of ministries was to be decided by cross-
community consent, and that gave an opportunity to delay on executive formation. It would be December 1998 before the parties reached agreement on ten
ministries after the UUP abandoned its demand for a seven-seat Executive in
which unionists would have had a 4:3 majority.

The protracted crisis over executive formation was, in principle, resolved in
mid-November 1999. Unionists accepted that executive formation would
occur—with the IRA appointing an interlocutor to negotiate with the International Commission on Decommissioning (IICD)—while actual decommissioning, consistent with the text of the Agreement, would not be required until
after executive formation. Senator George Mitchell in concluding his eleven-
week review of the Agreement, and with the consent of the pro-Agreement
parties, stated that 'Devolution should take effect, then the executive should
meet, and then the paramilitary groups should appoint their authorized repres-

entatives, all on the same day, in that order'. This was an honourable resolution to what looked like becoming a fundamental impasse. However, to get it passed by the Ulster Unionist Council David Trimble felt obliged to give his party a post-dated resignation letter—which meant that if there was no IRA decommissioning reported by February 2000 the UUP would walk out of the executive. No such IRA decommissioning occurred, though the IRA did appear to clarify that decommissioning would occur. Fearful that Trimble could not be resurrected as First Minister, the Secretary of State Peter Mandelson sought new powers from Westminster and suspended the Executive and the Assembly.

The consociational criterion of cross-community executive power-sharing was clearly met in the Agreement, but there were special features of the new arrangements that differed from consociational experiments elsewhere. Ministers took a 'Pledge of Office', not an 'Oath of Allegiance'. This cemented the binationalism at the heart of the Agreement: nationalist ministers did not have to swear an Oath of Allegiance to the Crown or the Union. The Pledge required ministers to:

(1) discharge their duties in good faith;
(2) follow exclusively peaceful and democratic politics;
(3) participate in preparing a programme of government; and
(4) support and follow the decisions of the Executive Committee and the Assembly.

The duties of office included a requirement to serve all the people equally, to promote equality and to prevent discrimination—which means, according to the UK's doctrine of ministerial responsibility, that civil servants were bound to run their departments consistent with these obligations.[8] They included a requirement that the 'relevant Ministers' serve in the North-South Ministerial Council, a duty that, in conjunction with other clauses, was designed to prevent parties opposed to this aspect of the Agreement, such as the DUP, from taking office in good faith—*cf* Wilford, in Chapter 6 of this volume.

The special skill of the designers and negotiators of the Agreement was to create strong incentives for executive power-sharing and power-division, but without requiring parties to have any prior formal coalition agreement—other than the institutional Agreement—and without requiring any party to renounce its long-run aspirations. The dual premiership was designed to tie moderate representatives of each bloc together, and to give some drive towards overall policy-coherence. The d'Hondt mechanism not only ensured inclusivity but also saved on the transaction costs of bargaining over portfolios. Distinctive coalitions could form around different issues within the Executive, permitting flexibility, but inhibiting chaos—given the requirement that the budget be agreed by cross-community consent. In these respects and others the Agreement differed positively from the Sunningdale experiment.

What was not foreseen was that failure to timetable the formation of the rest of the Executive immediately after the election of the First and Deputy First

Ministers might precipitate a protracted crisis of Executive-formation. Amendments to the *Northern Ireland Act* (1998) could be adopted by the UK Parliament, or by the Assembly, that would be consistent with the Agreement, to prevent any recurrence of this type of crisis. In future, candidates for First and Deputy First Minister could be obliged to state the number of executive portfolios that will be available, and the formation of the executive should be required immediately after their election. Otherwise the election of the First Minister and Deputy First Minister should be rendered null and void. That would plug this particular constitutional hole. It may, however, be unnecessary because it is not likely that future candidates for First and Deputy Ministers will agree to be nominated without a firm agreement from their opposite number on the number of portfolios and the date of cabinet formation.

Forms of Proportionality

Consociational arrangements are built on principles of proportionality. The Agreement met this test in four ways: in the d'Hondt procedure for executive formation discussed above; in the Assembly's committees—see Wilford, in Chapter 6 of this volume; in the electoral system for the Assembly; and in recruitment and promotion policies within the public sector.

The Assembly's Committees

The Assembly was to have committees scrutinizing each of the departments headed by ministers. Committee chairs and deputy chairs were allocated according to the d'Hondt rule. Committee composition was in proportion to the composition of the Assembly. Each committee had to approve any proposed new law within its jurisdiction tabled by ministers, and indeed committees could initiate legislative proposals. In consequence, a committee dominated by other parties could block the legislative initiatives of a dynamic minister; and it could initiate legislation not to that minister's liking—though the success of such proposals would be subject to cross-community special procedures. Thus, the committee system effectively combines the consociational principles of proportionality and veto-rights. The principles were reinforced by the stipulation in the *Northern Ireland Act* (1998) that the committees could not be chaired or deputy chaired by ministers or junior ministers, and the further requirement that they be organized in such a way that the chair and deputy chair were drawn from different parties from the relevant minister.

The Assembly's Election System: Corrections for Lijphart and Horowitz?   Elections to the 108 member Assembly used a proportional representation system, the sin-

gle transferable vote, STV, in eighteen six-member constituencies—though the Assembly could choose, by cross-community consent procedures, to advocate change from this system. The Droop quota in each constituency was therefore 14.3 per cent of the vote, which squeezed the very small parties, or, alternatively, encouraged them to form electoral alliances.[9] Thus, the smaller of the two loyalist parties, the Ulster Democratic Party (UDP), won no seats in the first Assembly election. However, minor parties which can gather lower order preferences from across the unionist and nationalist blocs, such as the Women's Coalition, have shown that the system need not preclude representation for small parties amongst the 'others'.

This voting system is not what Lijphart recommends: he is an advocate of party-list PR systems, principally because he believes they help make party leaders more powerful, and better able to sustain inter-ethnic consociational deals.[10] Those who would like to see David Trimble in greater control of his party might have hankered after Lijphart's preferred form of proportional representation. The Northern Ireland case, however, suggests that a modification of the consociational prescriptive canon is in order. Had a region-wide list-system been in operation in June 1998 the UUP would have ended up with fewer seats—fewer even than the SDLP—rendering the implementation of the Agreement even more problematic. There is a further and less contingent argument against party list-systems, especially important where the relevant ethnic communities are internally democratic rather than sociologically and politically monolithic. A region-wide party list election gives incentives for the formation of a wide variety of micro-parties. In Northern Ireland it would have fragmented and shredded the votes of the major parties which made the Agreement. Hard-liners under party-list systems have every reason to form fresh parties knowing that their disloyalty will penalize more moderate parties, but without necessarily reducing the total vote and seat share of the relevant ethno-national bloc. This objection to Lijphart's favoured prescription is not merely speculative. The 1996 elections to the Northern Ireland Peace Forum used a mixture of a party-list system and 'reserved seats'. Party-proliferation and the erosion of the UUP first preference vote[11] were some of the more obvious consequences.[12]

STV, of course, does not guarantee party discipline as multiple candidates for the same party in a given constituency may present different emphases on party commitments. Yet, combined with higher effective thresholds than under most forms of party-list PR, the system makes it more likely that parties will remain formally unified, and therefore able to make and maintain consociational deals. At the very least the prescriptive superiority of the party-list system for these purposes is unproven, and Lijphart's consistent counsel in this respect should be modified.[13]

As well as achieving proportionality STV has the great merit of encouraging inter-ethnic 'vote-pooling':[14] in principle, voters could have used their lower-order preferences (transfers) to reward pro-Agreement candidates at the expense of anti-Agreement candidates.[15] In this respect STV looks tailor-made to achieve the 'inter-ethnic' and 'cross-ethnic' voting favoured by Donald Horowitz, a critic of consociational thinking but a strong advocate of institutional and policy devices to facilitate conflict-reduction.[16] Consistent, however, with his general premises, Horowitz believes that the STV system damages the prospects for inter-ethnic co-operation because the relatively low quota required to win a seat in six-member constituencies (14.3 per cent) makes it too easy for hard-line parties and their candidates to be successful.[17] He also thinks that the Agreement's other institutions, biased towards the key consociational partners—nationalists and unionists—compounded this effect by weakening the prospects of cross-ethnic parties, such as Alliance, which he believed impaired conflict-reduction.

The Northern Ireland case suggests that normative and empirical challenges to Horowitz's reasoning are in order. Horowitz would generally prefer the use of the Alternative Vote (AV) in single-member constituencies in Northern Ireland, as elsewhere, because its quota—50 per cent plus one—would deliver strong support to moderate ethno-national and cross-ethnic candidates. The problem with this prescription is straightforward. The outcomes it would deliver would be majoritarian, disproportional, and unpredictably so, and they would be disproportional both within and across blocs. They would, additionally, have much more indirectly 'inclusive' effects than STV. In some of Northern Ireland's constituencies there would be unambiguous unionist and nationalist majorities—and thus AV would lead to the under-representation of minority voters within these constituencies, and to local fiefdoms. Secondly, while candidates would have to seek support for lower-order preferences under AV, it would not be obvious that their best strategy would be to seek lower-order preferences across the ethno-national divide because the imperative of staying in the count would dictate building as big an initial first and second preference vote tally as possible.[18] Lastly, AV would never be agreed by hard-line parties entering a consociational settlement if they believed that it would be likely to undermine their electoral support. Since the Agreement was made possible by encouraging 'inclusivity', by facilitating negotiations which included Sinn Féin—the party that had supported the IRA—and the PUP and the UDP—the parties that had supported the UVF and the UDA—it would have been perverse for their leaders to have agreed an electoral system that minimized their prospects.

Indeed STV arguably worked both *before and after* the Agreement to consolidate the Agreement's prospects. It had helped to moderate the policy stance of Sinn Féin. After its first phase of electoral participation in elections in Northern Ireland in the 1980s, and in the Republic in the latter half of the 1980s, the party discovered that it was in a ghetto. Its candidates in some local government constituencies accumulated large numbers of first-preference ballot papers, only to remain unelected as a range of other parties' candidates overtook them to achieve quotas on the basis of lower-order preferences. They received very few lower order preferences from SDLP voters. But once the party moderated its stance, once it promoted the IRA's cease-fire(s), and became the champion of a peace process and a negotiated settlement, it found that its first-preference vote, its transfer-vote, and its seats-won all increased.

The constitutional design argument that can be extracted from this story is this: once there has been party fragmentation within ethno-national blocs then STV can assist accommodating postures and initiatives by parties and candidates, both intra- and inter-bloc.[19] Horowitz's electoral integrationist prescriptions are most pertinent at the formation of a competitive party system. However, once party formation and pluralism have occurred there will be few agents with the incentives to implement Horowitz's preferences, and if a third-party or outside power did so it would be a provocation to the less moderate parties, and would therefore most likely reignite ethno-national tensions.[20] This argument is, of course, a very qualified one: STV is certainly not enough, and it may not be appropriate everywhere. But it can help both to promote accommodative moves and consolidate consociational deals in ways that region-wide party-list systems and the AV system in single member districts cannot.

There has been some empirical confirmation of the merits of STV since the Agreement was made—see Mitchell, in Chapter 3 of this volume. 'Vote-pooling' occurred within the first Assembly elections—as we can surmise, to an extent, from actual counts[21] and, as Geoffrey Evans and I can confirm from a survey we helped design.[22] In our survey, approximately 10 per cent of each bloc's first-preference supporters gave lower-order preference support to pro-Agreement candidates in the other bloc. Within-bloc rewards for moderation also occurred: Sinn Féin won lower order preferences from SDLP voters, and the PUP had candidates elected on the basis of transfers from other candidates.

The *Northern Ireland Act* 1998 and the *Northern Ireland (Elections) Act* 1998 opened one novelty in the practice of STV in Ireland. Both Acts left it open to the Secretary of State to determine the method of filling vacancies: through by-elections, substitutes, or through whichever method the Secretary of State deems fit. By-elections are anomalous in a PR system.[23] A candidate who wins the last seat in a six-member constituency and who subsequently resigns or dies is unlikely to be replaced by a candidate of the same party or persuasion in a by-election—which becomes the equivalent of the alternative vote in a single-member constituency. The *Northern Ireland Assembly (Elections) Order* of 1998 provided for a system of alternates, or personally nominated substitutes with a provision for by-elections if the alternates system fails to provide a substitute. The disproportionality possibly induced by by-elections—with consequent unpredictable ramifications for the numbers of registered nationalists and unionists and the cross-community rules—needed to be engineered out of the settlement, and it was encouraging that the parties co-operated with this concern in mind.

Recruitment and Representativeness in the Public Sector Proportionality rules combined with accommodative incentives did not stop with the Executive, the committee system, or with the electoral system. The Agreement was consistent with past and future measures taken to promote fair employment and (modest) affirmative action in the public sector that will, one hopes, eventually ensure a representative and non-discriminatory civil service and judiciary.

Most significantly, the Agreement envisaged a representative police force— see Walker, C. in Chapter 8 of this volume. The Patten Report published in September 1999 was an able expression of democratic thought on policing and fulfilled the mandate of the Agreement.[24] Given that the parties could not agree on police reform, the Commission had to propose policing arrangements consistent with the internal and external spirit of the Agreement. Patten delivered, including on recommendations for better-structured cross-border co-operation with the *Garda Siochana* in the Republic. Significantly, the Report's recommendations mostly do not depend upon the Agreement's institutions for their implementation. The commissioners explicitly recommended most of their changes come what may.[25] Policing is thus in principle scheduled for full-scale transformation.

In short, in the entirety of the important posts in the public sector the principles of representativeness and proportionality are to be applied, either in the form of party representativeness, or in the form of representative bureaucracies and public services. There is one exception left: the judiciary, and here the proposal to have a judicial appointments commission may eventually perform the same task.

Communal Autonomy and Equality

Consociational settlements avoid the compulsory integration of peoples. Instead they seek, through bargaining, to manage differences equally and justly. They do not prevent voluntary integration or assimilation; and to be liberal, such settlements must protect those who wish to have their identities counted differently, or not as collective identities.

The Agreement left in place the recently established arrangements for primary and secondary schooling in Northern Ireland in which Catholic, Protestant, and integrated schools are equally funded. In this respect Northern Ireland is fully consociational but liberal—one can avoid Catholic and Protestant schools. The Agreement also makes new provisions for the educational use, protection, and public use of the Irish language—along the lines used for Welsh within the principality—thereby adding linguistic to educational protections of Irish nationalist culture.

Most importantly, the Agreement completes the equalization of both major communities as national communities, that is, as British and Irish communities not just, as is so misleadingly emphasized, as Protestants and Catholics. The

European Convention on Human Rights—which is weak on the protection of collective rights and equality rights—will be supplemented by measures that will give Northern Ireland its own tailor-made Bill of Rights, to protect both national groupings as well as individuals. The worst illusion of parties to the conflict and some of its successive managers, based in London, Belfast, or Dublin, held that Northern Ireland could be stable and democratic while being either British or Irish. The Agreement promises to make Northern Ireland binational—and opens up the prospect of a fascinating jurisprudence, not least in the regulation of parades and marches.

The Agreement did not neglect the non-national dimensions of local politics, nor did it exclude the 'Others'. All aspects of unjustified social equalities, as well as inequalities between the national communities, were recognized in the text of the Agreement, and given some means of institutional redress and monitoring. The Agreement addresses national equality, the allegiances to the Irish and British nations, *and* social equality, that is, other dimensions that differentiate groups and individuals in Northern Ireland: religion, race, ethnic affiliation, sex, and sexuality. And equality issues, be they national or social, were not left exclusively to the local parties to manage and negotiate, which might be a recipe for stalemate. Instead, under the Agreement, the UK Government has created a new statutory obligation on public authorities. They will be required to carry out all their functions with due regard to the need to promote equality of opportunity in relation to people's religious background and political opinions; and with respect to their gender, race, disabilities, age, marital status, and sexual orientation. This commitment entails what McCrudden labels 'mainstreaming equality'.[26] The UK Government has also established a Human Rights Commission under the Agreement, tasked with an extended and enhanced role compared with its predecessor, including monitoring, the power to instigate litigation, and drafting a tailor-made local Bill of Rights.

Minority Veto Rights

The final dimension of an internal consociational settlement is the protection of minorities through tacit or explicit veto rights. The Agreement fulfilled this criterion in the Assembly, in the courts, and through enabling political appeals to both the UK and Irish Governments.

The Assembly has procedures—parallel consent, weighted majority, and the petition of concern—that protect nationalists from unionist dominance. Indeed they did so in such a comprehensive manner that the rules designed to protect the nationalist minority were deployed by hard-line unionist opponents of the Agreement to wreck its initiation and development. Indeed, their threatened use by 'No' unionists was the immediate excuse employed by the Secretary of State to suspend the Assembly. The 'Others' were less well protected in the Assembly—they could be outvoted by a simple majority, and any nationalist-unionist super-majority, and their numbers left them well short of being able to trigger a petition on their own. However, the 'Others' were not at the heart of the conflict so it is not surprising that they were not at the heart of its pacts—though it is not accurate to claim that they were excluded.

In the courts, the 'Others', as well as disaffected nationalists and unionists, will have means to redress breaches of their human and collective rights. The content of the European Convention on Human Rights is well known. What is less clear is what package of collective rights the new independent Northern Ireland Human Rights Commission will recommend. But the new policing arrangements, if they follow the Patten Report, will be infused with a human rights culture see Walker, C. in Chapter 8 of this volume. The incorporation of the European Convention into public law, and Northern Ireland's forthcoming provisions to strengthen the rights of national, religious, and cultural minorities, will ensure that policing arrangements have to perform to higher standards.

The Agreement provided for a review of the criminal justice system that would include 'arrangements for making appointments to the judiciary'. It was a vital, though delayed, part of embedding the settlement that a judicial appointments body ensure that the judiciary reflected, meritoriously, the different communities in the North, and be committed to the human and minority rights provisions that it will increasingly interpret. The Criminal Justice Review which made these recommendations was published late, after the suspension of the Assembly—its lateness apparently the product of resistance to possible 'read across' effects in Scotland and Wales.

Non-national minorities were not forgotten. A civil society forum was to be created in the North, with a Southern counterpart, and through the Intergovernmental Conference of the British and Irish Governments, mechanisms have been established to ensure that 'Others' will be able to express their voices and ensure that the new 'rights culture' does not exclude them.

The External Settlement: Confederal and Federal Elements

The Agreement was not, however, only internally consociational: it was also externally confederalizing, and federalizing, and as such is novel in comparative politics. Let me make it plain why the Agreement is both confederalizing and federalizing, though my emphasis is on the former. The argument rests on these stipulative definitions: confederations exist when political units voluntarily delegate powers and functions to bodies that can exercise power across their jurisdictions; and a federal relationship exists when there are at least two separate tiers of government over the same territory, and when neither tier can unilaterally alter the constitutional capacities of the other.[27]

The all-Ireland confederal relationship

The first confederal relationship was to be all-Ireland in nature: the North-South Ministerial Council (NSMC). It was to bring together those with executive responsibilities in Northern Ireland and in the Republic, and to be established after the Assembly had come into being and completed a programme of work—the specific deadline for which passed on 31 October 1998. That date passed without agreement, because no Executive had been formed in Northern Ireland to engage with its counterpart in the Republic. Instead the two sovereign governments encouraged the parties to complete this programme of work 'behind the scenes'. They did so.

What was intended by the Agreement was clear. Nationalists were concerned that if the Assembly could outlast the North-South Ministerial Council, it would provide incentives for unionists to undermine the latter. Unionists, by contrast, worried that if the NSMC could survive the destruction of the Assembly, nationalists would seek to bring this about. The Agreement was therefore a tightly written contract with penalty clauses. Internal consociation and external confederalism go together: the Assembly and the Council are 'mutually interdependent'; one could not function without the other.[28]

The NSMC satisfactorily linked northern nationalists to their preferred nation-state, and was one means through which nationalists hoped to persuade unionists of the attractions of Irish unification. Consistent with the Agreement, the Irish Government agreed to change its constitution to ensure that the NSMC, and its delegated implementation bodies, were able to exercise island-wide jurisdiction in those functional activities where unionists were willing to co-operate. The NSMC was intended to function much like the Council of Ministers in the European Union, with ministers having considerable discretion to reach decisions, but remaining ultimately accountable to their respective legislatures. The Council was to meet in plenary format twice a year, and in smaller groups to discuss specific sectors—say, agriculture, or education—on a 'regular and frequent basis'. Provision was made for the Council to meet to discuss matters that cut across sectors, and to resolve disagreements. In addition, the Agreement provided for cross-border or all-island 'implementation' bodies. What scope and powers these North-South institutions would have developed remained uncertain, 'yes unionists' minimizing their importance, nationalists and 'no unionists' doing the converse. The Agreement did, however, require a meaningful Council. It stated that the Council '*will*'—not 'may'—identify at least six matters, where 'existing bodies' will be the appropriate mechanisms for co-operation within each separate jurisdiction, and at least six matters where co-operation will take place through cross-border or all-island implementation bodies. The latter were agreed: inland waterways, food safety, trade and business development, special EU programmes, the Irish and Ulster Scots languages, and aquaculture and marine matters. The parties further agreed on six functional areas of co-operation, including some aspects of transport, agriculture, education, health, the environment, and tourism—where a joint North-South public company was established. These zones and modes of co-operation were to be decided during a transitional period between the Assembly elections and October 31 1998, but were not in fact resolved until December 18 1998. The Agreement provided an Annex listing twelve possible areas for implementation but left it open for others to be considered.

The NSMC differed from the Council of Ireland of 1974, and not just in name. There was no provision for a North-South joint parliamentary forum, as there was in the Sunningdale Agreement of 1973, but the Northern Assembly and the Irish *Oireachtas* were asked 'to consider' developing such a forum. Nationalists wanted the NSMC to be established by legislation from Westminster and the *Oireachtas*—to emphasize its autonomy from the Northern Assembly. Unionists preferred that the NSMC be established by the Northern Ireland Assembly and its counterpart in Dublin. The Agreement split the differences between the two positions. The NSMC and the implementation bodies were brought into existence by British-Irish legislation. During the transition it was for the Northern executive and the Republic's government to decide, by agreement, how co-operation should take place, and in what areas the North-South institutions should co-operate. The Northern Ireland Assembly could not alter this body of work, except by cross-community consent.

The Agreement also linked Ireland, North and South, to another confederation, the European Union. It required the Council to consider the implementation of EU policies and programmes as well as proposals under way at the EU, and made provisions for the Council's views to be 'taken into account' at relevant EU meetings.

The signatories to the Agreement promised to work 'in good faith' to bring the NSMC into being. There was not sufficient good faith to prevent the first material break in the timetable scheduled in the Agreement, but the signatories were required to use 'best endeavours' to reach agreement and to make 'determined efforts'—language that echoed that used in the Anglo-Irish Agreement of 1985—to overcome disagreements in functions where there is a 'mutual cross-border and all-island benefit'.[29]

Several economic and sociological developments might underpin the new confederalism. As the Republic's 'Celtic Tiger' continues to expand, Northern Ireland's ministers and citizens, of whatever background, should see increasing benefits from North-South co-operation. And if the European Union continues to integrate, there will be pressure for both parts of Ireland to enhance their co-operation, given their shared peripheral geographical position, and similar interests in functional activities such as agriculture and tourism, and in having regions defined in ways that attract funds.[30] Northern Ireland may even come to think that it would benefit from membership of EMU.

The British-Irish confederal relationship

This is the second, weaker, confederal relationship established by the Agreement. It affects all the islands of Britain and Ireland. Under the new British-Irish Council—see Walker, G. in Chapter 7 of this volume—the two sovereign Governments, all the devolved governments of the UK, and all the neighbouring insular dependent territories of the UK, can meet, agree to delegate functions, and may agree common policies. This proposal meets unionists' concerns for reciprocity in linkages and provides a mechanism through which they may in future be linked to the UK, even though Northern Ireland has become part of the Republic. Unionists originally wanted any North–South Ministerial Council to be subordinate to a British-Irish, or East–West, Council. This did not happen. There was no hierarchical relationship between the two Councils. Indeed, there are two textual warrants for the thesis that the North–South Council was more important and far-reaching than its British-Irish counterpart. The Agreement required the establishment of North–South implementation bodies, while leaving the formation of East–West bodies a voluntary matter. While the Agreement stated explicitly that the Assembly or North–South Council cannot survive without the other, it made no equivalent statement concerning the British-Irish Council.

A UK-Northern Irish Federalizing Process

The Agreement was perhaps the penultimate blow[31] to unitary Unionism in the UK—already dented by the 1997–8 referendums and legislative acts establishing a Scottish Parliament and a Welsh Assembly.[32] But was the Agreement simply a case of 'devolution within a decentralized unitary state'? That was certainly the unionist perspective. Arguably, however, matters were reasonably construed differently: Northern Ireland would become a 'federacy' if the Agreement stabilizes. Two Unions make up the UK: the Union of Great Britain and the Union of Great Britain and Northern Ireland. The constitutional basis of the latter Union is now distinctly different to the former see Hadfield, in Chapter 5 of this volume.

The Agreement was embedded in a treaty between two states, and based on the recognition of Irish national-self-determination. The UK officially acknowledged that Northern Ireland had the right to join the Republic, on the basis of a local referendum, and it recognized, in a treaty, the authority of Irish national self-determination throughout the island of Ireland. Moreover, the Agreement's institutions were brought into being by the will of the people of Ireland, North and South, and not just by the people of Northern Ireland—recall the interdependence of the North–South Ministerial Council and the Assembly. In consequence, the UK's relationship to Northern Ireland, at least in international law, was explicitly federal because the Westminster Parliament and executive could not, except through breaking its treaty obligations, and except through denying Irish national self-determination, exercise power in any manner in Northern Ireland that is inconsistent with the Agreement.

That is why, in Irish nationalist eyes, the unilateral suspension of the Assembly and the NSMC by the UK in February 2000 was regarded as a breach of the new constitutional arrangements. This step violated the will of the people of Ireland, North and South, expressed in two referendums: neither the Agreement, nor the people(s) had mandated the suspensory power. The Secretary of State and the UK Parliament may have believed they were acting from the best of motives—though that can certainly be debated—but they acted without any serious scrutiny of the constitutional consequences. Their action ripped apart the negotiating work of the last ten years—breaking the UK's commitment to the principles of consent, and the recognition of the Irish people's right to national self-determination, North and South. No UK parliamentarian can now look an Irish republican in the face and say that a united Ireland *will* occur if there is local majority consent, because any such promise, like every other element of the Agreement, is now vulnerable to the infinitely revisable dogma of parliamentary sovereignty. A state which lets its Parliament break international law, override a referendum, and suspend—without its assent—an Assembly built upon unprecedented levels of local consent in a referendum, is one which nationalists complain is incapable of being constitutionalized.

The federalizing possibility, or federacy, that has now been put into deep storage, might have been enhanced if the UK and Northern Irish courts had come to treat Northern Ireland's relationships to Westminster as akin to those of the former Dominions—which had a federal character—as they did in the period of the Stormont Parliament (1921–72).[33] Maximum feasible autonomy for Northern Ireland while remaining within the Union was achievable, provided there was agreement to that within the Northern Assembly. Legalist Diceyians and unionists insisted that Westminster's sovereignty in Northern Ireland remained ultimately intact—ultimately to disastrous effect in February 2000. Nationalists, by contrast, believed that the repeal of section 75 of the *Government of Ireland Act* of 1920 was intended to place the status of Northern Ireland and its institutions in the hand of its people, and not in Westminster's absolute determination. If the Agreement beds down, the political development of a federacy might be assured, but the prospect remains uncertain.

Irish Federalizing Processes

The Agreement opened federalist avenues in the Republic of Ireland—hitherto one of the most centralized states in Europe. Nationalists saw the NSMC, North and South, as the embryonic institution of a federal Ireland: first confederation, then federation after trust had been built. This stepping-stone theory was most loudly articulated by 'No Unionists', but they are not wrong in their calculation that many nationalists see the North-South Council as 'transitional'. Sinn Féin says so. Fianna Fáil says so.

The Irish Government and its people did not abandon Irish unification when they endorsed the Agreement. Upon the change of the Irish Constitution, it became 'the firm will of the Irish nation, in harmony and friendship, to unite all the people who share the territory of the island of Ireland, in all the diversity of their identities and traditions, recognizing that a united Ireland shall be brought about only by peaceful means with the consent of a majority of the people expressed, in both jurisdictions in the island' (from the new Article 3). The amended Irish Constitution therefore officially recognizes *two* jurisdictions that jointly enjoy the right to participate in the Irish nation's exercise of self-determination. Unification is no longer linked to 'unitarism', and therefore is entirely compatible with either full confederation or federation.

Irish unification cannot be precluded because of present demographic and electoral trends, which have led to a steady rise in the nationalist share of the vote across different electoral systems.[34] The nature of any eventual unification envisaged in the redrafted Irish Constitution is, however, now very different. It no longer has anything resembling a programme of assimilation. Respect for 'the diversity of . . . identities and traditions' connects with both consociational and con/federal logic. The Republic is bound by the Agreement to structure its laws, and its protection of rights, to prepare for the possibility of a con/federal as well as a unitary Ireland. The Agreement recognizes Northern Ireland as a legal entity within the Irish Constitution. So its eventual elimination as a political unit is no longer a programmatic feature of *Bunreacht na hEireann*. The Agreement also envisages the subjection of both jurisdictions in Ireland to the same regime for the protection of individual and group rights—a situation entirely compatible with a subsequent formal confederation or federation.

What might happen if a majority emerged for Irish unification within Northern Ireland—a possibility that is not, of course, guaranteed? If nationalists acquired local majority support it would not necessarily be in their considered interests to promote the region's immediate administrative and legal assimilation into the Republic. They would then have a new interest in preserving Northern Ireland as a political entity within a federated Ireland—after all they would be a 'local' majority. So would the governing coalition in the Republic whose calculations might be disturbed by the entry of Northern participants. Conversely, some unionists faced with this prospect might prefer a unitary Ireland as the lesser evil—calculating that their chances of being key players in government formation in a bigger arena might protect them better than being a minority in Northern Ireland. But that is simply one possible future.

The con/federal dimensions of the Agreement were not merely pan-Irish or pan-British. They could have evolved within a European Union which has its own strong confederal relationships, and many ambitious federalists. There would have been no obvious organizational or policy-making contradictions, though multiple networking clashes, that would have arisen from this extra layer of con/federalizing, and they might have helped to transfer some of the heat from binary considerations of whether a given issue is controlled by London or Dublin.

Double Protection and Co-Sovereignty

The subtlest and so far least implemented part of the Agreement went well beyond standard consociational thinking. This is its tacit 'double protection model' laced with elements of co-sovereignty. The Agreement was designed to withstand major demographic and electoral change and promised to entrench the protection of rights, collective and individual, on both sides of the present border in functionally equivalent ways. In effect, it promises protection to Northern nationalists now on the same terms that will be given to Ulster unionists should they ever become a minority in a unified Ireland. Communities are to be protected whether they are majorities or minorities, and whether sovereignty lies with the UK or the Republic—whence the expression 'double protection'.

The two states not only promise reciprocity for the local protection of present and future minorities, but they have created two intergovernmental devices to protect those communities. One is the successor to the Anglo-Irish Agreement, the British-Irish intergovernmental conference that guarantees the Republic's government access to policy formulation on all matters not (yet) devolved to the Northern Assembly or the North-South Ministerial Council—and which can be expected to develop a greater role in what were devolved matters in the event of continuing suspension of the Agreement. The other is the British-Irish Council—see Walker, G. in Chapter 7 of this volume. If Irish unification ever occurs, the Republic's government would find it politically impossible not to offer the British government reciprocal access in the same forums.

It is important to note what did *not* happen between the two sovereign states. Formal joint sovereignty was not established—though elements of co-sovereignty exist because both states are parties to a treaty that creates institutions which cross their jurisdictions and are interdependent with their core governing institutions. Unionists claimed that they have removed the 1985 Anglo-Irish Agreement in return for conceding a North-South Ministerial Council. This claim is, at best, exaggerated. Under the new Agreement the Irish Government will retain a say in those Northern Irish matters that have not been devolved to the Northern Assembly, as was the case under Article 4 of the Anglo-Irish Agreement. Moreover, as with that agreement, there will continue to be an intergovernmental conference, chaired by the Minister for Foreign Affairs and the Northern Ireland Secretary of State, to deal with non-devolved matters. This conference will continue to be serviced by a standing secretariat—

and under suspension of devolved government it can expect a growth in its remit.

The new Agreement, moreover, promised to 'intensify co-operation' between the two governments on all-island or cross-border aspects of rights, justice, prison, and policing unless and until these matters are devolved to the Northern executive. There is provision for representatives of the Assembly to be involved in the intergovernmental conference—a welcome parliamentarization—but they will not have the same status as the representatives of the governments of the sovereign states. The Anglo-Irish Agreement fully anticipated these arrangements.[35] Therefore it is more accurate to claim that the Anglo-Irish Agreement has been fulfilled than that it has been removed.

The Military and Political Nature of the Agreement

The institutional nature of the Agreement is complex, but matches the conceptual categories I have deployed. There is no need to evolve new terms for what has been agreed, except, perhaps, for what I have called the 'double protection' model. The Agreement was wide-ranging, multilateral and had something in it for everyone who signed it. Its institutions addressed the 'totality' of relationships between nationalists and unionists in Northern Ireland, between Northern Ireland and the Republic, and between Ireland and Britain. It was neither a victory for nationalists, nor for unionists. Both could maintain their central aspirations, their core identities, and protect or express better their interests. But describing constitutional architecture is one thing; informal political reality is often different.

The Agreement in its totality was an immensely subtle institutional construction and vulnerable to the play of either Orange or Green cards by hardline loyalists or republicans, and to miscalculations by softer-line politicians. Its successful implementation has proved more difficult than its formulation. The fracas at 'Drumcree 4' in July 1998, the massacre at Omagh in August 1998, and the continuing crisis over executive formation and decommissioning jointly revealed these difficulties. There were, however, reasons to be cheerful about the robustness of these institutions if we analyse the military and political nature of the settlement, though there were also reasons to be cautious.

The Agreement on Ending the Armed Conflict.

The Agreement promised a path to unwind armed conflict, though formally speaking, no military or paramilitary organizations negotiated the Agreement. The Agreement encompassed decommissioning, demilitarization, police reform, and prisoner release. It addressed these issues in this textual order, and though all these issues are interlinked they were not explicitly tied to the construction or timing of the new political institutions—with one exception.

Decommissioning   The Agreement is clear on decommissioning, despite the difficulties it has occasioned. No paramilitaries that abide by the Agreement have to engage in formal surrender to those they opposed in war. The IICD, chaired by Canadian General John de Chastelain, was to assist the participants in achieving 'the total disarmament of all paramilitary organizations'. The parties that (informally) represented paramilitary organizations in the negotiations are required to 'use any influence they may have to achieve the decommissioning of all paramilitary arms *within two years* following endorsement in referendums North and South of the agreement and *in the context of the implementation of the overall settlement*' (The Agreement, page 20, para: 3, emphases mine).

The italicized passages clarify the termination point for decommissioning, not the moment of commencement, and they make it plain that decommissioning is linked to the implementation of the overall settlement—including the establishment of the governance structures—North, North-South, and East-West—and to police and judicial reform. That is why David Trimble's demand that Sinn Féin achieve a start to decommissioning by the IRA before executive formation in the North, was regarded as a breach of any reasonable interpretation of the text of the Agreement. Without executive formation in the North none of the formal institutions of the Agreement that required the co-operation of the local parties could get underway. Sinn Féin nominated a representative to the International Commission; issued a statement to the effect that the war was over; and for the first time issued an outright condemnation of other republicans—of the Real IRA whose members carried out the Omagh bombing. But until November 1999, David Trimble and some of his senior colleagues were unprepared to regard this activity as sufficient evidence of good intentions. Each move on Sinn Féin's part merely led the UUP to request more. The Mitchell Review of the Agreement, caused by the impasse, recommended an agreed way forward. Devolution, executive formation—triggering the entirety of the institutions of the Agreement—and the appointment of interlocutors to the IICD by the paramilitaries were scheduled to occur, in that order. The scenario duly materialized. However, to win support from his party for reversing his position David Trimble demanded that Sinn Féin achieve an actual start to decommissioning by the IRA otherwise he and his colleagues would resign. Sinn Féin could not or would not deliver the IRA in the way required—and they were not bound legally bound by the Agreement to do so at that time, though their political obligations were clear. This led to a showdown with Peter Mandelson unilaterally deciding to suspend the Assembly to save David Trimble from his own threat of resignation.

Demilitarization, Police Reform, and Prisoner Release   The Agreement promises, and the UK Government has begun, a series of phased developments to 'demilitarize' Northern Ireland. 'Normalization' was explicitly promised; reductions in army deployments and numbers, and the removal of security installations and emergency powers were promised 'consistent with the level of overall threat'. There was also a commitment to address personal firearms regulation and control—The Agreement, page 21, paras: 1–4 an extraordinary proportion of Northern Ireland's citizens, mostly Protestants and unionists, have legally held lethal weapons. Demilitarization, however, has been stalled: both by the impasse over decommissioning and security concerns occasioned by dissident republicans and loyalists.

Police reform—see Walker, C. in Chapter 8 of this volume—was addressed through an Independent Commission[36] whose terms of reference required it to propose how to establish a police service that would be 'representative', 'routinely unarmed', 'professional, effective and efficient, fair and impartial, free from partisan political control; accountable. . . [and] conforms with human rights norms'. (The Agreement, page 22, paras: 1–2). Due to report some nine months before decommissioning was scheduled to finish, it is difficult to believe that this timetable agreed by the makers of the Agreement was an accident. The public outline of police reform was to be available as a confidence-building measure for republicans and nationalists before the major part of republican decommissioning could be expected. Some otherwise pro-Agreement unionists publicly wish to prevent the full implementation of the Patten Report, despite their obligations under the Agreement to support the implementation of all its aspects, so further trouble lies ahead on this issue.

The early release of paramilitary prisoners sentenced under scheduled offences, and of a small number of army personnel imprisoned for murders of civilians, has, by contrast, proceeded with less disruption than might have been anticipated. Measures to assist the victims of violence have helped ease the pain occasioned in some quarters by these early releases. The early release scheme also worked in creating incentives for some dissident paramilitary organizations, for example, the Loyalist Volunteer Force, agreed to establish a cease-fire in order to benefit their prisoners. So there was an agreement on how to unwind the military and paramilitary conflict. Movement has taken place on some dimensions, much more slowly in some cases than others, notably on decommissioning and demilitarization. But before I address the obstacles to complete implementation let me examine the political nature of the Agreement.

The Political Nature of the Agreement

Recognition The Agreement was an act of recognition between states and national communities. The Republic of Ireland has recognized Northern Ireland's status as part of the United Kingdom, subject to the implementation of the Agreement. The United Kingdom has recognized the right of the people of Ireland to exercise their national self-determination, albeit conjointly and severally. It has confirmed that Northern Ireland has the right to secede, by majority consent, to unify with the Republic of Ireland. The Republic of Ireland has recognized unionists' British political identity. The United Kingdom has recognized Northern nationalists as a national minority, not simply as a cultural or religious minority, and as part of a possible future Irish national majority. The two states have, in effect, recognized the paramilitaries that have organized cease-fires as political agencies. They have not required them to surrender to their respective authorities and have accepted the release of their prisoners on the assurances of their organizations' cease-fires. The paramilitaries on cease-fires have, with some minor exceptions, recognized one another. Unionists have recognized nationalists as nationalists, not simply as Catholics or as the minority. Nationalists have recognized Unionists as unionists, and not just as Protestants. Nationalists and unionists have recognized 'others' who are neither nationalists nor unionists. There was no just shortage of recognition: the Agreement would warm the cockles of Hegel's heart.[37]

Balance of Power   The Agreement also rested on a recognition of a balance of power. The Anglo-Irish Agreement of 1985 led to a new but ultimately productive stalemate. Republicans were left with no immediate prospect of significant electoral growth and their military capacity 'to sicken the Brits' proved limited. Loyalists reorganized in the late 1980s and by the early 1990s were able to raise the costs of sustaining violence within the republican constituency. Unionists discovered the limits of just saying 'No' as British or bigovernmental initiatives occurred over their heads. There was a military stalemate and a political stalemate.

But there were also structural changes beneath the 'frozen surface' that were noted by the late John Whyte.[38] These included greater equality of opportunity and self-confidence amongst nationalists and a shift in the demographic (and therefore) electoral balance of power between the communities—together these changes underlined the fact that any political settlement could not return nationalists to a subordinate status. The initiatives of John Hume and Gerry Adams responded constructively to this new stalemate. Much work had to be done before their initiative bore fruit.[39]

The Bargain   There was a bargain at the heart of the Agreement. Nationalists endorsed it because it promised them political, legal, and economic equality now, plus institutions in which they would have a strong stake, with the possibility of Irish unification later. They would get to co-govern Northern Ireland, rather than being simply governed by either unionists or the British Government. Moreover, they would get this share of government with promises of further reforms to redress past legacies of direct and indirect discrimination. Republicans in Sinn Féin and the IRA could trade a long war that they could not win, and could not lose, for a long march through institutions in which they could reasonably claim that only their means have changed, not their end: the termination of partition—see McIntyre, in Chapter 11 of this volume.

Nationalist support for the Agreement was not difficult to comprehend. For them it was a very good each-way bet. But why did the UUP and the loyalist parties make this consociational-plus bargain? In my judgement the unionists who supported the Agreement were concerned not so much to end the IRA's long war but rather to protect and safeguard the Union—see Aughey, in Chapter 10 of this volume. Their calculus suggested that only by being generous now could they reconcile nationalists to the Union, and protect themselves against possibly seismic shifts in the balance of demographic power. Unionists would get a share in self-government now, avoid the prospect of a British Government making further deals over their heads with the Irish State, and have some prospect of persuading northern nationalists that a newly reconstructed Union offers a secure home for them. In short, they made the Agreement to stave off something worse. It is not surprising therefore that there has been greater rejectionism within the unionist bloc. They are conceding more, and some maintain there is no need to concede anything, at least, not yet.[40] Nevertheless, significant proportions of supporters of the 'No' unionist parties, especially in the DUP, tell pollsters they would like the Agreement to work, which implied they were convertible to its merits.

Ideas Recognizing identities and interests are necessary but not sufficient conditions of a constitutional settlement. Ideas, however loosely understood or flexibly deployed, were also important in the making of the Agreement. Their development, dissemination, and impact is harder to trace, but that does not mean the task cannot be accomplished. Fresh language and policy learning were evident in the making of the Agreement—though so were policy obstinacy and recalcitrance within the highest echelons of the dying Major government[41]—see Patterson, in Chapter 9 of this volume—and of the spread-eagled rainbow coalition in Dublin during 1995–7. The crafters of the ideas were many and varied. Defining and understanding the sources of the conflict in national terms—rather than as issuing from religious extremism or terrorism—was vital. Without this shift, the Anglo-Irish Agreement, the 1995 *Framework Documents*, and the Agreement itself would not have been possible. Intimations and imitations of changes elsewhere—the end of the Cold War and its repercussions, political change in South Africa and the Middle East—all had their local register—see Guelke, in Chapter 13 of this volume. The traditional explanations of the causes of the conflict had increasingly ceased to move the local participants, and many were open to compromises and political institutions that would mark a shift from the limitations of either London's or Dublin's conceptions of good governance.

The beauty of the Agreement as a bargain was that both nationalists and unionists had sound reasons for their respective assessments of its merits, that is, for believing that they were right about the long term. They could not be certain that they were right, and so they were willing to make this elaborate settlement. There were incentives for each bloc to accommodate the other precisely in order to make its vision of the future more likely, that is, both had reasons to act creatively on the basis of self-fulfilling prophecies. The treat of the double protection model was to promise to ease the pain for whoever got it wrong about the future. The confederalizing and federalizing possibilities in the Agreement ensured that both national communities would remain linked, come what may, to their preferred nation-states.

Prospectus

Northern Ireland between April 1998 and January 2000 looked like a success story in the annals of ethno-national conflict-regulation. It had a new, if slightly precarious and slightly unbalanced, binational super-majority. The Assembly and its Executive Committee had demonstrated that they could work, and become mechanisms for accommodating the diverse peoples of the North. There would have been difficulties in agreeing a budget and a broad programme of government, and die-hards or kill-hards would have been hoping to capitalize on them. Managing the twilight of the second Protestant ascendancy in Irish history, and the re-rustication of militant republicanism, would not have been easy tasks, but they were not impossible. This optimistic picture was shattered in February 2000. It was broken on the stubborn refusal of the IRA to clarify unambiguously its commitment to end its war and to deliver 'product' on decommissioning; and on the equally stubborn refusal of the UUP to settle for the informal decommissioning, the silence of the IRA's guns; and, lastly, on the constitutionally untutored response of the Westminster Government. It will take skill and luck to unwind suspension and restore the Agreement; and in my view will require the full repeal of the Suspension Act to restore the original Agreement.

   The Agreement's political entrenchment required that some short-term advantage-maximizing and game-playing temptations be avoided, and that leaders remained in control of their parties and movements. These temptations have not been avoided. At the heart of this Agreement lay four internal political forces—the SDLP and the UUP amongst the historically moderate nationalists and unionists, and Sinn Féin and the PUP/UDP amongst the historically hardline republicans and loyalists. Maintaining the Agreement required these political forces to evolve as informal coalition partners while preserving their bases. Let me focus on just two of these constellations.

The UUP

The UUP was always the most likely short-term maximizer and game-player. It split more than any other party under the impact of the making of the

Agreement. It made very significant concessions on internal power-sharing and on all-Ireland dimensions. It lost votes to the 'No Unionists'; and subsequently lost some further dissenters that were elected on its platform to the Assembly. The temptation of its leaders was to renegotiate the Agreement in the course of its implementation. That way they could hope to refortify the party, and draw off support from the 'soft No' camp amongst unionists.

The UUP would have preferred an Agreement which was largely internal to Northern Ireland, and which involved them co-governing Northern Ireland with the SDLP in a weaker Assembly, on the lines established in Wales, and without the elaborate dual premiership and inclusive executive. It would have strongly preferred to govern without the formal participation of Sinn Féin in government. In consequence, the UUP's most tempting game plan was to use the decommissioning issue to split what their supporters saw as a pan-nationalist bloc. The signs of this game were a phoney 'legalism', adversarial and petty-minded interpretation of the Agreement, postponement and prevarication, and brinkmanship. Centre-stage in this game was David Trimble, the UUP's leader.

His rise to prominence did not bode well for the peace process then underway, but, to his eternal credit, the victor of Drumcree modified his previous policy commitments, one by one, and went on to win a Nobel prize with John Hume of the SDLP. Trimble won the prize, which he felt was 'premature', because of his decision to negotiate with two governments and eight other parties, including Sinn Féin; his role in the production of the Agreement; and his subsequent promise to build 'a pluralist parliament for a pluralist people'. He would say, correctly, that he had done it all his way, in defence of the Union.

The UK government suspended the Assembly 'in order to save David Trimble' as one Labour minister recently told me in justification. This breach of the Agreement—and international law—did not save Trimble from the wrath of his party's rejectionists who subsequently persuaded 43 per cent of fellow members to demonstrate that they prefer the 69 year old Reverend Martin Smyth MP as their leader. Trimble's political future looks bleak. He has shown more skill in winning power than in its exercise. He displays capacity to surprise, but rarely for effective follow-through. He is still trying to conciliate his party's irreconcilables and those who have personally betrayed him. His major gamble and praiseworthy risk in making the Agreement required him to win his battles with the 'No' unionists, inside and outside his party, and to build an informal and sustainable coalition with Sinn Féin and the SDLP. It was an extremely difficult task, not made easier by republican intransigence on decommissioning, but it is fair to say that Trimble, and his advisors, consistently mishandled their management of their party, their referendum campaign, and all the ensuing elections. By failing to reform their party they kept its Orange Order rejectionists armed with internal votes within their own camp. By appeasing their rejectionist critics they helped them reorganize and recover. By seeking in the implementation of the Agreement to recover what they had lost in its negotiation they crucially reduced republican and nationalist goodwill, and gave further ammunition to their rejectionists when they finally decided to do what they had agreed to do. David Trimble in consequence is now a First Minister in deep freeze, a leader presiding over a party whose members seem unlikely to recover their senses unless and until two blows come their way—the next Westminster general election and the 2001 census. Trimble is not politically dead, but he looks in mortal danger, with neither republicans nor hard-line unionists willing to lift a finger to help him.

Republicans

The other constellation is republican. Republicans too have been tempted to engage in game-playing, of a different kind. They insisted on the full letter of the Agreement from all other parties in order to sustain their constituency and their long-term political strategy, even if this insistence created great difficulties for the UUP and the SDLP, their informal partners. Republicans thought they had an each-way bet: if the UUP and the UK government delivered on the Agreement well and good; if the UUP did not then Sinn Féin would position itself to ensure that unionists got the blame for its non-implementation. As it happens a mixed scenario emerged. The UUP was late on its obligations on executive formation and agreeing North-South institutions, but it eventually delivered and then challenged Sinn Féin to get the IRA to deliver on decommissioning. That did not happen, although Sinn Féin did deliver two statements from the IRA in February, the second of which was as close as the organization had come to indicating its willingness to decommission. Trimble's and the UUP's unilateral deadline to republicans to deliver on decommissioning by the end of January had not been an explicit part of the Mitchell Review so Sinn Féin was able to insist, correctly, that the UUP's demands were outside the Agreement. The Secretary of State's suspension of the devolved institutions to prevent Trimble's resignation as First Minister meant that blame for the institutional freeze was distributed across three agents—the UUP, republicans, and the UK Government.

The hardest of IRA hard-liners appeared unwilling to deliver any decommissioning, because they consider it to be an act of surrender, unnecessary, and because they fear their arsenals might get into the hands of dissidents. For some hard-liners, non-implementation of parts of the Agreement within Westminster's remit—police reform, judicial reform, equality measures, and demilitarization—may yet provide a pretext for a return to war, though most seem committed to a permanent cease-fire. Their view, roughly speaking, is that they wish to retain their weapons 'just in case'. They expect others to trust them but are not willing to trust those others. By contrast, softer-liners appear willing to consider decommissioning but are having great difficulties taking their colleagues with them. Soft-liners would only sanction any return to violence if governmental or loyalist forces were responsible for the first military breach. Even then, fully politicized republicans believe their movement has more to gain electorally both within Northern Ireland and the Republic through becoming a wholly constitutional opposition movement—even if that is to an Agreement without devolved institutions. Republicans, in short, were tempted by hard legalism: extracting the full letter of the contract with the UUP, at the risk of damaging the informal political coalition that made the Agreement. It is ironic to see republicans demanding the restoration of devolved government, insisting, correctly, that the UK's suspension is a breach of international law. The Irish Government has refused to recognize the suspension partly to prevent Sinn Féin initiating legal proceedings in the Republic.

To be fully resurrected this consociational and con/federal agreement requires two things. First, immediate, daily, vigorous and continuing British and Irish co-operation to encourage the Agreement's full implementation—both in institutions and confidence-building measures such as police reform and demilitarization. The governments must use all their available tools to this end. Secondly, it requires greater recognition among the informal coalition partners, especially within the UUP and Sinn Féin, that they may benefit more in the long run from not seeking maximum short-run advantage from one another's difficulties, and from not over-hyping their own—and it requires some joint agreement on managing the matter of decommissioning.

Conclusion

The Mitchell Review of the Agreement temporarily renewed the inspiration that surrounded the making of the Agreement. But even if the full Agreement is not immediately resurrected it will continue to be partially implemented in its non-devolved dimensions. The UK government wants to avoid antagonizing any party or bloc too much. To maintain the major paramilitary organizations' cease-fires, prisoner-releases are likely to continue accompanied by warnings that punishment-beatings will be treated as violations of cease-fires. To create the conditions for legitimate policing where paramilitaries are presently dominant, police reform as recommended by Patten will begin, though delays can be expected to mollify unionist sentiment. The reform of Northern Ireland, embedded in the human rights and mainstreaming equality provisions in the Agreement are likely to be followed through, albeit more slowly than might otherwise be the case. In short, the dimensions of the Agreement that do not require the local parties to co-operate in government may be delivered, slowly, by the two governments of the sovereign states. The British-Irish intergovernmental conference will, gradually, become an active site for policy formulation, and in time encourage sensible functional cross-border co-operation in the zones marked out for the North–South Ministerial Council and the British–Irish Council.

This is a feasible and but less attractive scenario than the full Agreement. We may be moving into a world of a cold peace with traits of a local cold war, reform without significant devolution tempered by atrocities from the Continuity–Real IRA and the LVF, and their kindred spirits. Wrong moves by any parties might destabilize the cease-fires. Party politics might become more polarized: 'yes unionists' may lose electoral ground to 'no unionists', while the SDLP may lose electoral ground to Sinn Féin within a demographically and electorally growing nationalist bloc, and Sinn Féin may obtain a kingmaker role in southern Irish coalition politics. The Alliance Party, the Women's Coalition, and the reconstructed loyalist parties are unlikely to flourish or make major breakthroughs. And the longer the devolved components of the Agreement persist in institutional limbo the more likely it will be that other options will be considered.

A radical plan B might tempt some: *de facto* co-sovereignty in and over Northern Ireland by the UK and Irish Governments. In the absence of agreed devolution the two governments might increase rather than reduce their co-operation. A formal declaration of shared sovereignty would not, and need not be rushed. Its gradual emergence might act as a standing invitation to unionists to win some control over their own destiny through meaningful devolution, and it might persuade republicans that there is more to be gained through reforming intergovernmentalism than a return to war. Co-sovereignty has many merits, especially when considered from the perspective of justice. But, having just presided over a major institutional failure, the two governments are unlikely to move rapidly to a formal settlement of this kind, though coherent models of how it might operate have been sketched.[42]

The evolution of co-sovereignty could accompany two local government options. The unionist preference may be for a Northern Assembly on the Welsh model, with Stormont stripped of legislative powers and of its strongly consociational rules. Nationalists are unlikely to co-operate with this option. Though they may become interested in reducing the veto-powers of 'no unionists' they are not likely to want a form of majoritarianism from which they might suffer. A second local government strategy would be to abandon the project of one devolved government. Significant multi-functional competencies could be devolved to (reorganized) local governments willing to adopt institutions of the type made in the Agreement. Local governments on the border, mostly dominated by nationalists, could be permitted to develop significant cross-border arrangements with their southern counterparts and the Dublin government. This would isolate the heartlands of unreformed majoritarian unionism while giving nationalists significant incentives to work within a reformed Northern Ireland. The principal danger of this option is that such cantonization might encourage further ethno-national segregation and thereby promote repartitionist thinking.

The moral of this analysis is clear. The most feasible alternatives to the Agreement are not likely to improve the lot of either 'Yes' or 'No' unionists— though the latter may see a rise in their vote-share they are unlikely to be able to halt reforms for long. The fact is that the Agreement offers unionists a better chance of preserving the Union with their meaningful participation than the alternatives. That is why the 'yes unionists' signed it. Even if republicans are held primarily culpable for the failure of the Agreement's institutions because of their failure to co-operate on decommissioning, it does not follow that they will be politically isolated or that unionists will be able to block the human rights, equality and policing reforms contained in the confidence-building measures promised by the UK Government. Pressure from unionists to halt the release of republican paramilitary prisoners has, so far, not been effective. Demands from the UUP to both keep the unreformed RUC and for a scaled-down Assembly on the Welsh model, are not likely to be fully met. For most republicans any plausible cost-benefit analyses on renewed militarism are clear: they stand to gain more, North and South, through electoral politics, and the implementation of the reforms promised by the Agreement, than they do from an IRA which resumes assassinations or bombings.

The normative implications of this analysis are, I hope, clear. Consociational and confederal devices provide the best repertoires to address ethno-national disputes where a sovereign border has separated a national minority living in its homeland from its kin-state, and where a historically privileged formerly settler colonial portion of a *Staatsvolk* cannot control, or are refused permission to control, the relevant disputed territory on their own. These devices are capable of being constructed without guidance from constitutional designers—though plainly diffusion of institutional repertoires is one of the neglected dimensions of what some call 'globalization'. Comprehensive settlements, after inclusive negotiations, which incorporate hard-liners looking to come in from the cold, and that address the identities, interests, and ideological agendas of all parties, are likely to produce complex, interlinked institutional ensembles that look vulnerable. Referendums may assist their legitimation, and the consolidation of the pre-agreement pacts. Preferential voting in the STV mode enables cross-ethnic 'vote-pooling', and benefits hard-liners willing to become less hard-line. Double protection models offer imaginative ways to make possible changes in sovereignty less threatening, both now and later. But where any bloc is divided over the merits of such a settlement, and where its leaders respond more to the threat of being outflanked than they do to the imperative of making the new (tacit) cross-ethnic coalition work, it may prove impossible to implement the agreement. These agreements are precarious equilibria, but are infinitely better than their alternatives—fighting to the finish, or the panaceas proposed by partisan or naïve integrationists.

OFFICIAL PUBLICATIONS

The Agreement: Agreement reached in the multi-party negotiations (No place of publication, No date, UK Government).
House of Commons, Official Report. Vol. 319, November 18 1998.
Northern Ireland Act 1998 (HMSO: Westminster).
Northern Ireland (Elections) Act 1998 (HMSO: Westminster).
Northern Ireland Assembly (Elections) Order of 1998 (HMSO: Westminster)
Official Report of the New Northern Ireland Assembly, Belfast, 15 July 1999, 317–37.
Report of the Independent Commission on Policing for Northern Ireland (the Patten Report), September 1999 (Belfast, no publisher cited, and published on the web at http://www.belfast.org.uk/report.htm).

ENDNOTES

* This is an edited version of a paper presented at the Conference on 'Constitutional Design 2000' held at the University of Notre Dame, Indiana, US, December 1999. It draws freely and extensively upon a number of my previous publications: 'The 1998 British-Irish Agreement: Power-Sharing Plus', (London: Constitution Unit, Summer 1998); 'The 1998 British-Irish Agreement: Consociation Plus', *Scottish Affairs*, 26 (1999): 1–22; 'The Implications for Political Accommodation in Northern Ireland of Reforming the Electoral System for the Westminster Parliament', *Representation*, 35 (1999): 106–13; 'The Nature of the Agreement', *Fordham Journal of International Law*, 22 (1999): 1628–67; 'The Nature of the British-Irish Agreement', *New Left Review*, 233 (1999): 66–96. A United States Institute of Peace Grant and the Staff Research Fund at LSE facilitated research. The thanks given to colleagues and friends in these previous publications still stands, particularly to Geoff Evans, John McGarry, and Christopher McCrudden. I would also like to thank the participants at the Notre Dame Constitutional Design 2000 Conference for their comments, especially Bernard Grofman, Donald Horowitz, Arend Lijphart, Andrew Reynolds, Ben Reilly, Fred Riggs, Cheryl Saunders, and Giovanni Sartori.

1. See *inter alia* Lijphart, A., *Democracy in Plural Societies: A Comparative Exploration* (New Haven, CT, London: Yale University Press, 1977); and Walzer, M., *On Toleration* (New Haven, CT: Yale University Press, 1997).

2. Lijphart claims that Dutch politicians in 1917, and by their Lebanese (1943), Austrian (1945), Malaysian (1955), Colombian (1958), Indian (in the 1960s), and South African (1993–4) counterparts, invented consociational rules later in the century. One does not have to agree with the citation of any of these cases to accept that politicians are more than capable of doing theory without the aid of theorists—see *inter alia* Lijphart, A., 'Foreword: One Basic Problem, Many Theoretical Options—And a Practical Solution?', in J. McGarry and B. O'Leary (eds.), *The Future of Northern Ireland*, (Oxford: Clarendon Press, 1990) vi–viii; and Lijphart, A., 'The Puzzle of Indian Democracy: A Consociational Interpretation', *American Journal of Political Science*, 90 (1996).

3. One of the makers of the Agreement, Dr Mowlam, the UK Secretary of State for Northern Ireland (1997–9), had an academic consociational heritage, and at least one of her former academic advisors has had an abiding interest in the subject. Consociational thinking had an impact on the drafting of the Framework Documents of 1995. See O'Leary, B., 'Afterword: What is Framed in the Framework Documents?', *Ethnic and Racial Studies*, 18 (1995): 862–72.

4. The Assembly was not allowed to legislate in contravention of the European Convention on Human Rights or European Union law, modify a specific entrenched enactment, discriminate on grounds of religious belief or political opinion, or 'deal with' an excepted power except in

an 'ancillary way'—which roughly means it may not enact laws which modify UK statutes on excepted matters such as the Crown.

5. According to the UK's legislative enactment, the *Northern Ireland Act* (1998), the Assembly could expand its autonomy only with regard to *reserved*—not *excepted*—matters.

6. The *Northern Ireland Act* (1998) enabled the top two Ministers to hold functional portfolios, Clause 15 (10).

7. On July 15 1999 in a hand-written note to the Initial Presiding Officer, the Secretary of State introduced an additional Standing Order to the running of d'Hondt, namely 'On the completion of the procedure for the appointment of Ministers (designate) under this Standing Order, the persons appointed shall only continue to hold Ministerial office (designate) if they include at least 3 designated Nationalists and 3 designated Unionists'. This order, authorized under the *Northern Ireland (Elections) Act* 1998, in my view, was the first breach of the letter of the Agreement by the UK government. Given that the parties had agreed that the executive should consist of ten Ministers in addition to the First and Deputy First Ministers, the standing order, in effect, gave a veto-power to both the UUP and the SDLP over executive formation because each party was entitled to three seats on the basis of its strength in seats. The standing order was introduced in a hurry to stop executive formation leading *either* to an all-nationalist executive as would have transpired given the decision of the UUP to fail to turn up to the Assembly when the process of executive formation was triggered, and the decision of the 'no unionists' not to take their designated ministerial entitlements, *or* to an executive in which there would have been no pro-agreement unionists (See *New Northern Ireland Assembly*, Thursday 15 July 1999, Belfast, 317–37). This panic measure, introduced for high-minded motives, subtly changed the executive incentive-structures agreed by the SDLP and the UUP in the negotiation of the Agreement, and was subsequently abandoned. It was consociational, but it was not negotiated by the parties, was not endorsed in the referendums, and encouraged moderate unionists to over-bargain, knowing that they could veto executive formation. Insecure 'moderates' as well as 'hard-liners' can be troublesome in consociational systems.

8. McCrudden, C., 'Mainstreaming Equality in the Governance of Northern Ireland', *Fordham International Law Journal*, 22 (1999): 1696–775.

9. The Droop quota used in STV is V/(N+1) +1, where V = Total Valid Votes, and N = Number of Assembly members to be elected.

10. Lijphart also argues for this system rather than STV because it allows for a high district magnitude enabling greater proportionality, is less vulnerable to gerrymandering, and is simpler for voters and organizers (see Lijphart, A., 'Electroal Systems, Party Systems and Conflict Management in Divided Societies', in R. Schrire (ed.), *Critical Choices for South Africa* (Cape Town: Oxford University Press, 1990), 2–13). In the main text I argue implicitly for high thresholds to reduce fragmentation—as a trade-off against 'better' proportionality. Contra Lijphart, I would maintain that STV, legislatively enacted with uniform district magnitudes, and supervized by independent electoral commissions tasked to create uniform electorates, is not more vulnerable to gerrymandering than regional party-list PR. I concede that STV is only suitable for numerate electorates, but otherwise its complexities are not especially mysterious.

11. The nature of executive formation in the Agreement should have acted as one possible check on the possibilities of fragmentation under party-list PR, but that is true of any electoral system combined with this executive.

12. See Evans, G. and O'Leary, B., 'Frameworked Futures: Intransigence and Inflexibility in the Northern Ireland Elections of May 30 1996', *Irish Political Studies*, 12 (1997); and Evans, G. and O'Leary, B., 'Intransigence and Flexibility on the Way to Two Forums: The Northern Ireland Elections of 30 May 1996 and Public Opinion', *Representation*, 34 (1997): 208–18.

13. My co-researcher John McGarry and I used to assume the prescriptive superiority of the party-list system, see for example McGarry, J. and O'Leary, B., (eds.), *The Future of Northern Ireland* (Oxford: Oxford University Press, 1990), 297. Facts and reflection have made me reconsider the merits of STV: O'Leary, B., 'The Implications for Political Accommodation in Northern Ireland of Reforming the Electoral System for the Westminster Parliament', *Representation* 35/2–3: 106–13; and O'Duffy, B. and O'Leary, B., 'Tales from Elsewhere and an Hibernian Sermon', in H. Margetts and G. Smyth (eds.), *Turning Japanese? Britain with a Permanent Party of Government* (London: Lawrence and Wishart, 1995), 193–210.

14. Horowitz, D., *Ethnic Groups in Conflict* (Berkeley, CA: University of California Press, 1985).
15. This option is also open to anti-Agreement voters, but DUP and UKUP voters are unlikely to give their lower order preferences to Republican Sinn Féin—should that party ever to choose to stand for elections.
16. See Horowitz, D., *Ethnic Groups in Conflict*; Horowitz, D., 'Ethnic Conflict Management for Policymakers', and 'Making Moderation Pay: The Comparative Politics of Ethnic Conflict Management' in J. P. Montville (ed.), *Conflict and Peacemaking in Multiethnic Societies* (Lexington, MA: Heath, 1989) 115–30, 451–75; Horowitz, D., *A Democratic South Africa? Constitutional Engineering in a Divided Society*, (Berkeley, CA: University of California Press, 1991).
17. Personal conversations with Donald Horowitz during his period as a distinguished visiting professor at the London School of Economics, 1998–9.
18. It may be that AV's presumptively 'Horowitzian' moderating effects materialize better in multi-ethnic political systems with no actual or potentially dominant group in given districts—a situation that does not describe Northern Ireland.
19. The corollary is that STV's positive affects apply to already polarized and pluralized party systems in ethno-nationally divided societies. If there has been no prior history of ethnicized party polarization within a state, or of pluralization of parties within ethno-national blocs, the merits of its implementation may be doubted on Horowitzian grounds. This point raises what may be the key problem with Horowitz's electoral integrationist prescriptions: they apply best to forestalling or inhibiting ethnic conflict and are less effective remedies for cases of developed, protracted, and intense ethnic and ethno-national conflict.
20. The primary normative objection that can be levelled against Horowitz's position is that proportionality norms better match both parties' respective bargaining strengths, and their conceptions of justice. Once party pluralism has already occurred, some form of proportionality is more likely to be legitimate than a shift to strongly majoritarian systems such as AV, or to systems with *ad hoc* distributive requirements that will always be (correctly) represented as gerrymanders—albeit well-intentioned.
21. Sinnott, R., 'Centrist politics makes modest but significant progress: Cross-community transfers were low', *Irish Times*, 29 June 1998.
22. Evans, G. and O'Leary, B., 'Northern Irish Voters and the British-Irish Agreement: Foundations of a Stable Consociational Settlement?', *Political Quarterly*, 71 (2000).
23. Gallagher, M., 'Does Ireland Need a New Electoral System?', *Irish Political Studies*, 2 (1987): 27–48.
24. O'Leary, B., 'A Bright Future and Less Orange (Review of the Independent Commission on Policing for Northern Ireland)', *Times Higher Education Supplement*, 19 November 1999, 22–3.
25. This analysis has benefited from discussions with four members of the Patten Commission, and from the author's attendance at a conference at the University of Limerick on 2 October 1999.
26. See McCrudden, 'Mainstreaming Equality in the Governance of Northern Ireland', and his 'Equality and the Good Friday Agreement', in J. Ruane and J. Todd (eds.), *After the Good Friday Agreement: Analysing Political Change in Northern Ireland* (Dublin: University College Dublin Press, 1999), 96–121.
27. My definition is a necessary element of a federal system. Whether it is sufficient is more controversial. Normally a federation has sub-central units that are co-sovereign with the centre throughout most of the territory of the state in question. My point is that any system of constitutionally entrenched autonomy for one region makes the relationship between that region and the centre functionally equivalent to a federal relationship. Elazar calls such a system 'a federacy'.
28. The Agreement did not consider what would happen if one government unilaterally suspended its set of institutions—because neither government expected that to occur.
29. The possibility of a Unionist minister refusing to serve on the Council appeared very grave. However, this seemed to be ruled out in practice: participation in the North-South Council was made an 'essential' responsibility attaching to 'relevant' posts in the two administrations—'relevant' means, presumably, any portfolio a part of which is subject to North-South co-operation. This left open the possibility that a politician opposed to the North-South Council

might take a seat on it with a view to wrecking it. *But* Ministers were required to establish the North-South Institutions in 'good faith' and to use 'best endeavours' to reach agreement. Since these requirements were presumably subject to judicial review it is unlikely that potential wreckers would have been able to sustain a negative role in the North-South Council for very long.

30. Tannam, E., *Cross-Border Cooperation in the Republic of Ireland and Northern Ireland* (Basingstoke: Macmillan, 1999).
31. The formation of an English Parliament would be the last blow.
32. Hazell, R. and O'Leary, B., 'A Rolling Programme of Devolution: Slippery Slope or Safeguard of the Union?' in R. Hazell (ed.), *Constitutional Futures: A History of the Next Ten Years* (Oxford: Oxford University Press, 1999), 21–46.
33. Legal friends advise me that the UK's legislative enactment of the Agreement may have modified the pertinent precedents in this previous jurisprudence by changing the nature of the '*vires*' test that the courts will use to deal with jurisdictional disputes.
34. .O'Leary, B., 'Appendix 4: Party Support in Northern Ireland, 1969–89', in J. McGarry and B. O'Leary (eds.), *The Future of Northern Ireland* (Oxford: Oxford University Press, 1990), 342–57; O'Leary, B., 'More Green, Fewer Orange', *Fortnight*: 12–15 & 16–17 (1990); McGarry, J. and O'Leary, B., *Explaining Northern Ireland: Broken Images* (Oxford and Cambridge, MA: Basil Blackwell, 1995); O'Leary, B. and Evans, G., 'Northern Ireland: *La Fin de Siecle*, 'The Twilight of the Second Protestant Ascendancy and Sinn Féin's Second Coming', *Parliamentary Affairs*, 50 (1997): 672–80.
35. O'Leary, B., and McGarry, J., *The Politics of Antagonism: Understanding Northern Ireland*, 2nd Edn. (London: Athlone Press, 1996), chs. 6–7.
36. McGarry, J. and O'Leary, B., *Policing Northern Ireland* (Belfast: Blackstaff Press, 1999).
37. For sophisticated discussions of recognition see *inter alia* Ringmar, E., *Identity, Interest and Action: A Cultural Explanation of Sweden's Intervention in the Thirty Years War* (Cambridge: Cambridge University Press, 1996); and Taylor, C., *Multiculturalism and the Politics of Recognition* (Princeton, NJ: Princeton University Press, 1992).
38. Whyte, J., 'Dynamics of Social and Political Change in Northern Ireland', in D. Keogh and M. Haltzel (eds.), *Northern Ireland and the Politics of Reconciliation* (Cambridge: Cambridge University Press 1993), 103–16.
39. See Mallie, E. and McKittrick, D., *The Fight for Peace: The Secret Story Behind the Irish Peace Process* (London: Heinemann, 1996); McKittrick, D., *The Nervous Peace* (Belfast: Blackstaff Press, 1996).
40. See Evans and O'Leary, 'Northern Irish Voters and the British-Irish Agreement'.
41. O'Leary, B., 'The Conservative Stewardship of Northern Ireland, 1979–97: Sound-bottomed Contradictions or Slow Learning?', *Political Studies*, 45 (1997): 663–76.
42. O'Leary, B., Lyne, T., Marshall, J., and Rowthorn, B., *Northern Ireland: Sharing Authority* (London: Institute of Public Policy Research, 1993).

5

Seeing it Through? The Multifaceted Implementation of the Belfast Agreement

Brigid Hadfield

Introduction

The document, commonly referred to as the Belfast Agreement, actually consists of a novel form of double annexation of two Agreements, the one to the other. There is, first, the multi-party Agreement which, beginning with a Declaration of Support, deals with constitutional issues, specifically the constitutional status of Northern Ireland,[1] the three-stranded political structures, rights, safeguards and equality of opportunity, decommissioning, security, policing and justice, and prisoners. An annex to the multi-party Agreement is the Agreement between the British and Irish Governments, dealing with the elements of the former agreement which have interstate dimensions.[2] Its four Articles, therefore, deal respectively with: the status of Northern Ireland, the obligations incumbent upon whichever Government exercises sovereignty with regard to it, and related citizenship questions to which that Agreement's Annex 2 also refers; the implementation of those parts of the multi-party Agreement which require formal interstate agreement, namely, the North South Ministerial Council, the implementation bodies, the British-Irish Council, and the British-Irish Intergovernmental Conference; the cessation of the Anglo-Irish Agreement 1985 and its replacement by this British-Irish Agreement 1998; and the requisite conditions which need to be satisfied before the entry into force of this Agreement. Annex 1 to the British-Irish Agreement is the multi-party Agreement itself—hence the double annexation mentioned above. This Agreement was brought into force on 2 December 1999 in Dublin, following the exchange of notifications between the two Governments as required by its Article 4.

Whatever the significance of the substance of the multi-party Agreement, however, in terms of the processes of negotiation, or of its comparative value, or the appositeness of any given constitutional label, its provisions can have no legal force without being incorporated into the domestic law of the United Kingdom. Consequently, the Long Title of the *Northern Ireland Act* 1998 refers to its purpose 'of implementing the agreement reached at multi-party talks on Northern Ireland set out in Command Paper 3883'. The *Northern Ireland Act* began its parliamentary stages on 15 July 1998 and received the Royal Assent on 19 November 1998, the same day as the *Scotland Act*. The *Northern Ireland (Sentences) Act* 1998 was likewise enacted to give effect to the provisions in the Belfast Agreement on the accelerated release on licence of qualifying prisoners, essentially those paramilitary prisoners affiliated to organizations maintaining a complete and unequivocal cease-fire. As paragraph 4 of the Prisoners section of the Agreement required the end of June 1998 as the commencement date for the discharge of this undertaking, these provisions had to be included in a 'free-standing' Act—the *Northern Ireland (Sentences) Act* 1998—rather than await implementation in the *Northern Ireland Act* itself, which, given its nature and size, clearly required a more detailed and therefore slower parliamentary passage.

Before the Northern Ireland Bill was introduced into the House of Commons, the New Northern Ireland Assembly had already been elected under the provisions of the *Northern Ireland (Elections) Act* 1998, section 1(1) of which conferred upon the Assembly 'the purpose of taking part in preparations to give effect to' the multi-party Agreement. Section 1(2) empowered the Secretary of State to refer to the Assembly 'specific matters arising from the Agreement' and such other matters as the Secretary of State thought fit. The dominance of the Secretary of State—initially Dr Mo Mowlam—*vis-à-vis* the New or Shadow Assembly—the adjective 'New' is part of the Shadow Assembly's formal title and disappeared on 'devolution day', the 2 December 1999[3]—was also to be found in provisions in the schedule to the Elections Act. Paragraph 1 provided that Shadow Assembly meetings were to be held when and where the Secretary of State directed; paragraph 3 gave her the power of appointment of the Initial Presiding and Deputy Presiding Officer; and paragraph 10 gave her the power to determine the content of the New Assembly's Initial Standing Orders.[4] Under the terms of Initial Standing Order 14,[5] David Trimble of the Ulster Unionist Party and Seamus Mallon of the SDLP were, on 1 July 1998, elected First Minister and Deputy First Minister Designate respectively, and to them the Assembly delegated the following matters which the Secretary of State had referred to it under section 1(2) of the Elections Act:

(1) agreement on the number of Ministerial posts[6] and the distribution of executive responsibilities among those posts;
(2) preparations for establishing the North-South Ministerial Council and associated matters for co-operation and implementation;
(3) preparations for the establishment of the British-Irish Council;
(4) the establishment of the consultative Civic Forum.

The final report, as produced by the First Minister and Deputy First Minister, was approved by a cross-community majority vote in the Assembly in February 1999;[7] and the Assembly's Committee on Standing Orders produced—subject to later amendment—on 9 March 1999 the Standing Orders for the post-devolution Assembly.[8] On the previous day in Dublin, the two Governments entered into the four Treaties required by Article 2 of the British-Irish Agreement: on the British-Irish Council, the British-Irish Intergovernmental Conference, on the North-South Ministerial Council—all short treaties, their contents being simply references to the relevant part of the multi-party Agreement—and on the implementation bodies—drawing heavily in substance on the report approved by the Assembly in February 1999.

International treaties cannot, however, change the law of the United Kingdom or impose certain powers and obligations directly upon individuals or bodies, and where an international agreement seeks to do this incorporating legislation is required by Westminster. The first three Dublin Treaties established the named body; sections 52 to 54 of the *Northern Ireland Act* provide the requisite statutory powers concerning participation in and representation at their various meetings. Section 55 of the Act—which section came into force on the day on which the Act received the Royal Assent—empowered the Secretary of State, by Westminster legislation, to make provision for the six initial implementation bodies. Consequently, the *North/South Co-operation (Implementation Bodies) (Northern Ireland) Order* 1999 gave legislative force to the fourth March Dublin Treaty.[9]

In addition, there was a raft of other Westminster legislation of a technical nature but essential to secure the 'mechanics' of the new devolved system: the *Departments (Northern Ireland) Order* 1999 primarily to establish five new Northern Ireland Departments and to rename some existing Departments, in accordance with the Assembly's February Report;[10] the *Modification of Enactments Order* 1999 primarily to amend or repeal certain statutory provisions so as to give full effect to the *Northern Ireland Act* 1998;[11] the *Northern Ireland (Royal Assent to Bills) Order* 1999 prescribing the standard form for the Letters Patent signifying the Royal Assent to Assembly Bills;[12] and most significantly of all the *Northern Ireland Act (1998) Appointed Day Order* 1999, made under section 3 of the 1998 Act on 1 December 1999, bringing into force Parts II and III of the Act, that is, initiating devolution.

The purpose of referring to this legislation is threefold. The first purpose is a narrow one and is essentially a lawyer's point, but is no less important for that. The broad-sweep provisions of the Belfast Agreement must yield to the detailed provisions of (primarily) the *Northern Ireland Act* 1998, although parts of the Agreement are incorporated by reference in the Act. This has the basic consequence of requiring both those operating within, and those evaluating and analysing from outside, the devolved and cross-border institutions to work from the statutory provisions in all their complex detail and not primarily from the Agreement. The law must no longer be the concern of solely lawyers. There are other consequences too. The need to translate the provisions of the Belfast Agreement into the clauses of the *Northern Ireland Act*, which has 101 sections and fifteen schedules, meant that the 1998 Act was placed upon the pre-existing devolved structures—which had administratively remained in place—of the *Northern Ireland Constitution Act* 1973, and to a lesser, or partially deriva-tive, extent from the devolved system contained in the *Government of Ireland Act* 1920. There are thus not only political peculiarities distinguishing Northern Ireland devolution from devolution to Scotland, but legal ones too; but also—and these two points may in places pull against each other—the Scotland Bill and the Northern Ireland Bill proceeded through Parliament at effectively the same time, and therefore discussion of and amendments to the Scotland Bill affected in places the content of the Northern Ireland Bill, subject, of course, to the overriding concern of the Government not to deviate or depart from the principles of the Belfast Agreement in so far as they addressed the point in issue. Thus the legislative history of the *Northern Ireland Act* must also be considered along with its political genesis.

The second purpose in referring to the legislation is this: once legislation enters the domain, questions or issues which are or may be regarded as political become (also or even solely) legal questions and hence may receive a judicial answer, determining the future course of events. So, for example, the broad pro-visions in the Belfast Agreement on the accelerated release of qualifying prison-ers were translated into the detailed provisions of the Sentences Act which in turn gave rise to three quite different judicial review applications.[13] The courts will, through the resolution of questions concerning the powers of, for example, the Northern Ireland Assembly and Ministers, have a not inconsiderable role to play in the evolution and development of Northern Ireland devolution.

The third purpose in referring to the raft of legislative provisions is this: leg-islation goes so far and no further. This is not a point to take us back towards political analysis but rather towards a consideration of what may be termed the 'paralegal', including in this the Westminster Government's Memorandum of Understanding and Concordats produced to regulate the relations between Westminster and the devolved *governments*,[14] and rules of parliamentary/assem-bly procedure reflecting the relations between the various *legislatures*. The cross-border and all-Ireland dimensions of Northern Ireland devolution are of crucial, central importance; but Northern Ireland will also operate—for the first time, unlike the two previous experiences of devolution[15]—within a 'devolved United Kingdom'. The nexus of relationships so created and so regulated will have a fundamental impact upon the nature of devolution in Northern Ireland. Devolution will not only involve the establishment of its internal structures, but also a series of sometimes interconnecting relationships: Belfast and London concerning aspects of non-devolved matters peculiar to Northern Ireland; London, Belfast, Edinburgh, and Cardiff, in, for example, the Joint Ministerial Committee; Belfast and Dublin in the three tiers of 'consultation, co-operation, and action';[16] the British-Irish Council, involving the United Kingdom's Parliaments and Assemblies, the Dáil and the legislatures of the Isle of Man and the Channel Islands; the British-Irish Intergovernmental Conference, dealing with matters on the East-West axis as well as certain Northern Ireland matters for as long as they are not devolved.

Of necessity, this chapter has to be selective. In order to place the Belfast Agreement in a wider setting which may not always be immediately apparent from its terms, and to illustrate the significance of what is *omitted* from the Agreement, it will consider various central 'external' elements of this wider context, including the cross-border dimensions, the (parliamentary) procedural, the intergovernmental, and the judicial. It is necessary, however, to provide first an 'internal' and comparative outline of the *Northern Ireland Act*'s salient characteristics, and their evolution from the terms of the Belfast Agreement.

Setting the Terms of the 'Internal' Structures

The Belfast Agreement in its Strand One section on 'Democratic Institutions in Northern Ireland' deals with—although not in this sequence: legislation, executive authority, safeguards, operation of the Assembly, and relations with other institutions, including in that last heading the Secretary of State and the Westminster Parliament. Paragraph 4 of Strand One indicates that the Assembly 'will be the prime source of authority in respect of all devolved responsibilities'—a statement as much reflecting the peculiar nature of the relationship between a multi-party, power-sharing executive and the legislature, as reflecting the formal source of executive or ministerial power.

Strand One is in fact remarkably brief on the electoral provisions concerning the Assembly, mentioning only its size (108 members) and the electoral system (PR, STV). The other provisions in the *Northern Ireland Act* itself draw largely—but with some amendments on disqualifications—on the *Northern Ireland (Elections) Act* 1998. One matter which both Acts left open—open in the sense of being determined by the Secretary of State—is the method of filling vacancies; it may be done by by-elections, substitutes, or such other method as the Secretary of State 'thinks fit'. This issue is of singular significance in a situation which combines the STV electoral system—which can mean that a party winning, say, the fifth or sixth seat in a constituency at a general election stands little chance of winning the seat at a similarly conducted by-election—and the d'Hondt method of constituting the executive—under which entitlement to a ministerial post derives from the number of seats held in the Assembly.

The *New Northern Ireland Assembly (Elections) Order* 1998,[17] made under the Elections Act 1998, provides for a system of alternates or personally nominated substitutes with a fall-back provision for by-elections should the alternates system not provide the way of filling the vacancy. This current legislative provision may be modified by the Secretary of State exercising the general statutory power indicated above. The position has thus been left undetermined in order to enable the Secretary of State to consult with the Northern Ireland political parties about the implications in this regard of the *Registration of Political Parties Act* 1998, which also received the Royal Assent on 19 November 1998.

Of greater significance, concerning the relationship between the Secretary of State and the Assembly, were the provisions originally in the Bill on dissolution and prorogation. The silence of the Belfast Agreement on this matter at first induced the Government to confer upon (in effect) the Secretary of State considerable powers of dissolution and prorogation—addressing a situation where the Assembly, and particularly the members of the Executive Committee, were unable to carry out their functions. These clauses were, after consultation with the Northern Ireland political parties, removed from the Bill at the House of Lords Committee Stage.[18] The Bill was then 'radically restructure[d]'[19] to include the equivalent of the provisions in the Scotland Bill on the calling of extraordinary general elections, in which the issue is left to a resolution of two-thirds of the membership of the legislature rather than to Secretary of State direction. These provisions, actual or proposed, were not adumbrated in the Belfast Agreement; nor was section 93, which enables the Secretary of State for Northern Ireland to require the Northern Ireland Department of the Environment to make available to him any property on the Stormont Estate, other than the Parliament Buildings.[20] Yet all these provisions impinge upon the debate about the crucial nature of the relationship between the Westminster Government and the devolved legislature. They may indeed be of minor importance compared with what is contained within the Agreement, but the issues are of significance none the less.

The theme of Westminster control carries through into the legislative implementation of those parts of the Belfast Agreement which deal with the legislative competence of the Northern Ireland Assembly. Strand One, paragraph 3 states that the Assembly: '. . . will exercise full legislative and executive authority in respect of those matters currently within the responsibility of the Six Northern Ireland Departments with the possibility of taking on responsibility for other matters as detailed in this agreement.'

These last few words cover only 'policing and (criminal) justice issues'—subject to the outcome of the two Commissions established to review the two matters, to consultation with the Irish Government and to the broad agreement of the Northern Ireland political parties. Paragraph 3 is also subject to paragraph 33 which indicates that the power of the Westminster Parliament to legislate for Northern Ireland after devolution remains unaffected. Paragraph 27 states that 'the Assembly will have authority to legislate in reserved areas with the approval of the Secretary of State and subject to [Westminster] Parliamentary control', and paragraph 33(a) provides that, subject to paragraph 27, the Westminster Parliament will legislate for non-devolved issues. Strand 1 also provides for the 'necessary safeguards' controlling the exercise of the legislative power devolved to the Assembly. Some of the safeguards relate to, put broadly, procedural mechanisms, such as cross-community voting procedures and a role for multi-party committees in the legislative process. The major substantive safeguard relates to the European Convention on Human Rights and any later additional Bill of Rights for Northern Ireland: any Assembly legislation contrary to its terms will be rendered null and void—the Agreement indicating that 'disputes over legislative competence will be decided by the Courts', a principle to be considered further below. The Assembly itself is also to be placed under an obligation to 'proof' its Bills against this obligation to comply with the ECHR. Also considered below is the import of paragraph 26(d) of the Agreement which refers to the introduction of: '. . . mechanisms, based on arrangements proposed for the Scottish Parliament, to ensure suitable co-ordination, and avoid disputes, between the Assembly and the Westminster Parliament.'

At the time of the Belfast Agreement, April 1998, these proposals were to be found in the White Paper which preceded the Scotland Bill, *Scotland's Parliament*,[21] issued in July 1997 and the Scottish Office's *Guide to the Scotland Bill* of December 1997. Paragraph 4.13 of the White Paper stated that 'Departments in both administrations will develop mutual understandings covering the appropriate exchange of information, advance notification and joint working'; while the Scottish Office Guide, on the proposed liaison machinery, explained the requisite links between the Governments: 'there will be a series of non-statutory agreements (or concordats) between Departments'.

The Belfast Agreement's provisions on the division of power between Westminster and the Northern Ireland Assembly actually relate to an already existing three-fold division of legislative responsibility. Under the *Northern Ireland Constitution Act* 1973—and before it, but not identically, the *Government of Ireland Act* 1920[22]—there were three categories of legislative power: listed excepted matters including matters of national or international concern, being the sole responsibility of Westminster; listed reserved matters including the criminal law, policing, law and order, being regarded as generally suitable for devolution only in a stable society, in the interim being legislated on by Westminster, with provision for the Assembly exceptionally to do so, subject to Secretary of State consent and Westminster oversight[23]; and transferred matters, consisting of the unenumerated residue being the responsibility of the Northern Ireland Assembly and Executive. The administrative structures, for example, the six Northern Ireland Government Departments, underpinning this system of devolution remained in place even after the transferred or 'devolved' legislative and executive powers were returned to, or reclaimed by, Westminster in 1974.

It is, therefore, important to appreciate that the Belfast Agreement and the implementing sections of the *Northern Ireland Act* 1998—for example, sections 4, 5(b), 8, 15, 85, and schedules 2 and 3—provide for *three* categories of legislative power as paragraph 3 of Strand 1 of the Agreement, quoted above, illustrates. Legal developments subsequent to the Constitution Act 1973 have meant that the substance of particularly the reserved category has had to be updated, but the 1973 principles have completely moulded the 1998 Act. This is more than being simply a point of legislative history: it relates to comparisons to be drawn with the Scottish Parliament and, more broadly, to an understanding of the varying nature of Westminster's relations with the devolved legislatures. First, the Westminster Government in drafting the Northern Ireland and Scotland Acts has used, with regard to the latter, what may be regarded as unfortunate terminology. The Northern Ireland Act, as stated, builds on the 1973 Act; apart from (strong) arguments, based on substance, it would, technically, have been immensely, if not disproportionately, time-consuming to have unpicked the existing legal structures. So, the *Northern Ireland Act* 1998 has three categories of legislative power: excepted matters listed in schedule 2 are matters of national/international concern and may be legislated on only by Westminster. If the Northern Ireland Assembly were to deal with an excepted matter, other than in an ancillary way, its law would be *ultra vires*. Section 6(2)(b) of the Act makes this perfectly clear. The only way in which a *change* may be made to the excepted list is by an Act of the Westminster Parliament. Amending the Northern Ireland Act is itself an excepted matter—with the exception of some provisions which fall into the reserved category[24]—and the Assembly cannot, therefore, extend its legislative powers into the excepted domain.

Reserved matters are listed in schedule 3; there are forty-two reserved matters, including most notably the criminal law, criminal justice, and policing. Laws may be made in any one of three ways with regard to a reserved matter for as long as it is a reserved matter.[25] The Assembly may, with the consent of the Secretary of State[26] and, in certain situations, the approval of the Westminster Parliament,[27] legislate on a reserved matter. Otherwise the power to do so resides at Westminster. Westminster is required to legislate on a reserved matter by Act of Parliament, unless it is listed in paragraphs 9 to 17 of schedule 3, in which case the law may take the form of a (statutory) Order in Council, to be made only after the Assembly itself has been consulted on the draft.[28] Transferred matters are (unenumerated) devolved matters and consist of everything not listed in schedules 2 and 3. Under section 4, a reserved matter may become a transferred matter, and vice versa, by way of Westminster Order in Council, but only with the cross-community consent of the Assembly.

It is thus sometimes stated that the Assembly can enlarge, or for that matter, contract, its own legislative autonomy. This is indeed the case but only with regard to reserved and *not* excepted matters. This point is also used as a point of contrast with the Scottish Parliament. This is where the unfortunate terminology comes in. The Scotland Act has two and not three legislative categories: reserved or non-devolved, and devolved. Scotland's reserved category does not equate to the Northern Ireland reserved category but to its excepted category—

although the content of both lists is not identical. Under section 30(2) of the Scotland Act, (as read with schedule 7) a reserved matter may become a devolved matter by way of delegated legislation approved by both the Westminster and Scottish Parliaments. As paragraph 4.4 of the White Paper *Scotland's Parliament*[29] explains, this 'will enable the boundary between reserved and devolved matters to be adjusted as appropriate and as the need arises'. Thus the position of the Scottish Parliament *vis-à-vis* the statutory allocation of legislative powers is more open-ended than that of the Northern Ireland Assembly.

As far as the exercise of power within the Northern Ireland Assembly's transferred or devolved areas is concerned, section 6 of the Northern Ireland Act embodies the broad statement of the Agreement concerning the European Convention on Human Rights: a provision is outside the legislative competence of the Assembly if it is incompatible with any of the Convention rights.[30] Section 6, however, also provides other limitations upon the Assembly's power: it may not legislate incompatibly with European Community law; discriminate on the ground of religious belief or political opinion—this is a re-enactment of section 17 of the Constitution Act 1973;[31] modify a specified entrenched enactment including those dealing with the *European Communities and the Human Rights Act* 1998; or 'deal with' an excepted matter, except in an 'ancillary' way. The Scotland Act contains equivalent[32] provision. In terms of understanding the preclusion from the Assembly's legislative competence of legislation '*dealing with*' an excepted matter, the legislative history of this phrase has to be explored and compared with that provided in the Scotland Act.[33] The *Government of Ireland Act* 1920 prevented the Northern Ireland Parliament from lawfully legislating 'in respect of' an excepted matter. Such *vires* questions were for resolution by the courts[34] and in terms of the extent of the preclusion created by the phrase 'in respect of' two decisions are of major importance, namely *Gallagher v Lynn*[35] and *R (Hume) v Londonderry Justices*.[36] The phrase 'in respect of' was *not* followed in the Constitution Act 1973, however, which, further, sought to preclude recourse to the courts on *vires* questions on all but anti-discrimination issues.[37] Section 5 of the 1973 Act used the phrase '*dealing with*' an excepted matter, but the phrase was not defined. Under the *Northern Ireland Act* 1998 unlike the 1973 Act but like the 1920 Act—where, however, a different test was employed—it is possible for all *vires* questions to be aired before the courts. Probably as a consequence of this, the phrase 'deals with' is defined in the 1998 Act. It may be that the original intention of those drafting the Bill was to use the 'in respect of' test, although the Bill as published for its Second Reading employed the 'deals with' test, but the definition of 'deals with' was only added (it is section 98(2)) without debate at the House of Lords' Report stage:

For the purposes of this Act, a provision of any enactment, Bill or subordinate legislation deals with the matter, or each of the matters, which it affects otherwise than incidentally. (House of Lords Debates, 10 November 1998, vol. 594, col. 730, *per* Lord Dubs.)

By contrast the Scotland Act adopts for the preclusion from the Scottish Parliament's powers of reserved matters—the equivalent of Northern Ireland excepted matters—the 'relates to' test. In brief, section 29(2) states that a provision is outside that Parliament's legislative competence if it 'relates to reserved matters'. Section 29(3) defines 'relates to' by reference to 'the purpose of the provision, having regard (among other things) to its effect in all the circumstances'. In the debate on the Scotland Bill, a spokesperson for the Government[38] explained this test by reference to the principles articulated in *Gallagher v Lynn*, although no reference was made to *Hume*. The test in *Gallagher* is not as straightforward as some assume—especially if closer attention is paid to what was said in *Hume*—but in essence the dominant purpose and the means by which it is sought to be achieved are required to lie within the devolved domain.[39] There is an argument—probably of some strength—that the Government's intention for the Scottish devolution scheme—'relates to' as defined—was to give greater power or scope to that Parliament than to the Northern Ireland Assembly—'deals with' as defined. There is but little room regarding the 'deals with' test for debates on purpose or dominant purpose—anything which *affects* an excepted matter other than in an ancillary[40] way is unlawful. Although the *Gallagher v Lynn* test was laid down in a Northern Ireland House of Lords case in a previous devolved system—and drew on a Canadian federal test, heightening arguments that the 1920 system was a quasi-federal one[41]—there is no room for the *Gallagher* test in the application of the Northern Ireland Act. Although arguments generally of quasi-federalism or quasi-federalist potential may re-echo yet again in the Act's wake, these arguments may be put on the specific *vires* test basis concerning the Scottish Parliament, but not the Northern Ireland Assembly. It may be possible for other reasons to argue that the Northern Ireland system—indeed any system of primary legislative devolution—is a quasi-federal one, but it cannot be done on the basis of the statutory test imposed for *vires* questions in the *Northern Ireland Act* 1998.

The Belfast Agreement in Strand 1 also deals with the formation of the Executive in terms which are perhaps its best known feature. Paragraph 14 provides for executive 'authority to be discharged on behalf of the Assembly by a First Minister and Deputy First Minister and up to ten Ministers with Departmental responsibilities'. The Agreement also provides that after their election 'the posts of Ministers will be allocated to parties on the basis of the d'Hondt system by reference to the number of seats each party'—not always an easy concept when parties may tend to fragment—'has in the Assembly'. Other proportionality or 'weighting' elements in the Agreement include the allocation of chairs and deputy chairs in the Assembly Committees, committee membership, cross-community voting[42] on certain specified 'key' issues, and a mechanism for 'petitions of concern'. Against this broad background—faithfully reflected in the terms of the Northern Ireland Act—it is intended to consider two broad issues stemming from the nature of Executive power thus created:

the nature of *intra*governmental relations and the nature of the relationship between the members of the Executive and the Assembly. Again the details of the 1998 Act add very significant 'overlay' to the silences of the Agreement.

The keys to the balance of Executive power are: the 'dyarchy' of the First Minister and Deputy First Minister—and in no place whatsoever in the legislation is the one separated from the other; an entitlement to sit in the Executive Committee deriving from the number of seats won in the Executive and not, for example, from First/Deputy First Ministerial choice; and the requirement for all Northern Ireland Departments to be headed by a Minister required to liaise with his or her Departmental statutory shadow committee. The question that arises, therefore, is how can a balance be secured between the requisite Departmental individuality—which must be maintained so as to preserve the full import of resort to the d'Hondt formula, and which may be enhanced by an increasing tendency to appoint 'specialist' and 'political' advisers from outside the Civil Service—and the requisite collegiality necessary to deal with, for example, cross-cutting issues, the agreement of priorities, the budget and expenditure from the agreed budget, and external relations. The Agreement seeks to secure this balance in paragraphs 19 and 20 of Strand 1, incorporated by reference into section 20(3) of the Act dealing with the powers of the Executive Committee. The members of the Executive Committee are also required to take the Pledge of Office prior to taking up office, and this requires each Minister to 'participate with colleagues in the preparation of a programme for government' and 'to operate within the framework of that programme when agreed within the Executive Committee and endorsed by the Assembly'.[43] One additional factor in the Act, however, not in the Agreement and pertinent to this point, concerns the 'Department of the First and Deputy First Ministers', sometimes known as the Department or Office of the Centre. The statutory provision for this is to be found in section 21(3) which made its first appearance in the Northern Ireland Bill at the House of Lords Report stage.[44] Earlier, at the Lords' Committee stage, provision had been made for the appointment of Junior Ministers,[45] also not mentioned in the Agreement, but provided for in the Scotland Act and also in the previous devolved administrations in Northern Ireland. Lord Dubs in explaining to the House the 'interest shown by some of the parties during the consultation process in creating a department of the centre', stated:

Such a Department has obvious parallels in Whitehall. There was also a similar department in existence during previous periods of devolution in Northern Ireland. Its functions would be entirely for the Northern Ireland parties in the Assembly to determine but could include both *policy co-ordination* and possibly statutory functions as well. (House of Lords Debate, 10 November 1998, vol. 594 col. 660. Emphasis added.)

One can clearly present arguments that Westminster/Whitehall and the first Northern Ireland devolved administration being single-party governments are not analogous to a d'Hondt government. None the less, it is interesting to note,

selectively, the functions which the First and Deputy First Ministerial pro-
gramme—approved by the Assembly in February 1999[46]—plans to allocate to
the Office of the Centre: Economic Policy Unit, Equality Unit, liaison with the
North-South Ministerial Council including the Secretariat, liaison with the
British-Irish Council, liaison with the Secretary of State on excepted and
reserved matters, European Affairs/International Matters, Information Services,
Executive Committee Secretariat, Legislation Progress Unit, Freedom of
Information, Machinery of Government, Policy Innovation Unit, and Cross-
Departmental Co-ordination.

Within the context of central power, which may also be expressed in terms of
the necessary search for some collective or cohesive power, consideration needs
to be given to the introduction, post-Agreement, of the concept of Junior
Ministers. The Northern Ireland Act, by section 19, enables the FM and DFM
acting jointly to determine, subject to Assembly approval, the number of Junior
Ministers and the procedure to be employed for their appointment. There is no
statutory requirement to follow the d'Hondt procedure, although presumably it
may be recommended in the FM/DFM determination to the Assembly. Section
22 precludes an Assembly Act from conferring functions on a Junior Minister.[47]
These provisions reflect a possible lack of 'consensus as to what functions they
should exercise or how they should be appointed'.[48] The likelihood that two
Junior Ministers would be appointed to the Office of the Centre—perhaps with
the specific remits of Equality and Economic Policy—was, in the event, realized,
and it is clearly possible for a system to be recommended and approved whereby
each departmental Minister serves with a Junior Minister. The overall nature of
the Executive power and the various intragovernmental relationships are thus
not as clear as the starker provisions of the Agreement might indicate.

Equally uncertain is the precise nature of the relationship between the
Executive Committee and the Assembly. Clearly each Minister is responsible
both in law and politically to the Assembly for the formulation and discharge of
his or her responsibilities.[49] The Assembly will, however, also have considerable
power located in its statutory committees, including the powers to *initiate* legislation and to take the Committee stage of relevant primary legislation.[50] These
important powers—*initiative* located outside an Executive is an important power
for any legislature—must be understood in the context of the 'opposition' role
which the 1998 Act gives the Committees, a role, again, not foreshadowed in
the Belfast Agreement. Sections 29(5) and (6) were inserted into the Bill at
House of Commons' Report Stage,[51] without any discussion, and they, respectively, prevent Ministers including Junior Ministers, from becoming the chair or
deputy chair of a committee and require where possible the people holding such
a position to be of a different political party from the Minister who heads the
department which their committee shadows.

The point about provisions in the Act which have no counterpart in the
Agreement should not be overstated: the Act does seek faithfully to reflect the

broad provisions of the Agreement, and non-Agreement elements of the Act
either reflect routine necessity—on for example, a Northern Ireland Assembly
Commission, remuneration of members, financial provision, and the saving of
existing laws—or reflect the outcome of consultations with the parties as the Bill
proceeded through Parliament. Well over 400 amendments were put to the Bill
in the House of Lords—the Bill was guillotined in the Commons—and it is
hardly surprising that much consultation took place, as the Bill progressed
through Parliament, on working out the implications of the Belfast Agreement's
provisions. None the less, the fact remains that the main focus now for the operation of devolution in Northern Ireland is the legislation and not the Agreement;
and the Act itself has engendered, in the processes of its enactment and will
engender in the processes of its operation and (judicial) interpretation, a
dynamic, if not distinct from, then certainly additional to those dynamics engendered by the Belfast Agreement itself.

This may, before turning to the post-enactment parliamentary and intergovernmental developments, be briefly illustrated by reference to the variable commencement provisions of the Northern Ireland Act.[52] Certain provisions in the
Act came into force on the giving of the Royal Assent, but otherwise it was, as
is the traditional case, left to the Secretary of State to determine the commencement day for the remaining provisions and 'different days may be
appointed for different purposes'.[53] Although the Belfast Agreement indicated
no preferred commencement date for its proposed Human Rights Commission
and Equality Commission, the Secretary of State brought into operation the provisions of the Northern Ireland Act relating to them in advance of the commencement of devolution. From one point of view, it would have been clearly
unacceptable constantly to delay the introduction of these Commissions pending the resolution of the decommissioning impasse, especially given the
Government's *commitment* to these bodies as a matter of priority. Furthermore,
although the Agreement in its Declaration of Support paragraph 5 makes it clear
that certain institutional and constitutional arrangements are interlocking and
interdependent, the two Commissions are not mentioned there. From another
point of view, it may be argued that the Human Rights Commission—which
itself preceded the Equality Commission—has been given an opportunity to formulate the human rights agenda, and to a certain extent the Equality agenda,[54]
in a way which may not have happened had the Northern Ireland Act been
implemented in its (virtual) entirety on the same day. Thus partial implementation of the Belfast Agreement—or, it may be, implementation in a series of
steps—has the potential to create a quite different situation from that which may
have developed had the Agreement been implemented in its entirety on one day.
Prime responsibility for the protection, promotion, and enhancement of human
rights should rest with a legislature; the role of a Human Rights Commission in
a (potentially) devolved entity with no legislature, even initially, takes on a different role or essence of its own.

External Dimensions

In terms of identifying the nature of the Northern Ireland devolved system, consideration must be given to its external as well as its internal aspects. In so far as the devolved scheme is a part of United Kingdom structures, then there will be a (greater or smaller) commonality between Westminster and the devolved Parliament/Assemblies. These relationships have parliamentary, intergovernmental, and judicial aspects. Also, of course, built into the Northern Ireland devolved system is a series of quite distinct relationships[55] with another sovereign State, namely the Republic of Ireland. This set of relationships will, clearly, take on a particular significance with regard to, for example, European Union matters where the United Kingdom and Irish governments may espouse different policy preferences. Paragraph 17 of Strand 2 of the Belfast Agreement requires the North-South Ministerial Council (NSMC):

To consider the European Union dimension of relevant matters, including the implementation of EU policies and programmes and proposals under consideration in the EU framework. Arrangements to be made to ensure that the views of the Council are taken into account and represented appropriately at relevant EU meetings.

In order to facilitate the legal development of the Belfast-Dublin relationship—given the general inability of a devolved legislature to enter into international agreements[56]—paragraph 3 of schedule 2 of the Northern Ireland Act, whilst generally withholding international relations from the legislative competence of the Assembly, does not withhold 'the exercise of legislative powers so far as required for giving effect to any agreement or arrangement entered into' in the NSMC or by or in relation to the cross-border implementation bodies.[57]

There has been much debate about the nature of the all-Ireland bodies delineated in the Belfast Agreement and created subsequently by intergovernmental Treaty and legislation in both Westminster and the Dáil. In particular the question, not itself clearly answered in the Agreement,[58] asked is: 'Is the NSMC an executive body?' or, more diffusely, what is the nature of the all-Ireland dimension so created—dynamic or static? In so far as the word 'executive' requires the double element of *both* policy formulation *and* implementation, then it may be argued that the NSMC is not an executive body in that *implementation* of its decisions rests elsewhere, specifically in the implementation bodies created by the Assembly/Westminster and the Dáil. The Agreement itself refers to the Assembly and the NSMC and their functioning as being interlocking and interdependent, and under sections 52 and 53 of the 1998 Act, Ministers participating in the Council are answerable to the Assembly, which is responsible for enacting any requisite legislation emanating from NSMC decisions. It may, therefore, be argued that the NSMC and implementation bodies are 'delegates' of the Northern Ireland Assembly; that the implementation bodies are limited in number and operating in limited areas; and that the future ambit of the NSMC's powers, the development of implementation bodies, and consequently the nature or force of the all-Ireland dynamo are tied to the wishes of the Assembly. By contrast, Article 3 of the British-Irish Agreement of March 1999 on the cross-border implementation bodies states that each such body '. . . shall in particular implement any decisions of the [NSMC] on policies and actions relating to matters within the scope of the Body's functions' and the remit of each implementation body indicates a very close relationship between it and the NSMC, for example, relating to the power to appoint the body's membership, the obligation of the body to report to and to advise the NSMC, the submission of corporate plans, and of annual reports which are also to be laid before the respective legislatures. Each body is to be subject to the Ombudsman of the relevant jurisdiction and close liaison is likely between the law officers concerning any legal challenges or queries. There is thus an argument that policy and implementation are so closely linked in the chain that the word 'executive' is not inappropriate for the NSMC either alone, or with the implementation bodies.

Thus with regard to matters falling within the devolved responsibilities of the Northern Ireland Assembly and Ministers, there is already an all-Ireland dimension of not insignificant proportions.[59] The NMSC has within its remit 'matters of mutual interest within the competence of the two Administrations, North and South'. This does mean, of course—a factor not always fully appreciated—that there is a mutuality in these arrangements—that they may and will lead to as many changes in the laws of the Republic of Ireland as in Northern Ireland; that policies for the former jurisdiction will have to be reached through agreement with Ministers from Northern Ireland as approved by the Assembly; that a sovereign State is accepting such changes being wrought as a consequence of agreements with a non-Sovereign legislature and government.

Thus with regard to transferred matters—with regard to which Westminster retains the power to legislate[60]—there is a three-fold dimension: Westminster, Northern Ireland, and cross-border. It is highly probable that the latter two will play a more significant role in these matters than will Westminster, but it is none the less important to consider the likely attitude of the Westminster Government towards an exercise of its powers in the transferred areas, for, all else apart, this impinges on the 'quasi-federal' debate.

During the life of the Northern Ireland Parliament from 1921 to 1972, the quasi-federal analogy was used with regard to the relationship between London and Belfast.[61] The relationship, as defined by the terms of the 1920 Act, was clearly not federal—there were not two Parliaments of co-ordinate status, operating within mutually exclusive areas of competence. None the less it was argued that the strictly non-federal structure had been 'softened' to become quasi-federal in essence. Two factors which contributed to this argument were, first, the resort by the court in *Gallagher v Lynn*[62] to a principle for determining the *vires* of devolved legislative competence from the Canadian, that is, a federal, jurisdiction. The second factor which contributed to quasi-federalist arguments were the constitutional conventions, in the form of Speakers' rulings,[63] preventing the Northern Ireland Parliament from debating non-devolved matters and Westminster from debating transferred matters. This was coupled with a convention that Westminster would not exercise its (statutory) power to legislate in the devolved area without the consent of the devolved Government and Parliament.[64]

Suggestions that the current system of devolution constitute quasi-federalism are again being heard. It is, therefore, essential to consider Westminster's attitudes to the matters referred to above. Before doing so, however, the overall context of the debate in terms of its constitutional and judicial parameters should be mentioned—there are differences this time between the current devolved structures and that pertaining only for Northern Ireland, for the fifty years beginning in 1921. Previously there was only the Belfast-London, or Belfast-Great Britain, link to consider. This time, there are within the United Kingdom three relationships between the regional/national capitals and London to consider. Those relationships are not identical; the powers devolved to the three regions/nations are not identical; and as far as Northern Ireland specifically is concerned the cross-border element is not the same as that actually in existence under the *Government of Ireland Act* 1920.[65] So while 'quasi-federalism' may be used to describe one of those relationships, for example that between London and Edinburgh, *in isolation from the others*, the label becomes less persuasive when all three 'linkages' are considered with all their differences and in the light of cross-cutting factors such as the British-Irish Council. Secondly, the likelihood of future judicial resort to *Gallagher v Lynn* style reasoning should not be assumed *simpliciter*. Certainly, it was referred to in the debates on the Scotland Bill as indicating what lies behind the wording of section 29(2)(b)—the 'relates to' test—as explained in section 29(3)—'relates to' to be determined by reference to the 'purpose of the provision and its effect in all the circumstances'—although the test cannot be fully understood without considering the far more restrictive test in *Hume*.[66] The 'relates to' test, however, does not apply in Northern Ireland—the 'deals with' test does not lend itself to quasi-federal analogies—as explained above, and, given the more limited form of devolution to Wales, will not be at the heart of the judicial resolution of *vires* questions under the *Government of Wales Act* 1998. There is thus, as it were, asymmetrical 'judicial devolution' too. Furthermore, however, the role of the courts is now very different from that pertaining in the 1930s when *Gallagher v Lynn* was decided—and, for that matter, in the 1970s when *Hume* was decided. The expansion of judicial review, the (future) role of the courts in the protection of human rights, and the judicial formulation (and protection) of constitutional principles all reflect an expansive (and formalized) attitude of the courts to public power. When the Scottish courts, against the background of their constitutional history, constitutional principles, and evolving judicial role, consider the 'relates to' test, why should they automatically resolve the issue in accordance with *Gallagher v Lynn* or any other federal case? Devolution instead of being regarded as 'quasi-anything' should be analysed as a system—indeed as several different systems—in its or their own right. The courts of England, Scotland, Wales,[67] and Northern Ireland, with their own evolving and maybe varying public law jurisdictions and jurisprudence, will be key players in this regard, *pace* the Westminster Government which seems to believe (or hope) that they have only a minor role to play.[68] A prediction of the courts' future role should include reference to *Gallagher* and other federal, including specifically Commonwealth cases, but *Gallagher* will not *resolve* the issue—not (arguably) for Scotland, and certainly not for Northern Ireland and Wales.

If, however, the Westminster Government is correct and the courts will have only a minor role to play, then arguments based on quasi-federalism cannot anyway place too much reliance on *Gallagher*, but must instead place greater emphasis on the conventions, concordats and rules of (parliamentary) procedure which also relate to the nature of the relationship between Westminster and devolved power.

In the absence of a devolved government, Northern Ireland was not a party—other than through the Secretary of State—to the Memorandum of Understanding between the Westminster, Scottish, and Welsh Governments and the accompanying concordats—on Co-ordination of European Policy issues, Finance Assistance to Industry, International Relations and Statistics[69]—but it is a realistic assumption that they will in due course apply without significant amendment, other than with regard to the European Union concordat which may need some adjustment to cope with Belfast-Dublin relations on EU matters. In the context of this chapter, some of the key elements of these documents—which are essentially 'management' documents, written in centralist not quasi-federalist language—are paragraphs 13 to 15 of the Memorandum of Understanding and the remit of the Joint Ministerial Committee, on which a supplementary agreement has been reached.

Paragraphs 13 to 15 are, in their language—both words used and tone or stress—quite distinct from the 1920s Westminster Speaker's ruling preventing MPs debating (Northern Ireland) devolved matters and vice versa:

The United Kingdom Parliament retains authority to legislate on any issue, whether devolved or not. It is ultimately for Parliament to decide what use to make of that power. However, the UK Government will proceed in accordance with the convention that the UK Parliament would not normally legislate with regard to devolved matters except with the agreement of the devolved legislature.[70] The devolved administrations will be responsible for seeking such agreement as may be required for this purpose on an approach from the UK Government.[71]

The United Kingdom Parliament retains the absolute right to debate, enquire into, or make representations about devolved matters. It is ultimately for Parliament to decide what use to make of that power, but the UK Government will encourage the UK Parliament to bear in mind the primary responsibility of devolved legislatures and administrations in these fields and to recognize that it is a consequence of Parliament's decision to devolve certain matters that Parliament itself will in future be more restricted in its field of operation. The devolved legislatures will be entitled to debate non-devolved matters but the devolved executives will encourage each devolved legislature to bear in mind the responsibility of the UK Parliament in these matters.

These principles are reflected in the terms of reference of the Joint Ministerial Committee (JMC)—always to be chaired in whatever its format by a Minister in the Westminster Cabinet—which include consideration of non-devolved matters which impinge on devolved responsibilities and vice versa; and, 'where the UK Government and the devolved administrations so agree' the consideration of devolved matters in terms of their respective treatment in the different parts of the United Kingdom.[72] The JMC is also the forum for the resolution of disputes, including *vires* questions. As against that as the Agreement makes clear, the JMC 'is a consultative body rather than an executive body and so will reach agreements rather than decisions. It may not bind any of the participating administrations. . . . Nonetheless, the expectation is that participating administrations will support positions that the JMC has agreed'.[73]

From a management and/or efficiency point of view, such intergovernmental agreements—to be found also in federations—are essential for the smooth resolution of questions concerning the scope of power and for avoiding unnecessary and potentially divisive recourse to the courts. Such documents seek to oil the machinery of structures allocating, on a territorial basis, powers and responsibilities. The point being made is not a point against such documents—though there are, none the less, issues worthy of fuller exploration, such as their legal status, the political accountability of the decision-making processes, and scrutiny by the legislature—but rather to indicate the centralist nature of the ones agreed between Westminster and the Scottish and Welsh Governments.

As far as parliamentary procedure is concerned, the proposed situation is rather more towards the quasi-federalist part of the spectrum without being the same as that which obtained during the life of the Northern Ireland Parliament. This issue has been considered in various forums, not least the Westminster Select Committee on Procedure[74] and an *ad hoc* committee of the New Northern Ireland Assembly on the Procedural Consequences of Devolution.[75] The Belfast Agreement, in Strand 1 paragraph 33(c) in effect gave a commitment to the continuation of the Northern Ireland Grand and Select Committees,[76] especially for the scrutiny of the responsibilities of the Secretary of State. The Government has expressed its opinion that the 'territorial' Select Committees 'will play an important role in fostering good relations between Westminster and the respective devolved legislature. It is possible that they will also conduct inquiries in conjunction with committees of the devolved legislatures into subjects for which responsibility is shared'.[77]

The overall guiding principle for the Westminster Government in this area is that 'parliamentary procedure or custom should not be called in aid'[78] to undermine the principles inherent in devolution itself, while at the same time avoiding the rigidity of the previous system. Hence questions of Ministers will (generally) be confined to matters within their responsibility but with the possibility of also exploring matters, for example the subject of intergovernmental liaison or discussion. Thus the legislatures and executives will not enter upon rigidly exclusive domains, but rather into a set of interweaving relationships surrounding largely discrete areas of responsibility. The possibility for mutual influence in such situations is also not inconsiderable, as may perhaps be illustrated by, for example, the decision of the Scottish Nationalist Party to lay a motion on the provisions of the *Act of Settlement* 1700\1, in the Scottish Parliament in December 1999, thus engendering a wider debate about the issues which the *Act of Settlement* raises.

The insight given by labels such as quasi-federalist has been considerable—and will continue to be so, although it appears highly unlikely that a federalist United Kingdom will emerge from the operation of the current devolved structures. The constitutional structures of Northern Ireland, Scotland, and Wales—not discounting England—may possibly follow different paths, although it is accepted that to use quasi-federalist analogies does not necessarily imply that a federal solution is the *terminus ad quem*. Although the Westminster Government often gives the impression of regarding the consequences of the introduction of devolution as a series of opportunities to resort to *ad hocery*, it is also (probably) true to state that it is seeking to forge 'devolution' as a distinctive constitutional structure, or set of structures. The matter may not of course, indeed, will not, be solely in their hands. The courts, the devolved legislatures, the cross-border institutions, the cross-cutting alliances of the British-Irish Council will all play a significant role too. Devolution as it is, and how it may evolve, has to be placed in the context of governance in a multilayered democracy. Cross-cutting constitutionalism has arrived.

ENDNOTES

1. See Hadfield, B., 'The Belfast Agreement, Sovereignty and the State of the Union', *Public Law*, (1998): 599–616. Sections 1 and 2 and schedule 1 of the 1998 *Northern Ireland Act* came into force on the same day as the changes to Articles 2 and 3 of the Irish Constitution.
2. See also the multi-party agreement's section on 'Constitutional issues'.
3. The *Northern Ireland Act* 1998, s.4(5).
4. See New Northern Ireland Assembly, Initial Standing Orders, 28 June 1998. The most accessible source is House of Commons Research Paper, *The Northern Ireland Bill: Some legislative and operational aspects of the Assembly*, 98/77, 26–36. Subsequent additions were made to the Standing Orders, for example in March 1999, concerning the appointment of Ministers, and chairpersons and deputy chairpersons to the shadow statutory committees as then projected.

5. SO 14(1): 'The First Minister and Deputy First Minister shall be jointly elected by the members'. The nomination procedure was itself of a 'joint slate' nature. See the later enacted *Northern Ireland Act* 1998, s.16. Section 16 covers resignation from office; SO 14(1) does not. Mr Mallon 'offered to resign' and was generally believed to have resigned his position on 15 July 1999. On 29 November, an Assembly motion passed by 71 votes to 28 requested Mr Mallon to withdraw his offer of resignation. For the pertinent Assembly debates see N.I.Ass.Debs. 29 November 1999. The Motion thus obviated a need for a new 'joint slate' re-election obtaining the requisite cross-community support.

6. The Belfast Agreement, Strand 1, para.14 refers to '. . . up to ten Ministers with Departmental responsibilities'. *The Northern Ireland Act* 1998, s.17(4) provides: 'The number of Ministerial offices shall not exceed 10 or such greater number as the Secretary of State may by order provide'.

7. New Northern Ireland Assembly (NNIA) 7, February 1999.

8. NNIA 9, March 1999.

9. See SI 1999 No.859 as amended by SI 1999 No.2062. Irish legislation was also required: see the *British Irish Agreement Act* 1999. See also the *Human Rights Act* 1999 and the *Criminal Justice Release of Prisoners Act* 1998.

10. SI 1999 No.283 (NII.), made under the *Northern Ireland Act* 1974.

11. SI 1999 No.663, made under s.49(1) of the 1998 Act.

12. SI 1999 No.664, made under s.49(1) of the 1998 Act.

13. See *In re the Home Secretary (Mr Jack Straw)* 29 March 1999, *In re Thomas Anthony Burke* 3 September 1999, and *In re Michelle Williamson* (19 November 1999), all NI QBD, Unreported. The judgment in *Williamson*—which, unlike the leave application, received limited publicity—was to the effect that the Secretary of State's evaluation under the *Sentences Act* that the IRA were maintaining a complete and unequivocal cease-fire was not irrational and that the correct statutory test had been applied. The judgment in the case was delivered on the day after Senator Mitchell has issued the final report on his Review of the Belfast Agreement stating his opinion that there was sufficient consensus between the parties for devolution to commence and decommissioning to occur.

14. See Cm. 4444, October 1999. As at the time of writing, there have also been a number of specific supplementary or bilateral concordats between a Westminster Department and its Scottish counterpart setting out their working practices with the aim of ensuring 'a close and effective working relationship'. These include one between the Cabinet Office and the Scottish Administration.

15. Under the *Government of Ireland Act* 1920 and the *Northern Ireland Constitution Act* 1973.

16. This refers respectively to the responsibilities of the North-South Ministerial Council, the cross-border areas of co-operation, and the cross-border implementation bodies. The essential difference between the latter two is that the former areas relate to co-operation through existing bodies. A cross-border implementation body is one body for both jurisdictions, its powers being derived from, respectively, Westminster/Northern Ireland Assembly legislation and Dáil legislation.

17. SI 1998, No.1287.

18. See Clauses 24(4) and 43 of the Bill as originally published.

19. Lord Dubs, H.L.Debs., vol.593, col.1295, 19 October 1998.

20. '[This] will facilitate the kind of close and constructive working relationship with the new institutions which the Government certainly want to develop', *per* Lord Dubs, H.L.Debs., vol.593, col.1489, 21 October 1998. Mr Peter Mandelson was appointed Secretary of State for Northern Ireland on 11 October 1999. It will, therefore, fall to him to avail of this power.

21. Cm. 3658.

22. See Hadfield, B., *The Constitution of Northern Ireland* (Belfast: SLS Legal Publications, 1989), chs. III and IV.

23. See also section 3 of the Constitution Act on alterations in devolved responsibilities. *Cf* section 4 of the *Northern Ireland Act* 1998, discussed below.

24. See schedule 2, para.22.

25. Again, see the similarity to the *Constitution Act* 1973, sections 3, 5, 6 and schedule 3.

26. The *Northern Ireland Act* 1998, section 8. The Secretary of State, after devolution, remains responsible for reserved and excepted matters unless one of the latter matters lies within the

responsibility of one of the other Westminster Departments. In moving the draft *Northern Ireland Act 1998 (Appointed Day) Order* 1999, the 'devolution Order', the Secretary of State said: 'In the exercise of my authority in those important residual areas, I will consult the Assembly whenever proper and appropriate to ensure that local concerns and issues are taken into consideration in relation to the exercise of my responsibilities'. H.C. Debs., col.254, 30 November 1999.

27. *Northern Ireland Act* 1998, section 27.
28. *Ibid.*, section 85. This section is a response to many of the criticisms levelled against the method of legislating for Northern Ireland during direct rule: laws falling within the transferred and reserved areas under the 1973 Act were legislated on by Westminster usually by (statutory) Order in Council. For a criticism of this procedure, see Hadfield, B., 'Legislating for Northern Ireland: Options for Reform' in *18th Annual Report of the Standing Advisory Commission on Human Rights*, H.C. 739, 111–28.
29. Cm. 3658.
30. The *Human Rights Act* 1998, an Act applying throughout the United Kingdom, was also at this time in the process of being enacted. It requires all public authorities to act compatibly with the European Convention and enables the courts—subject to some exceptions—to set aside incompatible subordinate legislation, which includes Acts of the Northern Ireland Assembly. The interrelationship between the Human Rights Act itself and the human rights provisions of the Northern Ireland Act does not seem to have been fully thought through—for example, there could be differences under the two Acts concerning the rules of construction, time limits and the powers of the courts—but certain provisions of the Northern Ireland Act cross-refer to the Human Rights Act: see, for example section 71(3) and (4). Under the *Northern Ireland Act* 1998, schedule 14, paragraph 1, the *Human Rights Act* 1998 applies on and from devolution day to the powers of the Assembly and Northern Ireland Ministers and Departments. There are comparable provisions in the Government of Wales and Scotland Acts. Otherwise, the Human Rights Act comes into force on 2 October 2000.
31. For the case-law arising under this section and section 19 (see section 76 of the 1998 Act), see Hadfield, B., 'The Northern Ireland Constitution Act 1973: Lessons for Minority Rights' in P. Cumper and S. Wheatley (eds.), *Minority Rights in the 'New' Europe* (The Hague: Kluwer, 1999), 129–46.
32. But not identical: see the *Scotland Act* 1998, section 29. It omits reference to the anti-discrimination provision found in the Northern Ireland Act and includes reference to the position and powers of the Lord Advocate.
33. This chapter does not deal with the equivalent limitations on the powers of the Northern Ireland Ministers and Departments. On these, see the 1998 Act, sections 24, 25, 26, and 27.
34. Either as arising during other proceedings—for example, as in both *Gallagher* and *Hume*, see below—or 'directly' under section 51 of the 1920 Act, which gave rise to only one case.
35. [1937] AC 863.
36. [1972] NI 91.
37. See s.4(5), ss.17–23 of the 1973 Act, and para.55 of Cmnd.5259, March 1973: *Northern Ireland Constitutional Proposals*—the White Paper preceding the 1973 Act.
38. *Per* Lord Sewel, H.L.Debs., vol.592, col.818 *et seq.*
39. In *Gallagher v Lynn*, n.35, at 870, Lord Atkin, drawing on Canadian federal authorities, spoke of, the 'true nature and character of the legislation' . . . its 'pith and substance'. If that fell within the transferred area, the Act would be upheld as valid. In *Hume*, greater emphasis was placed upon the need for the means to the lawful end themselves to be valid.
40. Defined in the 1998 Act, s.6(3).
41. In *Gallagher*, resort to a federal system—and a legally different system from that pertaining in Northern Ireland—was used to base an argument that the clearly non-federal elements of the 1920 Act had been—and for other reasons too—'softened' into a form of quasi-federalism, expansive of the devolved legislature's power. Also during the life of the Northern Ireland Parliament, another analogy was used—of less relevance now and not to be confused with arguments on quasi-federalism which relate to relationships *within* a State. The second analogy is that Northern Ireland was, in practice, in spite of obvious differences in both law and status,

moving closer to enjoying a 'Dominion-status' relationship with Westminster like that of the Dominion Parliaments. See, for example Calvert, H., *Constitutional Law in Northern Ireland* (London and Belfast: Stevens, 1968), ch. 4.

42. See on designation of identity (for cross-community voting purposes) Initial Standing Orders, SO 3(1), the Northern Ireland Act 1998, section 4(5), and NNIA 10, March 1999, SO 3(7) and (8). SO 3(8) provides: 'A Member may change his/her designation of identity on no more than one occasion during the life of an Assembly. Any such change takes effect thirty calendar days after notification in writing is submitted to the Speaker'.

43. Section 30 of the 1998 Act provides for the exclusion of Ministers from office for, *inter alia,* any failure to observe the terms of the pledge of office.

44. H.L.Debs., vol.594, cols.659 *et seq.*, 10 November 1998.

45. H.L.Debs., vol.593, col.1276, 19 October, 1998.

46. NNIA 7, February 1999.

47. See also the *Departments (Northern Ireland) Order* 1999, articles 2(3) and 2(4). A Junior Minister is required to take the pledge of office and may be excluded from holding office for non-observance of that pledge: see ss.19(3) and 30(1).

48. See, for example, H.L.Debs., vol.593, cols.1277–9, 19 October, 1998.

49. See, for example, s.24 of the Northern Ireland Act and NNIA 10, SO 18 and 19. Of broad interest here concerning the relationship between Ministers and civil servants in the context of expenditure and audit are the provisions inserted into an Act of the Scottish Parliament: the *Public Finance and Accountability (Scotland) Act* 1999, sections 14 *et seq.*

50. See the 1998 Act, s.29(3) of which incorporates paragraph 9 of Strand of the Belfast agreement, and s.44.

51. H.C.Debs., vol.217, col.585, 30 July 1998.

52. See, for example, Commencement Nos. 1, 2 and 3 Orders, SI 1999, No.340, SI 1999, No. 1753 and SI 1999, No.2204, and the *Equality Commission for Northern Ireland (Supplementary Provisions) (Northern Ireland) Order* SI 1999, No.1804. The remainder of the Act—other than Parts II and III, which are dealt with separately—were brought into force by the final Commencement Order made at the same time as the Devolution Order.

53. The *Northern Ireland Act* 1998, s.101(3). The commencement of devolution is dealt with under section 3.

54. See the Human Rights Commission Draft Strategic Plan 1999–2002 generally, and specifically the HRC's assumption that it will be a designated public authority under section 75(3)(a) of the 1998 Act. The powers of the Human Rights Commission are to be found in sections 69 and 70; those of the Equality Commission in sections 73 to 75 and schedules 8 and 9. The role of the Equality Commission in overseeing the operation of section 75 begins on 1 January 2000. The role with regard to human rights, additional to those found in the European Convention— see section 69(11)—will have a very considerable impact in terms of broadening the human rights agenda in Northern Ireland beyond the Convention Rights. See also in this regard, the 1998 Act, sections 14(5) and 26.

55. But see, for example, the role and powers of, especially, the British-Irish Intergovernmental Conference and, to a lesser extent, the British-Irish Council.

56. See the Scotland Act, schedule 5, para.7. *Cf* the Northern Ireland Act, schedule 2, para.3.

57. Section 55, under which the Secretary of State made the relevant delegated legislation, for the initial six implementation bodies, confers the power on the Northern Ireland Assembly, should it so wish, to legislate for further such bodies.

58. Strand 2, paragraph 1: '. . . the [NSMC] . . . to bring together those with executive responsibilities in Northern Ireland and the Irish Government, to develop consultation, co-operation and action within the island of Ireland—including through implementation on an all-island and cross-border basis—on matters of mutual interest within the competence of the Administrations, North and South'. See also para.5(iii).

59. For the non-devolved matters all-Ireland dimension, see the powers and responsibilities of the British-Irish Intergovernmental Conference.

60. The *Northern Ireland Act* 1998, section 5(6). See also section 87(1) with regard to the need for parity between Northern Ireland and Great Britain on social security, child support, and pensions. These matters were previously devolved and remain so, subject to the 1998 Act's

statutory requirements. They are not devolved under the Scotland Act; see schedule 5, Head F. For Westminster's powers over Scottish devolved matters, see section 28(7).

61. See, for example, Calvert, *Constitutional Law in Northern Ireland*, n.42, ch. 6; Hadfield, *The Constitution of Northern Ireland*, n.22, 80–8; and Palley, C., 'The evolution, disintegration and possible reconstruction of the Northern Ireland Constitution' *Anglo-American Law Review* (1972): 368–476, especially at 383–8, where she discusses both quasi-federalism and the (distinct) Dominion analogy.

62. [1937] AC 863; section 4(1) of the 1920 Act used 'in respect of' not 'relates to'.

63. That is, rulings from the Speaker of the Westminster Parliament and of the Northern Ireland Parliament.

64. See Calvert, *Constitutional Law in Northern Ireland*, n.42 at 87–9.

65. On the 1920 Act's cross-border provisions, see Hadfield, *The Constitution of Northern Ireland*, n.22, Chap.2.

66. [1972] NI 91. See per Lowry L.C.J. at 113: 'The argument in favour of a liberal construction . . . of the 1920 Act may be based on the proposition . . . that the subordinate legislature ought to be master in its own house. . . . The flaw in this reasoning is that it tends to disregard the limitations expressly imposed on the subordinate parliament'.

67. Judicial review cases involving Welsh devolution issues may be heard in Wales.

68. See, for example, Mr Henry McLeish, then Minister of State in the Scottish Office, in his evidence to the Scottish Affairs Select Committee into *The Operation of Multi-Layer Democracy*, 1997–8, H.CV. 460-II, 2 December 1998, Qs.323 and 4: 'If you have confidence in the judiciary . . . then this is a process whereby we can resolve that very small band of technical legal issues which have not been resolved further down the line'. See also the *Memorandum of Understanding*, Cm.4444, October 1999, paras. 26 and 27. The provisions of section 101 of the Scotland Act and of section 83 of the Northern Ireland Act—requiring an interpretative presumption in favour of the validity of devolved legislation—should also be noted in this regard. The Human Rights Act jurisprudence generally and the fact that (European Convention) human rights issues in Scotland, Northern Ireland, and Wales are 'devolution issues' will also be of considerable importance in these regards.

69. Cm.4444, October 1999. See the references in the Concordat on International Relations to the role of the Foreign Office with regard to agreements reached in the British-Irish Council: D3.7. See also related text and footnotes 4 and 6 of the same document.

70. This repeats a reassurance given by the Government during the debates on what is now section 28(7) of the Scotland Act.

71. See the debate in the Scottish Parliament, Vol.1, No.8, Session 1, 9 June 1999.

72. See Cm.4444, October 1999, Supplementary Agreement on JMC.

73. *Ibid.*, para. AI.10. See also concerning intergovernmental relations, the announcement of Mr Gordon Brown, the Chancellor of the Exchequer, on 1 December 1999, of the institution of three new 'cabinet committees' to co-ordinate policy between Westminster and Scotland. These 'joint action committees', designed to ensure the smooth operation of matters where the responsibilities of Westminster and Edinburgh overlap, are to cover pensions, child poverty, and 'knowledge technology'.

74. See, for example, its Fourth Report on the Procedural Consequences of Devolution (H.C.185, 1998–9), and the First Special Report from the Committee (H.C.814) containing the Government Response, and the Commons' debates thereon on 21 October 1999, cols.606 *et seq.*

75. NNIA 3 and 4, October 1998.

76. HC SO 109–16 on the Northern Ireland Grand Committee—little use has so far been made of its extended powers—and SO 152 on the Select Committee.

77. HC 814 at n.76, para.6.

78. Drawing on the principles formulated by the Procedure Select Committee itself.

6

The Assembly and the Executive

RICK WILFORD

Introduction

The adoption of the consociational (plus) template to pattern the Agreement's architecture structured the logic of choice in the design of both the Assembly and its Executive arm—see O'Leary, in Chapter 4 of this volume. In this chapter the focus turns to these institutions and the means by which they were intended to interact. To gain further insight, we examine the process of implementing the infrastructure of the Assembly, including its committee system, and the ways in which a number of features of the consociational model—power-sharing, proportionality, and the unanimity rule—were effected in mobilizing Strand One of the Agreement. A subtext of the chapter is the extent to which the application of those features provides for the realization of joined-up government, a principle that underpins not only Strand One but also the wider Agreement given the mutual interdependence of its political structures.

Constraints of Design

One might begin by observing an apparent paradox in the design of the Assembly. The rules of the classical consociational 'game' are intended to remove uncertainties, anxieties, and threats among contending élites by building in decision-rules and procedures that eliminate reliance on simple majoritarianism. Yet, this is true only up to a point in the case of the decision-rules prescribed for the Assembly since the Agreement does provide for simple majority voting. Conformity with the proportionality rule via weighted voting is confined to 'key' decisions, some of which are predetermined by the Agreement while others may be designated as such via a 'petition of concern' moved by 30 Assembly members. Given the fine balance between pro- and anti-Agreement unionists in the Assembly—see Mitchell, in Chapter 3 of this volume—the petition device could be interpreted as a means of producing gridlock on the floor of the chamber. During both the 'shadow' and 'live' phases of the Assembly, however, the only attempts to move a petition were made by the DUP. On three occasions it sought to exclude Sinn Féin from the chamber on the ground that it was not committed to 'non-violence and exclusively peaceful and democratic means', an obligation for all Members of the Legislative Assembly (MLAs) and reinforced by the terms of the ministerial 'Pledge of Office'. Although the DUP's attempts failed, the delicacy of unionist arithmetic in the Assembly, coupled with concern about the cohesiveness of the UUP's Assembly group, threatened to make its operation, if not untenable, then certainly difficult. The vexatious use of the cross-community voting procedures undoubtedly had the capacity to, at best, frustrate the handling of business in the Assembly and, at worst, to bring it to a grinding halt.

The framers of the Agreement could not have anticipated fully such potential difficulties since they were contingent upon the outcome of the Assembly elections, down to the counting of the last transfers. Thus, while the calculation of the Agreement's signatories may well have been that there was safety in numbers—in this case 30—as a defence against a troublesome anti-Agreement bloc within the unionist/loyalist camp, the intention that lay behind the provision for a petition of concern was not entirely cynical. It also supplied a potential check to any attempt by the proposed Executive Committee to bulldoze the Assembly in a particular legislative or policy direction. In that sense, the petition device was entirely consistent with the power-sharing principle characteristic of consociational democracy: in this case, partnership between legislature and executive—for which read between ethno-national communities, since both were designed to be expressly binational in their composition.

The constraints of a divided society, as O'Leary pointed out earlier, are manifest in a number of key features of the Assembly's design. Initially, each of the 108 MLAs—elected by means of PR STV, itself of course an expression of the proportionality principle—had to designate him/herself either as a 'Nationalist', a 'Unionist' or 'Other'.[1] Such self-ascription was required to enable the explicit tests of cross-community support to be applied to 'key' decisions, whether predetermined by the Agreement or designated as such via the petition device. The former, including the election of the Assembly's Presiding Officer (Speaker), the determination of its standing orders, the adoption of the Executive's programme of government, budgetary procedures, and expenditure allocations to the devolved departments, are subject to two alternative special voting procedures, each designed to realize the principle of bicommunalism: namely 'parallel consent' and 'weighted majority.[2]

The procedures were applied first to the twinned election of David Trimble and Seamus Mallon as, respectively, First and Deputy First Minister Designate at the inaugural meeting of the shadow Assembly on 1 July 1998.[3] Their joint-election epitomized the power-sharing philosophy of the Agreement: they were designedly co-equal, a shared status that exemplified the spirit and the flesh of accommodative politics. Together with any Junior Ministers appointed to the departments—see discussion in 'Junior Ministers' later in this chapter—the First and Deputy First Ministers were the only two members of the Executive subject to a legitimizing vote in the Assembly. Following the protracted inter-party negotiations concerning the size and configuration of the Executive that were concluded in December 1998, its remaining ten[4] members were eventually nominated—almost a year later—by the relevant (four) parties, as were their preferred departments, through the application of the d'Hondt mechanism.

The fact that the ministers did not require the endorsement of the Assembly meant that the extent of executive patronage available to Trimble and Mallon was limited. It applied only to those from within their own parties who were nominated either to take seats around the 'cabinet' table or to the chairs and deputy chairs of the Assembly's committees, and to any Junior Ministers appointed to their own Office—although the latter are also subject to a simple majority vote by the Assembly. Consequentially, the only members of the Executive who could be sacked by Trimble and/or Mallon are those from within their own parties. This idiosyncratic method of constituting the Executive did not, however, render the Assembly utterly powerless. Were an incumbent to lose the confidence of the Assembly, the Agreement provides that s/he could be removed by way of a resolution moved by at least thirty MLAs and which secures sufficient cross-community support on the floor of the chamber.[5] In such cir-cumstances, the Minister or indeed any party that was to lose the Assembly's confidence would be excluded from office for not less than 12 months. This pro-cedure, besides providing the opportunity for anti-Agreement parties to unsettle the operation of the devolved institutions, also supplies a check on ministerial autonomy by offsetting the possibility that a department could be turned into a party redoubt. In that sense, as with the voting procedures that govern 'key' deci-sions, it embodied the principle of partnership that was intended to animate the new institutions. Hence, a bloc vote by unionists—the only 'grouping' capable of mustering a simple majority in the Assembly—would be insufficient to exclude a Minister. Were an incumbent to be excluded, his/her successor would be nom-inated from within the ranks of the same party. If, however, a party was to lose the confidence of the Assembly then d'Hondt would be reapplied and the Executive seats would be reallocated to that party with the next highest number of MLAs or, in the event of a tie, the party with the higher or highest number of first preference votes cast at the Assembly election.

Following the restoration of devolution at the end of May 2000, the DUP—buoyed by the UUC's narrow endorsement (53 per cent to 47 per cent) on 27 May of David Trimble's recommendation that he and his fellow Ministers should re-enter the Executive—again sought to move a 'Petition of Concern' designed to exclude Sinn Féin from Ministerial office. On this occasion, they were successful in attracting the thirty signatures required to trigger a debate and a vote because Pauline Armitage, one of the Ulster Unionist MLAs, added her name to the petition. Although the motion failed on the ground that it did not attract cross-community support, as the DUP knew it would, it provided the anti-Agreement unionist parties with the opportunity to mobilize a majority of unionist members against the participation of Sinn Féin in government. And they succeeded. Armitage was joined in the division lobby by two other UUP members, Derek Hussey and Roy Beggs Jr. Together with Peter Weir, who had earlier resigned the UUP whip, these three 'defectors' increased the number of unionist MLAs opposed to Sinn Féin's presence in the Executive Committee to thirty-two out of a total of fifty-eight unionist members. Provided it remains stable, that new balance of unionist forces within the Assembly means that future petitions can be moved almost at will. This would enable anti-Agreement parties to at least slow down Assembly business and embarrass David Trimble or, at worst, erode the level of support for the First Minister from within his own party to a point where he would be forced to resign from office, effectively signalling the end of the Assembly.

Committees

The legislative competence of the Assembly is consistent with prior attempts to devolve power to Northern Ireland in that its scope is limited primarily to 'transferred' matters—see Hadfield, in Chapter 5 of this volume.[6] The Assembly was not, however, designed to be a mere legislative cipher or rubber-stamp for the Executive Committee. In addition to its more conventional legislative and scrutinizing roles, the Assembly was intended to enjoy considerable authority, notably via its statutory committees. These committees—dubbed 'statutory' by the shadow Committee on Standing Orders—were charged by the Agreement to 'advise and assist' each of the departments with which they were associated 'in the formulation of policy'. In addition, they were enabled to examine draft legislation from their associated departments and were themselves empowered to introduce primary legislation. Thus, law-making was not vested solely in the Executive Committee but was shared by the statutory committees, whose composition was broadly proportional to relative party strengths in the Assembly. The bargain struck by the UUP and SDLP in December 1998 to create ten departments—alongside the First and Deputy First Ministers' Office—meant, in due course, that the parties would nominate a total of twenty chairs and deputy chairs to these committees, again by means of d'Hondt. In making their nominations, the parties were encouraged by the Agreement to 'prefer Committees in which they do not have a party interest'. This 'rule' prevented the Minister and either the chair or the deputy chair of the relevant committee from being drawn from the same party, another means of realizing the power-sharing principle.[7] A further injunction prevented either a Minister or a Junior

Minister from occupying these positions, thereby both consolidating the distinction between legislature and executive and cementing the planned partnership between the Assembly and the departments.

Monitoring the 'Centre'

No provision, however, was made in the Agreement or the Act for the Office of the First and Deputy First Ministers, the 'Office of the Centre' as it was subsequently designated, to be subject to scrutiny by a statutory committee.[8] This omission provoked considerable controversy within the shadow Assembly[9] and was to spill over into its devolved phase between 2 December 1999 and 11 February 2000. Given the multidimensional nature of the Office[10] and its role as the key co-ordinating department, MLAs were concerned that it should be made fully accountable to the Assembly. To that end, during the shadow phase, the all-party Committee on Standing Orders—itself jointly chaired by a unionist and a nationalist—made provision for a 'Committee on Conformity with Equality Requirements' (CCER) to scrutinize the management of the 'Equality Unit' that was to be located within the Office. However, following the devolution of powers, on 6 December 1999 the Standing Orders Committee revisited the matter. It tabled two motions, duly endorsed by the Assembly, proposing in the stead of CCER, two new standing committees: 'Equality, Human Rights and Community Relations' and 'European Affairs'. A week later, David Ford (Alliance Party) moved a new standing order to create a third standing committee to examine and report on the remaining functions carried out by the Office of the Centre. However, the First and Deputy First Ministers tabled an amendment to the motion, seeking to revoke the creation of the two new committees and replace them with a single 'Committee of the Centre'.[11] The purpose of the joint motion was to insulate some aspects of the Office's—and the Executive Committee's—work against the focused scrutiny of an Assembly committee:

It is essential that discussions which take place in determining the decisions reached by the Executive Committee or the negotiating position for the Northern Ireland Administration in relation to the North/South Ministerial Council or the British-Irish Council should remain private. (*Northern Ireland Assembly Reports*, 14 December 1999.)

The shared view of Mallon and Trimble was that such matters, more particularly those pertaining to Strands Two and Three, were more properly dealt with on the floor of the Assembly rather than in the close confines of a committee room. However, their motion drew stiff opposition from among others Sinn Féin, the DUP, Progressive Unionists, and the Women's Coalition, each concerned at the limited scope of the proposed committee. Nevertheless, the combined weight of the UUP and SDLP MLAs assured a sufficient level of cross-community support for the Trimble/Mallon motion to succeed. Thus, where there were two, and potentially three, Assembly committees to scrutinize the Office of the Centre, now there was one enjoying a narrow remit.

This episode was instructive in a number of respects. First, it demonstrated the readiness of rival parties to act in a common cause—in this case, to further provide for the kind of executive-legislative partnership that was intended for the other departments and the Assembly's statutory committees. Secondly, and perhaps more ominously, it demonstrated the capacity of the Trimble/Mallon dyarchy to mobilize their Assembly parties in order to free their hands—as well as those of their Executive colleagues—to deal with a range of strategic issues, especially in relation to north-south matters. Such mobilization confirmed a growing suspicion among the other parties that a UUP/SDLP duopoly was emerging at the heart of the administration which was at odds with the inclusivity of the Agreement's basic design.

Junior Ministers

This suspicion was enhanced when Trimble and Mallon sought to enlarge the ministerial 'team'. Unlike the nomination procedure for both ministerial heads of departments and committee chairs and deputy chairs, no formula was specified in the Agreement for the nomination of Junior Ministers, save that the First and Deputy First Ministers could, at any time, determine the number that may be appointed and the functions they should exercise. On 14 December 1999 they tabled a determination, seeking to appoint two Junior Ministers to their Office, one from the UUP, the other from the SDLP, subject to a simple majority vote in the Assembly.[12] This also angered the other parties. Nigel Dodds, one of the DUP's two ministers, described the proposal as a case of 'jobs for the boys', a view echoed by Sinn Féin's Mitchel McLaughlin who likened the Office to 'a closed shop'. A common observation among the parties was that the nominations further belied the Agreement's spirit of inclusiveness. This charge was rebutted by Trimble and Mallon on the ground that the appointees had to command their confidence. On this they had a decided point: had they opted for, or been constrained to nominate, members drawn from any two of the other parties, especially their ostensible 'partners' in the voluntary coalition, the DUP and Sinn Féin, their confidence would have likely been sorely tried. Following a lengthy and ill-tempered debate, the nominations were endorsed by 49 votes to 38, the UUP and SDLP members voting *en bloc* in support of the determination, notwithstanding the fact that there was a deliberate vagueness about the functions the Junior Ministers would perform.

This, too, proved an instructive episode. Apart from demonstrating that the UUP/SDLP partnership was emerging as the efficient, albeit open, secret at the heart of devolved government, it also signified the limits of trust in Northern Ireland style consociationalism. Once the decision was made in December 1998 to create a twelve-strong, four-party, voluntary coalition, few would have disputed that it was an unlikely setting in which the convention of collective responsibility could take root, especially since the Executive would include the resolutely anti-Agreement DUP, albeit at one remove from the other Ministers. While the convention was undeniably assisted, or rather, enforced, by the application of the unanimity rule to all key decisions, including the programme for government and the operation of the North-South Ministerial Council—see discussion in 'North-South' later in this chapter—Trimble and Mallon were clearly averse to increasing the risk that it might be breached. Insisting that the Junior Ministers in their Office would be drawn from within the ranks of their own parties provided the insurance that its day-to-day operations would remain confidential and jealously guarded.

Centering Equality

During the Assembly's shadow phase, the Committee on Standing Orders proposed the creation of a number of standing committees which, besides the small Audit Committee, were to include a representative from each party. With the later exception of the Committee of the Centre, they were endorsed with little or no controversy and included the Business, Procedures, Standards and Privileges, and Public Accounts Committees. Like the statutory committees, their chairs and deputy chairs were appointed via the d'Hondt mechanism and, with the exceptions of the seventeen-strong Committee of the Centre and the five-member Audit Committee, were each to have eleven members.

The Committee of the Centre includes within its remit the 'Equality Unit', lodged in the Trimble/Mallon Office. The decision to locate it there was one outcome of the negotiations on the reshaping of the departments concluded in December 1998. The Agreement had suggested that the creation of a free-standing 'Department of Equality' should be considered as part of the new devolved landscape.[13] However, the placement of the Unit in the Office of the Centre was the product of both a 'positive' and a 'negative' calculation. The more positive interpretation was that the authority of the Office and its two lead Ministers would ensure that the equality agenda was taken seriously by all Departments: that a stand-alone Department, headed by one Minister enjoying the same status as his/her peers would simply not carry enough clout. The negative interpretation was that its placement was a conflict-avoidance measure adopted by the UUP's and SDLP's negotiators, designed to avoid a fully-fledged Equality Department from falling into the hands of either Sinn Féin or the DUP via the d'Hondt mechanism. The former preferring a maximalist interpretation of the equality agenda, the latter a minimalist one, the likelihood was that an Equality Minister drawn from either quarter and with a strategic, intrusive brief, would cause severe difficulties caused by, respectively, over- or under-ambition.[14] Whatever the exact reasoning behind the decision, the creation of the Unit copper-fastened the statutory obligation upon MLAs 'to promote equality of opportunity' and the Agreement's stress upon equality and human rights. The Unit's tasks included ensuring that Departments and other designated public bodies, in formulating and reviewing policies and in delivering services, comply with 'Policy Appraisal for Fair Treatment', first implemented as a set of administrative guidelines for Northern Ireland's Departments in 1994 and made a statutory duty by the *Northern Ireland Act* 1998. Sifting policies and legislative proposals through the fair treatment net is further proof of the Agreement's intention to mainstream equality of opportunity, ensuring that they do not exert a disparate impact upon potentially vulnerable groups within the wider population. A further safeguard is provided by the requirement to seek the view of the new and independent NI Human Rights Commission, also created under the terms of the Belfast Agreement, as to whether a Bill, draft Bill or legislative proposal is compatible with the European Convention on Human Rights and any future Northern Ireland Bill of Rights—and, of course, there is further protection through the courts which can overrule Assembly legislation on grounds of inconsistency.

Committee of the Centre

Draft legislation, whether emerging from the Executive Committee or the relevant statutory committee—voting on a cross-community basis—could be referred to what, in the event, became the Committee of the Centre to test its consistency with equality requirements. Moreover, the Assembly also had to agree any ensuing report by the Committee on a cross-community basis. With the renewal of devolution, the prospective task confronting the Committee of the Centre is immense, not least because, although limited, its remit extended to twelve of the twenty-six functions allocated to the First and Deputy First Ministers Office. Its role in the equality-proofing process will require it to scrutinize all legislative proposals, including those that constitute the Executive's programme for government, so that a clogged agenda seems unavoidable.

Apart from its size, which itself threatened to make it unwieldy, the Committee's initial internal dynamics did not augur well as a setting for the realization of consociational practice. During its brief existence—it met in private on just three occasions before the reimposition of direct rule—each of its sessions lasted for just a few minutes and all ended in utter disarray. Its chair, Gregory Campbell (DUP), refused to acknowledge the existence of its Sinn Féin members, let alone involve them as full and equal members of the Committee—a stance wholly inconsistent both with its remit and the wider principle of inclusivity that suffuses the Agreement.

The inauspicious start to the Committee of the Centre was not characteristic of the other standing or, more significantly, the statutory committees. During the seventy-two days of devolution, the ten statutory committees held a total of sixty-two meetings, mostly with civil servants and interest groups, in order to draw up a programme of work and to familiarize themselves with the agendas and resources of their partner departments. Unlike practice in the Welsh Assembly, only a fraction of the meetings were open to the public. But, by the time devolution was suspended, all bar one of the statutory committees—Culture, Arts, and Leisure—had met with their relevant Minister on at least one occasion and each had agreed an initial major inquiry. That is, they had begun to realize their scrutinizing role but, given the lack of progress on the programme for government, had not had the opportunity to work in tandem with the relevant Departments on legislation and policy. However, one committee—Health, Social Services, and Public Safety—was involved in a very public disagreement with the Minister, Sinn Féin's Bairbre de Brun.

Health

The conflict—which centred on the provision of maternity services in Belfast[15]—excited widespread debate not only about the merit of the Minister's decision, but also because it seemed wholly inconsistent with the model of partnership between Departments and statutory committees adumbrated by the Agreement. In short, a majority of the committee voted in favour of one option whereas the Minister took the other. Subsequently, the matter was taken to the floor of the Assembly where members voted by simple majority to endorse the committee's view. However, since the issue was not designated as a key decision—and was thereby free from both the cross-community voting procedures and the unanimity rule within the Executive—and did not require legislation, the Minister was able to act under existing executive authority in taking her decision. The matter was interpreted widely as being incompatible with at least the spirit if not the letter of the Agreement, certainly by those health care professionals adversely affected by the Minister's action and, of course, the majority of the committee. In such a case it seemed that the only available recourse was to seek a judicial review of the decision: which the supporters of the alternative duly did. The episode implies that, in like circumstances, the prospect of shared decision-making by Ministers and committees may be more apparent than real—or realizable—and that the Minister's view will prevail. If nothing else, it was certainly an inauspicious start to the relationship between the Health Minister and the committee.[16]

Executive Unanimity

Provision for the unanimity rule, or mutual veto, although not applicable to the above decision, was made by the Agreement in relation to the procedures of the Executive Committee. Given the DUP's antipathy towards the Agreement in general—and, in particular, to Sinn Féin's participation in government[17]—there was little likelihood that full meetings of the Executive Committee could occur unless and until full and verifiable decommissioning by the IRA had taken place. Of course, neither did. This raised some intriguing questions about its standard operating procedures, although there is clear guidance for the Executive in the Agreement, especially in relation to key decisions and the operations of the North-South Ministerial Council.

For instance, the Executive is charged by the Agreement to 'provide a forum for the discussion of, *and agreement on*, issues which cut across the responsibilities of two or more Ministers, for prioritising executive and legislative proposals and for recommending a common position where necessary'. In addition, it 'will *seek to agree each year*, and review as necessary, a programme incorporating *an agreed budget linked to policies and programmes*, subject to approval by the Assembly, after scrutiny in Assembly Committees, on a cross-community basis'. The Agreement also states that 'Ministers will have full executive authority in their respective areas of responsibility, *within any broad programme agreed by the Executive Committee* and endorsed by the Assembly as a whole'. All Ministers must, as a condition of their appointment, also affirm the terms of the 'Pledge of Office' set out in the Agreement which, *inter alia*, requires them to 'participate with colleagues in the preparation of a programme for government'; 'operate within the framework of [a] programme [for government] *when agreed within the Executive Committee and endorsed by the Assembly'*; and '*to support, and to act in accordance with, all decisions of the Executive Committee and the Assembly'* (my emphases throughout).

The Pledge reinforces the interlocking and interdependent relationship between the Executive and the Assembly. Indeed, the insistent provision for cross-community checks and balances in the Agreement, coupled with the requirement for agreement on key decisions, including a 'programme', lends distinctive meaning to the phrase 'joined-up government'. Moreover, and this seems paradoxical given the inclusion of emphatically anti-Agreement parties in the Assembly, the lack of a formal—let alone loyal!—opposition underlines the uniqueness of the Northern Ireland case.

Programme for Government and Public Expenditure

During its shadow existence, virtually no attempt was made by the prospective Executive to discuss, let alone agree, a programme for government. Apart from an initial exploratory meeting in January 1999 involving the party's policy advisers at which civil service briefing papers were tabled, and a follow-up 'brainstorming session' later that month, no substantive progress was achieved towards a common programme.[18] Moreover, the parties were and are at variance on a wide range of policy issues including, for instance, the transfer procedure—Northern Ireland's version of the 11+, a grading test for 11 year olds—Sinn Féin and the SDLP want it abolished, while the UUP and the DUP support its retention. Equally, while all four parties share the goal of regenerating the economy, both Sinn Féin and the SDLP understand that objective to be best served in an all-Ireland context, a view not shared by the UUP and the DUP.

Habituated to opposing the Northern Ireland Office (NIO) and one another, both within and across the political divide, the process of agreeing a programme for government confronted the parties with a steep learning curve. During the Assembly's shadow phase, there was a 'transitional programme' organized by the NIO for its members, designed to familiarize them with the work, agendas, and resources of both the Departments and their associated bodies.[19] In addition, the parties were faced with a raft of policy proposals from the NIO's ministerial team, including a regional economic strategy, a regional planning strategy, and controversial plans for the reform of acute hospital provision.

The Executive also inherited the Government's expenditure plans for Northern Ireland for 1999–2000 to 2001–2 announced on 10 December 1998. The announcement followed the outcome of the first Comprehensive Spending Review, which injected an additional £1.4bn into the NI block. During the early stages of negotiating the spending review with the UK Treasury, the then Secretary of State consulted the parties, district councils, trades unions, representatives of business, commerce, and the voluntary and community sectors to obtain their views about which expenditure programmes should be given priority. Following the outcome of the national review in July 1998, Dr Mowlam decided that there should be a further round of consultation with Messrs Trimble and Mallon and with the shadow Assembly, when she had reached a provisional view on programme allocations.[20]

The consultation exercise provided an unprecedented degree of access into the public expenditure process in the period prior to final decisions and was undertaken on the (mistaken) assumption that devolution would proceed in the early spring of 1999. It was a means of induction into the realities of governing for the parties, although the Government recognized that the expenditure plans could change in the light of the announcement on 18 December 1998 when Trimble and Mallon unveiled the new Departmental structure. Following the announcement, work continued by the First and Deputy First Ministers (Designate) that was designed to flesh out its details. In tabling their report on this work to the shadow Assembly in mid-January 1999, the incumbents set out their joint agenda for the programme, albeit in understandably broad terms. Stressing the need for 'urgency in seeking to address the social, economic and cultural challenges facing the whole community', their shared priorities were: 'to address the needs of the most vulnerable and disadvantaged; to imbue the community with a sense of enterprise and self-reliance; to tackle educational disadvantage; [and] to put behind us the tragic years of trauma and separation'. In words reminiscent of the Blairite, New Labour project, Messrs Trimble and

Mallon also stated: 'We want to agree upon and implement a programme for government that will succeed in delivering efficient, accountable and transparent government and enable us to achieve economic growth and development, the benefits of which will be shared throughout the entire community'.[21] However, the deepening impasse over decommissioning, fraying relationships among the pro-Agreement parties and the unflinching posture of the DUP, effectively stymied the prospect of an agreed, budgeted programme for the new Departments. Following devolution and the choice of portfolios by the four eligible parties, in early December 1999 the Executive Committee turned its attention to both the programme and the allocation of resources to each of the eleven Departments: what was an already sharp learning-curve, immediately steepened.

The delay in implementing the Agreement meant that the ministers had no alternative other than to adopt the spending plans bequeathed by the NIO.[22] While this entailed a lack of autonomy, it at least freed the Executive Committee from the risks of further delay caused by the need to achieve unanimity over budgetary procedures and their cross-community endorsement by the Assembly. More positively, it also meant that ministers could focus on the programme and ready themselves for the looming negotiations on the new comprehensive spending review. This was a tight schedule: the programme had to be agreed unanimously by the Executive and be accepted by the Assembly, voting on a cross-community basis, before the end of March 2000. Initial work on the programme did get underway in December and was accelerated in January when the Economic Policy Unit (EPU) in the Trimble/Mallon Office became operational. The EPU was charged with assisting the First and Deputy First Minister 'in determining, within the Executive Committee, the Administration's detailed strategic goals and inputting them to the Programme of Government and the allocation of financial resources (in conjunction with the Minister for Finance and Personnel)'. This paper, endorsed by the Executive on 11 January, proposed that the programme should include 'long term strategic objectives' and would, in line with the prescriptions within the Agreement, be subject to 'annual revision, annual incorporation of a budget and annual approval by the Assembly'.[23] It also reaffirmed the Pledge of Office in stating that each Minister was required to both participate in and operate within the programme's framework.[24] Led by Trimble and Mallon, the programme was to be the mortar holding the four-party voluntary coalition together, providing the only visible means of support for the convention of collective ministerial responsibility.[25] However, the act of suspension on 11 February 2000 meant that what would have been a test of coherent, joined-up government was unable to be met.

With devolution restored, the Executive Committee sought to introduce some momentum to the programme by announcing, under the broad theme of 'Moving Forward Together', an 'Agenda for Government' following its meeting of 29 June 2000. Four days later, on 3 July, the First and Deputy First Ministers made a joint statement to the Assembly fleshing out some of the details of the Agenda. With new resources available, derived from underspending by the existing Departments during the previous financial year and new monies derived from Gordon Brown's March budget, Messrs Trimble and Mallon announced a first tranche of £27.6m that was to be allocated across a range of spending programmes including health, education, the economy, the environment, tackling disadvantage and social exclusion, and the modernization of public services.

The announcement of the Agenda was clearly presented as a preliminary step, a paving measure in effect, towards the achievement of the programme, the first draft of which was planned to be available for consideration by the Assembly in the autumn. As far as the Executive Committee was concerned, it also signalled, as Mallon put it, 'our determination to work together for the benefit of all. We know that we can make real improvements to people's lives when we move forward effectively together'.[26]

Although the DUP had decided to reassume its two Executive Committee seats when devolution was restored, this was only on the basis that it would reshuffle the Ministers from among its MLAs as and when it saw fit. Indeed, the first such reshuffle was scheduled to occur on 27 July 2000, when its two incumbents Nigel Dodds and Peter Robinson were to be replaced by Gregory Campbell and Maurice Morrow, thereby causing some further disruption to the handling of Executive business, already hampered by the steadfast refusal of the DUP to participate in meetings of the 'cabinet'. Nevertheless, the readiness of the DUP's Ministers to participate in the devising of the Agenda may indicate that when the stiffer test of agreeing a programme arises they will not be found wanting in the process of priority setting and resource allocation—even if their participation is undertaken at one remove from the full Executive Committee.

North-South

The stiffness of the putative test was compounded by Strand Two of the Agreement which institutionalized the relationship between Belfast and Dublin. The outcome of the protracted—and at times acid—negotiations on Strand Two was for there to be six new cross-border implementation bodies and a further six matters for co-operation effected through existing bodies in each separate jurisdiction.[27] Though the detail and substance of these bodies is significant, what is of interest here is their standard operating procedures and their consistency with the consociational template. The first, somewhat paradoxical, point to note is the seeming incongruity with that template. The 'Pledge of Office' contained in the Agreement requires Ministers 'to discharge in good faith *all* the duties of office' (my emphasis). Given the indispensability of the North-South Ministerial Council, one might conclude that participation in it by Ministers was not an option. Indeed, the Agreement stipulates that such participation is an 'essential responsibility' for Ministers. However, the same paragraph also states: 'If a holder of a relevant post will not participate normally in the Council, the Taoiseach in the case of the Irish Government, and the First and Deputy First Minister in the case of the Northern Ireland Administration, to be able to make alternative arrangements'.[28] Besides lending new meaning to the word 'essential', this provision enabled the DUP's two Ministers—Nigel Dodds and Peter Robinson—to boycott the Council without, on the face of it, breaking the Pledge of Office. It allowed the First and Deputy First Ministers to make proxy arrangements in order to assist the Council's work. Though politic, even expedient, this provision sat uneasily with the intention to facilitate inclusive government that is a hallmark of consociationalism. It meant that only three of the four parties in the Executive participated in the cross-border Council and, in theory, enabled the DUP to frustrate at least some of its business. This is because the agenda of each Council meeting was to be agreed in advance and all decisions it made were also to be agreed, between or among both NI Ministers and their counterparts in the Republic. Moreover, any Council decisions that are 'beyond the defined authority of those attending' must achieve the consent of both the Assembly, on a cross-community basis, and of the *Oireachtas*. There is, in effect, provision for a reciprocal veto on each side of the border although it was clear that the North-South Ministerial Council would enjoy a measure of autonomy, provided its participants could agree on the adoption of common policies and their implementation.

East-West

The North-South Ministerial Council was one aspect of the Agreement's confederal character. The other is contained in Strand Three, which deals with the British-Irish Council—see Walker, G., in Chapter 7 of this volume—and the British-Irish Intergovernmental Conference (BIIC). The latter, which 'subsumes' the Anglo-Irish Intergovernmental Council and Intergovernmental Conference established by the 1985 Anglo-Irish Agreement (AIA), has attractions for both the unionist and nationalist communities. For the latter it underpinned the binationalism of the Agreement by providing for the continuing involvement of the Irish Republic in the internal affairs of Northern Ireland but without derogating from the sovereignty of either Government, thereby assuaging unionist anxieties concerning joint authority.

The remit of the Conference is to foster 'bilateral co-operation at all levels on all matters of mutual interest within the competence of both Governments', essentially those that are not to be devolved in the first instance. These include prisons, policing, and criminal justice, issues upon which the Republic's

Minister for Foreign Affairs as 'co-chair' alongside the Secretary of State 'may put forward views and proposals', given the Irish Government's 'special interest in Northern Ireland'. Both Governments will 'intensify co-operation on the all-island or cross-border aspects of these [non-devolved] matters' and any decisions it makes will be on an agreed basis—indeed, the Agreement commits them to 'make determined efforts to resolve disagreements'. Unanimity was clearly intended to be the rule for the BIIC's participants.

This new exercise in Anglo-Irish co-operation, welcomed by the nationalist and republican communities alike, was also perceived by many unionists to be more acceptable than the intergovernmental conference established by the 1985 Anglo-Irish Agreement. There are three reasons for this. First, its meetings were to be attended by 'relevant' members of the Executive Committee; secondly, they would participate in the triennial reviews of the 1998 Agreement conducted under the aegis of the Conference; and finally, the Conference would be unable to 'override' the democratic institutions and processes created by the Agreement. It was the accessibility to, and relative transparency of, these new arrangements that made it more palatable for pro-Agreement unionists.

Conclusion

Though its trajectory can be traced back to 1973, none can deny the novelty and subtle complexity of the Belfast Agreement. Bolstered by a new regime of human rights and a commitment to a culture of equal opportunity, it has something for (nearly) everyone. Steeped in a pluralist, inclusive philosophy, the Agreement represented an imaginative attempt to move from a condition of zero-sum to positive-sum politics. For its proponents, whether nationalist, republican, loyalist, unionist, or 'other', it proved a difficult consociational bargain: as David Trimble put it in commending support for the Agreement at the referendum, 'It's as good as it gets'—see Aughey, in Chapter 10 of this volume. Though a rather *sotto voce* rallying cry, it helped to achieve the desired effect as the unionist/loyalist electorate narrowly endorsed it at the referendum in May 1998, although it was to hedge its bets at the subsequent election.

That the Agreement left the future constitutional status of Northern Ireland contingent upon the popular will of its electorate was a necessary exercise in open-endedness, albeit that many voters are less than open-minded. Besides underlining Northern Ireland's binationalism, the Agreement placed a premium upon political and, more especially, electoral mobilization by the parties. This is especially the case for Sinn Féin, which, by pursuing politics with both hands, may reasonably anticipate junior partnership in a future coalition government in the Republic. Recourse to political violence will do nothing to further such ambition. Were it to achieve the status of a governing party in the Republic then, allied to its presence in an Executive in Northern Ireland, the dynamics of politics on the island of Ireland would be significantly altered. However, dissident republicans construe the 'transitionalism' articulated by the Sinn Féin leadership to be meaningless when it is made conditional upon the politics of majority consent in the north: for them, 'the long war' remains a live—and doctrinally 'correct'—strategy.

The future is, of course, always uncertain: even hours before Good Friday in 1998 few anticipated that an Agreement was attainable. That it compounded an open-ended future for Northern Ireland was, in the judgement of its serried proponents—and significant majorities at both the referendum and the election—a path worth taking: at least, up to a point. Decommissioning, initially prior to, then concurrent with and, finally, shortly after the transfer of power, was the only obstacle to the restoration of devolved government. After eleven weeks of discussions and negotiations in both Belfast and London, on 18 November 1999 the Chair of the review of the implementation of the Agreement, George Mitchell, felt able to state: 'I believe that a basis now exists for devolution to occur, for the institutions to be established and for decommissioning to take place as soon as possible'.[29] In respect of decommissioning, his belief proved unfounded, albeit that 'as soon as possible' was an elastic form of words. That no paramilitary weapons had been put out of, or beyond, use—or dealt with by the De Chastelain Commission in some other way—by 11 February meant that the initial phase of renewed devolution lasted for less than half the period of the Sunningdale 'experiment' in 1974.

The suspension of devolution left a heavy question hanging in the air: 'could it have worked?' In the event, protracted Anglo-Irish efforts to effect a start to the process of decommissioning bore fruit when on 6 May 2000 the IRA released a statement reiterating its commitment to 'a just and lasting peace' and reassured the public that the IRA represented 'no threat to the peace process'.[30] The resumption of contact with the IICD by the IRA shortly afterwards and its commitment to put in place a confidence building measure 'within weeks' paved the way for devolution to be restored on 29 May 2000, once David Trimble had mustered majority support within the UUC two days earlier for his recommendation that the UUP should re-enter devolved government.

Trimble's slim margin of victory, at just 53 per cent of the UUC, does not inspire overweening confidence that the new devolved institutions will prove to be overly robust. And yet, the fact that they have survived both the period of suspension and the absence of a tangible beginning to decommissioning by all paramilitary organizations, suggests that some measured optimism my not be entirely misplaced. Moreover, the rapid implementation of the institutions created by the Agreement during the first phase of devolution also encouraged many to the view that Northern Ireland was embarking on a new era. Following the passage of the devolution Order by Parliament on 30 November 1999, within a matter of days the new arrangements were in place. On 2 December the existing Articles 2 and 3 of the Irish Constitution were replaced and, on the same day, papers were exchanged in Dublin between the British and Irish Governments bringing into being the new British-Irish Treaty, formally establishing the North-South Ministerial Council, and the British-Irish Council. The Executive Committee—minus the two DUP Ministers—met for the first time on 3 December; on 6 December the Assembly created its statutory committees; the North-South Ministerial Council—again minus a DUP presence—met in Armagh for the first time on 13 December—without protest; and the inaugural meeting of the British-Irish Council took place in London on 17 December. Thus, after a delay of nineteen months the Belfast Agreement had taken almost full effect.[31]

The flurry of necessary formalities did not, however, disguise the fact that a number of political tests were not met during the initial phase of devolution. While Assembly members from all parties did work together in the committee rooms both before[32] and after powers were devolved, and although debates in the chamber were not unusually disruptive, there were evident strains among, and within, the parties. The most palpable source of interparty tension was between the DUP and Sinn Féin, both on the floor of the Assembly and in the committee rooms, although it was not vented around the cabinet table given the DUP's boycott of the Executive Committee. Although it never met in full, and was thereby spared slanging matches between the DUP and Sinn Féin Ministers, there was a lingering doubt that the convention of collective responsibility could flourish within the Executive. Such doubt rests not only on policy differences and matters of personality; it is implicit within the design of the Agreement. Notwithstanding their configuration, and the policy co-ordination role allocated to the Trimble-Mallon Office, each the outcome of the December 1998 bargain on executive formation, the Agreement created the possibility that the Departments would become the petty fiefdoms of their Ministers. Attempts by Sinn Féin and/or the smaller parties to create thematic Departments— notably 'Equality'—or Departments defined by 'target groups' in the population, such as 'Women' or 'Children', failed during the negotiations on executive formation.

In the view of their proponents, thematic Departments would have been conducive to the realization of joined-up government. The Blair Government's commitment to 'cross-cutting working'[33]—to what others have styled 'holistic' government'[34]—as a means of overcoming the insularity of narrow departmentalism, seems either to have fallen on deaf ears among Northern Ireland's political leaders, or to have succumbed to the imperatives of ethnic competition. The bargaining over executive formation between the UUP and SDLP was dominated more by arguments over the number of Departments assigned to the rival blocs, than to clear considerations of what the Departments might do by way of achieving agreed policy outcomes. The prescription offered by the Cabinet Office—that policies should be designed 'around shared goals and carefully

designed results, not around organizational structures or existing functions'[35]—
appears to have been overwhelmed by a more mundane, if explicable, concern
for equal status among the coalition 'partners'. In the event, the calculations of
the UUP/SDLP negotiators revolved around a much less imaginative axis.
They preferred to opt for functional 'silos', reallocating responsibilities in a
somewhat improvised fashion[36] across the eleven departments that were eventually agreed, and relying on the dual premiership of Trimble and Mallon to
effect co-ordination, coherence, and clout.

There was more than a whiff and a prayer about both the design of the
Executive and the capacity of the First and Deputy First Ministers to implement the UK Government's credo for Ministers and officials: to 'act as cham-
pions for cross-cutting policies and services and so help to create a culture
conducive to cross-cutting working'.[37] Inheriting, in conjunction with the
Equality Commission, responsibility for the implementation of the equality
agenda from the direct rule regime,[38] and for integrating two strategic policy
objectives bequeathed by the NIO—'targeting social need' and the 'promotion
of social inclusion'—into legislation and policy meant that the Executive was
nudged towards 'joined-upness'. This was reinforced by the SDLP's determination to ensure, during the negotiations on Executive formation, that each of
the Departments would embrace both social and financial responsibilities.
However, between early December 1999 and mid-February 2000, there was
nothing to prevent the Ministers from retreating into their respective silos: as
one of the DUP's two Ministers put it to me, he had spent the period in his
'Departmental bunker'.

While the latter is something of an overstatement,[39] not least because the two
DUP Ministers did participate in the process of agreeing the Agenda for
Government announced within weeks of the restoration of devolution, the risk
that the Executive Committee could yet prove to be less than the sum of its
parts remains a real one. The continuing refusal of the DUP to play a full part
in the Executive Committee has complicated its operation and could thwart the
unanimity that is required for the Programme for Government. As yet, it is not
clear how these difficulties may be resolved. Moreover, the looming prospect of
local government elections in May 2001, and perhaps a simultaneous general
election, will embolden the DUP and other anti-Agreement unionists to act in
an increasingly disruptive manner within the Assembly where they currently
hold a majority on the matter of Sinn Féin's participation in government.

The former Secretary of State for Wales, Ron Davies, once remarked that
devolution is 'a process not an event': on 11 February 2000, when devolution
was suspended, one might have been justified in adding the caveat, 'except in
Northern Ireland'. Now that devolution has been restored, the qualification is a
redundant one—at least for the immediate future. However, should the devolved
institutions fail at some point, there are aspects of the Agreement that will survive and, perhaps, even flourish. In that respect, the legacy of the Agreement is

likely to prove durable, even if some of its architects become future electoral casualties. As O'Leary noted in Chapter 4, there are a number of thinkable alternative futures for Northern Ireland, though few are practical or feasible.[40] The Belfast Agreement may, or may not, be 'the only show in town', whether it as construed as an imaginative exercise in political accommodation or, conversely, an act of appeasement of terrorism. However, unlike its vaunted and failed predecessor, the Sunningdale Agreement, the operative cause of suspension lay less in its architecture and much more in the level of trust accorded to primarily republican paramilitaries. While the relative silence of the guns was a necessary condition for devolution to occur, it was not enough to sustain it indefinitely. The IRA's confidence building measure, namely the inspection of a number of its arms dumps, certainly paved the way for devolution to be restored, at least in the short-run. But, in the longer term, unless it is followed by actual acts of decommissioning, it too is likely to be insufficient as a means of nourishing the trust that is required to maintain the devolved institutions.

ENDNOTES

1. When Monica McWilliams and Jane Morrice, the Northern Ireland Women's Coalition's MLAs signed the members' register at the first meeting of the shadow Assembly on 1 July 1998, they designated themselves initially as 'Nationalist, Unionist, Other'. In the face of objections from other members, notably the DUP, they redesignated themselves as 'Inclusive Other'. The Initial Presiding Officer, John (Lord) Alderdice, ruled that the operative word in the redesignation was 'Other' and was hence acceptable. See *New Northern Ireland Assembly Report* (*NNIAR*) 1, 1 July 1998. Note: Following devolution, the prefix 'New' was dropped from the official record of proceedings in the Assembly. The Standing Orders adopted by the shadow Assembly in March 1999 allow that a political party's designation may be changed once during the life of an Assembly, provided that 30 days written notice is given to the Presiding Officer.
2. 'Parallel consent' requires a majority of those present and voting, including a majority of those designated as unionists and nationalists. A 'weighted majority' requires 60 per cent of those present and voting, including 40 per cent of both unionists and nationalists.
3. Sinn Féin abstained from the vote endorsing the Trimble/Mallon ticket. John Alderdice, who had been nominated by the Secretary of State as 'Initial Presiding Officer', has remained in the Chair throughout the existence of the Assembly. By the time direct rule had been reimposed, he had not been confirmed as Presiding Officer by means of election. Three Deputy Speakers were elected by the Assembly on a cross-community basis: Jane Morrice (Women's Coalition); Sir John Gorman (UUP); and Donovan McClelland (SDLP). The DUP's nominee, William Hay, was not elected. See *NIAR*, 31 January 2000.
4. The ten departments and their respective ministers were: Agriculture and Rural Development (Brid Rogers, SDLP); Culture, Arts, and Leisure (Michael McGimpsey, UUP); Education (Martin McGuinness, Sinn Féin); Enterprise, Trade, and Investment (Sir Reg Empey, UUP); Environment (Sam Foster, UUP); Finance and Personnel (Mark Durkan, SDLP). Health, Social Services, and Public Safety (Bairbre de Brun, Sinn Féin); Higher and Further Education, Training, and Employment (Sean Farren, SDLP); Regional Development (Peter Robinson, DUP); Social Development (Nigel Dodds, DUP). See *NNIAR 7*, 15 February 1999 for a complete list of departmental functions.
5. For other grounds on which a minister may be removed from office, see the *Northern Ireland Act* 1998, Section 9.

6. The Assembly may legislate on 'reserved' matters, including policing and the criminal law, only with the consent of the Secretary of State and of Parliament at Westminster. See also Hadfield, B., 'The Nature of Devolution in Scotland and Northern Ireland: Key Issues of Responsibility and Control', *Edinburgh Law Review*, 3 (1999): 3–31.

7. The chairs and deputy chairs, respectively, of the statutory committees are as follows. Agriculture and Rural Development, Ian Paisley (DUP), George Savage (UUP); Culture, Arts, and Leisure, Eamon O'Neill (SDLP), Mary Nelis (SF); Education, Danny Kennedy (UUP), Sammy Wilson (DUP); Enterprise, Trade, and Investment, Pat Doherty (SF), Sean Neeson (Alliance); Environment, William McCrea (DUP), Carmel Hanna (SDLP); Finance and Personnel, Francie Molloy (SF), James Leslie, (UUP); Health, Social Services, and Public Safety, Joe Hendron (SDLP), Tommy Gallagher (SDLP); Higher and Further Education, Training, and Employment, Esmond Birnie (UUP), Mervyn Carrick (DUP); Regional Development, Dennis Haughey (SDLP), Alan McFarland (UUP); Social Development, Fred Cobain (UUP), Michelle Gildernew (SF).

8. The co-chair of the shadow Standing Orders Committee, Denis Haughey, in moving the motions to establish the two Standing Committees, remarked: 'Other functions of the Office of the First Minister and Deputy First Minister . . . will need to be scrutinised, but we did not agree how this might be done, and a motion about this will be put before the Assembly in the future'. See *NIAR*, 6 December 1999.

9. The shadow Committee on Standing Orders expressed concern about the lack of such a committee in its Report to the Assembly tabled on 1 March 1999: *NNIAR* 9, I and II. The Report was debated on 8 and 9 March. On the second day of the debate, Peter Robinson (DUP) moved an unsuccessful amendment to establish a 'Special Scrutiny Committee' with a remit to scrutinize the Office of the First and Deputy First Ministers.

10. The following functions of the Office of First and Deputy First Minister fall within the remit of the Committee: economic policy, other than the 'programme for government', equality unit, civic forum, European affairs and international matters, community relations, public appointments, freedom of information, victims, Nolan standards, public service improvement, emergency planning, and women's issues. The functions that lay beyond the Committee's remit were: liaison with the North-South Ministerial Council, liaison with the BIC, British-Irish intergovernmental conference, relations with the secretary of state, the International Fund for Ireland, machinery of government, honours, policy innovation, legislation progress unit, executive committee secretariat, cross-departmental co-ordination, Assembly ombudsman, Office of the legislative counsel, and information services. See *NNIAR* 7, 15 February 1999.

11. When d'Hondt was reapplied for the purpose of nominating the chair and deputy chair of the Committee, both were drawn from the DUP: Gregory Campbell and Oliver Gibson, respectively.

12. The two junior ministers were Denis Haughey (SDLP) and Dermot Nesbitt (UUP). On appointment, each had to resign his seat on the relevant statutory committees.

13. See para. 7, strand one. *The Agreement* committed the British government to create a statutory obligation on public authorities in Northern Ireland 'to carry out all their functions with due regard to the need to promote equality of opportunity in relation to religion and political opinion; gender; race; disability; age; marital status; dependants; and sexual orientation'. See the section on 'Rights, Safeguards and Equality of Opportunity' para. 3, *The Agreement*.

14. There was also the possibility that the relationship between an Equality Department and the new Equality Commission could be problematic, or lead to at least some functional overlap. It is certainly the case that the Sinn Féin negotiating team was insistent that a free-standing Department was a necessary part of the new configuration. However, they felt 'badly let down by both the SDLP and the Irish government' when the announcement was made on 18 December 1998. Interview with Mitchel McLaughlin, March 2000.

15. The issue turned on the choice between the Royal Victoria and City hospitals as the site for centralized maternity services. The former, located in west Belfast—the constituency of both the Minister and the health committee chair, Joe Hendron—was chosen by de Brun in preference to the latter, located a mile away in the neighbouring constituency of south Belfast. The Assembly debated the matter on 31 January 2000 and voted by a simple majority in favour of the City option. De Brun's decision entailed a commitment to build a new facility on the Royal

Victoria's site. However, a fellow member of the Executive Committee insisted to the author that the Minister had not sought approval for the necessary funding from the Department of Finance and Personnel, nor her ministerial colleagues. Consequently, his view was that de Brun would have been 'ambushed in the long grass' by the Executive Committee when she sought the necessary finance.

16. Relationships between the Minister and many unionist MLAs, including those on the statutory committee, had already been soured by two earlier decisions taken by de Brun. One was to pulp the department's existing stationery and replace it with a bilingual version, the other to halt the flying of the Union flag on the department's properties. Relations were further strained when, shortly before suspension, she appointed a former republican prisoner as her special advisor—an individual, like herself, with no previous experience of health and associated Departmental responsibilities. Procedurally, the Minister's insistence on answering oral questions in full in both Irish and English also caused controversy. Members complained that this practice effectively reduced the number of questions that could be answered in the thirty-minute slot allocated for Ministerial questions and the matter was referred to the Assembly's Procedure Committee shortly before suspension.

17. During its shadow phase, two DUP members, Dr Ian Paisley and Peter Robinson tabled an undated motion on the Assembly's Order Paper seeking to exclude Sinn Féin members from holding ministerial office for a period of twelve months. See 'All Party Notices: List of Motions', *NNIAR*, 30 March 1999. The authors of the motion sought to move it as a 'Petition of Concern' on 15 July and 29 November 1999 and again on 8 February 2000, the last occasion the Assembly met in plenary session prior to suspension. On each occasion they failed narrowly to accrue the thirty signatures necessary to trigger a vote.

18. At the 'brainstorming session' held on 13 January 1999, participants were provided with a copy of the programme for government agreed by the Fine Gael, Labour Party, and Democratic Left coalition forged in 1994. The intention was to demonstrate the possibility of brokering such a programme despite the diverse backgrounds of these parties and their conflicting social policies. Private information.

19. The Transitional Programme's series of seminars began at the end of July 1998. For the most part they involved briefings by civil servants and academics concerning the machinery of government and particular policy sectors.

20. Beginning in September 1998, the Northern Ireland Office held a series of weekly meetings with the First and Deputy First Ministers Designate 'for wide-ranging discussions designed to bring them into the heart of government in Northern Ireland'. Another rite of ministerial passage, these 'Heart of Government' meetings enabled Trimble and Mallon to be 'fully briefed to help the smooth transfer of power'. Northern Ireland Information Service, *Press Release*, 9 September 1998.

21. 'Report from the First Minister (Designate) and Deputy First Minister (Designate)', *NNIAR* 6, 18 January 1999, Para. 3.7.

22. The spending proposals were laid before the Assembly by Mark Durkan, Finance and Personnel Minister, on 15 December 1999. Totalling almost £9bn, the largest beneficiaries were health and social services which were allocated almost £2bn, and schools which received £1.2bn. See *NIAR* 15 December 1999. A month later, a further £32m was reallocated to increase Departmental budgets for the current financial year, the lion's share going to health (£6.3m) and agriculture (£7m). See *NIAR* 11 January 2000.

23. Private information.

24. The DUP's refusal to participate in full meetings of the Executive created real difficulties in the process of designing the programme for government. The party's two Ministers did request separate briefing and debriefing meetings on the programme with Trimble and Mallon prior to and shortly after relevant meetings of the Executive: the request was refused. Private information.

25. At the end of January, the 'Ministerial Code' became available to members of the Executive Committee, but its capacity to effect collective responsibility also remained untested given that suspension occurred shortly afterwards. Separate interviews with a number of ministers confirmed that the ten attending Executive members had on occasion resorted to a simple majority vote to resolve disagreements. The absence of the DUP's two Ministers from Executive

meetings was costly. During separate interviews with the author, two fellow Ministers insisted that 'millions' had been reallocated to other Departments because 'the DUP's Ministers weren't there to fight their corners'.

26. NIAR 3, July 2000.
27. The six implementation bodies were: Inland Waterways, Food Safety, Trade and Business Development, Special EU Programmes, Language, and Aquaculture and Marine Matters. The six matters for cross-border co-operation were: Transport, Agriculture, Education, Health, Environment, and Tourism. See *NNIAR* 7, 15 February 1999.
28. *The Agreement*, Para. 2, strand two.
29. *Irish Times*, 19 November 1999.
30. *Republican News*, 11 May 2000.
31. The one institutional aspect of the Agreement that was not in place before suspension was the 'Civic Forum'. It was planned to be up and running in May 2000. The review of the criminal justice system was published in March 2000.
32. Despite, perhaps, every appearance to the contrary, members of all parties co-operated in a variety of committees throughout the shadow period. These included, the 'Committee to Advise the Presiding Officer', the 'Committee on Standing Orders', and the 'Shadow Assembly Commission'. In addition, two *ad hoc* committees were established. The first, the 'Committee on the Procedural Consequences of Devolution', considered 'the procedural consequences of devolution as they are likely to affect the relationship between, and the working of, the Northern Ireland Assembly and the United Kingdom Parliament'. The Committee submitted its report to the Assembly (*NNIAR* 5) on 9 November 1998 and it was then forwarded to the Procedure Committee of the House of Commons. The Committee also produced an interim report, *NNIAR* 3, on 5 October 1998. The second was the '*Ad Hoc* Committee (Port of Belfast)'. Its purpose was to 'consider the proposals of the Belfast Harbour Commissioners regarding the future of the Port of Belfast and their affect on the other ports in Northern Ireland'. Its report (*NNIAR* 12) was published on 22 July 1999. Had suspension not occurred, the proposed sale of the port would have realized a significant sum of money that would have been ploughed into Departmental spending programmes.
33. Performance and Innovation Unit, *Wiring It Up: Whitehall's Management of Cross-Cutting Policies and Services* (London: Cabinet Office, 2000), 7.
34. Leicester, G. and Mackay, P., *Holistic Government: Options for a Devolved Scotland* (Edinburgh: Scottish Council Foundation, 1998).
35. Cabinet Office, *Modernizing Government* (London: HMSO, 1999), Cm 4310.
36. The clearest instance of such improvisation related to the functions of the Trimble/Mallon Office. Between mid-December 1998 and mid-January 1999 when they reported to the Assembly, the number and range of their responsibilities increased significantly although, according to one Minister, David Trimble was 'adamant' that the 'Office of Law Reform' would not be lodged in his and Mallon's Office.
37. Performance and Innovation Unit, 'Wiring It Up'.
38. The White Paper, *Partnership for Equality*, Cm 3890, was published on 10 March 1998. It contained the Government's proposals for future legislation and policies on employment equality in Northern Ireland. The outcomes of the consultation on the proposals were announced by the Secretary of State, Mo Mowlam, four months later. See Northern Ireland Information Service, 10 July 1998.
39. Both DUP ministers were in regular communication with all bar their Sinn Féin counterparts, and within days of their appointment were the first to contact the new Minister for Finance and Personnel, Mark Durkan (SDLP), to discuss the budgets of their Departments.
40. See Mitchell, P., 'Futures' in P. Mitchell and R. Wilford (eds.), *Politics in Northern Ireland* (Boulder, CO: Westview Press, 1999), 265–84.

7

The British–Irish Council

GRAHAM WALKER

Introduction

The British–Irish Council (BIC), more popularly known as 'the Council of the Isles', constitutes one part of Strand Three of the Belfast Agreement of 10 April 1998.[1] It is one of the institutions connecting the governments and nations of the United Kingdom and the Republic of Ireland, and is the subject of an international treaty between the two states, attached to the Agreement. The BIC brings together representatives of the British and Irish Governments, devolved institutions in Scotland, Wales, and Northern Ireland, and representatives of the Isle of Man and the Channel Islands.

The official purpose of the Council, as stated in the Agreement, will be 'to promote the harmonious and mutually beneficial development of the totality of relationships amongst peoples of these islands',[2] and to 'exchange information, discuss, consult and use best endeavours to reach agreement on co-operation on matters of mutual interest within the competence of the relevant Administrations'.[3] Two summit-level meetings of all the representatives of the Council are to be held annually, and sectoral meetings involving Ministers responsible for specific areas as and when required. The Cabinet Office document outlining the *modus operandi* of the BIC stated that there was 'no theoretical limit to the matters which could be put forward for discussion',[4] although the Belfast Agreement specifically instances examples such as transport links, environmental issues, cultural issues, education, and approaches to European Union (EU) matters.[5] It is as yet unclear whether the Council will be a forum in which policy is formulated in these areas, or whether it may function as a means to the end of co-ordinating policies between the different participants. Certainly, a clause in the Agreement providing for two or more members to develop bilateral or multilateral arrangements between them goes beyond 'consultation' into the possibility of 'joint decision-making' on matters of mutual interest.[6] This is a section which would appear to have implications in particular for the devolved governments in respect of the possible development of intergovernmental relationships between them.[7] Questions of budgeting and of the location and composition of a permanent secretariat remain to be worked out.

The inclusion of the BIC in the terms of the Agreement was designed to provide an institutional expression of East-West relations as a balance to the provisions of Strand Two: the North-South Ministerial Council comprising Ministers from the Northern Ireland Assembly and the Irish Government, and implementation bodies to cover specific subject areas. Whereas Strand Two was shaped towards Irish nationalist demands and aspirations, so Strand Three, especially the BIC, was conceived to offer reassurance to Ulster unionists. Indeed, the inclusion of the BIC in terms of the Agreement appears to have been fundamental to the Ulster Unionist Party's acceptance of the whole package. The UUP leader, David Trimble, stated in March 1998 that the creation of the British Isles-wide Council 'makes it possible for Unionists to contemplate an institutionalised relationship between Belfast and Dublin'.[8] Ideally, unionists wished to have the North-South bodies made subordinate to the BIC, a position given expression in an earlier draft of the terms of Agreement by the British Government which occasioned much nationalist alarm.[9] Instead, the Agreement provided for the separate operation of the North-South and East-West bodies with the clear implication that a spirit of independence was to hold both, along with the Northern Ireland Assembly, together. However, it has been pointed out that the North-South dimension is bound more tightly to the Northern Ireland Assembly, and that the development of the BIC is not as clearly predetermined as that of the North-South bodies.[10]

British and Irish Government Ministers have stressed the flexibility which is built into the new constitutional arrangements for Northern Ireland,[11] and there is an open-ended quality to the BIC which suggests that the shape it takes will depend largely upon the motivation and the vision of its members. Strictly speaking, it is an intergovernmental executive body, but the possibility of it developing into a means of strengthening interparliamentary links, especially between the new devolved assemblies, has been clearly underlined.[12] On the other hand, as has been recently observed in an academic investigation,[13] the BIC takes its place in an already crowded area of intergovernmental and interparliamentary activity. It joins the British-Irish Interparliamentary Body which has deliberated since 1990, a new British-Irish Intergovernmental Council which 'subsumes' that established by the Anglo-Irish Agreement of 1985, and the recently announced Joint Ministerial Committee (JMC) on devolution.[14] The question thus arises as to the definition of a distinctive role for the BIC.

The Council was described by the former Secretary of State for Northern Ireland, Mo Mowlam, as 'an idea whose time has very much come'.[15] The British Government's perception of the BIC is of a body designed to develop further the relationship between the UK and the Republic of Ireland, and to provide a context in which the Northern Ireland problem can be truly resolved. In his speech to the Irish Parliament, the Dáil, in November 1998, Prime Minister Tony Blair explicitly related the BIC to his hopes for the development of a common approach and a new era of co-operation between the UK and the Republic of Ireland.[16] The ultimate goal here seems to be a more coherent 'British-Isles' voice in the EU.

The Inaugural Summit of the BIC

The BIC formally came into effect on 2 December 1999 with the devolution of power from Westminster to the new Northern Ireland Assembly. The inaugural session of the body took place in London on 17 December 1999.

The latter meeting approved a memorandum on the working procedures of the BIC, and drew up a list of issues for initial discussion and consultation. Different administrations were assigned to take the lead in each sectoral area in preparation for the following summit meeting of the Council scheduled for June 2000 in Dublin. There were five key areas specified: drug trafficking and abuse (the Irish Government), the main issue for discussion in June 2000; social exclusion (the Scottish Executive and Welsh Cabinet); transport (the Northern Ireland Executive); the environment (the British Government); and the knowledge economy (Jersey). Other suitable issues for the Council were specified, including consideration of the development of interparliamentary links.[17] In the Northern Ireland Assembly during questioning on the BIC inaugural meeting, the Deputy First Minister, Seamus Mallon, said later that Assembly members would be encouraged to participate in any interparliamentary activity arranged through the BIC.[18]

The Ulster Unionist Party—whose leader David Trimble described the inauguration of the BIC as a 'revolutionary political development'—produced a document prior to the meeting which discussed how the Council might function.[19] The most publicized suggestion was that a successful future bid on the part of England to host the World Cup football tournament should result in some matches being played in both Northern Ireland and the Republic of Ireland.[20] The idea raised the prospect of future British-Irish co-operation regarding the hosting of sporting events. The UUP takes the view that a body like the BIC will reconnect the Republic of Ireland to the affairs of the UK, and the comments of the Taoiseach, Bertie Ahern, following the BIC inaugural meeting, emphasized the issue of the renewal of relationships within the British Isles. Ahern added that the new institutional architecture signalled the widening of these relations beyond the connotations of the 'Anglo-Irish' terminology hitherto so widely used.[21] As a positive response to the new constitutional arrangements put in place by the Blair Government, and the advent of the BIC, the Irish Government had earlier established Consulates-General in Edinburgh and Cardiff. These will remain in place, despite the fact that the reintroduction of direct rule in February 2000 has jeopardized the BIC's future.

The Thinking behind the 'Council of the Isles'

The Ulster Unionists have been widely credited with the idea of the BIC, but the roots of it arguably date back at least as far as the time of Gladstone and the initial Irish Home Rule controversy. In this period many Liberals, and a few Conservatives, envisaged relations between the different countries of the British Isles taking on a loosely federal, or quasi-federal, character.[22] As Meehan points out, Ireland, North and South, is central to historical analysis of British flirtations with federalism.[23] The Irish Home Rule issue for a time raised the possibility that the UK would take a 'Union State' rather than a 'Unitary State' direction:[24] a decentralized system of governance reflecting the multinational nature and distinctive identities of the archipelago.

Much of the spirit of this concept informs the BIC, notwithstanding changed circumstances and, particularly, the creation of an independent Southern Irish State. The Blair government appears to have arrested the unitary trends in British State territorial management, accelerated by the Conservative governments of Thatcher and Major, instead signalling the resumption of a 'Union State' outlook. The BIC might be said to be emblematic of this change, as well as an idea evidently in tune with the regional consciousness of the European Union and the impact of EU developments in weakening traditional concepts of national sovereignty and borders and of relationships between nations and states.[25]

In this altered context it is necessary to appreciate the intellectual effort expended on the idea of a 'Council of the Isles' by political thinkers such as Richard Kearney and Simon Partridge.[26] These thinkers have approached the concept in a broadly 'post-nationalist' spirit, seeking to transcend the obstacles put in place by traditional ideas of nation-states, sovereignty, and borders. They view a body such as the BIC has become, to have the potential to refashion relationships in these islands around genuinely pluralist values and an acceptance of the reality of fluid and multiple, or multilayered, identities. The writings of such thinkers challenge established polarities—the either/or mindset in relation especially to matters of identity—and encourage the notion of cultural complementarity and interaction. With particular reference to the Northern Ireland problem, they see such a structure as the BIC as a means to the end of transcending the deadly political 'endgame' between unionism and nationalism in which the 'zero-sum' mentality is prevalent on both sides. They challenge both the 'supremacy of Westminster' brand of unionism and the anglophobic 'Four Green Fields' version of Irish nationalism/republicanism. Moreover, they make a 'common-sense' case for a body like the BIC, adopted by Government Ministers like Mowlam,[27] around the realities of population movements and inter-mixing in these islands. Partridge states, for example, that one quarter of Britons have an Irish relative, and that only a small fraction of British people consider the Irish to be 'foreign'.[28]

Kearney, Partridge, and others have for some time urged politicians to take a lead from the example of the Nordic Council,[29] and the BIC, as defined in the Agreement, clearly bears some of its hallmarks. Like the Nordic Council, the BIC is not made up exclusively of sovereign states and involves autonomous territories. The BIC also is intended to deal with similar subject areas and issues as the Nordic Council. On the other hand, the Nordic Council emerged from the 'bottom up', while the BIC is being driven at present by the two sovereign governments. The composition of the Nordic Council includes five sovereign states, while only two will feature in the BIC. The Nordic Council is essentially an interparliamentary body, while the BIC, by the terms of the Agreement, is meant primarily to be intergovernmental. Moreover, as Bogdanor points out, the Nordic Council was a product of consensus, while the BIC hopes to create consensus to resolve the long-running conflict of Northern Ireland.[30]

The evidence thus far does not suggest that either unionists or nationalists in Northern Ireland have come to view the BIC in the spirit of the 'post-nationalist' intellectuals, or have given much thought to the Nordic Council parallel. Nationalists have regarded the BIC as a concession to unionists, and many appear to believe that it will be likely merely to function as a talking shop.[31] Pro-Agreement unionist attitudes will be discussed more fully below, although special mention should be made of the contribution of the small loyalist party, the Ulster Democratic Party (UDP),[32] while anti-Agreement unionists concur with nationalists about the likely ineffectiveness of the BIC in practice.[33] To get beyond old dichotomies it may well be the case that the BIC will have to develop a civic dimension in the manner called for by commentators like Hassan,[34] a forging of a meaningful connection with civic institutions throughout the two islands to render the body more democratic and less ministerial and bureaucratic.

The BIC and Devolution

The BIC forms part of the new governmental and institutional framework constructed by the Blair government. Just as much discussion has already taken place about the grey areas relating to devolution, and the subject of intergovernmental relations in particular,[35] so the BIC's relationship to new devolved structures of government is likely to give rise to debate, negotiation and perhaps friction.

The British Government has made clear its wish to see matters arising between the new devolved assemblies and the central government dealt with through the Joint Ministerial Committee and the respective sets of concordats.[36] Concordats relating to co-ordination of European Union policy issues, international relations, financial assistance to industry, and statistics have been drawn up. However, the inclusion in Strand Three of the Belfast Agreement of an invitation to the participants in the BIC to develop bilateral or multilateral arrangements, perhaps to the point of joint decision-making, raises the possibility of devolved governments deciding matters with legal, financial, and policy implications. Moreover, it is open to the devolved governments to strike up similar arrangements with the Government of the Republic of Ireland, something reaffirmed in the British Government's concordats document.[37] The British Government does not wish devolution matters to impinge on a body like the BIC which will contain a foreign government, yet ambiguities appear to remain in respect of the overlap between BIC issues and devolution. The critical reception accorded to the concordats in some Scottish quarters[38] suggests that resentments may build up over perceived restrictive tendencies on the part of central government, and could yet express themselves in an outlet such as the BIC. It is not inconceivable that a Scottish Executive at odds with London may view the BIC as a context in which it can exert autonomy and pursue an independent course in relation to initiatives with other partners, including the Republic of Ireland. Such scenarios are a long way from the visions of the BIC entertained by the British Government and promoted by the Ulster Unionist Party in the context of the Northern Ireland peace process.

The inclusion of the BIC in the Belfast Agreement represented a vindication of the UUP's efforts over several years to play up the theme of East-West links. Under the leadership of James Molyneaux the party pushed for more developed links especially to Scotland, and at Westminster in the years of the Major Government unionists exposed to good effect the inconsistencies in that government's approach to constitutional-devolution questions pertaining to Northern Ireland and to Scotland respectively. On the election of Tony Blair, the UUP leader, David Trimble, stressed the need to include Northern Ireland in the new Labour Government's decentralization plans. Thus the Government's blueprint for a Northern Ireland Assembly in conjunction with the BIC could be regarded by Ulster unionists as a welcome change from previous policy initiatives which had centred on the North-South dimension in Ireland alone, and in which Northern Ireland's status within the UK was anomalous. The unionists were able to argue that the new proposals offered more security for the Union, and indeed, through the medium of the BIC, reinvolved the Republic of Ireland in a 'British' context.[39] In stark comparison with Sunningdale (1973) and the Anglo-Irish Agreement (1985), the East-West dimension was firmly acknowledged and provided for in the Belfast Agreement. North-South proposals were, in unionist eyes, counterbalanced by the idea of the BIC.

However, it quickly became clear that unionists might have to struggle to maintain this equilibrium by ensuring that the BIC was not allowed to become a cosmetic body. Though progress was made on the establishment of the remit of the North-South Ministerial Council and the six implementation bodies, the BIC's profile fell; media attention focused on North-South matters rather than

East-West. Unionists had desired to see the JMC and the concordats put within the framework of the BIC,[40] but the British Government by the summer of 1998 had made it evident that only an exclusively UK process would be appropriate for the resolution of devolved matters. By the end of 1998 David Trimble was urging Tony Blair to give more attention to the BIC, and in February 1999 Northern Ireland Minister Paul Murphy produced a memorandum suggesting possible work areas for the BIC. These built on those stipulated in the Agreement itself, namely transport, tourism, the environment, culture, education, and dealings with the European Union. Indeed, the evidence suggests that the Government has always regarded the BIC as potentially meaningful, even as a means to the end of successfully managing the transition to devolution in the UK and making the project work, notwithstanding the establishment of the JMC and the concordats for this purpose also. In October 1998 the then Northern Ireland Secretary of State, Mo Mowlam, talked about the successful operation of devolutionary arrangements in Scotland and Wales helping the situation in Northern Ireland, and expressed the hope that Scotland and Northern Ireland, for example, might exploit the opportunity presented by the BIC to interact more positively with one another.[41] Notwithstanding the intention of the concordats to pre-empt friction between central government and devolved parliaments, it may still prove to be the case that the BIC will function partly as a body in which the devolved administrations will draw closer together, perhaps to the point of forming territorial alliances, as suggested by Vernon Bogdanor.[42] In the case of the Scotland–Northern Ireland relationship, there is the common ground of the legislative competencies of the respective assemblies, against the backdrop of well-documented cultural and historical ties.

On the other hand, the BIC may also help to exacerbate 'the English problem' inherent in the Blair Government's constitutional reform project.[43] Even before it first convened, the BIC highlighted the 'Who speaks for England?' issue: for England is represented in the BIC by the UK Government.[44] The problematic nature of this question was not addressed at the inaugural meeting of the BIC. A perception of unfairness and lopsidedness which looks set to take root in England may thus be reinforced by the perception that the BIC will in effect be a body dominated by the 'Celtic fringe'. A jaundiced English view of Blair—remodelling the constitution according to the whims of the non-English parts of the UK—may prove prejudicial to the project's ultimate chances of success.[45] In addition, the possible development of English regionalism, apparently desired and encouraged by the Government, may create problems for a body like the BIC if it results in the latter being overloaded by English regions.[46] Thus a new problem regarding balance and perception of fairness could be created.

Questions surrounding the BIC Agenda

The suggested initial agenda of the BIC, as set out at the inaugural meeting, is geared towards practical and 'common sense' co-operation between the different parts of these islands over issues of common concern. Thus it is unlikely that much controversy will attend BIC deliberations and initiatives in areas such as drugs, transport links, tourism, and environmental affairs, although the question of dumping nuclear waste in the Irish Sea has already proved a thorny matter of British-Irish governmental relations.

Strengthening regional economic links may not run into many obstacles, but there could be competing pressures in the Irish context to prioritize the harmonizing of economic ventures between North and South. The UUP's BIC spokesman, Esmond Birnie, has long favoured the idea of a Belfast-Glasgow economic corridor which would benefit both the North-East of Ireland and South-West Scotland in terms of trade and jobs, and the Northern Ireland CBI appears to hold ambitious ideas for the BIC and East-West links in general.[47] Co-ordination of investment and planning strategies across the UK appears to be one of the main purposes of the recently-produced concordats, but the BIC might play a role in developing this, as well as providing a space for the possible inclusion of the Republic of Ireland in such plans.

Education is a field apparently ripe for new initiatives between participants in the BIC, and perhaps further development of existing schemes. Educational exchanges are established practice between North and South in Ireland and might be extended eastwards. The opportunity also exists for joining curriculum projects and joint field trips. Ulster unionists are likely to press in a future educational sector of the BIC for the removal of the Irish language qualification which currently stands in the way of many teachers wishing to apply for posts in the Republic of Ireland. They are also likely to argue that the BIC address the East-West dimensions of the matters on the agenda of the North-South Ministerial Council and its implementation bodies.[48]

The British Government, through the provision of the Belfast Agreement, has approved of the idea of the BIC dealing with European Union affairs. As stated earlier, the objective appears to be the construction on an islands-wide basis of a common voice in European matters, and the exertion of greater influence within the EU. Many European issues may indeed lend themselves to co-operation, yet commentators on the relationship between EU matters and the Blair Government's constitutional reforms, have highlighted the potential which exists for disharmony within these islands.[49] There is certainly the risk, for example, that a future Scottish Executive, at odds with the central government, will want to exert itself in Europe more directly, and be unwilling to fit in with the central government's European policy. The stipulations on the EU—as in other subject areas—in the current concordats document may come to be contested. In this respect, the BIC could again find itself the context for the struggle between central and devolved governments and the forging of the territorial alliances and coalitions mentioned above.[50] Given the regional dimension to European funding and policy-making, there may also be the possibility of regional alliances being formed in the BIC which could cut across national boundaries and identities.

Questions of Culture and Identity

But perhaps the most intriguing, if potentially divisive, questions pertaining to the form the BIC will take are those surrounding culture and identity. The BIC, by its very nature, will be central to the future of the Union and British identity, and may even play a vital role in determining that future.

The New Labour constitutional project is directed at shaping a 'New Union Politics'.[51] Along with the process of decentralization it is hoped that a renewed sense of collective identity can be forged. This 'New Unionism' or new Britishness will not be based, as in the past, on the 'unwritten constitution' and the totem of parliamentary sovereignty; far less will it draw on the emotional patriotism of an Imperial Britishness, strongly Protestant, and nurtured by war until 1945. Rather it is a concept that harks back to the notion of a 'Union State' rather than a unitary one, and styles itself as a modern pluralist outlook reflecting the multinational, multiethnic, and regionally diverse character of the UK. It is a broad-based and expansive form of identity orientated towards federalism.[52] Britishness, it is argued, can supplement other identities and accommodate in a manner alien to monocultural nationalisms. It can take on the role of a secondary, 'umbrella' form of identity.[53] It is promoted in the context of the argument for moving beyond old concepts of both unionism and nationalism in Northern Ireland, and also in Scotland.[54] In the election campaign for the Scottish Parliament in May 1999, the Scottish National Party (SNP) was put under pressure regarding the dual sense of identity (Scottish-British) which polls suggest that most Scots still feel, and a senior party figure later advocated that the SNP should acknowledge the significance of British identity and attempt to accommodate it.[55] However, there remains a strong body of traditionalist opinion in the SNP, while commentators from a nationalist or republican standpoint in Northern Ireland insist on seeing a predatory British nationalism, hopelessly wedded to an imperialist mindset, which has to be eradicated for peace to come to the Province.[56]

The British Government, in the spirit of the 'New Unionism', appears to desire the BIC to help develop an expansive and impeccably civic form of Britishness and smooth the path of the radical changes it has embarked upon. This may well be uncomfortable for those unionists, especially in Ulster, whose

British allegiance is decidedly of an ethnic and exclusivist variety. It certainly serves up a challenge to unionists to adapt to a subtler ideological defence of their position in which the Union represents the cultural interaction of the islands, rather than any notion of triumphalism or superiority. If Ulster unionists approach the business of the BIC in the manner of their forebears they will breach the spirit of the idea which politically they fought for in the context of the Northern Ireland peace process.

However, it is an open question whether the BIC will help to revitalize British identity in any form. It might as plausibly be argued that it would give a fillip to separatism and contribute to the actual dissolution of the Union. The Scottish National Party's enthusiasm for the BIC to date can be read this way. The SNP views the BIC as akin to the Nordic Council and a potential structure for co-operation between independent states on these islands. They view the BIC as a forum in which the separate 'Celtic' identities can be enhanced and Britishness will continue its inexorable decline.[57] In addition, the then SNP has indicated that the BIC could be a means of renewing ties between Scotland and Ireland, in effect the Republic of Ireland. In August 1998 the SNP leader Alex Salmond spoke enthusiastically of re-establishing links between Scotland and Ireland which had been 'dislocated by the affairs of the United Kingdom', and pointed to the Council of the Isles as a structure 'which can allow us to communicate directly, work together on shared interests and influence each other by example'. Salmond listed four priority areas for such exchanges—education, culture and the media, transport, and Europe—and held out the possibility of a shared television channel on one of the digital multiplexes.[58]

Others outside nationalist political parties have also situated the BIC in the context of a 'post-Union' or 'post-British' world. According to the influential Scottish thinker and commentator Tom Nairn, British identity is in a 'terminal' condition, and the constitutional changes unleashed by Blair will be likely to lead to 'an archipelago-system of effectively independent polities'.[59] In this context, suggests Nairn, the BIC might function as the forum in which they meet to discuss or decide questions of common interest, and the European Union will provide a framework for this whole process to occur successfully and to avoid the perils of 'break-up'.[60] This is a vision reluctantly shared by the Conservative academic John Barnes who regards such a role for the BIC as the only thing to be salvaged out of the post-UK world which he thinks the Blair Government's incoherent and unstable programme of change will bring about. However, Barnes also feels that a BIC composed of independent polities will not be able to exert the same influence on the EU as the UK.[61]

Such speculations serve to confirm the arrival of the BIC as an important idea, particularly in the context of debates about identity, even before the body has started to function in earnest. It would not be pushing speculation too far to suggest also that the BIC will constitute one of the conditions which will test the health and nature of British identity when the historical 'English

Constitution' is removed and the balance is altered, as in the BIC itself, in favour of the 'periphery' over the centre.[62]

In the realm of cultural matters the BIC might reflect the divisions over identity discussed. Given the body's close relationship to the Northern Ireland peace process there could be friction within it over competing claims made by Gaelic lobbies in Ireland and Scotland and that of the Ulster-Scots, the latter politically galvanized by unionists in response to Irish nationalism's politicization of Gaelic culture. Language and sporting issues are likely to figure in the cultural sector of the BIC, and both are extremely divisive in Northern Ireland.[63] Again, it is a moot point whether the spirit of multiculturalism which infuses the concept of the Council of the Isles will be able to prevail.

Thus, in spite of government spokespersons playing down the ideological dimensions to the BIC and promoting it in terms of practicalities, competing unionist and nationalist agendas are likely to be brought to it. This is not in the 'post-nationalist' and 'post-unionist' spirit of the concept as expounded by intellectual figures like Kearney, or argued for by New Labour thinkers, but traditional notions of exclusive identity, allegiance, and sovereignty will die hard, and cultural matters will carry the potential for political friction. Such friction may be more likely if nationalist or separatist pressures constantly assail devolutionary arrangements.

Conclusion

The BIC as an idea has gripped the imaginations of many people in these islands, independently of its connection to the Belfast Agreement. In Scotland, in particular, it has raised hopes of closer relationships being refashioned with Ireland, North and South, and has matched the mood there of a growing sense of cultural self-confidence and adventurousness.[64] In the context of the contemporary European Union and its planned expansion, the BIC appears as a possible way forward politically, socially, culturally, and economically for the British Isles as a whole. There remains, however, the question of whether the structural reforms in the UK, to which the BIC inevitably relates, will result in the long term maintenance of a UK state, however altered in terms of sovereignty and capability. There remains, too, the question of achieving enduring peace and stability in Northern Ireland without which the development of a new set of relationships within these islands will be rendered extremely problematic and perhaps elusive. The BIC, it would seem, could either contribute to a resolution of the conflict, or fall victim one way or another to its continuation.

ENDNOTES

1. Hereafter referred to as *The Agreement*.
2. *The Agreement*, 14, para. 1.
3. Ibid., 14, para. 5.
4. The Constitution Unit, *The British–Irish Council: Nordic Lessons for the Council of the Isles* (London: Constitution Unit, 1998), Appendix B.
5. *The Agreement*, 14, para. 5.
6. Ibid., 14, para. 10.
7. Hassan, G., (ed.), *A Guide to the Scottish Parliament* (Edinburgh: Centre for Scottish Public Policy, 1999), 148.
8. *Irish Times*, 18 March 1998.
9. Ibid., 12 January 1998.
10. O'Leary, B., 'The 1998 British–Irish Agreement: Power-Sharing Plus', *Scottish Affairs*, 26 (1999): 14–35.
11. *The Herald* (Glasgow), 15 October 1998.
12. The Constitution Unit, *The British–Irish Council*, Appendix B; Mowlam, M., 'The Good Friday Agreement', *The Parliamentarian*, April 1999.
13. The Constitution Unit, *The British–Irish Council*, 17–18.
14. For which see Cornes, R., 'Intergovernmental Relations in a Devolved United Kingdom: Making Devolution Work', in Hazell, R., (ed.), *Constitutional Futures* (Oxford: University Press, 1999).
15. Mowlam, 'The Good Friday Agreement'.
16. *Belfast Telegraph*, 26 November 1998.
17. *Irish Times*, 18 December 1999.
18. *Northern Ireland Assembly Report*, 4/4, 17 January 2000.
19. *Irish Times*, 18 December 1999; The Ulster Unionist Party, *The British–Irish Council—A Work Programme*, 13 December 1999.
20. *Irish Times*, 17 December 1999.
21. *The Herald* (Glasgow), 18 December 1999.
22. See Kendle, J., *Federal Britain* (London: Routledge, 1997).
23. Meehan, E., 'The Belfast Agreement and UK Devolution', *Parliamentary Affairs*, 52/1 (1999): 19–31.
24. See Mitchell, J., 'Conservatives and the Changing Meaning of Union', *Regional and Federal Studies*, 6 (1996): 30–44; and Bogdanor, V., 'Devolution: Decentralisation or Disintegration?', *Political Quarterly*, 70 (1999): 185–94.
25. For an interesting discussion of such questions in relation to Northern Ireland, see McCall, C., *Identity in Northern Ireland* (Basingstoke: MacMillan Press, 1999).
26. See Kearney, R., *Postnationalist Ireland* (London: Routledge, 1997); and Partridge, S., 'The Irish diaspora and devolved democracy in the British–Irish islands', *Times Change*, 16 (1998/9): 15–18.
27. Mowlam, 'The Good Friday Agreement'.
28. Partridge, 'The Irish diaspora'.
29. For an exploration of the parallels between the two bodies, see The Constitution Unit, *The British–Irish Council*.
30. Bogdanor, V., 'The British–Irish Council and Devolution', *Government and Opposition*, 34 (1999): 287–98.
31. See Walker, G., 'The Council of the Isles and the Scotland–Northern Ireland Relationship', *Scottish Affairs*, 27 (1999): 108–23.
32. See for example, UDP written submission in Northern Ireland Forum for Political Dialogue, *Relationships within the British Isles and the Implications of Decentralisation throughout the Regions of the UK*, 24 April 1998.
33. See for example, comments of Nigel Dodds (Democratic Unionist Party) in *The News Letter*, 23 December 1999.
34. Hassan, G., 'A New Union Politics', in G. Hassan (ed.), *A Guide to the Scottish Parliament*, 143–50.

35. See Cornes, 'Intergovernmental Relations'.
36. Memorandum of understanding and supplementary agreements, Cm. 4444, October 1999.
37. Ibid., 33.
38. See *Sunday Herald* (Glasgow), 3 October 1999.
39. See Walker, 'Council of the Isles'; and McCall, *Identity in Northern Ireland*, 160–3.
40. Information from Esmond Birnie.
41. *The Herald* (Glasgow), 15 October 1998.
42. Bogdanor, 'The British-Irish Council'.
43. Bogdanor, 'Devolution'.
44. Scottish Affairs Committee, *The Operation of Multi-Layer Democracy*, Vol. I, HC 460-I (HMSO, 1999), xv.
45. Scottish Affairs Committee, *The Operation of Multi-Layer Democracy*, Vol. II, HC 460-II (HMSO, 1999), 86–8 (evidence of John Barnes).
46. Bogdanor, 'The British-Irish Council'.
47. Birnie, E., 'British-Irish Council can keep UK together', *The NewsLetter*, 19 September 1998. Birnie was appointed Chair of the Northern Ireland Assembly Statutory Committee on Higher and Further Education, Training and Employment with the establishment of devolution on 2 December 1999.
48. Information from Esmond Birnie.
49. Scottish Affairs Committee, *The Operation of Multi-Layer Democracy*, Vol. I, xv–xvi; also Robbins, K., 'Britain and Europe: devolution and foreign policy', *International Affairs*, 74/1 (1998): 105–18.
50. Bogdanor, 'The British-Irish Council'; Cornes, 'Intergovernmental Relations'.
51. See Hassan, 'A New Union Politics'.
52. Or, perhaps, the confederalism exemplified by the Belfast Agreement.
53. See Lloyd, J., 'These Islands', *Prospect*, 41 (1999): 10.
54. Hassan, G., 'Essay', *The Herald* (Glasgow), 17 July 1999.
55. *Sunday Herald* (Glasgow), 19 September 1999.
56. See O'Dowd, L., '"New Unionism", British nationalism and the prospects for a negotiated settlement in Northern Ireland', in Miller, D., (ed.), *Rethinking Northern Ireland* (London: Longman, 1998).
57. Walker, 'The Council of the Isles'.
58. Salmond, A., 'Scotland and Ireland', *Scottish Affairs*, 25 (1998): 68–77.
59. Scottish Affairs Committee, *The Operation of Multi-Layer Democracy*, Vol. II, 81; see also Nairn, T., *After Britain* (London: Granta, 2000).
60. Scottish Affairs Committee, *The Operation of Multi-Layer Democracy*, 86; see also MacCormick, N., 'Does a Nation need a State? Reflections on Liberal Nationalism', in Mortimer, E., (ed.), *People, Nation and State* (London: I. B. Tauris, 1999).
61. Scottish Affairs Committee, *The Operation of Multi-Layer Democracy*, Vol. II, 90.
62. Bogdanor, 'The British-Irish Council'; see also Langlands, R., 'Britishness or Englishmen? The historical problem of national identity in Britain', *Nation and Nationalism*, 5 (1999): 53–69.
63. See Walker, 'Council of the Isles'.
64. See comments of the poet Edwin Morgan in *Scotland-on-Sunday*, 31 October 1999; and the report of speech by Scotland First Minister Donald Dewar in *Irish Times*, 30 October 1999; and special supplements on Scottish-Irish relations to mark President MacAleese's visit to Scotland in *Irish Times* and *The Scotsman*, 30 November 1999.

8

The Patten Report and Post-Sovereignty Policing in Northern Ireland*

CLIVE WALKER

Introduction

Policing in Northern Ireland has been hurtful and divisive. Hurt is felt by the police—302 Royal Ulster Constabulary (RUC) officers have been killed since 1969, and several thousands injured. Equally, many detainees and even communities have suffered harassment, discrimination, abuse, assaults, and ill-treatment at the hands of the RUC, who have also shot dead many suspects and are alleged to have colluded with Loyalist paramilitaries.[1] Division arises because policing is a fundamental attribute of statehood—the police are 'the locus of ultimate coercive power' and inevitably show 'partisanship in favour of a dominant order'.[2] Put simply, if Northern Ireland is a political entity whose very existence and legitimacy is challenged, then it follows that all major attributes of the entity will also be challenged, and the police in Northern Ireland, the RUC, are prime candidates for this treatment:

If citizens perceive state institutions as alien or as ethnically skewed, they may become less compliant to state authority. Community-police relations become essentially inter-communal relations, with one group wearing uniforms and carrying weapons while the other is handicapped by limited authority. (Enloe, C. H., *Ethnic Soldiers* (Harmondsworth: Penguin, 1980), 88.)

As well as this fundamental attribute of epitomizing a contested state, other features of policing in Northern Ireland have also given rise to controversy and disaffection. Some relate to the consequences of the association—the fact that the RUC have had to contend with paramilitary challenges of a scale and nature unparalleled elsewhere in western Europe mean that they have remained militaristic and remote from the public. The result is a distortion both of the RUC's approach to policing and the community's attitude to policing(Patten: 1.4).[3] In addition, there have been persistent concerns about the standard of police performance, especially in the security field.

For all of these reasons, it has long been recognized that changes to policing form an integral part of any political settlement in Northern Ireland. That point was recognized in the Anglo–Irish Agreement of 1985, article 7 of which emphasized the need 'to improve relations between the security forces and the community'. Likewise the Mitchell Report expressed 'the hope . . . that policing in Northern Ireland can be normalised as soon as the security situation permits'.[4] Yet, when the moment came for change with the Belfast Agreement, the issue proved beyond the bounds of consensus (Patten: 1.2). Rather than see the Agreement falter, the parties decided to throw the balls back up into the air by setting up a commission to take over the issue. To this end, Chris Patten, the erstwhile Conservative Cabinet minister and Governor of Hong Kong, was appointed as commission chair, and seven others also received the call in June 1998. There followed a major consultation exercise, including meetings attended by over 10,000 members of the public and an opinion survey. The report was published in September 1999. This chapter will describe and analyse its main recommendations.

The Context of Policing in Northern Ireland

The current 'troubles' since 1968 are of greater persistence and arguably entail greater dangers to police officers than earlier periods of cyclical paramilitary violence experienced in Northern Ireland.[5] Nevertheless, the majority nationalist rejection of the RUC,[6] including a paramilitary republican fringe prepared to resort to violence, has been endemic since the inauguration of the province.[7]

Full histories of the evolution of policing in Ireland and the more contemporary life of the RUC may be left in detail to others.[8] However, it may be noted that by 1969 the relationship between police and community was widely viewed with dissatisfaction and prompted the establishment of the Advisory Committee on Police in Northern Ireland—the 'Hunt Committee'. The Hunt Committee identified the military/security role of the RUC as the 'most striking difference' between it and British counterparts.[9] The solution imposed made few concessions to local difficulties. In the short term, the RUC was to be relieved of its military/security duties, and it was expected that the British Army and a new, mainly part-time, Ulster Defence Regiment would replace the police in this field. In the long-term, the aim was to impose English policing models.

While some commentators[10] viewed the reform package as superficial, it did result in a substantial programme of legislative change. Thus, the *Ulster Defence Regiment Act* 1969—now the *Reserve Forces Act* 1980—secured the replacement of the Ulster Special Constabulary. The conduct of serious public prosecutions was transferred from police hands to the Director of Public Prosecutions by the *Prosecution of Offences (Northern Ireland) Order* 1972. In the meantime, the RUC itself was reshaped by the *Police Act (Northern Ireland)* 1970.

The most innovatory feature of the new Police Act was the establishment of a Police Authority for Northern Ireland, which subsumed many of the important functions previously exercised by the Minister of Home Affairs. However, the composition of the Police Authority in Northern Ireland under schedule 1 of the 1970 Act, sharply differs from the norm in England in that the Authority is a wholly appointed body, which contains no leading politicians.

The police complaints system has proved equally contentious.[11] The Chief Constable was placed under a duty by section 13 to record and investigate complaints. However, the only independent oversight was by the Police Authority and that was limited to situations where a complaint was so generalized or serious that an inquiry in the public interest was required (section 13) or where charges were brought against senior officers (section 25(3)). This system has since been renovated on two occasions prior to 1998. First, the *Police (Northern Ireland) Order* 1977 provided for a civilian Police Complaints Board for Northern Ireland.[12] In turn the Board was replaced by the Independent Commission for Police Complaints (ICPC), which was invested with extra powers under the *Police (Northern Ireland) Order* 1987—amended further in 1995— to direct and supervise investigations.[13]

In many ways, the Hunt Report represented a false dawn in the imposition of a British ethos on the RUC, for, like many other institutions in Northern Ireland, it was soon engulfed by the political violence which took hold after 1970. A number of results, counterproductive in Hunt Report terms, soon followed. One was that the rearming of the police began in 1971; in short, the police gradually reassumed a security role and became the primary security force after 1976 in pursuit of broader British security strategies of Ulsterization and criminalization.[14] The Police Authority became secretive and defensive; it neither provided a 'buffer' between police and political goals and pressures[15] nor did it bring the RUC into a closer relationship with the community by making it answerable to its representatives.

A later attempt to ally police and community was the *Police (Northern Ireland) Act* 1998,[16] by which the Police Authority is placed under a duty to make arrangements to obtain the views of the public about policing and the co-operation of the public in preventing crime (section 7), and becomes responsible for drawing up annual policing objectives and performance targets (section 15) and for approving an annual policing plan, the draft of which is provided by the Chief Constable (sections 16, 17). These requirements may be viewed primarily as the counterpart to the *Police and Magistrates' Courts Act* 1994 in England and Wales, and followed two Northern Ireland Office papers, *Policing in the Community* (1994) and *Foundations for Policing* (1996). However, the Police Authority, the composition of which is left largely unchanged, is weakened in the process. It loses significant financial control to the Chief Constable—and even direction of its own civilian staff—and its plans are subjected to the policing objectives set by the Secretary of State (section 14), and there is also a strategic plan produced by the Chief

Constable to contend with (section 15). In addition, both Police Authority and Chief Constable are subjected to much more direct control by the Secretary of State than found in Britain. The mechanisms include a power to issue a statement of policing principles (section 37) and general guidance on the exercise of policing functions (section 39), and to require the use of specialized equipment, facilities, or services (section 40). Despite the conjunction of the passage of the 1998 legislation and the Patten Review, the latter was expected to build upon, rather than dismantle, the main themes of centralized control and managerialism. In the event, the Patten Report expresses some irritation with the 1998 Act and certainly does not accept its degree of centralized control, as shall be seen. The Police Authority itself undertook a major consultation exercise and published its findings and proposals in *Everyone's Police* (1996). More radical reform models were floated by the Northern Ireland Office in a paper in 1998, *Your Voice, Your Choice*. However, these papers were overtaken by the Patten Review.

The efforts of the RUC itself to gain cross-community acceptance have also had limited impact, as may be evidenced by the level of Catholic recruitment, which fell to 8 per cent by 1998. The reasons for this level of support are probably two-fold. One is the widespread nationalist ambivalence towards the police, which means that relatively few members of that community will receive encouragement from their peers or families to join.[17] The second problem is intimidation: it is not by chance that Catholic officers of the RUC have been statistically the most likely victims of paramilitary attack, both on and off duty.[18]

Attempts to establish local liaison committees have been sustained and widespread but have again produced, at best, mixed results.[19] Parallel to English models,[20] the concept of local liaison committees has been built upon and has also received much encouragement from the Police Authority, especially after it was placed under a duty to ascertain the views of the community on policing by article 82 of the *Police and Criminal Evidence (Northern Ireland) Order* 1989— the 'PACE Order'. Likewise, direct community input into policing has been attempted by the device of lay visiting.[21] Lay visiting was instituted in respect of designated police stations in Northern Ireland after 1990, but notably not in relation to terrorist suspects detained in the special holding centres.[22]

In conclusion, the policing reforms after 1969 have proven 'apparently extensive and significant',[23] and the RUC has become 'the most modern and professional of those forces which police ethnically divided societies'.[24] There has been liberalization in the RUC, but it is in check because of the security situation. Furthermore, democratization has not occurred at all.

The Details of the Patten Report

The fundamental difficulty in regard to policing in Northern Ireland, its political associations and identity, is readily recognized in the Patten Report (1.3):

Policing has been contentious, victim and participant in past tragedies, precisely because the polity itself has been contentious. . . . [The] identification of police and state is contrary to policing practice in the rest of the United Kingdom. It has left the police in an unenviable position, lamented by many police officers. . . . Policing therefore goes right to the heart of the sense of security and identity of both communities and, because of the differences between them, this seriously hampers the effectiveness of the police service in Northern Ireland.

It is not that nationalists are opposed to policing *per se*—the basic problem is alienation, not anarchy or even gangsterism. So, opinion surveys commissioned by the Patten Commission in fact found a high level of public satisfaction with police performance in response to the experience of mundane contacts within the previous two years—77 per cent Catholic and 69 per cent Protestant—but a much more divided view in regard to overall satisfaction—43 per cent Catholic and 81 per cent Protestant—(Patten: 3.14–3.15), 'a view owing more to political considerations than to policing concerns.' (Patten: 3.21)

In this light, it is to be expected that, according to Chris Patten himself, 'the nub is the need to depoliticise policing',[25] and this overall objective is indeed reflected in the tests adopted by the Patten Report (1.10):

1. Does this proposal promote effective and efficient policing?
2. Will it deliver fair and impartial policing, free from partisan control?
3. Does it provide for accountability, both to the law and to the community?
4. Will it make the police more representative of the society they serve?
5. Does it protect and vindicate the human rights and human dignity of all?

These tests seem appropriate and are similar to the overarching aims and objectives adopted recently for the Police Service in England and Wales.[26]

At their most abstract, the Patten objectives can be achieved by the reorientation of policing towards the support of active and equal citizenship rather than the support of a sovereign statehood. In this way, policing is to be tied directly to the aspirations and demands of the communities of Northern Ireland rather than to those of the political élites and sovereigns. At an intermediate level, this can be achieved by an overt attachment to, and furtherance of, solely those policing goals and values which, if not universal, then at least can be easily shared across communities. These include effectiveness and efficiency, representativeness, impartiality, and respect for human rights and dignity. And more specifically, the objective can be furthered by, one the one hand, banishing political personnel or political bric-a-brac from connection with police government, and, on the other hand, achieving 'normalization' so as to bring the RUC more into line with the regular features of British policing. The question to be discussed next is how far the Patten Report follows this strategy in a logical and effective manner.

Reorientation of Policing Towards the Community

The reorientation of policing comprises an emphasis on accountability to the community and community policing—institutional and stylistic changes are both canvassed.

Taking first the institutional aspects, the existing arrangements for democratic accountability are seen as deficient from the Police Authority downwards. The Police Authority is said to lack democratic credentials since it is neither elected nor sufficiently open, while the involvement of the Secretary of State—who lacks any local franchise—is seen as too direct (Patten: 5.5–5.6). There are also doubts about legal and financial accountability.

The central institution in the new regime will be a Policing Board which will replace the Police Authority. Aside from the cosmetic change of name, there may be at least four features of the new Board which represent significant changes. The first is that it is given powers to set medium term—three to five years—and annual policing objectives (Patten: 6.5–6.6). These will fit with the power of the Secretary of State—or possibly the First Minister and Deputy First Minister in due course—to set long-term objectives, and the duty of the Chief Constable to take all levels of policy aspirations into account when setting shorter-term tactical plans. However, this is not a radical change since the *Police (Northern Ireland) Act* 1998 already allows for some planning by the Police Authority and a non-statutory forerunner was produced for 1998–9. So, the main effect seems to be that the new regime is expressed in clearer terms and without some of the statutory constraints that allowed the Secretary of State to prevail over the civilian body.

The Policing Board is additionally to have responsibility for appointing all chief officers and civilian equivalents and for determining the length of their contracts, subject to approval by the Secretary of State—or Northern Ireland's First and Deputy First Ministers, the Secretary of State's successors after devolution—and subject to consultation with the Chief Constable (Patten: 6.9).

Next, the functional isolation of police government is to be ended. In future, 'the Policing Board should co-ordinate its work closely with other agencies whose work touches on public safety, including education, environment, economic development, housing and health authorities, as well as social services, youth services and the probation service, and with appropriate non-governmental organizations.' (Patten: 6.10) This would be a major innovation but again is less radical than it seems for it is very much based around partnership approaches[27] culminating in the *Crime and Disorder Act* 1998 in England and Wales.

Perhaps most eye-catching is the proposed membership of the Police Board, which is to consist of nineteen members, with ten members from the parties—and in proportion, along the d'Hondt lines—comprising the Northern Ireland Executive and nine independent members appointed by the Secretary of State from business, trade unions, voluntary organizations, community groups, and the legal profession (Patten: 6.11–13).

Community involvement is not to be limited to the Policing Board, but will become localized. Rather than rely upon the existing Community and Police Liaison Committees (CPLCs) which suffer from élitism and obscurity, a more systematic set of District Policing Partnership Boards (DPPBs) is to be established (Patten: 6.26).[28] These Boards will each consist of between fifteen to seventeen members, the majority being nominated by District Councils with a minority appointed by the Policing Board. Some of their functions would be similar to the CPLCs—advisory, explanatory and consultative—which would be achieved by monthly meetings with the police district commander who would have to take their views into account. But the Patten Report (6.33) also steps beyond this agenda and suggests that the DPPBs be allowed to raise 3p in the pound to be spent on local policing. This power is more extensive than the equivalents in England and Wales: under section 163 of the *Criminal Justice and Public Order Act* 1994, the ever-popular CCTV is the expenditure in mind; patrolling services can also be purchased to protect council property under the *Parks Regulation Acts* 1872–1974; *Public Health (Amendment) Act* 1907; *Minister of Health and Local Government Provisional Order Confirmation (Greater London Parks and Open Spaces) Act* 1967. The locus of Northern Ireland immediately gave rise to the allegation that this provision would allow Sinn Féin dominated councils the power to find jobs for redundant paramilitaries. Whilst the pluralization of policing is a desirable objective, perhaps it would be wise to specify some limits on the type of expenditure as in England and Wales[29] and some safeguards such as the registration checks under Part V of the *Northern Ireland (Emergency Provisions) Act* 1996 in relation to private police recruits.

As for policing styles, there is further impetus toward policing with the community. 'Community policing' should become the core function of policing (Patten: 7.9). In practice, this objective requires the adoption of the precepts of problem-oriented policing, including neighbourhood policing teams dedicated to a locale over a period of time and working in association with groups and official agencies to identify and resolve policing and safety issues within the area.[30] Conversely, the police should move away from the trappings of militarism—fortified buildings, armoured vehicles, and reliance upon Army support. But disarming the police is seen as unwise and possibly unlawful under health and safety legislation, as well as giving rise to liability in negligence such as was established in the case of the IRA mortar attack on Newry police station: *Donaldson v Chief Constable of the Royal Ulster Constabulary and the Police Authority for Northern Ireland*.[31] At best, the routine issuance of firearms should be kept under review and alternatives to plastic baton rounds be investigated (Patten: 8.19, 9.16).

The new community-style policing must also be reflected in changes in management and personnel. The current structure is criticized as akin to military hierarchical command rather than civilian management.[32] This disposition can be altered by flattening the chain of command by phasing out chief superintendents, and granting greater local power to district police commanders—mostly superintendents who would then work in divisions based on District Council boundaries alongside the proposed District Policing Partnership Boards; by the introduction of greater civilianization of posts and contracting out of functions, and by personnel rotation so that service in a specified community becomes the norm rather than service in detached squads such as Special Branch (Patten: 10.7, 10.16, 10.22, 12.4, 12.9). The Special Branch, a 'force within a force' consisting of around 850 officers, is to be reduced and more embedded within the Crime Branch (Patten: 12.11).

Whatever the changes in institutions and style to achieve democratic and devolved accountability, it is emphasized that policing is to remain unitary. Thus, there is to be no two-tier system in which local community policing is divorced from central crime squads as advocated by some commentators.[33] Any such division makes little sense in terms of principle, and it may prove practically impossible to distinguish the local/central or civil/political functions. Furthermore, the central police would face even deeper antagonism than the RUC, and that hostility could have repercussions on the standing of the local police, amounting to 'a gross waste of public funds and a threat to civil liberties'.[34] Likewise, the Patten Committee (12.8):

. . . would certainly reject any idea of an upper tier of policing superior to neighbourhood police officers, and implicitly excused from community policing obligations [which would] seem likely to exacerbate the divisions in Northern Ireland society rather than heal them. . . . There are also salutary experiences elsewhere in the world of localising police services to the point of fragmentation . . . A multiplicity of police services would not lead to effective or efficient policing.

A community patrol scheme was rejected by the Secretary of State in 1974 on RUC advice,[35] and the Hunt Report[36] likewise suggested that they are likely to be less efficient than the experienced and professional main police body. Secondly, they would 'lessen the likelihood of uniformity in matters of policy requiring sensitive but strong central direction'. Herein lies the heart of the problem. For local forces to remain acceptable both to participants and the populace, they must to some extent reflect the ethos of their locality. If this means, say, in South Armagh, condoning the activities of dissident republican paramilitaries, their existence becomes pernicious rather than helpful.

Nor is decision-making to be diffused across agencies: '. . . the Chief Constable should be deemed to have operational responsibility for the exercise of his or her functions and the activities of the police officers and civilian staff under his or her direction and control. Neither the Policing Board nor the Secretary of State (or Northern Ireland Executive) should have the power to direct the Chief Constable as to how to exercise those functions.' (Patten: 6.21)

However, explanatory accountability will remain in cases where subordinate accountability is overridden, subject to 'national security, sensitive personnel matters and cases before the courts' (Patten: 6.22). The Police Board will also be entitled to initiate an inquiry (6.23) or to require the Police Ombudsman, the Inspectorate of Constabulary or the Audit Office to conduct or contribute to an inquiry into policing matters in the same way as the Home Secretary can intervene under section 44 of the *Police (Northern Ireland) Act* 1998. This is a vital reform and should improve upon the *ad hoc*, badly designed, and secretive inquiries such as the Stalker/Sampson investigation into police shootings in 1982.[37]

Overall, the reorientation towards community policing tessellates well with policing trends in Britain and so should suit RUC managers (Patten: 10.4). It is also acceptable to political masters in London, for the Northern Ireland Office paper, *Policing in the Community*[38] likewise was based around a new Police Commission which would establish community policing and represent the community. Police-community partnership is enshrined within the *Crime and Disorder Act* 1998, while problem-oriented policing is favoured by the influential Audit Commission.[39] The objective also could be said to fit with the overall ethos of the Belfast Agreement, which emphasizes power-sharing and power-spreading and de-emphasizes sovereign statehood. However, the engagement of the community is uneven. On the one hand, the powers of the Police Board appear rather diluted. Some profile-raising will undoubtedly be achieved by more open working styles—including the requirement to publish annual reports under section 47 of the 1998 Act: a stark contrast to the three reports it managed in its first 20 years—and by liaison with the DPPBs. But there are dangerous exceptions to its ambit in relation to national security and sensitive personnel matters that may obstruct its usefulness. On the other hand, the powers granted to DPPBs appear somewhat generous, given their lack of practical policing experience and oversupply of partisanship. Reliance upon elected representatives is likely to emphasize majoritarianism rather than plurality.

Attachment to Universal Goals and Values

If Queen and country can no longer offer rallying calls around which to inspire the duty and valour of police officers, then a new morality must take its place and one which can appeal across the sectarian divide. That new morality lies principally in human rights: 'It is a central proposition of this report that the fundamental purpose of policing should be, in the words of the Agreement, the protection and vindication of the human rights of all.' (Patten: 4.1) The choice is predictable but no less worthy for being so.[40] It chimes with the forthcoming implementation of European Convention rights under the *Human Rights Act*

1998, and it also sits well with the overall ethos of the Belfast Agreement pursuant to which a new Northern Ireland Human Rights Commission has been established under Section 68 of the *Northern Ireland Act* 1998.

This emphasis upon human rights is reflected in a number of ways in the Patten Report. First, it proffers a new oath to be taken by officers:

I hereby do solemnly and sincerely and truly declare and affirm that I will faithfully discharge the duties of the office of constable, and that in so doing I will act with fairness, integrity, diligence and impartiality, uphold fundamental human rights and accord equal respect to all individuals and to their traditions and beliefs. (Patten: 4.7)

The amended oath in Schedule 2 of the *Police (Northern Ireland) Act* 1998 had already removed the English-based reference to the Queen, but the expression of values recommended by Patten goes a stage further.

There is to be a new code of ethics, replacing the code established in 1987. The new version—which could be issued under sections 37 and 38 of the 1998 Act—will include substantive guidance on covert policing along the lines signalled by the Association of Chief Police Officers, but it is not clear how far it will otherwise differ from the existing RUC Code, *Professional Policing Ethics*, which was produced in 1987.[41] Respect for the Code is part of the unilateral undertakings as to service delivery in the RUC Charter of 1995. For the most part, the results have been intangible. Its contents comprise barely more than a collection of worthy platitudes, such as reminders to policemen to act with impartiality, courtesy, sense, and restraint in their private lives, matters which are already required by the police discipline code. More worthwhile and specific guidance, such as a description of good police practices in different situations and the regulation of membership of organizations which may be viewed as divisive, is omitted.

The next step in the new rights regime involves the reorientation of training. It is viewed as highly unsatisfactory that 'of 700 sessions of training there are only 2 sessions dedicated to human rights, compared with 40 of drill and 63 of firearms training; the preponderance of these last two subjects reflects the security situation that has afflicted Northern Ireland and its distorting effect on policing, including the integration of human rights into policing culture' (Patten: 4.5). Once trained, human rights awareness will become a matter on which officers are periodically appraised.

The human right of privacy is given especial prominence. Therefore, the Home Office's pending legislation on these matters, which will build upon the *Interception of Communications Act* 1985 and the *Police Act* 1997, is welcomed,[42] but it is suggested that there should be a specific Northern Ireland Commissioner and complaints tribunal to oversee the system of issuance of police warrants and authorizations (Patten: 6.44). Transparency is to be improved, such as by public meetings held by the Policing Board and the DPPBs; in addition, the police codes of practice should be publicly available

(Patten: 6.38). Finally, there will be an in-house lawyer to be consulted over human rights issues.

Another universal moral goal around which to construct policing in Northern Ireland is impartiality. This is in part to be achieved by the emphasis on human rights, whereby requirements of due process and non-discrimination are undoubtedly relevant. In addition, impartiality is to be primarily reflected in personnel changes, the hope being that a more representative police force will not only be less likely to be perceived as entertaining sectarian outlooks but also will encourage the community to see itself as having 'a stake in the police service as a whole' (Patten: 14.3). The low proportion of Catholic officers—8 per cent of the full-time complement—is the primary focus, understandably in the context of the implementation of the Belfast Agreement, though it is recognized that women and ethnic and other minorities are also under-represented. Achieving representativeness at the same time as downsizing will require considerable adroitness, but the expectation is that half of serving officers will have been recruited after 1998 within 10 years (Patten: 13.15). This turnover—aided by the retirement of the large numbers of officers recruited in the 1970s—allows for major reconfiguration of the profile of the police population, and so the aim is to double Catholic representation in four years and to achieve around 30 per cent—still a shortfall on a population of 43 per cent—within 10 years (Patten: 14.10). The retained part-time RUC Reserve faces even larger changes since it is overwhelmingly Protestant in composition (Patten: 12.18). But, given it is to expand from 1300 to 2500, it is set to reach a 40 per cent Catholic profile in 10 years (Patten: 14.12).

Can these targets for sectoral recruitment realistically be met? There is some hope that in the circumstances of peace and community involvement in policing, Catholic recruitment will naturally progress—during the precarious ceasefires in 1995 and 1998 it rose to around 20 per cent. But more must be done to achieve the suggested targets, and the envisaged measures include: the removal on community bars to recruitment, including the opening up of Catholic schools to police visits and the repeal by the Gaelic Athletic Association of its rule 21, which prohibits members of the police in Northern Ireland from being members of the Association; a police cadet scheme; and the civilianization of recruitment by the use of a recruitment agency (Patten: 15.4–15.8). However, in order to bring about the rapid dramatic change which is felt to be necessary, a quota system of 50/50 Catholic/Protestant recruitment is to be set for 10 years (Patten: 15.10). Though this balance broadly reflects the balance in the target population and is subject to an overriding requirement of merit, it would require legislative amendment since quotas of this kind breach of the *Fair Employment (Northern Ireland) Act* 1989—though it is asserted that, unlike any quota systems for men/women, there would be no breach of European Community laws. Nevertheless, positive discrimination in this way seems paradoxical, intrusive, and insulting—is it sufficient to be Catholic or must the recruit also be a true green nationalist, as suggested by O'Leary?[43] It is also probably unrealistic, given that it has been consistently rejected in all anti-discrimination legislation in Northern Ireland since 1969.[44] On the other hand, there may be no legal objection to the setting of targets,[45] nor arguably to the geo-demographic profiling of candidates, which, in pursuit of policing objectives, takes account of a much wider range of social characteristics—including place of residence—than religious affiliation.[46] It is also regrettable that Patten did not comment on the failure to bring the police within section 75 of the *Northern Ireland Act* 1998: the legal duty to have due regard to the need to promote equality of opportunity.

Two further very controversial aspects of the proposals on recruitment include the willingness to accept persons with relatively minor criminal offences—but certainly not serious or terrorist offenders (Patten: 15.13). Equally, membership of Loyal orders or groups such as the Ancient Order of the Hibernians should not disbar recruitments—the contrary was suggested by the Hunt Report[47]—but there should be a register of such membership, an idea reflecting the treatment of Freemasonry in English criminal justice professions (Patten: 15.16).[48] Though some commentators have argued for a complete ban,[49] a prohibition would entail a number of disadvantages. There might arise a breach of various European Convention rights, as alleged in the case of *Grande Oriente d'Italia di Palazzo Giustiniani v Italy* (1997)[50] in which the prohibition of judicial membership of Freemason lodges in Italy was questioned. There might also be a failure to adhere to the goal that community characteristics should be reflected back by the police. Any form of involvement which displays in public strong adherence to one community can be dealt with by police disciplinary rules.[51]

It shall be assumed that the United Kingdom Government does genuinely wish to increase Catholic recruitment into the RUC, despite ample evidence that, in general terms, 'state élites exploit ethnic divisions at the same time as they publicly deplore them'.[52] The likely outcome of the proposed changes will very much depend on the success of the overall 'peace process'. Without it, glossy advertising, familiarization, or special access courses and personal visits to applicants from the under-represented community will fail, as would the removal of republican intimidation and the establishment of non-conflict.[53]

A more general question-mark over attempted changes to police cultures in these ways is the extent to which they will be 'internalized' or simply seen as external obstacles to be circumvented. Internal cultures run especially deep in the RUC.[54] Here, the Patten Commission offers a more sophisticated and thorough overhaul than the Hunt review and also has the advantage of being located within the narrative of a 'peace process'. But even the Patten Report arguably underplays the difficulty of impacting on the closed world of police cultures, and arguably exacerbates the situation by accepting that the RUC's Training Centre at Garnerville is inadequate and that a new dedicated facility is required (Patten: 16.6). The isolation of the Northern Irish police in this way is not helpful—the model in Britain is much more regional or even national. On the other hand, a high degree of civilian input is to be introduced (Patten: 16.9), and the emphasis in the Report on human rights as a part of professionalization is likely to be fruitful over a period of years.[55]

Finally, the grand value of the rule of law—accountability to the law—is also to be respected. Here, the Patten Commission is content to defer to the work of one of its members, Dr Maurice Hayes, whose report, *A Policing Ombudsman?*[56] is viewed as 'a most effective mechanism for holding the police accountable to the law.' (Patten: 6.41).

The Hayes Report has been largely implemented by Part VII of the *Police (Northern Ireland) Act* 1998. At the core of the reformed system is a Police Ombudsman, an office which commenced in mid-2000 and filled by Nuala O'Loan. By section 51 of the 1998 Act, the Police Ombudsman is charged with ensuring efficacy, efficiency, and independence in the operation of the system and in a way which inspires confidence in both the public and the police. The emphasis is upon independence from the police,[57] and this is achieved in a number of ways. First, the receipt of complaints is the duty of the Police Ombudsman, who thereby, from the outset, has control over what counts as a 'complaint'—as opposed to a matter of operational direction or control which is either for the Chief Constable or Police Authority—and the way it is to be processed (section 52). Matters of concern not giving rise to any complaint by a member of the public can also be referred if desirable in the public interest by the Police Authority, Secretary of State, or Chief Constable or—by way of a new power to overcome the reluctance of the aforementioned to make referrals—can be taken up on the initiative of the Police Ombudsman. Furthermore, all police actions resulting in death must be referred by the Chief Constable (section 55). Reflecting the emphasis in the Hayes Report upon standards of service delivery as well as discipline—an idea also championed by the Northern Ireland Office[58]—there is next an encouragement for the informal resolution of complaints, provided the matter is not 'serious'—a much narrower exemption than under the previous formulation—and provided the complainant agrees (section 53). Even if these conditions are met, it remains for the Police Ombudsman to decide whether to refer the complaint and to take up the complaint again if not informally resolved.

Where the formal resolution of complaints is appropriate, the Police Ombudsman is again at centre stage. It is for the Police Ombudsman to decide how complaints—including complaints against senior officers previously falling under the jurisdiction of the Police Authority—are to be investigated (section 54), and there are three possibilities. If a complaint is 'serious'—involving especially allegations of death or serious injury cause by the police—then office of the Police Ombudsman must investigate. In other cases, either the Police Ombudsman's office itself conducts the inquiry (section 56) or may decide to leave it to the police (section 57). It is expected that most inquiries in the early days of the new system will be 'in-house', the opposite to the practice of the Garda Complaints Board in the Republic under section 6 of the *Garda Síochána (Complaints) Act* 1986.[59] In this circumstance, the Hayes Report envisaged mixed teams of both non-police and seconded police investigators.[60] To this end, the Police Ombudsman can ask for police officers, including from the RUC, to be seconded for the purpose (Schedule 3). The battle for non-police invest-igators in the complaints system has been long fought[61] and is made more rev-olutionary by the grant to them of constabulary powers (section 56(3)). But even when the investigation is left to the RUC, the Police Ombudsman remains in a supervisory position—with powers to determine and to direct the investigator (section 57). At the outcome of the investigation, the Police Ombudsman—and not the police—has control over the referral of the complaint to the Director of Public Prosecutions for possible criminal proceedings (section 58) or to make recommendations about disciplinary proceedings (section 59). The final decision on disciplinary proceedings against senior officers is left to the Police Authority. For lower-ranking officers, the Chief Constable has the power but must follow a direction to take proceedings, unless there is a later dispensation by the Police Authority.

With such a concentration of power in the hands of the Police Ombudsman, much will depend on the quality of that officer and those around her. All that remains to be undertaken in legislative terms is to address the forms and pro-cedures of disciplinary hearings. In particular, the Hayes Report sought to achieve a more variable standard of proof, a change also recommended by the existing complaints body[62] and already adopted by the courts in the Republic under the *Garda Síochána (Complaints) Act* 1986.[63] The Hayes Report also sug-gested a role for the Ombudsman in the presentation of cases and a greater inde-pendent element in decision-making. In response, section 25 allows for regulations to be made and 'a special procedure' may be established by section 59(8), so hopefully the details will follow in due course.

Removal of Political Bric-à-brac and Personnel

The divorce of policing from all aspects of political allegiances must be symbolic as well as substantive. The problem in Northern Ireland involves '. . . one com-munity effectively claiming ownership of the name of "our" police force, and the other community taking the position that the name is symbolic of a rela-tionship between the police and unionism and the British state. The argument about symbols is not an argument about policing, but an argument about the constitution.' (Patten: 17.4) Accordingly, symbols that emphasize the union with Britain are largely to be discarded. These symbols include the RUC name and badge and the flying of the Union flag, and so a restyled 'Northern Ireland

Police Service' (NIPS) is to emerge from the RUC. The Patten Report rightly emphasizes that in total these changes did not amount to the disbandment of the RUC (17.7)—it has already been remarked that in many ways a more typically British, and not Irish, police service is to emerge, and it remains a police service fastened upon the contested polity of Northern Ireland. In addition, the NIPS is itself not new—the concept was coined by the *Police (Northern Ireland) Act* 1998, section 2, to cover all public policing services in Northern Ireland. At the time, this umbrella title seemed 'a cosmetic exercise',[64] though its significance has now considerably grown. The new title appears appropriate—it fits the reforms undertaken in the *Police (Northern Ireland) Act* 1998, and it accurately describes the area and ethos of policing.[65]

Since symbolism is so important, it is therefore as expected that much initial public reaction to the Patten Report focused here. Accordingly, the change was received by unionists as an attempt to 'repudiate and insult what is currently one of the world's most professional police forces', and the Report itself was 'shoddy' and a 'gratuitous insult'.[66] The Police Federation for Northern Ireland interpreted the change of symbols as without community support and even 'a sop to Republican Terrorism',[67] its 400,000 signature petition in opposition was delivered to Downing Street in January 2000. Presumably to aid the process of digestion, as some symbols are discarded, so others are gained, in the shape of the George Cross, awarded to the RUC in November 1999 and presented by the Queen at a ceremony in Belfast in April 2000. The award could be seen as reasserting the very symbols of Britishness which are anathema to the alienated communities of Northern Ireland. On the other hand, an award to a police force about to cease to exist in its current guise could be seen as much as a retirement gong as an affirmation of continuing service.

Next, political personnel are made more distant by the recommended repeal of the power in section 39 of the *Police (Northern Ireland) Act* 1998 by which the Secretary of State may issue guidance to police as to the exercise of their functions. This power is unique to Northern Ireland and is seen as not only undesirable but also incoherent (Patten: 6.18). However, it may be necessary to replicate this power elsewhere in order to meet complaints under the European Convention that 'soft' police law cannot comply with the *Human Rights Act* 1998—as in the *Malone* case.[68] However, it is arguable that the power in section 38 to issue codes of practice, should suffice.

In other respects, the Patten Report arguably shows inconsistency with the goal of depoliticization. The political domination of the Policing Board and DPPBs runs against the strategy and produce disjunction with the aim of community acceptance: 'Even in less polarized nations, parochial community standards often fly in the face of the law and the wider public interest.'[69] The idea of an elective element within the police governing structures has been supported by the Hunt Report[70] and by the later White Paper, *Northern Ireland Constitutional Proposals*,[71] but neither had been implemented probably because of the concern that, far from being unrepresentative, it was feared that a body of elected representatives would too accurately reflect the deep sectarian divisions and political impasse which has long blighted Northern Ireland. In short, local political control could be 'recipe for disaster'.[72] It may therefore be wise at the outset to dilute the political cadre with more appointed, apolitical nominees at all levels and not just the Policing Board.[73]

Bringing the RUC Into Line with 'Normal' Policing

The 'normalization' of policing in Northern Ireland is by and large to be measured against British norms. It is perhaps remarkable that this assumption seems to be constantly made in the context of the enforcement of the Belfast Agreement and that so little effort is made either to consider precedents from the Garda Síochána or new hybrid models. The existing links with the south are indeed seen as rather stunted, but the Patten Report suggests merely that protocols about deeper co-operation be established (18.7), and that, in the meantime, exchanges of officers with either Britain or the Republic are to be confined mainly to training and work experience (18.10, 18.11, 18.17). While policing relations within the United Kingdom have been clarified by the *Criminal Justice and Public Order Act* 1994, Part X,[74] should there be a firmer North-South agenda including hot pursuit and, more importantly, cross-border policing squads, as well as the useful idea about a joint database on border criminality (Patten: 18.15)? Perhaps the unstated truth is either that these pragmatic changes would be interpreted as too suggestive of an embryo all-Ireland police or alternatively that little would be gained from adopting as a model the constitution and practices of the Republic's Garda Síochána, which far more faithfully preserves its nineteenth century origins than does the RUC.[75] Nevertheless, some attention should have been directed towards the experience of the relationship between the Republic's Minister of Justice, the police, and local communities, including the effectiveness of democratic accountability,[76] especially following its scrutiny in 1997 by the Steering Group on the Efficacy and Effectiveness of the Garda Síochána as part of the Strategic Management Initiative in the public service and the establishment in 1998 of an implementation group.[77]

An example of the British normative predominance might be the consideration of the appropriate 'peacetime' size of the RUC. It is assumed that Home Office models provide the benchmark, and, given that they would suggest a complement of 4,300 officers and 1,700 civilians, there is a perceived need to downgrade the size of the force. Nevertheless, accepting the special features of the continuance of paramilitary organizations and the possibility of severe public disorder—the national border and the distinctiveness of legal and political systems might also be counted as relevant factors—the Patten Report (9.7, 13.15) suggests a total of 7,500 (now 11,500) full-time officers and 2,500 (now 1,300) part-time reserves—retained because of the impracticality of police mutual aid and the undesirability of military aid—a reduction to be achieved in three years. The full-time reserves (around 2,900) are to be disbanded (Patten: 12.17), partly to create the flexibility for changes in the composition of personnel. These figures should also be adjusted for the civilianization of up to 1,000 posts (Patten: 10.23).

Another aspect of normalization concerns financial accountability. Her Majesty's Inspector of Constabulary[78] is critical of the current financial planning process, especially the absence of proper links between financial plans, policy plans, and strategic plans. These plans must be linked together to be effective, so the memorandum setting out the financial relationship between Secretary of State and the Policing Board should be so formulated as to ensure that there is no blurring of these responsibilities, and that the government does not, as in the past, become involved in what is properly the business of the Board: 'to determine the allocation of the budget to the Chief Constable and to hold him/her responsible for the efficient and effective use of resources' (Patten: 6.17). Greater use should also be made of the Audit Commission, the studies of which have had a major impact on British policing (Patten: 6.46).

Redolent of changes to policing styles, legal normalization is to involve the implementation of the Home Office white paper[79] on anti-terrorism laws (1998), subject to the further requirement that records be kept of stop-and-search powers—as under the *Police and Criminal Evidence (Northern Ireland) Order* 1989 (Patten: 8.14). This call is being met by the Terrorism Bill 1999–2000, clause 101 of which places a requirement on the Chief Constable of the RUC to make arrangements for records to be kept when such policing powers are exercised, unless, as will often be the case, there are reasons which make this impractical, such as weight of numbers being processed. In addition, the Patten Report (8.15) calls for the closure forthwith of the special holding centres, in which detentions and interrogations of terrorist suspects have taken place since 1972, a recommendation likewise already accepted in regard to the Castlereagh centre but not for the Gough or Strand Road (Londonderry) Centres. Next, all police custody suites are to be subject to the safeguards of video-recording and lay visiting (Patten: 8.16). These recommendations are not taken up by the first draft of the Terrorism Bill, but they are very much in line with those of the Independent Commissioner for the Holding Centres,[80] the continuation of whose office is left for future consideration by the Policing Board. Even more difficult to secure will be the suggestion that the use of plastic baton rounds also be based more firmly in legislation (Patten: 9.20). Though departmental guidelines have been issued, the security forces and their political masters have long preferred to rely upon the much looser criteria in section 3 of the *Criminal Law Act (Northern Ireland)* 1967.

Finally, one is shocked to learn of the limited use of information technology by operational RUC officers, the absence of automated fingerprint scanning and the brittle and slow command and control systems (Patten: chap.11). One expected the RUC to be at the forefront of electronic policing, but it has fallen behind British forces, which may have had the advantages of starting with later, more advanced technology and not having the temptation of putting all their eggs in the security basket. The existence of powers under section 40 of the *Police (Northern Ireland) Act* 1998 will ensure there is reform, though it is unlikely that they will formally be invoked.

Conclusions

The Patten Report can be judged according to whether the advocated reforms address the problems of Northern Ireland policing in ways which are not only relevant and helpful but also consistent with its expressed objectives. The broad answer must be in the affirmative, but many problems remain. Though the Patten Commission was supposed to resolve some of the abeyances at the time of the Belfast Agreement, much has been left uncertain and at the mercy of the discretion and interpretation of politicians and police, subject only to the scrutiny of a foreign oversight commissioner who should be in the post for five years (Patten: 19.4).

The uncertainty left in the wake of the Patten Report has been amplified by two ways in which the Secretary of State (Peter Mandelson) has reacted on behalf of the government in January 2000,[81] even though both the Patten Report (19.2) and the then Secretary of State (Dr. Mowlam) warned against cherry-picking. There are first of all uncertainties as to the pace of implementation. The Patten Report emerged initially in the unexpected, unpromising circumstances of no devolved government and no decommissioning. With the suspension of devolved government, the same or similar circumstances apply. The changes in the structural accountability of the police may still be feasible come what may, but even the Patten Report believes that the rest depends on the security situation (7.1), a contingency which others have underlined with even greater vehemence.[82] In response, the Secretary of State has guaranteed implementing legislation sometime during the 1999–2000 Parliamentary session[83] and has even emphasized that the reforms:

. . . stand alone on their own merits and independently from the Good Friday agreement. I intend that the reform of the police in Northern Ireland will continue, whatever cloud happens to gather over the institutions of the Good Friday agreement. (Mandelson, P., *Statement on the Patten Report*, HC Debs. 342 at col.854.)

But the pace of implementation of many of the changes—especially in regard to the size of the establishment and the treatment of the Special Branch—is expressed as contingent on the security situation which is expressly for the Chief Constable 'in the first instance'.[84]

Secondly, there are uncertainties as to the extent of implementation. It was always likely that the major fundamentals of reform would be actioned, since they fit with the discourses of managerialism and service delivery[85] which have prevailed for some years within the realm of British policing. Even the more radical values of equality and individual rights arrive at the opportune time when the police throughout the United Kingdom face up to the implementation of the *Human Rights Act* 1998 and the MacPherson Report on the Stephen Lawrence case[86]—both decisive steps towards ethical policing and away from the pragmatism of the Runciman Report.[87] In the event, Secretary of State Mandelson[88] has indeed accepted in outline the ethical reforms—including an emphasis on human rights, as embodied in a statutory code of ethics, and a new training college—as well as the main structural modifications, such as the reductions in overall personnel numbers but with increased Catholic recruitment, the establishment of a Policing Board, the reorganization of police service delivery based on district council boundaries and with greater empowerment of divisional commanders, reforms in technology, and an oversight commissioner.

But these reforms are not adopted exactly as the Patten Report envisaged. For example, the new oath of office will only apply to new recruits, and the registration of organizational membership is to be transcribed onto individual personnel files and not into a central database. Next, the DPPBs are shorn of their controversial executive features to purchase policing services or equipment—on the pretext of awaiting a wider criminal justice review. They emerge as rather more amorphous District Policing Partnerships (DPPs), and, in a further departure from the Patten Report, there is only to be one body instead of four for Belfast, diminishing any chance that a smaller political party such as Sinn Féin could gain control. In addition, the Special Branch is to remain distinct from the CID and under separate management, until the Chief Constable advises otherwise. Furthermore, the controversial recruitment quota is to be reviewed on a triennial basis. Presumably, the hope is that the device can be dropped sooner than planned. Finally, there are significant modifications in the implementation of the changes to name and emblems. It is accepted that there must be a new name 'to signal the new beginning'.[89] But the transition is eased by promising that it will not occur until autumn 2001. In an even more conciliatory gesture— at least to unionists—the design of new police emblems, if any, is left for the future and for the discretion of the new Policing Board.

In some respects, there has been silence in response to the Patten Report. As yet, no pronouncement has been made in relation to several important recommendations, including the timetable for implementation and the choreography of implementation—especially the question of how soon the DPPs and oversight commissioner will be in place so as to have any impact on the process. Nor has there been any mention of the sensitive security-related proposals such as oversight of covert surveillance or research on weaponry.

Even if implemented in full, what would be the result? The Patten Report emphasized that it was not intended to bring about disbandment, though the NIPS will be depicted in some quarters as the 'New Ireland Police Service', which may in part account for the government's emergent preference for the less adaptable title 'Police Service of Northern Ireland'.[90] However, rather than study the nuances of nomenclature, a wider perspective ought to be taken. The devil in the Patten Report is not in the detail. Rather, the concern surrounds the overall philosophy being pursued: a fissure between police and state, as dramatized through the removal of the symbolic linkages. The later evidence is that this symbolism is unacceptable to the unionist population whose representatives have claimed that the government's reform package 'degrades, demeans and denigrates an honourable force that has stood four-square between the law-abiding community . . . and the terrorists for the past 30 years . . .'.[91] A question then arises as to whether it is really such an important issue for nationalists and whether, if not implemented, the result would be to discourage recruitment. This debate reflects more deep-seated perceptions surrounding the Belfast Agreement itself. Is the peace process an olive branch or a fig leaf?[92] If it is an olive branch, then we should expect to witness fundamental changes of heart and a willingness to compromise and be inventive in order to create a new society. But if all that is on offer from either side is a fig leaf to cover up the embarrassment of concession and defeat of the other, then only cosmetic changes are on the table. The reaction to the Patten Report suggests that a large part of the unionist community still harbours a fig leaf mentality. If correct, there arise major problems concerning the local 'ownership' of the Patten process. The Patten blueprint already suffered from the problem that it did not involve at any stage a majority of residents of Northern Ireland but was delivered from the great and the good, most of whom were outsiders. Neither was its birth monitored by a Northern Ireland Assembly or Executive. And then there is the foreign oversight commissioner whose very existence suggests that the locals cannot be trusted to internalize the changes or to implement them with good grace.

At the other end of the scale, there are doubts whether the Patten reforms really would provide a sufficiently new beginning for policing in Northern Ireland. Other radical reforms around policing have been eschewed by the Patten Commission. These include the establishment of a truth and reconciliation commission and the outright abolition of special anti-terrorism laws (Patten: 1.6), though whether either reform would be productive is debatable.[93] Additional areas left unconsidered are the Royal Irish Regiment, whose origins give rise to a legacy of distrust,[94] and mechanisms of accountability such as coroners' courts or civil action. For his part, the current Secretary of State has likewise rejected a wider reform agenda involving the Royal Irish Regiment.[95]

Almost all Northern Ireland citizens share an interest in personal security, which might be drawn upon to foster interest in devices such as local liaison committees, lay visitors, partially elective police boards, and neighbourhood watch schemes. As the Patten Report identifies, only at such a popular level of involvement can there be located self-interest in contact with the police common to both communities in Northern Ireland. Only from such mutually beneficial contact can there grow respect between police and community in Northern Ireland. This scenario assumes that the RUC can reveal itself in its dealings with both sides of the political divide as fair, impartial, and effective. If, on the other hand, its true colours turn out to be as a sectarian oppressor, then this revelation will produce an unanswerable argument for more fundamental change amounting to disbandment. In the meantime, the hope must be that both police and community are prepared to make the radical foray into post-sovereignty policing as outlined by the Patten Report.

Since the completion of this chapter, the Police (Northern Ireland) Act 2000 has been passed by way of implementation of much of the Patten Report. The Act provides for the constitution of the Police Service of Northern Ireland (incorporating the Royal Ulster Constabulary), governed by the Northern Ireland Policing Board and District Policing Partnerships (which are not granted powers to purchase services on top of normal policing). An implementation oversight commissioner (Tom Constantine—former head of the US Drugs Enforcement Administration) has already been appointed.

ENDNOTES

* The author thanks his colleagues Dr Adam Crawford and Dr David Wall for valuable comments on this paper.
1. McPhilemy, S., *The Committee* (Boulder, CO: Roberts Rinehart, 1999).
2. Weitzer, R., *Transforming Settler States* (Berkley, CA: University of California, Press, 1990), 3–4.
3. Patten Report (The Independent Commission on Policing for Northern Ireland), *A New Beginning: Policing in Northern Ireland* (Belfast: Northern Ireland Office, 1999). Hereafter referred to in the text as (Patten).
4. Mitchell Report (1996), *Report of the International Body on Decommissioning*, Belfast: http://www.britainUSA.com/bis/nireland/mitchell.htm. Address correct as at June 2000.
5. Bowyer Bell, J., *The Secret Army: The IRA 1916–1979* (Dublin: The Academy Press, 1979).
6. Stringer, M., and McCluskey, K., 'Expectations in Ulster', *Policing*, 6 (1990): 363; Weitzer, R., 'Policing Northern Ireland today', *Political Quarterly*, 58 (1987): 88.
7. Weitzer, R., 'Policing a divided society', *Social Problems*, 33 (1985): 41.
8. See: Hezlet, A. R., *The B Specials* (London: Tom Stacey Ltd, 1972); Farrell, M., *Arming the Protestants* (London: Pluto, 1983); RUC, *The RUC—A History in Brief* (Belfast: RUC, 1988); Ryder, C., *The RUC: a force under fire* (London: Methuen 1989); Walker, C., 'Police and community in Northern Ireland', *Northern Ireland Legal Quarterly*, 41 (1990): 105; Brewer, J. D., *Inside the RUC* (Oxford: Clarendon, 1991); Guelke, A., 'Policing in Northern Ireland', in B. Hadfield, (ed.), *Northern Ireland: Politics and the Constitution* (Buckingham: Open University Press, 1992); Mapstone, R., *Policing in a Divided Society* (Aldershot: Avebury, 1994); Weitzer, R., *Policing under Fire* (Albany, NY: State University of New York Press, 1995); Brewer,

J. D., Guelke, A., Hume, I., Moxon-Browne, E., and Wilford, R., *The Police, Public Order and the State* 2nd ed. (Basingstoke: MacMillan, 1996); Hainsworth, P., 'Law and order', in A. Aughey and D. Morrow (eds.), *Northern Ireland Politics* (Harlow: Longman, 1996).

9. Hunt Report, *Report of the Advisory Committee on Police in Northern Ireland* (Belfast: HMSO, 1969), Cmnd 535, 80.

10. Hadden, T. and Boyle, K., (1969). 'The Hunt Report—convincing justice', *New Law Journal*, 121 (1969): 1176.

11. Topping, I., (1991). 'The police complaints system in Northern Ireland' in A. J. Goldsmith, (ed.), *Complaints against the Police* (Oxford: Clarendon, 1991).

12. See: Report of the Working Party for Northern Ireland, *The Handling of Complaints against the Police* (London: HMSO, 1976), Cmnd.6425; Weitzer, R., 'Accountability and complaints against the police in Northern Ireland', *Political Studies*, 9 (1986): 106.

13. See: Topping, I., 'The police complaints system in Northern Ireland', *Police Journal*, 60 (1987): 252; ICPC, 'Quis custodiet ipsos custodes?', *Northern Ireland Legal Quarterly*, 39 (1988): 185.

14. See: Hamill, D., *Pig in the Middle* (London: Methuen, 1985); Pockrass, R. M., 'The police response to terrorism', *Police Journal*, 59 (1986): 143.

15. Oliver, I., *Police. Government and Accountability* (Basingstoke: MacMillan, 1987); Hunter, J., 'Ulster's secret authority', *New Law Journal*, 138 (1988): 556; Dickson, B., 'The Police Authority for Northern Ireland', *Northern Ireland Legal Quarterly*, 39 (1988): 277.

16. Walsh, D., 'Annotations to the Police (Northern Ireland) Act 1998', in *Current Law Statutes* (London: Sweet & Maxwell, 1998).

17. Cf: Northern Ireland Affairs Select Committee, *Composition, Recruitment and Training of the RUC*, H.C. 337, 1997–8, 35, 37; and McGarry, J., and O'Leary, B., *Policing Northern Ireland* (Belfast: Blackstaff Press, 1999), 16.

18. Murray, R., 'Killings of local security forces in Northern Ireland 1969–1981', *Terrorism*, 7 (1984): 11.

19. Committee on the Administration of Justice, *Police Accountability in Northern Ireland* (Belfast: CAJ, 1988), Pamphlet No.11; Walker, 'Police and community in Northern Ireland'; Weitzer, R., 'Northern Ireland's police liaison committees', *Policing*, 2 (1992): 233.

20. Home Office, Circular No.54/1982, *Local consultative arrangements between community and police* (London: Home Office, 1982); Home Office, Circular No.2/1985, *Arrangements for local consultation between the community and police forces outside London* (London: Home Office, 1985); Morgan, R. and Smith, D. J., *Coming to Terms with Policing* (London: Routledge, 1989).

21. Home Office, Circular No 12/1986, *Lay Visiting to Police Stations* (London: Home Office, 1986); James, S., 'Guarding the Guardians', *Public Law*, 432 (1988); Kemp, C. and Morgan, R., 'The Lay Visitor', *Police Review*, 97 (1989): 650; Weatheritt, M. and Vieira, C., *Lay Visiting to Police Stations* (London: Home Office Research Study, 1998), 188.

22. Committee on the Administration of Justice, *Lay Visitors to Police Stations in Northern Ireland* (Belfast: CAJ, Pamphlet No.14, 1989); Dickson, B. and O'Loan, N., 'Visiting police stations in Northern Ireland', *Northern Ireland Legal Quarterly*, 45 (1994): 210; Walker, C. and Fitzpatrick, B., 'The Independent Commissioner for the Holding Centres: a review', *Public Law*, 106 (1998).

23. McGarry and O'Leary, *Policing Northern Ireland*, 35.

24. Brewer, *Inside the RUC*; 269.

25. Patten, C., 'Changing a symbol does not dishonour the dead', *The Times*, 10 September 1999.

26. Her Majesty's Inspector of Constabulary, *Annual Report* (London: 1998–9 HC 804, 1999), 13.26, and Appendix B.

27. Crawford, A., *The Local Governance of Crime* (Oxford: Clarendon Press, 1997).

28. Cf. Hayes, M., *A Policing Ombudsman?* (Belfast: Northern Ireland Office, 1997), 18, 20.

29. Police Federation for Northern Ireland (1999), *Independent Commission on Policing for Northern Ireland: Submission to Government*. Belfast: http://www.policefed-ni.org.uk/patten/response. pdf, 3.16. Address correct as at June 2000.

30. See: Leigh, A., Read, T., and Tilley, N., *Problem-Oriented Policing: Brit Pop* (London: Home Office Crime Prevention and Detection Series Paper 75, 1996); Leigh, Read and Tilley, *Brit Pop II: Problem-Oriented Policing in Practice* (London: Home Office Police Research Studies 93, 1998); Brownlee, I., and Walker, C., 'The Urban Crime Fund and total geographic policing initiatives in West Yorkshire', *Policing and Society*, 8 (1998): 125.

31. Belfast, Queens Bench Division, 1989 (LEXIS: NILAW).
32. Her Majesty's Inspector of Constabulary, *1998/99 Inspection. RUC* (Belfast: Northern Ireland Office, 1999).
33. Boehringer, G. H., 'The future of policing in Northern Ireland', *Community Forum*, 3 (1973): 22; Weitzer, 'Policing a divided society': 33; McGarry and O'Leary, *Policing Northern Ireland*, chapter 5.
34. O'Rawe, M. and Moore, L., *Human Rights on Duty* (Belfast: Committee on the Administration of Justice, 1997), 185.
35. Rees, M., *Northern Ireland: A Personal Perspective* (London: Methuen, 1985), 117.
36. Hunt Report (1969), 95.
37. Stalker, J., *Stalker* (London: Harrap, 1988).
38. Northern Ireland Office, *Policing in the Community* (Belfast: NIO, 1994).
39. Audit Commission, *Tackling Patrol Effectively* (London: HMSO, 1996).
40. O'Rawe and Moore, *Human Rights on Duty*, 88.
41. See: Association of Chief Police Officers and HM Customs and Excise, *Codes of Practice. Covert Law Enforcement Techniques* (London, 1999); RUC Chief Constable, *Annual Report for 1987* (Belfast, 1988); RUC Chief Constable, *Annual Report for 1988* (Belfast, 1989).
42. Home Office, *Interception of Communications in the United Kingdom* (London: The Stationery Office, 1999), Cm.4368.
43. O'Leary, B., 'A bright future and less orange', *Times Higher Education Supplement*, 19 November 1999.
44. O'Rawe and Moore, *Human Rights on Duty*, 46.
45. Standing Advisory Commission on Human Rights (SACHR), *20th Report* (London: 1994–5 HC 506, 1995); Northern Ireland Affairs Select Committee, *Composition, Recruitment and Training of the RUC*, 72.
46. McGarry and O'Leary, *Policing Northern Ireland*, 57–8.
47. Hunt Report (1969), 146.
48. See also: Home Affairs Committee, *Freemasonry in Public Life* (London: 1998–9 HC 467, 1999).
49. McGarry and O'Leary, *Policing Northern Ireland*, 75.
50. *Grande Oriente d'Italia di Palazzo Giustiniani v Italy* (1997). Strasbourg: Application no.35972/97. Decision as to admissibility 21 October 1999.
51. *R v Secretary of State, ex parte William and Stewart*, Belfast: Queen's Bench Division, 1996 (LEXIS: NILAW); See also Topping, I., 'Police officers and members of organisations', *New Law Journal*, 147 (1997): 63.
52. Enloe, *Ethnic Soldiers*, ix.
53. McGarry and O'Leary, *Policing Northern Ireland*, 16–24.
54. Brewer, J. D., 'Motivation in the RUC', *Policing*, 6 (1990): 440.
55. Dixon, D., *Law in Policing: Legal Regulation and Police Practices* (Oxford: Clarendon Press, 1997).
56. Hayes Report (1997).
57. Hayes Report (1997), 11.2.
58. Northern Ireland Office, *Police Discipline Procedure* (Belfast: NIO, 1993).
59. Walsh, D., *The Irish Police* (Dublin: Round Hall Press, 1998), Chap. 9.
60. Hayes Report (1997): 13.49, 13.64, and 13.67.
61. Ibid., 13.3 *et seq.*
62. ICPC, *Annual Report for 1997* (London: 1997–8 HC 670, 1998).
63. *Grant v Garda Síochána Complaints Board and Others*, Dublin: High Court, 1996.
64. Walsh, 'Annotations to the Police Act': 8.
65. McGarry and O'Leary, *Policing Northern Ireland*, 68.
66. Trimble, D., 'You've given in to the IRA, Chris', *The Times*, 27 August, 1999, 20; D. Trimble, 'Trimble's "shoddy" rap', *Belfast Telegraph*, 9 September, 1999.
67. Police Federation for Northern Ireland, *Submission to Government*, 14:5.
68. *Malone v United Kingdom* (1984). Application No. 8691/79, (1984) Judgement of Court Ser. A. vol. 82, (1985) 7 EHRR 14.
69. Weitzer, 'Accountability and complaints against the police in Northern Ireland', 108.
70. Hunt Report (1969): 85.

71. White Paper, *Northern Ireland Constitutional Proposals* (London: HMSO, 1973), Cmnd.5259.
72. Weitzer, 'Policing Northern Ireland Today', 89.
73. Police Federation for Northern Ireland, *Submission to Government*, 3.10, 3.15.
74. Walker, C., 'Internal cross-border policing', *Cambridge Law Journal*, 56 (1997): 114.
75. See: Allen, G., *The Garda Síochána* (Dublin: Gill & MacMillan, 1999); O'Sullivan, D. J., *The Irish Constabularies* (Dingle: Brandon Books, 1999); Herlihy, J., *The Royal Irish Constabulary* (Dublin: Four Courts Press, 1997); McNiffe, L., *A History of the Garda Síochána* (Dublin: Wolfhound Press, 1997); Walsh, *The Irish Police*, 8.
76. Walsh, *The Irish Police*, chapter 12.
77. Steering Group on the Efficacy and Effectiveness of the Garda Síochána, *Report*. (Dublin: Stationery Office, 1997); Walsh, *The Irish Police*, 172, 440.
78. HMIC, *1998/99 Inspection. RUC*.
79. Home Office, *Legislation Against Terrorism: A Consultation Paper* (London: The Stationery Office, 1998), Cm.4178.
80. Walker and Fitzpatrick, 'The Independent Commissioner for the Holding Centres: a Review'.
81. Mandelson, P., *Statement on the Patten Report* (London: House of Commons' Debates vol.342, 19 January 2000).
82. Police Federation for Northern Ireland 1999: 1.9
83. Mandelson, *Statement on the Patten Report*, col. 845.
84 Ibid., cols. 847, 852.
85. Raine, J. W., and Wilson, M. J. *Managing Criminal Justice* (Hemel Hempstead: Harvester Wheatsheaf, 1993).
86. MacPherson, Sir W., *The Stephen Lawrence Inquiry* (London: The Stationery Office, 1999), Cm.4262.
87. Runciman Report, *Report of the Royal Commission on Criminal Justice* (London: HMSO, 1993), Cm.2263.
88. Mandelson, *Statement on the Patten Report*, cols. 845–850.
89. Ibid., 848.
90. Ibid.
91. Maginnis, K., *Statement on the Patten Report* (London: House of Commons' Debates vol.342, 19 January 2000).
92. Walker, C., and Weaver, R., 'A peace deal for Northern Ireland? The Downing Street Declaration', *Emory International Law Review*, 8 (1994): 817.
93. Home Office, *Legislation Against Terrorism: A Consultation Paper*. Walker, C., 'The commodity of justice in states of emergency', *Northern Ireland Legal Quarterly*, 50 (1999): 164.
94. Ryder, C., *The UDR* (London: Methuen, 1991).
95. Mandelson, *Statement on the Patten Report*, col. 860.

9

From Insulation to Appeasement: the Major and Blair Governments Reconsidered

HENRY PATTERSON

Introduction

Until the archives in London, Dublin, and Washington are open and unless the IRA provides the minutes of its Army Council, it is impossible to do more than offer a provisional judgement on the roles played by the Major and Blair Governments in the peace process. Yet, it is at least possible to lay to rest one of the myths that has already gained credence in both journalistic and academic accounts, namely that the Belfast Agreement was possible only because the Blair Government broke with the approach of John Major. The Major administration's alleged failure to exploit constructively the first IRA cease-fire in 1994 is claimed to have resulted in its collapse, endangering the historic opportunity created by the work of the real authors of the peace process, John Hume, Gerry Adams, and Albert Reynolds.[1] It was Major's insistence that the IRA begin the process of decommissioning its arsenal that, according to critics, destroyed the first cease-fire. The peace process was only to be reconstructed after a change of government. Tony Blair's resounding electoral triumph in May 1997 provided him with such a massive majority in the House of Commons that, unlike Major, he was not dependent on the ten Ulster Unionist MPs and could move away from the pre-conditions that the Major Government had imposed upon 'inclusive' negotiations.

This chapter demonstrates that there are more elements of continuity between Major and Blair than conventional critical wisdom allows. Major was prepared to make significant constitutional concessions to Irish nationalists in order to maintain the IRA cease-fire and both he and his Secretary of State for Northern Ireland, Sir Patrick Mayhew, fudged the issue of the decommissioning of weapons. Blair's willingness to test David Trimble's modernizing brand of unionism almost to the point of destruction in *The Way Forward* document of July 1999 may well in part have reflected his impregnability at Westminster, but his disregard for what 'middle Ulster' could stomach was prefigured in Major's acquiescence in the green-garlanded Framework Document of 1995.

John Major and the Legacy of the Anglo-Irish Agreement

The British and Irish States entered the peace process with very different attitudes to the political and institutional legacy of the 1985 Anglo-Irish Agreement. The difference is apparent from the history of the failed attempt in 1992 to produce an agreement through an inter-party talks process, which included unionists and the SDLP but not Sinn Féin, and involved unionist acceptance of Irish governmental involvement in the process of negotiations. The British position was set out in the paper 'Fundamental Aspects, Common Interests and Theme, Other Requirements':

An outcome to these talks would attract a wide degree of allegiance and support among the Unionist community if it were to include agreement among all the participants that Northern Ireland is part of the UK, as well as agreement on the circumstances in which that status could change. (Bew, P., Patterson, H., and Teague, P., *Between War and Peace: The Political Future of Northern Ireland* (London: Lawrence and Wishart, 1998), 81.)

The British negotiators pressed the Irish government for the amendment of the Irish Constitution to remove the territorial and jurisdictional claims made in its Articles 2 and 3 on Northern Ireland. They argued that such a clear recognition of the legitimacy of partition would make it easier for unionists to accept a settlement including power-sharing in government with nationalists, and also a clear recognition of the Irish national identity of Catholics in Northern Ireland through the creation of north-south institutions to enhance co-operation and harmonization between the two Irish States. What is quite striking is the similarity between the architecture of the type of settlement envisaged by the Northern Ireland Office in 1992 and what the parties finally signed up to on Good Friday 1998.

Of course what was very unclear in 1992 and remained a major source of Anglo-Irish tension was the role that Sinn Féin would play in such a settlement. The immediate cause of the failure of the talks in 1992 was the unbending commitment of the leader of the SDLP, John Hume, to a proposal for a six-person commission to run Northern Ireland, three of whose members would have been the nominees of the British and Irish Governments plus the European Community. Hume had been convinced since the destruction of the Sunningdale Agreement by Ulster loyalists in 1974 that progress in Northern Ireland would have to be largely externally generated by a joint Anglo-Irish approach which would, if necessary, impose change over the heads of a recalcitrant unionist community.

For Hume the Anglo-Irish Agreement was something to be built upon, not diluted to placate what he depicted as unionist intransigence. However, behind the rigidity of his position was a much more immediate concern: to block any agreement that, like Sunningdale, was based on the major centre forces of union-ism and nationalism and which excluded the extremes. Hume and the Irish Government were convinced that a talks process that excluded republicans was bound to fail. The SDLP leader had been engaged in public and private dis-cussions with the republican movement since 1988 and was convinced, as was the Irish Prime Minister Albert Reynolds, that a joint declaration by the British and Irish Governments which engaged seriously with the republican analysis of the situation would produce a cease-fire. However, if from an Irish nationalist point of view, an inclusive peace process was to succeed then it seemed to demand an offer to the republican movement that could be presented by the Sinn Féin leadership as, at the very least, creating an institutional dynamic which would lead to a united Ireland within a twenty to thirty year transitional period.

Major's attitude to the concept of 'inclusiveness'—the belief in the necessity of bringing in the extremes of republican and loyalist paramilitaries—was ini-tially considerably less enthusiastic and wholehearted than that of the Irish Government and John Hume. He was also only willing to pay a limited price to bring about this objective. As early as 1990, British intelligence sources were informing the government of the possibility that a section of the leadership of the republican movement was seeking an end to the armed conflict. It was to encourage this process that the then Secretary of State for Northern Ireland, Peter Brooke, made a speech in November 1990 in which he declared that the British Government 'has no selfish strategic or economic interest in Northern Ireland'. A secret channel of communication with republicans was reactivated in 1990 and was used intensively in 1992 and 1993. Major justified his willingness to allow behind-the-scenes talks with republicans by claiming that British offi-cials had received a message from Martin McGuinness on 22 February 1993 which began by saying: 'The conflict is over but we need your advice on how to bring it to a close'. This was denied by republicans.[2] However, a subsequent message sent by the British to Sinn Féin on 26 February does imply that they had received a communication of some significance: 'We understand and appre-ciate the seriousness of what has been said. We wish to take it seriously and at face value. . . . In view of the importance of the message it is not possible to give it a substantive reply immediately'.

What is clear, even from the version of the correspondence published by Sinn Féin, is that there was no basis for the accusations of treachery levelled at Major by the DUP's leader, Ian Paisley, when the existence of the 'back channel' was revealed in November 1993. The documents showed that the British position was no different, nor more congenial to republicans, than the stated public posi-tion of the British Government. Thus it was made clear in the important nine-paragraph British document of 19 March 1993 that for republicans to enter into dialogue it had to be clear that 'violence had genuinely been brought to an end'.[3] But most important of all was paragraph six:

The British Government does not have, and will not adopt, any prior objective of 'ending of partition'. The British Government cannot enter a talks process, or expect others to do so, with the purpose of achieving a predetermined outcome, whether the 'ending of partition' or anything else. It has accepted that the eventual outcome of such a process could be a united Ireland, but this can only be on the basis of the consent of the people of Northern Ireland. . . . But unless the people of Northern Ireland come to express such a view, the British Government will continue to uphold the union, seeking to ensure the good government of Northern Ireland, in the interests of all its people, within the totality of relationships in these islands. (Cited in *Setting the Record Straight*, Sinn Féin, 1994.)

It was, thus, unsurprising that the Major Government refused to accept the central propositions of the joint document agreed by John Hume and Gerry Adams in the summer of 1993: that it recognize the collective right to self-determination of the Irish people and adopt the role of 'persuader' of Ulster Unionists for a united Ireland. Instead, after intensive and at times heated negotiations with the Government of Albert Reynolds, the British Government agreed the Downing Street Declaration of December 1993 which recognized the right to self-determination of the 'people of the island of Ireland' but only on the basis, anathema to Sinn Féin, of separate referendums north and south, thereby allowing the unionist majority in Northern Ireland control of their constitutional destiny. Thus, while the language of the Declaration was 'green' in tone the British Government had ensured that there was no reference to a role for it of 'persuader'.

For a variety of reasons the British attitude to the developing peace process *was* more ambiguous and certainly less enthusiastic than that of most Irish nationalists. First, it was the British State that had been the object of IRA violence for more than twenty years and as such suspicion of the authenticity of peace declarations by republicans was understandable. Secondly, there was clear evidence of real divisions within the republican movement over the strategy being pursued by Adams and McGuiness. Thirdly, even if the Adams/McGuinness axis was to prevail, it was also clear that the price they expected to be able to exact from the British was a series of political and sectarian victories over unionists. Essentially the republican leadership sought British concessions to destabilize relations between the British State and the majority community in Northern Ireland, thus making joint authority the most likely intermediate outcome of the process.

Yet, while the British had good reason to be wary, the prospect of an end to IRA violence was an inevitably attractive one. Although the leadership of the republican movement had accepted that the 'armed struggle' was no nearer to forcing a British withdrawal than it had been in the period of maximum IRA violence in the early 1970s, it was still capable of pulling off 'spectaculars' like the NatWest Tower bomb in April 1993 which caused over £1 billion worth of damage.[4] Dr Martin Mansergh, Albert Reynolds's special adviser on Northern

Ireland, has dismissed the republican 'myth' that this bomb moved the British, a view that is endorsed by the 'back channel' documents where the British Government makes it clear that 'events on the ground' will make a start to dialogue impossible. Yet it is unlikely that the opportunity to end such damaging and embarrassing assaults on key financial and commercial centres would be easily foregone. This helps to explain the very different unionist reaction to the Joint Framework Document agreed by the British and Irish Governments in February 1995 as compared to the Downing Street Declaration of December 1993. Major had been keen to keep the Ulster Unionist leader informed about the progress on negotiations over the Downing Street Declaration and he had been consulted on its content, as had the head of the Church of Ireland, Dr Robin Eames. As one insider observed, 'The lesson we learned from the 1985 Anglo-Irish Agreement was that we were not going to move anything forward in Northern Ireland if the Unionists rejected the initiative. We were very keen not to be on that territory again.'[5] Yet there was no similar British attempt to gauge unionist reaction to the document they were negotiating with Dublin that set out a shared understanding on what a comprehensive settlement would look like.

British reticence may have reflected Major's failure to persuade Albert Reynolds and his successor as Taoiseach, John Bruton, to give a positive response to the 'Corfu questions'. These were the two key issues that, from a British point of view, needed to be resolved if the Framework Document was to have any chance of unionist acceptance. Major had raised them at an EU summit in Corfu in June 1994. The British had wanted the Irish to agree to both amend Articles 2 and 3 of their constitution and to acknowledge the legitimacy of British rule.[6] Reynolds conceded neither, while Bruton was concerned that if he moved further than his predecessor he would provoke a wave of nationalist criticism from Fianna Fáil in opposition.

The amendments to the constitution which Bruton inherited from the previous government were judged by the Irish Attorney General to have 'probably' removed the jurisdictional claim in Article 3 but insufficient to deal with the territorial claim in Article 2. As for the British demand that the Framework Document recognize the legitimacy of its jurisdiction in Northern Ireland, this was rejected as too 'emotive': a far-reaching change which challenged directly the core tenet of the republican movement. The Irish response was a predictable and understandable one. They saw the Framework Document through a more 'principled' prism than the British. From the Irish perspective it was part of the process of 'bringing in the extremes': since the Northern Ireland 'moderates' had consistently failed to bridge the divide and neutralize their respective extremes, the Downing Street Declaration was read as a way of opening the process of negotiating a comprehensive settlement including the 'two extreme poles of the problem'. As well as failing to come up with the answers that Major wanted to his Corfu questions, the Irish were intent that Strand Two of the

Document—dealing with North–South relations—would provide a dynamic set of institutions with extensive 'executive', 'harmonizing', and 'consultative' functions.

Major has blamed himself for 'not injecting a wider political perspective into the drafting' of the Framework Document:

I was heavily preoccupied in 1994 with the build-up to the cease-fire. I did not focus adequately on the fine print and the tone of the draft texts until early 1995, by which time it was too late to reshape them fundamentally. Officials had done an expert job, but the end product was not user-friendly. The texts were long and dense. . . . And the language was more 'green' than the substance. (Major, J., *The Autobiography* (London: HarperCollins, 1999), 423.)

The leak of a draft of the Document to *The Times* and the interpretation put on it by Matthew d'Ancona, the pro-unionist leader writer who wrote the accompanying story, caused consternation in Downing Street and fury amongst Ulster Unionists. D'Ancona's comment—'The British and Irish governments have drawn up a document that brings the prospect of a united Ireland closer than it had been at any time since partition'[7]—may have exaggerated the prospects of a united Ireland but the Document was a recipe for a very advanced form of north–south co-operation, well beyond anything that would have been politically acceptable to unionists. Although Mo Mowlam, when she became Secretary of State, appeared to see the Northern Ireland Office as pro-unionist,[8] the negotiation of the Framework Document tells a different story. What seems to have been lacking, despite the involvement of some 'native' Northern Ireland civil servants in the negotiations over the functions of the north–south bodies, was any serious reflection on how such an apparently strong set of links with Dublin would play in 'middle Ulster', let alone the loyalist heartlands. Clearly one object lesson of the Anglo-Irish Agreement with its implicit disregard for the opinions of those senior 'natives' like Sir Kenneth Bloomfield, head of the Northern Ireland Civil Service (NICS), who was excluded from the negotiating process, was that advancement did not come to those locals whose critical comments might be read as signs of a unionist agenda. The NIO's willingness to accept transport networks as an area for executive action, including ports, and which the Irish negotiators interpreted as a willingness to accept an integrated transport plan for the island as whole, is difficult to explain in other terms. How the fiercely loyalist port of Larne would respond to being part of this all-Ireland initiative does not appear to have been considered.[9]

The leak had immediate effect in that transport and 'animal, fish and plant health'—which the Irish had pressed for inclusion in the 'executive functions' category—were demoted to the less frightening 'harmonizing level'. Nevertheless, the areas identified for executive functions, EC programmes and initiatives, and culture and heritage were, from Dublin's point of view, in themselves a significant improvement on that which had been on offer at

Sunningdale. In 1973 a proposal to allocate the Council of Ireland functions in the area of 'Culture and Arts' had been dismissed in a report by three officials, including the then head of the NICS: 'For a government to hand over its functions in respect of arts and culture to some international authority would be to abdicate its authority'.[10] In 1995 the leak produced concessions to realism if not to the coherence or inherent logic of the Document. Thus, in paragraph 28 the process by which the two governments would designate the various functions of the north–south body was now made less peremptory by the need to 'to seek agreement in discussion with the relevant political parties in Northern Ireland'. A new 'illustrative' paragraph 33 was added to reassure apprehensive unionists that in the proposed areas for 'harmonization', such as agriculture, the intent was to promote research and training, while in the field of education it entailed merely the 'mutual recognition of teacher qualifications'.

Despite these last-minute changes, the Document had, as Major recognized, 'failed conclusively' when unionist dissatisfaction with Molyneaux's inability to prevent another apparent political reverse forced his resignation. If 'cross-borderism' had been accompanied by a clear Irish commitment to remove the territorial and jurisdictional claim, events may have unfolded rather differently. But there was no such commitment. Moreover, despite the strong opposition of Sir Patrick Mayhew, the section on constitutional issues contained a restatement of Brooke's incentive for the Provisional IRA: 'they [the British Government] reiterate that they have no selfish strategic or economic interest in Northern Ireland'. In their eagerness to entice the Provisionals down the democratic road, the British pledged that 'their jurisdiction will be exercised with rigorous impartiality. . . . It will be founded on the principles of full respect for, and equality of, civil, political, social and cultural rights and freedom from discrimination for all its citizens, on parity of esteem, and on just and equal treatment for the identity, ethos and aspirations of both communities'.[11] Two things are evident from this language. First, the easy acceptance by the British of the discourse of the Department of Foreign Affairs on the nature of the subtext of the Agreement. The Irish argument, unchallenged by the NIO or Downing Street, was that in exchange for their acceptance of the consent principle, there had to be corresponding agreement on the conditions and relationships which would prevail 'for as long as Northern Ireland is under British jurisdiction'.[12] From this there seemed to flow, at least to many mainstream unionists, a demeaning willingness to accept the most lurid nationalist view not simply of the supposed infamies of unionist rule up to 1972, but even the current Sinn Féin view: that, despite the substantial expansion of the catholic middle class under two and a half decades of direct rule and the implementation of an extremely tough fair employment regime,[13] Northern Ireland is an 'apartheid state'.

It was the damage inflicted by the Framework Document on John Major's relationship with the majority community in Northern Ireland that, in part, explains what nationalists have criticized as his allegedly 'niggardly' and 'prevaricating' response to the first IRA cease-fire. Major had condoned a strongly 'green' document that the Irish Government had assured him was needed by Adams and McGuinness to maintain the cease-fire. Yet he knew that the IRA continued to recruit 'volunteers' and to target prospective victims and that there was substantial resistance to the Adams strategy within the organization. It is thus true that British insistence on the 'clarification' of the permanence of the first cease-fire and the associated demand for IRA decommissioning before Sinn Féin could enter into political talks was in part a result of unionist pressure. However this reflected not so much Major's narrow majority at Westminster, the factor cited by many nationalist and journalistic critics, as a genuine democratic and moral dilemma. Politically there was no point in satisfying republicans at the expense of driving mainstream unionists out of negotiations, unless London had the stomach for joint authority. Although an exotic pamphlet produced by some academics close to Kevin MacNamara, the former shadow Northern Ireland Secretary of State, had supported joint authority,[14] under Blair the party distanced itself from such ideas; there was no serious prospect of it being on the agenda in London. Progress therefore demanded that unionists be brought back into a more constructive relationship with London by adopting a fairly robust line on decommissioning. It could also be pointed out to those, like Garret Fitzgerald and Albert Reynolds, who criticized the British for introducing decommissioning as a precondition after the cease-fire when, they claimed, it had not been mentioned during the negotiations, that Sir Patrick Mayhew had made clear in a radio interview on 10 October 1993 that the IRA would have to make available its guns and explosives to show that violence was over. There was also the *Irish News* interview on 8 January 1994 where Gerry Adams criticized Mayhew for stating, after the Downing Street Declaration, that talks between Sinn Féin and the Government would concern the decommissioning of weapons.[15]

Major's alleged 'binning' of the Mitchell Report on decommissioning is usually at the centre of critiques of his handling of the peace process and is linked to Sir Patrick Mayhew's much criticized three point plan for decommissioning. This contained 'Washington Three', the demand for some actual decommissioning of arms before talks could include Sinn Féin. But, as Norton has pointed out, 'Washington Three' incensed Unionists and Conservative back-benchers because it was seen as a softening of the Government's position on arms which now amounted to a request for gesture from the IRA.[16] The central recommendation of the Mitchell Report:, for decommissioning to be carried on in parallel with the talks, had been denounced by Mitchell McLaughlin of Sinn Féin as 'Washington Three by instalments'. Moreover, there was mounting evidence of a shift in the balance of force within republicanism towards the more militaristic elements who were unhappy with the cease-fire. By the end of 1995 the IRA, using the *nom de guerre* 'Direct Action against Drugs' had killed six alleged drug dealers. Those who criticized Major were implicitly arguing that he should attempt to pressurize mainstream unionists to sit down with Sinn Féin at a time when, had they done so, their support base would have revolted against what loyalist ultras would have depicted as capitulation to the threat of renewed violence. The critics also conveniently ignore the fact that the decision to plant the Canary Wharf bomb of February 1996 had been made *before* the Mitchell Report had been published.

Major's only significant negative legacy to Tony Blair was the joint communiqué he agreed with the Taoiseach, John Bruton, on 28 February 1996 which provided for elections and a definite date for the start of all-party talks, the latter being a Sinn Féin demand. This gave the republican movement the distinct impression that bombs in British cities could produce political results. It slowed down the process by which those, like Adams, who were prepared to put an end to the 'armed struggle' but could still be tempted to use the threat of 'hard men' breathing down their neck to extract destabilizing concessions, were forced to rely solely on their substantial but limited electoral mandate. It also encouraged the notion within Labour's government-in-waiting that the first cease-fire could have been saved by a more 'flexible' attitude towards republicanism.

Major's private calculation—'I had to reckon on a long haul'—which would allow the costs Adams had to pay in lost support in Ireland and the US to force republicans to accept a democratic settlement, was fundamentally a sound one.[17] In the short term, Hume's bitter condemnation of him for 'sabotaging' the peace process was the conventional wisdom in nationalist Ireland although not in the US. Adams was successful in persuading even moderate nationalists that the 'Brits' were to blame and Sinn Féin's electoral star continued in the ascendant. Yet, the relatively half-hearted and ineffectual nature of the IRA's return to violence was a fundamental indicator that the 'long war' for national liberation, as the veteran republican Bernadette MacAliskey noted, had become little more than a squalid bargaining counter in Sinn Féin's struggle for more influence within a reformed partition settlement.[18]

New Labour and Northern Ireland

Tony Blair's first major speech on Northern Ireland contained a much more vigorous championing of the Union than anything delivered by his predecessor. This in part reflected the need to still traditional unionist fears of the pro-unity sentiments of sections of the Labour party. Blair had already removed the Irish nationalist sympathiser, Kevin MacNamara, from the position of shadow Northern Ireland Secretary. Moreover, the party's 'unity by consent' policy had been dropped in favour of a formulation favouring a settlement based on the reconciliation of the 'two traditions' on the basis of the principle of consent. However Mo Mowlam, MacNamara's replacement, had declared that the '*status quo* is not an option' and in her John Smith Memorial Lecture in June 1996 made it clear that a new IRA cease-fire should lead to rapid political move-ment.[19] Mowlam would never succeed in diminishing initial unionist suspicions that she had a pro-nationalist inclination. Indeed, there was very little evidence that she wanted to try or even that she understood her relationship with main-stream unionism to be a problem. An insouciant disregard for mastering the details of her brief was inevitably amplified as a problem by the serious illness which disrupted her time at Stormont. The result was that there was little effective senior political input from Belfast to the formulation of Blair's policy. What input there was tended to reflect the strong anti-unionist bias of those sec-tions of civil society in Northern Ireland with access to Hillsborough Castle.

This in particular contributed to the poor relationship Mowlam had with the Ulster Unionist leader, David Trimble. Blair was aware of the problem and explained it to leading Irish-American politicians:[20]

The Unionist community felt isolated in many ways. The Irish Government supported the Nationalist side, whereas the British government obviously had to take account of both communities. This led the Unionists to resist all change. . . . As far as Trimble was concerned he had come a good deal further than many Unionists wanted him to, for example accepting North-South structures. (*Irish Times*, 17 February 1998.)

Despite this perception Blair, like Major, continued with a policy that was seri-ously affected by the desire to restore the IRA cease-fire, even when this meant the adoption of positions which threatened Trimble's ability to sell a difficult deal to mainstream unionism. The Forum elections in May 1996 had shown a strengthening of the political extremes and, although Trimble's party remained the largest, there was no doubting the strong showing of his major critics, Paisley and to a lesser extent Bob McCartney.

Blair maintained the key role assigned to former Senator George Mitchell as chairman of the talks process, despite the fact that Mitchell's judgement on both the sincerity of the republican movement towards the decommissioning issue and its support for the principles of democracy and non-violence had been put in question by the ending of the first cessation. What the *Daily Telegraph* deplored as a demeaning 'internationalisation' of the negotiations[21] was an important indication of how the Major and Blair Governments maintained an implicitly contractualist view of the Union as far as Northern Ireland was con-cerned. Unionists could look to them to respect the principle of majority con-sent in relation to the question of the ultimate constitutional destiny of Northern Ireland. However, given the existence of a substantial dissident minority and the extent of Britain's financial and military support for the region, unionists should not object to Northern Ireland becoming a constitutional and social laboratory.

Blair's attitude to the republican movement was based on the acceptance that, while Adams and McGuinness wanted to travel a solely political path, their commitment was insufficient by itself given the long history of involvement in terrorist activity. However, this did not entail a hard line on decommissioning.

A new IRA cease-fire in July 1997 ushered the republican movement into the talks process in September and the swift and corresponding exit of Paisley and McCartney, but not Trimble. Rather than press Adams on the weapons issue, Blair wanted an acceptance by Sinn Féin of the consent principle which, he believed, 'would make a huge difference'.[22] Up to the signing of the Belfast Agreement the focus of the Prime Minister's involvement was on the constitutional problems that unionists had with the approach of the Framework Document, especially in the light of the failure of the Irish to move radically enough on the issue of Articles 2 and 3. Thus, the 'Heads of Agreement' document which he and the Taoiseach Bertie Ahern negotiated in January 1998, showed that both governments accepted that a key part of the Framework's conceptual apparatus—the notion of a Council of Ireland with explicit 'dynamic', 'harmonizing', and 'executive' powers—would have to be jettisoned. The same document also made reference to a Northern Ireland Assembly and provision for some east-west link, recalling the idea of a 'Council of the Isles' so beloved by Trimble's predecessor, Lord Molyneaux.[23] The republican response was swift: on 9 February 1998 the IRA shot dead an alleged drug dealer in Belfast and on the following day murdered a prominent loyalist, for which Sinn Féin was 'expelled' from the talks for less than a month.[24]

The republicans appeared to have again successfully used their 'Tactical Use of Armed Struggle' strategy. When the first draft of the proposed agreement was delivered by George Mitchell to the parties on the morning of the last Tuesday of the talks process, 7 April 1998, the approach of the 'Heads of Agreement' document towards Strand Two, that is, the north-south institutions, was abandoned. The text, written by the two governments, surprised Mitchell by the degree to which it returned to the ambitious north-south vistas of the Framework Document which, he realized, would be unacceptable to David Trimble.[25] When Lord Alderdice, then leader of the Alliance party and a largely uncritical supporter of the Framework Document, declared publicly that the talks had been propelled into crisis by the governments' proposals, Blair descended on Belfast armed with a characteristic sound-bite about feeling the 'hand of history' on his shoulder—and a ruthless disregard for the position he had recently agreed with Ahern. The key outcome was a return to the strictly limited version of an accountable and limited north-south body which, together with Ahern's acceptance of clear Irish constitutional recognition of the democratic validity of partition, did much to ensure Trimble's acceptance of the Agreement.

Tony Blair and 'Middle Ulster'

However, the problems that were to dog the implementation of the Agreement were clear from the moment it was signed. Blair had, in the last two days of frenetic renegotiations at Stormont, disappointed Adams by bursting the republican bubble of a free-standing north-south complex of institutions charged with knitting the two states together. The fact that he had been prepared to indulge this vision up to practically the last moment suggested that in the final phase of the talks Adams and Martin McGuinness had offered a radical shift on decommissioning—if the all-Ireland dimension of the Agreement was suitably grandiose.[26] Thus, having satisfied the prime unionist objection on Strand Two matters, it was unsurprising that the republican movement's anger would be assuaged elsewhere in the document. The fundamental concessions were on the deliberate vagueness over the relation between executive formation and decommissioning, and in the short period—two years—within which qualifying prisoners would be released on licence.

The potential for these issues to undermine support for Trimble was immediately clear, signalled first by Jeffrey Donaldson's walk-out on the very day the Agreement was signed. Blair, hemmed in by pressure from the Irish Government, the SDLP, and Clinton—as well as his own desire to do nothing that would undermine the cease-fire—tried to shore up Trimble's position by issuing a letter, in which he stated that he would support changes to the provisions of the Agreement within six months, if they were not effective in excluding Sinn Féin from office if the IRA had not begun the process of decommissioning.[27]

The letter was some defence against the unionist 'rejectionists' but, as the campaign for a 'yes' vote at the referendum developed, it became clear that it would have difficulty in winning over a clear majority of unionists. Trimble had secured the support of two-thirds—55 votes to 23—of the Ulster Unionist party Executive for the Agreement on 11 April and 72 per cent of the 850 strong Ulster Unionist Council a week later.[28] But, as Sinn Féin spokesmen continued quite correctly to point out, there was no decommissioning 'precondition' in the Agreement. When the party's special *ardfheis* gave a standing ovation to recently released IRA men responsible for a string of bombings in London during the 1970s,[29] the Prime Minister had to intensify his efforts to reassure unionist doubters. Although he failed with the Orange Order which announced on 1 May that it could not support the Agreement, Blair's intensive personal involvement in the later stages of the campaign no doubt helped Trimble to recover some ground. The result—a 71 per cent vote in favour—although it would have been seen as a resounding victory in more consensual polities, represented, at the most optimistic assessment, a small unionist majority in favour of the Agreement. Even this limited achievement was won on the basis of dangerous hostages to fortune created by a speech by Blair at Balmoral on 14 May. Here he had attempted to reassure 'middle Ulster' by stating that those parties which stood to benefit from the early release of prisoners and seats in government must prove their commitment to giving up violence for good by a number of 'tests'. These included a clear commitment that the 'so-called war is finished'; an end

to bombings, killings, and beatings, claimed or unclaimed; progressive abandonment and dismantling of paramilitary structures; and full co-operation with
the Independent International Commission on Decommissioning.[30]

At the election for the new Assembly on 25 June 1998 the Ulster Unionist
party turned in its worst ever performance, coming second to the SDLP with a
fairly disastrous 21 per cent of the first preference vote, compared to the DUP's
18 per cent—see Mitchell, in Chapter 3 of this volume. The fact that pro-
Agreement unionists, including the Progressive Unionist party, had a narrow
two-seat margin over anti-Agreement unionists of 30–28 seats, demonstrated
clearly the limited room for manœuvre available to David Trimble. Despite this,
and the May 2000 deadline for the completion of the decommissioning process,
Blair appeared in no hurry to press republicans on the arms issue. Meanwhile
the NIO pushed ahead with those aspects of the Agreement—the Independent
Commission on the reform of the RUC and the early release of paramilitary
prisoners—that played so badly in the unionist heartlands. It was Bertie Ahern
who, in an interview in the *Sunday Times* on 14 February 1999, first registered
impatience with republicans' lack of movement as 'illogical, unfair and unrea-
sonable', adding: 'Being a part of a government is not possible without at least
a commencement of decommissioning'. At Hillsborough on 1 April 1999 Blair
and Ahern proposed a sequenced process in which a shadow executive would be
formed and, within a month of its formation, during a 'collective act of reconciliation', some arms would be 'put beyond use on a voluntary basis' concurrent
with the devolution of powers to the new Executive. Within a week Martin
McGuinness was pronouncing that the IRA would not 'jump to any ultimatum'
and rejected the Hillsborough proposals out of hand as a product of demands
from Trimble and the 'British military establishment'.[31]

Republicans talked up the danger of a split[32] and the threat to the cease-fire
produced a quick reversal of policy, Blair now putting intense pressure on
Trimble to 'take a risk' for peace. The shift produced the inevitable and not
implausible charge from anti-Agreement unionists like Robert McCartney that
Blair's policy was dictated by fear of bombs in London. It is undoubtedly true
that, like Major, Blair was concerned about a resumption of the IRA's 'war' on
the mainland. However, there were also more short-term factors in play. The
war in Kosovo may have encouraged a new aggressive 'rush for a deal' on Blair's
part.[33] It is also possible that some public opinion surveys showing surprisingly
strong Protestant support for the Agreement influenced the shift. Whatever the
basis for the *volte face* it had a damaging effect on Trimble's leadership. The
damage mounted when it became known that, under pressure at a Downing
Street summit on 14 May, he had apparently agreed to try and sell a process
that would have involved Sinn Féin's entry into government without even
acceptance of an 'obligation' to decommission on the part of republicans.[34]

Keen to announce an Ulster deal to coincide with the inauguration of the
Welsh and Scottish assemblies, the Prime Minister set a deadline of 30 June for

a resolution to the impasse, ignoring the problems that Trimble might have in selling what a Blair aide referred to as a 'leap of faith'[35] to his party. Trimble's apparent initial preparedness to advocate such a deal to his party may have encouraged the Prime Minister to maintain the pressure. Blair's now almost solipsistic fixation on a deal by the 'absolute' deadline of the end of June appeared to have blotted out the results of the European elections in which Paisley came triumphantly top of the poll and the Ulster Unionist party had a terrible result: its lowest ever share of the popular vote, 17.6 per cent, meant it narrowly avoided an ignominious fourth place behind Sinn Féin.[36]

Downing Street's performance in the days leading up to the deadline showed a remarkable willingness to put trust in the *sotto voce* commitments of a few leading members of Sinn Féin, namely that they were 'confident' that their inclusion in government would lead to decommissioning by May 2000. Blair's aides told journalists he trusted Adams and McGuinness to deliver.[37] The two governments' *The Way Forward* document which they produced at the end of the elongated talks process on 2 July showed just how little Blair had been prepared to engage with Trimble's concerns. Its central provisions for 'sequencing' and a 'fail safe' mechanism in the event of IRA failure to deliver on decommissioning had been set out in an article which he had written for *The Times* on 25 June with the apocalyptic title, 'Looking into the face of disaster'. Journalists were informed that a 'seismic shift' had taken place in republican thinking on weapons. However, it was soon evident that in their reports back to activists the Sinn Féin delegation at the negotiations made it clear that they were making no commitments on the part of the IRA and that a central purpose in the talks was 'to create confusion and disunity among their political enemies'.[38] The government's media spin had seemed to go out of control as the deadline approached and then passed. There was intense denigration of Trimble, accompanied by reports of Blair's 'fury' at the UUP leader's refusal to grasp Sinn Féin's offer.[39]

Although the subsequent formal rejection of the 'Way Forward' by the Unionist Party Executive and the announcement of a review process in the autumn to be chaired by George Mitchell allowed some hope of an eventual deal, the prospects did not appear at all promising. A recrudescence of IRA punishment beatings and killing during the summer, along with the organization's probable involvement in an attempt to buy arms in the United States, strengthened the rejectionist camp as did the publication of the Patten Report on the RUC on 9 September. Despite all this there was no indication that Blair's position had shifted; essentially unionists should accept republicans in government without any guarantee from the IRA that decommissioning would even begin, let alone be completed, by May 2000. If the IRA failed to decommission the 'fail-safe' would mean the ending of the executive, not simply the exclusion of the party that had failed to deliver. The replacement of Mo Mowlam by Peter Mandelson, who Trimble had wanted as Secretary of State, may have improved the prospects for political progress but the problems remained formidable.

Despite the hostile reaction of the unionist mainstream to Patten—particularly the recommendations for a change to the name and symbols[40]—the eleven-week Mitchell Review produced an interim agreement. This involved David Trimble agreeing to the formation of a power-sharing executive with Sinn Féin ministers before any decommissioning by the IRA. Whether Trimble became convinced of republican willingness to decommission during the relaxed and informal talks with Adams and McGuinness at the American Ambassador's residence in London, or simply calculated that 'sequencing' was only way that unionism could expose republican insincerity remains unclear. However, whatever the motivation, the successful completion of the review created a wide gap between Trimble's view of the republican leadership and that of the ordinary unionist. With his deputy leader, John Taylor, openly sceptical of the result of the review process and substantial disquiet in the Assembly Party, Trimble had to face a special meeting of the Ulster Unionist Council to seek support for putting republicans into government *sans* action on weapons. With nothing more than a minimalist statement from the IRA in support of Sinn Féin and its agreement to appoint an intermediary to meet with General de Chastelain's decommissioning body, it was unsurprising that a *Daily Telegraph* poll of Ulster Unionist Council members taken the day before the Council meeting, predicted a narrow defeat for Trimble. In the event, the UUP leader was able to secure an uncomfortable victory—58 per cent in favour and 42 per cent against. This was achieved by means of an expedient—which he had resisted up to the last moment—a post-dated letter of resignation encompassing all UUP ministers in the proposed executive if there was no start to decommissioning by February 2000.[41] Gerry Adams's sharp protest that Trimble had violated the spirit of the review's conclusion by reintroducing an element of compulsion on decommissioning was an early indication of the problems the republican leadership was having in persuading the IRA base that a 'gesture' was needed on weapons. Northern Ireland entered the new millennium with a functioning government, including Sinn Féin ministers of Health and Education, but one that could be brought crashing down within weeks over the decommissioning issue.

Conclusion: An Appeasement that Worked?

The republican movement remained the axis around which the whole political process continued to revolve. John Major had been prepared to offer radical constitutional concessions to republicans and had begun to soften his line on decommissioning by the time he lost office. While unionism recovered some ground on constitutional issues in the Belfast Agreement, the pressure on them to accept a major fudge on decommissioning grew significantly under Blair. What this demonstrates is that as soon as a direct terrorist assault on the British State was lifted, if only temporarily, the longer-term British desire for insulation from this tiresome vestige of the Irish Question was reasserted. When unionism had the political, ideological, and military strength to force devolution on a reluctant British Government in 1921, the desire for insulation was bad news for northern nationalists. As unionism's political resources have shrunk since the 1960s, its major argument for the defence of the constitutional *status quo* had been that anything else would mean a capitulation to terrorist violence. The central calculation of republican revisionism was that a cessation of their armed assault on the British State would remove this last unionist argument and allow the British State to take on the role of 'persuader' for a united Ireland. Yet, there has never been a possibility of the British adopting that role for the simple reason that it would unify the vast majority of Protestants behind Paisleyism and provoke major instability and probably violence. At the same time, the open declaration of a lack of a 'strategic' or 'economic interest' in remaining in Northern Ireland reflects not simply long-standing realities, but also a disposition in favour of extrication on the part of a significant section of the British ruling élite.

The structural ambiguity of the British State's residual presence in Ireland means that, while British governments will not be party to the overt political, economic, or military coercion of unionists, they will make little secret of the fact that the search for stability in the north—and with it a gradual attenuation of Britain's direct involvement—demands that unionists grin and bear a process in which, if the 'cutting edge' of the IRA is removed from the scene—and it remains a big 'if'—it is at the price of major political and ideological concessions. This unquestionable dilution of what most unionists conceive of as the 'Britishness' of Northern Ireland was accepted as the price of peace by just over half of unionists at the time of the referendum. Almost two years on it is a price that a majority would reject, if they thought they had a choice. If the Agreement does eventually result in not only the formation but the consolidation of an inclusive government, it will be because 'middle Ulster' has a better grasp of the realities of the British State's attitude to Northern Ireland than some prominent journalists and academics. Major's and Blair's overwhelming desire to keep republicans on board has been factored, *faute de mieux*, into the realistic privatized world of those unionists who know that the price of a scarred and ambiguous peace will be the inclusion in government of those who still appear to believe that their movement was driven into almost three decades of sectarian carnage by an 'apartheid state'—and who remain publicly committed to the abolition of the very State they are administering. Critics of the peace process, like Robert McCartney and Conor Cruise O'Brien, are correct to detect more than a whiff of 'appeasement' in the approach followed by Major and Blair. Yet defenders of both governments could respond that, unlike Chamberlain's policy, this one has worked. There is increasing evidence that Adams and McGuinness have buried the republican project—see McIntyre, in Chapter 11 of this volume. There is certainly no inherent dynamic towards a united Ireland within the structures agreed on Good Friday 1998. But the price which the republican leadership has been able to extract for the forsaking of an objective which even they admitted was unrealizable in the short to medium term, has been a high one: an effectively binational polity when that segment of the electorate which can be defined as nationalist amounts to 40 per cent. The cumulative import of the policies of Major and Blair amounts to the constitutional triumph of unionism, combined with a certain political and ideological retreat. If they succeed it will be more to do with the bankruptcy of the rejectionist alternative than to any positive identification with them on the part of 'middle Ulster'. Whether, given a successful outcome on the issue of weapons, 'inclusive' institutions of government can help to build this identification will be the major challenge facing the province's new political élite.

ENDNOTES

1. This is the view in the main journalistic account, Mallie, E. and McKittrick, D., *The Fight for Peace: The Secret Story Behind the Irish Peace Process* (London: Heinemann, 1996). Brendan O'Leary provides the academic version in 'The Conservative stewardship of Northern Ireland, 1979–97: Sound-Bottomed Contradictions or Slow Learning', *Political Studies*, 45 (1997).
2. *Setting the Record Straight: A Record of Communications between Sinn Féin and the British Government October 1990–November 1993* (Belfast: Sinn Féin, 1994).
3. Ibid., 27.
4. Patterson, H., *The Politics of Illusion: A Political History of the IRA* (London: Serif, 1997), 243.
5. Quoted in Seldon, A., *Major: A Political Life* (London: Phoenix, 1998), 423.
6. Ibid., 525.
7. Seldon, *Major*, 528.
8. See *Sunday Business Post*, 3 August 1997.
9. Private information.
10. Bew, P. and Patterson, H., *The British State and the Ulster Crisis: From Wilson to Thatcher* (London: Verso, 1985), 73.
11. 'A New Framework for Agreement', par. 20, included in *Frameworks for the Future* (London: HMSO, 1995).
12. Private information.
13. On these questions see, Bew, Patterson, and Teague, *Between War and Peace*, 143–63.
14. O'Leary, B., Lyne, T., Marshall, J., and Rowthorn, B., *Northern Ireland: Sharing Authority*, (London: IPPR, 1993).
15. Patterson, *The Politics of Illusion*, 263–4.
16. Norton, C., 'Renewed Hope for Peace? John Major and Northern Ireland' in P. Dorey (ed.) *The Major Premiership Politics and Policies under John Major, 1990–1997* (London: MacMillan, 1999), 123.
17. Major, *Autobiography*, 489.
18. Patterson, *The Politics of Illusion*, 282.
19. Quoted in ibid., 293.
20. Contained in a NIO document leaked to Rev Ian Paisley: letter written by John Holmes, Principal Private Secretary to the Prime Minister, to Ken Lindsay in Dr Mowlam's office 6 February 1998 on Blair's Washington Breakfast meeting with Congressional Irish Lobby on 5 February.
21. 'But is there an Agreement on Northern Ireland?', *Daily Telegraph*, 17 April 1998.
22. Quote is from leaked NIO document on Washington Breakfast meeting.

23. Collins, S., 'Bertie sets test for Sinn Féin', *Sunday Tribune*, 18 January 1998.
24. See account in Mitchell, G., *Making Peace: The inside story of the making of the Good Friday Agreement* (London: William Heinemann, 1999), 139–40.
25. Ibid., 159.
26. Bew, P., 'Consent is the key', *The Times Literary Supplement*, 24 April 1998.
27. Mitchell, *Making Peace*, 179.
28. Bew, P. and Gillespie, G., *Northern Ireland A Chronology of the Troubles 1968–1999* (Dublin: Gill and MacMillan, 1999), 361.
29. Ibid., 363.
30. The Balmoral speech is reproduced in full in the *Irish Times*, 15 May 1998.
31. *Irish Times*, 8 April 1999.
32. See 'Adams and McGuiness believed to want the IRA to move on arms', *Irish Times*, 15 May 1999.
33. See for example de Bréadún, D., 'Governments again try to plot a course between foes', *Irish Times*, 22 May 1999.
34. Millar, F., 'Trimble's leadership in question in wake of summit', *Irish Times*, 22 May 1999.
35. Cracknell, D. and Murphy, J., 'The night that Blair looked into the abyss', *Sunday Telegraph*, 27 June 1999.
36. Millar, F., 'No way to soften the impact of Paisley's defiant triumph', *Irish Times*, 15 June 1999.
37. 'The night that Blair looked into the abyss', *Sunday Telegraph*, 27 June 1999.
38. Harnden, T., 'Secret report exposes Sinn Féin tactics', *Daily Telegraph*, 5 July 1999.
39. Millar, F., 'Blair observes niceties with no sign of shift in Trimble position', *Irish Times*, 2 July 1999.
40. Trimble denounced the report as 'shoddy' and a 'gratuitous insult', see Patterson, H., 'Shrill, hysterical Trimble? No, just pragmatic', *The Observer*, 12 September 1999.
41. Moloney, E., 'Unsatisfactory result sets up more hurdles', *Sunday Tribune*, 28 November 1999.

10

Learning from 'The Leopard'

Arthur Aughey

The Culture of Fatalism

Steve Bruce once described the political views of Ulster unionists as a 'dismal vision'. He noted that they 'fell easily into a self-pitying assumption that the world was against them'.[1] This observation has been repeated by others. Paul Bew, in a memorable phrase, once described the reaction of unionists to the politics of the peace process as 'an orgy of self-pity'.[2] Why should this particular characteristic be so frequently noted? Self-pity, it may be argued, is one of the consequences of a culture of political fatalism. The fatalist view is that any given situation can have only one outcome. In these circumstances 'fatalism is incompatible with deliberation, in that its truth would make deliberation over one's future actions not impossible but at any rate pointless'.[3] Traditional unionist suspicion of political 'initiatives' is partly explained by that disposition. It has been habitual to think that deliberation along such lines means undoing the Union. Such pessimism may seem at odds with what has also commonly been ascribed to unionism: a mentality of no surrender. However, both dispositions share a world of certainty and simplicity. Certainty, even the fatal certainty of betrayal, orders the world and arranges its materials, providing a defensive barrier against complexity and political ambiguity. Fatalism also has its psychological consolations in that it provides a ready excuse for both political failure and for political indolence—and the two may be related.

Indeed, some sympathetic commentators have even gone so far as to suggest that unionism may harbour a death wish.[4] If this is too strong a term then critics might substitute 'a preference for futility'. Futility in this sense has a double meaning. First, it implies a preference for projects that are ultimately self-defeating. The Drumcree march might fall into this category. Secondly, it implies a view of the world so conscious of the futility of schemes for political improvement that is almost Schopenhauerian in quality: 'No rose without a thorn. Yes, but many a thorn without a rose'.[5] Of course, these criticisms have been made of unionism for the better part of a hundred years. But it survives. So it is not necessarily the case that this culture of fatalism is without its political dividends. Furthermore, being able to survive in a hostile world and to manage this burden of fate encourages a curious form of self-esteem, a sort of ineffable sense of nobility and self-righteousness. That is the strength which has possibly found its greatest expression in 'Paisleyism'.

The response of unionists to the Belfast Agreement must be understood in terms of this historic culture of fatalism, a culture suspicious of the intentions of those outside the unionist 'family' and even more suspicious of the intentions, even the best intentions, of those within it. Yet it is a culture with some surprising and diverse effects. On the one hand, it has difficulty adapting to the sort of relentless optimism which has characterized New Labour policy. The natural disposition of many unionists, after 30 years of political violence and subversion, is indeed to follow Schopenhauer in always qualifying the noun 'optimism' with the adjective 'unscrupulous'. And a lack of scruple is what they believe to be a requirement of the Agreement—which is why a substantial proportion also refuse to be optimistic about it. Again, it should be stressed that this is not necessarily an unintelligent response to the world. In so far as wisdom emerges from what experience obliges one to believe, then unionists do perceive a world in which they have witnessed decline and sometimes marginalization. To what extent unionism is the author of its own misfortune remains an open question.

However, as was once suggested of the literary pessimism of Samuel Beckett, there exists in unionist culture a fragile optimism based on the consolation of survival.[6] This is the other side of the same fatalistic coin. It is a very austere form of optimism indeed and one that is easily ridiculed by its unionist critics. The attack on supporters of the Agreement is evidence of this. It is assumed to be at best foolishness or at worst, collaboration. Like its theological counterpart this is an optimism which affirms only a possibility. In the political sense it means that it is possible to secure one's interests in a world of paradox and ambiguity. It is not horrified by the challenge of deliberation. Living with political paradox is not the easiest thing for those in the unionist tradition, a tradition that seeks—like its dominant theology and like its republican opponents— absolutes. But politics is always paradoxical. The trick is to make the best of it. 'Trimble-ism' or the 'new unionism' is of that austerely fragile, optimistic character and as such, a delicate flower.

In sum, within a common fatalistic culture a number of dispositions arise. Three are relevant in the context of the Agreement. The first is apathy and resignation. Some commentators have detected this in the lower electoral turn-outs in unionist areas. If we set aside those who are apolitical, fatalism does have a certain appeal. This is especially the case if you believe that your future is behind you. Moreover, a diet of betrayal and humiliation, real or imaginary, helps to confirm a vision of the political that is beyond one's influence. Like Don Ciccio Tumeo in *The Leopard*, these people feel that British governments just ignore their opinion or simply transform it: 'I said black and they made me say white!' Many felt that Tony Blair's dismissal of the European election result in April 1999, when the unionist vote split 60/40 against the Agreement, was of that order. The second response is stubborn resistance to change, the great refusal which justifies itself in terms of some absolute index—the Union; principle and integrity; the will of the majority; righteousness. This refusal, too, is often based on a fatalistic sense. Why get involved in schemes for one's own undoing? Why move when movement can only be in a preordained, hostile direction? The third is the attempt to make the best of the hand which fate has dealt you. This game is not a game of political poker—as some have called it—but a game of political tarot. It is about, as R. A. Butler once put it, the art of the possible. It involves readings, interpretations, meanings, and deliberation in which fate may just possibly be made to bend at least some way to one's will. It may be no coincidence, therefore, that opponents of the Agreement believe that its unionist supporters have fallen for the wiles of political necromancers.

The Sicilian Connection

In a perceptive article in *The Times*, Michael Gove suggested that post-Agreement Northern Ireland in some ways resembled Sicily. By that he meant the existence of a mafia subculture—loyalist and republican paramilitarism—which Gove believed was corrupting the mainstream of political life.[7] However, the Sicilian analogy may be taken further by consideration of the novel *The Leopard*, by Guiseppe Tomasi di Lampedusa.[8] This work provides a way to examine the choices that the Belfast Agreement poses for unionists. All academic caveats about literary relevance fully acknowledged, the story of *The Leopard* can be said at least to 'speak to' the situation of contemporary unionism.

The Leopard is set in 1860 and is a tale of the upheaval attending the Italian *Risorgimento*. It chronicles the choice facing the Sicilian aristocracy, a choice between resisting the emerging order or reaching an accommodation with it. It is a tale of class politics, of course, but it is also a general political fable of how to adapt to circumstance by recognizing a possibility and turning it to advantage. It can be taken as an imaginative exploration of La Rochefoucauld's maxim: 'No occurrences are so unfortunate that the shrewd cannot turn them to some advantage, nor so fortunate that the imprudent cannot turn them to their own disadvantage'.[9] The novel reveals the way in which unfortunate circumstances can be turned to advantage even though the author has no illusions about the grandiose claims of politics. What is promised is not the future held out by Russo, that 'perfect specimen of a class on its way up'—whose Northern Ireland equivalent would possibly be the public sector professional—a future of 'liberty, security, lighter taxes, ease, trade. Everything will be better; the only ones to lose will be the priests'. What is promised, rather, is a future of petty compromise, manipulation, and manoeuvre in which decent values and old standards may be lost. Indeed, the novel suggests that the grander the political rhetoric the more likely it is that the reality will be sordid.

The central character of the story, Don Fabrizio, Prince of Salina—the Leopard—proposes that the aim of his generation is ultimately one of survival: 'Any palliative which may give us another hundred years of life is like eternity to us'. In this he proves successful—and for all its intellectual fatalism, the historical achievement of unionism has also been its capacity for survival. As one commentator put it, Don Fabrizio is 'burdened with the truly onerous responsibility of bequeathing a once vital past to a future that seems to have no place for it'.[10] This may be an equally good description of the task of a modern leader of unionism. And like the culture of unionism itself, the atmosphere of the novel is fatalistic. There are clear intimations of mortality for a whole way of life. Not only is there a sense of foreboding about the future, there is also a sense of loss about the past.[11]

Like many of his generation, Lampedusa (1896–1957) had great respect for the traditions of British constitutionalism. He was a sort of Italian Lord Molyneaux. His biographer has argued that he viewed the tragedy of Sicilian history in terms of a missed opportunity. It is this failure which informs the political fatalism of the book and has an obvious resonance in the recent history of Northern Ireland:

The 1812 constitution, established during the brief period of British control, was fatally undermined by a political class divided between those who thought it went too far and those who complained it had not gone far enough. For Lampedusa, the Sicilians' failure to support the constitution destroyed their chances of a decent future: their short-sightedness in those years ensured that the island would never experience the British form of constitutional development. (Gilmour, D., *The Last Leopard* (London The Harvill Press, 1996), 179.)

It was that missed opportunity which influenced Lampedusa's pessimistic judgement of the political abilities of his fellow Sicilians. Lampedusa's is a vision 'of a past consisting of recurrent themes, unexpected continuity and patterns of behaviour repeated down the centuries'.[12] If this is familiar it is because it corresponds to the understanding of a fine historian of unionism, A. T. Q. Stewart, in his *The Narrow Ground*. In that book Stewart argued that patterns of conflict:

cannot be changed or broken by any of the means now being employed to 'solve' the Ulster question. Neither pressure from London, nor pressure from Dublin, can alter them. . . . To say this is not to aver that the economic and constitutional situation of Northern Ireland will not change, or that its society will not change; it is, of course, changing constantly, but it changes in accord with intrinsic laws, and not at the dictate of the makers of instant blueprints. (Stewart, A. T. Q., *The Narrow Ground: Patterns of Ulster History* (Belfast: Prestani Press, 1986), 183–4.)

In his audience with the Chevalley di Monterzuolo, the representative of the modernizing Piedmontese administration—and for all the world the confident voice of New Labour, a man who believes that Sicily under the new regime, like Northern Ireland under the Agreement, 'is only now sighting the modern world, with so many wounds to heal, so many just desires to be granted'—Don Fabrizio replies with a worldly fatalism which echoes much of what has been said many times in Northern Ireland. Clever initiatives are intellectually appealing but they won't work. Indeed, it was this very fatalistic disposition which Tony Blair, like the Chevalley, tried to shift in his speech at Stranmillis College on 15 June 1999: 'People say this agreement will collapse like all the rest. . . . So people say: "nothing's changed. It's all going to collapse". The other side, but not me, are totally cynical. And I'm saying to people: "it's all rubbish". Things have changed'.[13]

Don Fabrizio's irritation at the Chevalley's assumption that the bad old ways have gone—'But that is all over, isn't it?'—illuminates the fatalistic suspicions at the heart of unionist politics. It was evident in the mainly hostile response to the exasperation obvious in Blair's Stranmillis speech. Like the distance between the Chevalley and Don Fabrizio there appeared to be a wide cultural gap between Blair's optimism and the fatalism he was challenging. The profound caution which verges on immobilism and which was embodied by the former Ulster Unionist leader, James Molyneaux, is captured in the Prince's opinion: 'I must say, between ourselves, that I have strong doubts whether the new kingdom will have many gifts for us in its luggage'. Furthermore, to the Chevalley's plea to 'collaborate' with the new spirit of the age Don Fabrizio responds by arguing 'that for a long time to come, there's nothing to be done. I'm sorry but I cannot lift a finger in politics. It would only get bitten'. The sense of an unavoidable fate, the unbreakable crust of custom, is expressed in terms frequently heard within Northern Ireland and without. 'I don't deny that a few Sicilians may succeed in breaking the spell once off the island; but they would', argued Don Fabrizio, 'have to leave it very young; by twenty it's too late; the crust is formed; they will remain convinced that their country is basely calumniated like all other countries, that the civilised norm is here, the oddities elsewhere'.

And what is the reason for this? In a penetrating insight which would be endorsed by British politicians from Churchill to the present sceptics, Don Fabrizio denies the Chevalley's assumption that the people universally want to improve—the venerable Gladstonian assumption which now animates New Labour: 'the Sicilians never want to improve for the simple reason that they think themselves perfect; their vanity is stronger than their misery'. This is indeed how things appear on both sides of the Garvaghy Road, a perspective at once arrogant and stupid. Those who hope to canalize Sicily or Northern Ireland 'into the flow of universal history'—surely the object of the Blairite 'project'?—are in for disappointment, if fatalism and self-regarding arrogance—unionist and nationalist—prevail. This view of the irredeemable quality of a political problem may be read as utter despair. This would do an injustice to the subtlety of the message of *The Leopard*. As one of Lampedusa's literary influences, Giacomo

Leopardi, once wrote: 'To enjoy life, a state of despair is necessary'.[14] And that is also the sort of paradox of which *The Leopard* partakes.

It is spoken by Don Fabrizio's nephew, Tancredi. Interpreters of the novel have taken this to be its central political message. The paradox—which might be called the Tancredi option—goes: 'Unless we ourselves take a hand now, they'll foist a republic on us. If you want things to stay the same things will have to change'. On this Emiliana Noether has written: 'This seemingly contradictory idea becomes a *leitmotif* in the Prince's thinking . . . the Prince understands Tancredi's motives and realises that Tancredi has made the right decision. To preserve the old, it is important to support the new order. Tancredi has shown more wit and acumen in assessing the situation than any other member of the family'.[15]

On the other hand, Lampedusa's biographer has argued that these lines have been consistently misunderstood. He notes that Don Fabrizio explicitly rejects them and settles for the objective of what today would be called gently managing decline.[16] After all, he tries to dissuade Tancredi from actively supporting those campaigning for change. And the whole purpose of the Chevalley's mission was to persuade the Prince to accept a seat in the Senate of the new Italy; to be, one might say, no longer part of the problem but part of the solution. Don Fabrizio declines. However, the Prince did secure the future for Tancredi, who was prepared to make his own accommodation with destiny, through an arranged marriage between his nephew and the daughter of the new style of political fixer, Don Calogero. 'Thus does the ancient Sicilian nobility find a place in a world that has no room for it'.[17] So one is still justified in believing, as does John Gatt-Rutter, that it is the Tancredi option 'which subtends the whole novel and could well be the historical judgement of the novel, beyond the intentions of its protagonists, [and it] cuts with both edges'.[18] This is the possibility which qualifies the fatalism of the novel. It does not displace it. Rather, it actually requires such fatalism to make any sense at all.

Thus, if the views of one historian of unionism, A. T. Q. Stewart, seem to reflect the opinion of Don Fabrizio, then the views of another historian of unionism seem to reflect the possibility implied in Tancredi's option. Brian Walker has argued that: 'As elsewhere, leaders and people in Ireland, both north and south, have a vital role to play in determining the shape of their own societies, and are not just hapless victims of a turbulent past. The myths of history must not be allowed to unduly affect peoples' minds and influence their judgement. It is important that when people try to deal with the very real problems confronting them, they do so without the unnecessary and harmful burden of "history's tune"'.[19]

David Trimble's wager on the Belfast Agreement of April 10 1998 may be taken as the unionist Tancredi option, an attempt to make history rather than to dance to its fatalistic tune. How do we explain this choice, given the 'dismal vision' of unionist politics and the very clear resistance to it not only from other unionist parties but also from within the Ulster Unionist party itself?

The Origin of the Tancredi Option

The attraction of the Tancredi option may be traced to the tentative emergence
of a 'new unionism' which began to claim the attention of some commentators
in the 1990s.[20] This was no single movement but, like all political changes, more
of an adjustment to circumstances. As the high tide of integrationist enthusiasm
began to wane with the demise of the Campaign for Equal Citizenship; as the
permanence of Anglo-Irish co-operation within which Northern Ireland's future
would be worked out was quietly acknowledged during the Brooke/Mayhew
Talks of 1991–2; so the energy of thoughtful unionism refocused on what
needed to change in order to secure its vital interests through the opportunities
of 'deliberation'.

A number of distinctions were drawn, distinctions designed to establish the
political space within which an historic compromise with Irish nationalism could
be made. A distinction was made between acknowledging an 'Irishness of place'
which could be shared by the 'greater number' in Northern Ireland, and a
'politicized Irishness' determined to destroy the entity of Northern Ireland
itself. A further distinction was made between self-government, a general movement throughout Western European democracies to devolve power to the
regions, and political exclusion, an attempt to attenuate the Union and to substitute an exclusively Irish context for decision-making. And a distinction was
made between accountable and practical cross-border co-operation between the
two parts of the island and co-operation driven ideologically by nationalist ambition, with new institutions developing an exclusively Irish political agenda.

Since the Anglo-Irish Agreement of 1985 it had been the fatalistic assumption
within unionism that the British government was pursuing a policy of 'separation by consent'. If the new unionism had a definitive parentage it was the child
of what was thought to be the appropriate alternative. That alternative was
'Union by consent'. It involved three key propositions. The first was that the
principle of consent should govern the political arrangements in Northern
Ireland and those between North and South. The second was that the notion of
any British Government 'facilitating' Irish unity should be finally abandoned.
The third was that in order to secure the proper atmosphere for relationships on
the island the Irish Government should remove the territorial claim in Articles
2 and 3 of its constitution. Here was Ulster Unionist thinking which implied
abandoning majoritarianism and embracing pluralism. Interestingly, it coincided
with a similar reassessment taking place within loyalist parties like the
Progressive Unionist party. If these were the strategic intimations of the new
unionism, what of the thing itself? Was it not rather like the 'post-nationalism'
of its opponents—something more often talked about than lived? There were and
are many difficulties in trying to realize the good intent of new unionism and
some of these have to do with the character of the so-called unionist 'family'.

Unionism is a broad community of views and interests. It is no surprise that opposition and antagonism within it is often as strong as that between unionism and nationalism. The Ulster Unionist party, the best hope of the new unionism and historically the broadest of political churches, has also had difficulty in managing its diversity. The course followed quite successfully by Molyneaux might be termed ambiguous equilibrium—which meant not doing very much in general about anything in particular. Its purpose was party unity. It was hardly a heroic strategy. But then it was not intended to be so. The essence of the Molyneaux 'long view' was to take no initiative and to compel opponents to struggle for everything. And in struggling for everything, they would dissipate their energy on small matters and never summon sufficient concentration of effort to make the big gains. It might be possible to view this logic as the real message of *The Leopard*, with Molyneaux as a sort of passionless Don Fabrizio. Certainly there is some similarity in their profound political scepticism. However, the difficulty with the Molyneaux style was clear. It appeared to most unionists that nationalists and republicans *were* making the big gains and had been doing so since at least 1985. And as the republican 'peace process' began to destabilize politics, Ulster Unionist activists, for a range of reasons, believed the Molyneaux style to be a demoralized and demoralizing strategy. The idea of a new unionism, then, represented one, but not the only, alternative—the other was to become still more resistant. The convincing moral was that unionists should become active participants in, rather than a passive victim of, political change. The themes of nationality, self-government, consent, and citizenship translated into a broad set of objectives that might ideally be achieved through negotiation in the peace process.

In brief outline that broad set of objectives was this. Unionists might accept an 'agreed Ireland', to use John Hume's phrase, in terms of a settlement that would be accepted as a just settlement and not simply as a stepping stone to something else. What might be created would be stable institutions based on consent, not ones designed to be transitional to Irish unity. If unionist consent was acknowledged as the requirement for constitutional change then unionists would have to acknowledge the need for nationalist consent to new arrangements within Northern Ireland. This would have implications for the functioning of any local administration and for the scope of an Irish dimension. But with unity off the agenda, and Articles 2 and 3 changed, then mutually beneficial co-operation between unionists and nationalists within Northern Ireland and between North and South could become a practical reality. However, all these things would pose difficulties of acceptance within unionism.

Possibly none of this would have been addressed seriously without David Trimble becoming leader of the Ulster Unionist party in 1995. Trimble promised to replace the 'do nothing' style of Unionist leadership.[21] This promise was not necessarily welcomed by those who felt that it was a sin to do anything at all. Unionism they felt, to use the Chevalley's term, should not 'collaborate'. The game, they believed, was still an Anglo-Irish one which was inimical to unionist interests. The task facing Trimble's 'active' style of leadership, was to be astute and imaginative enough to ensure that the peace process was transformed into something unionists could live with. That was a demanding task, given the generally pessimistic perception of where things were tending. When Trimble assumed the leadership three key ideas—balance, process, and consent—were at the centre of debate.

In the Downing Street Declaration of December 1993 the balance appeared to be between self-determination and consent. Unionists were uncertain whether London's conceding the principle of self-determination to the 'people of Ireland' in that document had made a fundamental concession to the goal of Irish unity. If it had, everything else, for instance the stipulation that this right could only be exercised by separate acts North and South, would be a façade. On the other hand, the acknowledgement by the Irish Government of the principle of consent for constitutional change could be read as guaranteeing that the statehood of Northern Ireland would continue to depend on the will of the 'greater number'. Equally, there were two opposed understandings of the term 'process'. The first would mean that the fact of the Union would be decisive. The Union, albeit a significantly reformed Union, would be 'safe'. The process would be biased towards stabilizing Northern Ireland as a part of the United Kingdom. The second meaning assumes a law of historical development moving inexorably towards the achievement of Irish unity. The peace process in this sense would project a predetermined course to that end beyond the power of unionists to frustrate. The third idea was the idea of consent. If one were to accept that the principle of consent took precedence over the principle of unity then the bias would be again towards a more inclusive Northern Ireland, a Northern Ireland based on parity of esteem yet still a Northern Ireland securely within the UK. If, on the other hand, the principle of unity were to take precedence then a very different set of expectations would emerge. In this case, the balance would be towards those structures designed to facilitate Northern Ireland's transition from its present UK status towards some form of all-Ireland arrangement.

The generality of unionists read the trend of policy fatalistically. After the Framework Document of February 1995 they understood the peace process to mean three things. First, that the policy based on it was not balanced but was tilted against them. Secondly, that the process unfolding represented a move towards Irish unity. Thirdly, that the objective of unity did indeed take precedence over the principle of consent. Things hardly looked propitious for the fledgling 'new unionism' or for the Tancredi option as the talks about the future of Northern Ireland began in 1996.

Swallowing the Toad

In a dramatic scene of *The Leopard*, Don Fabrizio must negotiate—without acknowledging that he was indeed *negotiating*—with the scheming and ambitious Don Calogero. The Prince is seeking to arrange the marriage between Tancredi and Don Calogero's daughter, a union designed to secure continuity in the fortunes of the family and to secure its future. The scene symbolizes what is often a political imperative: that one must swallow one's pride in order to secure one's interest. This is symbolized by the act of swallowing a (metaphorical) toad: 'the toad had been swallowed; the chewed head and gizzards were going down his throat; he still had to crunch up the claws, but that was nothing compared to the rest; the worst was over'.

In signing the Agreement, Trimble's UUP had to swallow the toad as well. It had to chew the heads and gizzards of the early release of terrorist prisoners. Crunching the claws meant accepting a place for Sinn Féin in the government of Northern Ireland. And, at this point some of Trimble's co-negotiators, like Jeffrey Donaldson, could not be persuaded that the worst was indeed over. Nor could most of his parliamentary party. His opponents in the DUP and UK Unionist party had already abandoned the 'Tar Baby' talks because, in the words of Robert McCartney, they were the 'killing fields' of the Union.[22] Having swallowed the toad, Trimble's problem was to get his own constituency to acknowledge that if the Agreement he signed was the best possible of all possible deals then there would have to be necessary evils.

This was a dialogue between fatalism and possibility. Fatalism can lead to a conservative judgement that nothing can ever be other than what it has been. The history of the last 30 years, the history of violence and confrontation, has made it understandably difficult for unionists to envisage a world in which things could be otherwise. This culture of (experiential) fatalism takes as its measure the thought that nothing which is proposed jointly by the British and Irish Governments and is, moreover, acceptable to John Hume and, apparently, to Gerry Adams, can ever be good for unionists. It found full expression in the character of the opposition to the talks and to the Agreement which married absolute defiance with absolute fatalism. The Agreement, in this view, is the worst possible of all possible deals and nothing in it is a necessary evil. Anglo-Irish policy will always betray the unionists. Logically, then, any set of proposals would be tainted by British perfidy and Irish hubris. In that logical but fatalistic reading of history there can be no way out. For instance, it was frequently argued that 'the devil is in the detail'. In the hunt for the politically satanic in every twist and turn of the talks it was assumed that the devil *must* be there. That there might be another way of interpreting the phrase 'devil in the detail' never seemed to occur. Intense textual criticism to discover satanic intent in the particular might prevent one discovering advantages and possibilities in the larger scheme of things. And that is precisely the charge made against their critics by David Trimble's supporters. Such pessimism, they felt, actually demonized the detail of the Agreement precisely because the whole was pre-judged to be hopeless.

If interpretation could not escape the influence of fatalism then political judgement could be also influenced by possibility. The Agreement appeared to provide unionists with a potential escape from the view that nothing could ever be otherwise. The culture of fatalism might now be infused with, if it could not be entirely replaced by, a new culture of self-confidence. The Tancredi option was expressed here in its local dialect. As Trimble put it, the Agreement is 'as good and as fair as it gets'.[23] That is a phrase which has an obvious Lampedusan ambiguity. Does it mean 'good'—that is, it is difficult to imagine a better deal for unionists? Or does it mean 'good'—that is, any other deal would be even worse than this one? It practice it really means both.

The DUP's deputy leader Peter Robinson did identify a truth about pro-Agreement Ulster Unionists when he argued: 'The excuse used by unionist sup-porters of the agreement, to explain their behaviour, is that unionists need to do a deal now as the deal they would negotiate in five or ten years time would be even less satisfactory'.[24] He was correct to detect this deeply fatalistic tendency in the UUP strategy. This was indeed true but it was not the whole truth about the pro-Agreement position. In Trimble's view, the difficulties which unionists would find in the Agreement were short-term ones—though critics could have responded appropriately with the words of Keynes: 'In the long run we're all dead'. The long-term could now look after itself on the basis of consent. As he argued an 'Agreement such as this may not come around again for another gen-eration'.[25] And he meant it.

The academic view tended to share that assessment. For instance, Paul Bew's view, in true Tancredian form, was that the Agreement asked unionists 'to go a long way to meet the concerns of the nationalist minority. It does not necessar-ily follow that it is not in the interests of the unionists to do so'. He believed there was no need for the present level of unionist pessimism. The price of change was worth paying in order to end the IRA's campaign, to secure the legitimacy of Northern Ireland's status and to remove the Republic's territorial claim.[26] Brigid Hadfield's legal analysis of the Agreement also favoured the Trimble view that it secured the Union.[27] In the UUP's clarification paper *Understanding the Agreement*, fatalism was evidently mixed with possibility. It noted fatalistically that many of those aspects of the Agreement which are objec-tionable could be introduced anyway by the Secretary of State over the heads of the unionist electorate. It noted further, realistically, that 'Unionists must make a judgement as to whether or not the features that bring us considerable constitutional gains outweigh those elements of the Agreement that we all find objectionable'.[28] The Trimble answer was clear.

The Troubles of David Trimble

On the eve of the referendum, the editor of the *Belfast Newsletter* also identified this delicate balance of judgement. He believed that unionist uncertainty was a result of people 'trying to weigh up the obvious benefits that would materialise from a long period of stability'—the Tancredi option of Trimble—against 'a gut instinct that tells them that what the agreement amounts to is rather more than a tampering with the edges of their society'—the message of Trimble's opponents.[29] How were these conflicting views put across?

To use a term of the Irish Government's adviser, Martin Mansergh, the DUP argued that the institutions and procedures of the Agreement would 'hollow out' Northern Ireland's Britishness. As the Chairman of the DUP, Nigel Dodds, put it: 'the Northern Ireland recognised in this document is a different one from the Northern Ireland that I knew prior to this Agreement. This is a Northern Ireland in transition to a united Ireland'.[30] The fatalism of the end is well captured by the familiar assertion of the DUP that: 'The Union binds Northern Ireland to the rest of the United Kingdom. This Agreement deliberately prises it away and enforces a rolling scheme of all-Ireland harmonisation and integration, with only one ultimate goal in view. Irish unification. No other outcome is anticipated'.[31]

One of the consistent objectives of British policy-makers, the DUP claimed, has been to find a unionist leader who would collaborate with their policy of disengagement. They had now in Trimble found their man: a man who, like Brian Faulkner before him, would do what was required of him. And what was required was collaboration in a process of moving inexorably towards Irish unity. Trimble 'purports to be a unionist yet is one of the architects of a united Ireland plan'.[32] Despite this betrayal, the DUP and the UK Unionists still had faith that this 'process' would eventually be rejected by ordinary unionists who 'will not allow a conflicting principle of consent, whereby the Government sets in place a process to unite Ireland and then tells the people of Northern Ireland that they have no power to control it'.[33] It was merely defeatism or surrenderism to believe otherwise. This is the politics of the great refusal and suggests determined faith in the will to triumph against circumstance. As such it appears to be at the opposite pole to fatalism. What does define its fatalism, however, is the notion that the course is already set. Drawing upon all the cultural resource of siege and resistance, Peter Robinson could tell his party that: 'We are being tested to determine how long we can endure. They are asking you if you are ready to submit to a shady surrender and sue for an unprincipled peace'.[34]

Ian Paisley Jr argued that the Agreement is 'not about finding a real, lasting or just peace, but about finding what will be enough political concessions to buy the support of the IRA/Sinn Féin'.[35] The persuasiveness of this approach was assisted by the refusal of the IRA to disarm. Robert McCartney played on the worry that the intimidation and punishment beatings would soon be visited on districts of middle class affluence which had voted 'yes'. Soon these people may not need to enquire, argued McCartney, 'for whom the bell tolls in the ghettos, for by then it may also be tolling for both them and their children'.[36] The republican struggle had simply entered a new phase. The provisions of the Agreement would be now the focus of a revitalized campaign of destabilization. McCartney's argument touched a real moral nerve. Sammy Wilson went so far as to claim that: 'Unionists are even accepting that the IRA should be allowed to act as "defenders of their own communities"'.[37] Like Russo's assurance to the Prince of Salina, given with 'amiable irony', that he was not to worry about events because no harm would come his way—'Villa Salina will be quiet as a convent'—the real concern which Wilson expressed is this: how can unionists accept assurances of security from those who remain their political adversaries and who refuse to move towards exclusively peaceful means? For these mafias will enjoy the rules of democratic practice and the civilities of a liberal society while denying them to others. In language which found an echo in these denunciations of the morality of the Belfast Agreement, Don Fabrizio had already warned the determined Tancredi: 'You're mad, my boy, to go with those people. They're all mafia men, all crooks'. That was the mood of a substantial vector of unionist support. The publication of the Patten Report on policing in September 1999 confirmed for many the process of the hollowing out of Ulster's Britishness and also the horrible vision of paramilitary policing.

The appalling prospect which these thoughts conjured up provoked one of the more surprising, though perfectly logical, responses. It was that of McCartney's UKUP ally, Conor Cruise O'Brien. In his *Memoir*, O'Brien advocated unionist 'inclusion in a united Ireland: an inclusion negotiated on terms which would safeguard the vital interests of the Protestant community'. As he contended 'in the conditions of the late 20th century, no other way to safeguard the vital interests of the Protestant community in Northern Ireland is available'.[38] His reasoning was simple. Doing a deal with southern nationalists is much to be preferred to the one that had just been done with the SDLP and Sinn Féin. For if the Belfast Agreement is a great betrayal of Ulster unionism, if the British Government is intent on destroying the Union, if the strategy is simply one of appeasement, a daily diet of aggravation and cumulative humiliation—and Trimble's opponents did profess all these things—then the Agreement is only death by a thousand cuts. Better to make an end of it now and recognize the inevitable. That was O'Brien's own distinctive Tancredi option.

This fatalistic culture of unionism—one side of it perfectly intuited by someone not of a unionist background at all like O'Brien—has tended to think in eternal truths. There is little room for ambiguity or paradox. Nor is there much appreciation of the limits of political endeavour, noted by Don Fabrizio, in which nothing can be permanently secured. 'We may worry about our children and perhaps our grandchildren; but beyond what we can hope to stroke with these hands of ours we have no obligations'. Indeed, it is that very contingency of politics—a world without permanence—which engenders pessimism among many unionists. However, it may also engender its own qualified optimism. Political life, as a tissue of contingencies, is just as contingent for one's opponents as it is for oneself. Those who believe in historical inevitability—as Sinn Féin seems to do—are more often than not, to use a phrase of Brian Faulkner's, wrong-footed by history. Indeed, one of the problems of unionist politics has been, by demonizing Sinn Féin, also to invest it with demonic powers. In this sense unionists tend to believe the worst and to assume that their opponents have secret knowledge of the fabric of things. This is an illusion, though one assiduously cultivated by the propagandists of Sinn Féin. It was this style of politics which Trimble's supporters have been trying to change.

In a series of speeches and articles Trimble was compelled to justify his judgement that the Agreement was as good as it gets. In a speech to the Northern Ireland Forum on 17 April 1998, Trimble claimed fidelity to long-standing unionist objectives. He argued that the Belfast Agreement represented 'the culmination of a process begun by the current leader of the DUP and my predecessor, Lord Molyneaux'. For Trimble, the Agreement had achieved the unionist goal 'proposed separately by the UUP and the DUP in the 1992 Talks' of placing Northern Ireland's future within a wider British-Irish context than the Agreement of 1985. He addressed the central conceptual issue of the priority of consent over unity: 'As both Governments and all the political parties at Stormont, with the exception of Sinn Féin, admitted, the settlement arising out of this process is a partitionist one based on the principle of consent'. Trimble's assertion, contradicting the charge against him, was that one key unionist objective had been now achieved. 'We have sought and secured a permanent settlement, not agreed to a temporary transitional arrangement.' He pointed to the Irish Government's commitment to modify Articles 2 and 3 of its constitution as evidence of this. The Tancredian message addressed what Trimble believed to be the one-dimensional flaw in his opponents argument. Dismissing change was insufficient in itself for what would stay the same would be equally intolerable: 'What is their alternative? The truth is they have none except the *status quo*; and that means the continuation of the Anglo-Irish Agreement; no control over our destiny; and a continual dilution of the Union'.[39] In other words, if we want what is valuable to stay the same some things will have to change.

Of course there was acknowledgement that the Agreement was not perfect. But in the circumstances Trimble felt that there was little value in trying to destroy the Agreement by saying that things should be even better. The truth is, as we find in *The Leopard*, 'the world is an imperfect place and we have to deal with political realities as we find them'. Trimble admitted that 'the situation I inherited seemed to be leading from the Anglo-Irish Agreement to something much worse'. But he had 'reversed this and can look forward to working with democratic nationalists to build a better Northern Ireland'.[40] There might be some appreciation too of the Prince's very political response to the criticisms of his priest for accommodating himself to new circumstances: 'We live in a changing reality to which we try to adapt ourselves like seaweed bending under the pressure of water'. There would be less agreement on the fatalistic assumption that there was nothing which could be done to change the pressure—though his opponents believe that the course of the debate about IRA decommissioning confirms it. Trimble has kept to a publicly optimistic position holding to the opinion that 'former paramilitaries have nowhere else to go other than into exclusively democratic politics'.[41] That optimism has fluctuated but it has never fully deserted him.

Furthermore, in an address to the Irish Association in November 1998, Trimble implied that the Agreement had created a new situation in which the old antagonism between North and South could be overcome. 'Economic co-operation, we trust, is no longer advanced as a strategy for creeping unification. After the Agreement there is no longer any need to engage in such tactical manoeuvres and a growth in co-operation is consequently possible'. Though there might be a large measure of wishful thinking in that assessment, a more fruitful approach was proposed. 'Is it not better to say: "This area has proven potential, let us see how we can build upon it", rather than, "This was on the agenda in 1965 and 1975 and the situation now demands more?"'. Trimble's Tancredian vision was one of practical co-operation leading an end to the 'cold war' on the island.[42] This view of North/South matters complemented his vision for Northern Ireland set out in a speech to business and community leaders in Belfast a few months earlier. 'We can now get down to the historic and honourable task of this generation: to raise up a new Northern Ireland in which pluralist unionism and constitutional nationalism can speak to each other with the civility which is the foundation of freedom'.[43]

Conclusion

As Trimble asserted at his party conference on 9 October 1999, 'the true glory lies not in a grand beginning, but in carrying it on until all is completed'.[44] And the message of his conference speech, recommitting his party to the principles of the Agreement, had a clear warning for his opponents who believed that a safer Union would emerge from that Agreement's demise. Like the carcass of the Prince's faithful hound, Bendico, his opponents might catch a brief glimpse of former glory only to witness the ultimate dissolution of their illusion: 'what remained of Bendico was flung into a corner of the yard. . . . During the flight down from the window its form recomposed itself for an instant; in the air there seemed to be dancing a quadruped with long whiskers, its right foreleg raised in imprecation. Then all found peace in a little heap of livid dust'. That would be (fatalistically) the final lesson from *The Leopard*, not Tancredian but Ozymandian.

The difficulty in persuading the culture of fatalism, even persuading union-ist supporters of the Agreement, of the possibility of positive completion lay ultimately in this. The subtlety of the Tancredian paradox is easily lost on a large proportion of the electorate. Many unionists could only see things chan-ging and changing to their disadvantage. They remained unpersuaded that the things they valued would stay the same or, even if they did, that it was worth making the required changes to secure that end. The impact on unionist opin-ion of the report of the Patten Commission into the RUC is a classic example of that. What did appear to stay the same was the intransigence of their oppo-nents. Republicans did not seem willing to move to exclusively peaceful means. Trimble's marginal success for his strategy among unionists in the referendum in May 1998 illustrated the problem clearly, a problem starkly revealed by divi-sions within his own party and by the leaching of support to his opponents in the European election of 10 June 1999. Those opponents, although divided amongst themselves, can now claim to represent the majority unionist view.

For Trimble, the nut to be cracked was that of delivering a credible compro-mise on the devolution/decommissioning question. In essence, the Trimble pro-posal was that republicans and unionists should set aside the objective of winning the ideological argument over guns and government and should con-centrate instead on sharing the political risks. Both should accept risk manage-ment, or what might be called the principle of 'simultaneity'—colloquially known as 'jumping together'—as a way to avoid the politics of blame and to secure both parties from their critics. In Sicilian fashion, neither would lose face. An act of decommissioning at the same time as devolution would satisfy honour on both sides. Even this proved unacceptable to Sinn Féin. The pressure shifted again onto Trimble to compromise. In the sectarian dynamic of Northern Ireland politics this shift represented a victory for republicans and a defeat for unionists. And this posed serious problems for the UUP leadership.

If the position was conceded then critics could argue that the UUP had resiled from a principled position and capitulated yet again to political pressure. There did exist a strong feeling amongst many in Trimble's Assembly group that the UUP was being asked to take all the risks and to suffer all the potential dam-age. Moreover, it seemed to put the future of the party into the hands of the IRA and that is a position, they felt, which no unionist leader should be put in. Nor did there appear to be sufficient evidence that if the UUP did take the risk of accepting republican *bona fides* that there would be appropriate insurance for that risk. Few believed the word of the British Government that, in the event of IRA default on decommissioning, Sinn Féin would carry the blame for the collapse of the Agreement.

Therefore, on 27 November 1999, Trimble took an enormous gamble in try-ing to secure his party's consent to trigger the establishment of the Executive and the devolution of power *before* IRA decommissioning. His success was marginal but sufficient—58 per cent of the Ulster Unionist Council supported him. His performance was a classic example of politics as 'arrangements', one of the central lessons of *The Leopard*. This holds that bending and adapting to circumstance will affect the opportunities of politics itself. This is the novel's enduring appeal, not just one of literary solace in the face of loss but also of the dignity to be found in responding with courage to change. There was no doubting Trimble's courage and his dignity in the face of unpalatable choices. Nor was there any doubting the sense of unease about and potential loss in the enterprise upon which his party was embarked. The journalist Sion Simon captured the fatalistic mood of the Ulster Unionist decision when he wrote, in Lampedusan fashion: 'The Unionist compromises are concluded in resigned anticipation of defeat, in the spirit of Abraham, who expected neither mercy nor return. The Irish problem, as historically defined, is not susceptible to a loserless ending'.[45] Trimble has made a different calculation, that the future has surprises in store for those who believe in the inevitability of Irish unity.

ENDNOTES

1. Bruce, S., *The Edge of the Union: The Ulster Loyalist Political Vision* (Oxford: Oxford University Press, 1994), 63.
2. Bew, P., 'One Side Self-Pity, The Other, Self-Deception', *Parliamentary Brief*, 3/5 (1995): 6.
3. Small, R., 'Fatalism and Deliberation', *Canadian Journal of Philosophy*, 18/1 (1988): 15.
4. Harris, E., 'Still time to keep the faith', *The Sunday Times*, 19 September 1999.
5. Schopenhauer, A., *Studies in Pessimism: A Series of Essays*, trans. T. Bailey Saunders (London: Swan Sonnenschein and Company, 1892), 138.
6. Rosen, S. J., *Samuel Beckett and the Pessimistic Tradition* (New Brunswick, NJ: Rutgers University Press, 1976), 38.
7. Gove, M., 'And no one stops to think', *The Times*, 30 March 1999.
8. Tomasi di Lampedusa, G., *The Leopard*, trans. A. Colquhoun (London: The Harvill Press, 1996).
9. La Rochefoucauld, *Maxims*, trans. L. Tancock, (Harmondsworth: Penguin Books, 1959), 44.
10. Saccone, E., 'Nobility and Literature. Questions in Tomasi di Lampedusa', *MLN*, 106, (1991): 169.
11. Ruthenberg, M., 'Death of an epic, death of an Epoch. Ariosto and Tasso in Tomasi di Lampedusa's "Il Gattopardo"', *Forum Italicum*, 32/2 (1998): 411.
12. Gilmour, D., *The Last Leopard* (London: The Harvill Press, 1996), 175.
13. Cited in *The Belfast Telegraph*, 15 June 1999.
14. Carsaniga, G., *Giacomo Leopardi: The unheeded voice* (Edinburgh: Edinburgh University Press, 1977), 43.
15. Noether, E., 'The Old Order Confronts the Risorgiomento: The Leopard as History', *Forum Italicum*, 21/1 (1987): 31.
16. Gilmour, *The Last Lepoard*, 179.
17. Rubino, A. C., 'A Bomb Manufactured in Pittsburgh, Pennsylvania. Past, Present and Future in The Leopard', *Forum Italicum*, 21/1 (1987): 18. See also Duncan, D., 'Lifting the Veil: Metaphors of Exclusion in Il Gattopardo', *Forum for Modern Language Studies*, 29/4 (1993): 323–35.
18. Gatt-Rutter, J., *Writers and Politics in Modern Italy* (London: Hodder and Stoughton, 1978), 29.

19. Walker, B., *Dancing to History's Tune: History, myth and politics in Ireland* (Belfast: Institute of Irish Studies, 1996), 158.
20. See, for example, O'Dowd, L., 'Intellectuals and political culture: a unionist-nationalist comparison', in E. Hughes (ed.), *Culture and Politics in Northern Ireland 1960–1990* (Milton Keynes: Open University Press, 1991), 151–73.
21. See Aughey, A., 'Ulster Unionist Party leadership election', *Irish Political Studies*, 11 (1996): 160–8.
22. McCartney, R., 'Talks that won't do the union any good', *Northern Ireland Brief*, (December 1995): xiv.
23. Trimble, D., 'Platform', *The Belfast Newsletter*, 18 April 1998.
24. DUP, *Statement by Peter D. Robinson MP*, 7 May 1998.
25. Trimble, 'Platform', 18 April 1998.
26. Bew, P., 'The unionists have won, they just don't know it', *The Sunday Times*, 17 May 1998.
27. Hadfield, B., 'The Belfast Agreement, Sovereignty and the State of the Union', *Public Law*, (Winter 1998): 599–616.
28. UUP, *Understanding the Agreement*, May 1998, 4.
29. Martin, G., 'Wavering unionists fear havoc a strong no vote could cause', *Irish Times*, 20 May 1998.
30. Dodds, N., 'Accept and we are on the road to a united Ireland', *Parliamentary Brief*, 5/6 (1998): 21.
31. DUP, *The Big Lie*, 12 May 1998.
32. DUP, *Statement by Peter D. Robinson MP*.
33. Robinson, P., 'Belfast deal just pushes the same problems further down the track', *The Irish Times*, 12 June 1998.
34. DUP, *Speech to Party Conference by Peter Robinson MP*, 28 November 1998.
35. DUP, *Statement by I. Paisley Jr: 'Yes Parties are Wreckers of The Belfast Agreement'*, 23 April 1999.
36. McCartney, R., 'North's hope of a bright future is fast becoming a nightmare', *Irish Times*, 12 January 1999.
37. DUP, *Statement by Sammy Wilson: 'Is Trimble Caving In Again?*, 1 September 1998.
38. O'Brien, C. C., *Memoir* (Dublin: Poolbeg Press, 1998), 440.
39. UUP, *Speech by Rt. Hon. David Trimble MP to the Northern Ireland Forum*, 17 April 1998.
40. UUP, *Rt. Hon. David Trimble MP: Where I Stand Now*, 4 June 1999.
41. UUP, *The Commitment to Peace and Democracy: Speech in Canada by Rt. Hon. David Trimble MP*, 28 May 1999.
42. UUP, *Speech by Rt. Hon. David Trimble MP, First Minister, to the Annual Conference of The Irish Association in Wicklow*, 20 November 1998.
43. UUP., *Speech by Rt. Hon. David Trimble MP to business and community leaders in Belfast*, 22 June 1998.
44. Cited in the *Irish Times*, 11 October 1999.
45. Simon, S., 'Trimble: a Moses, not a Judas', *The Daily Telegraph*, 29 November 1999.

11

Modern Irish Republicanism and the Belfast Agreement: Chickens Coming Home to Roost, or Turkeys Celebrating Christmas?

Anthony McIntyre

The Defeat of the Provisional IRA

The peace process in the North of Ireland has occasioned considerable debate as to whether or not Provisional republicanism has undergone a major transformation. While some unionists may reassure themselves with a rhetorical question—'Why do Martin McGuinness and Bairbre de Brun maintain the illusion that they are inheritors of Sean Russell's Irish Republic rather than Ministers of the British Crown?'[1]—there has clearly been a deep unionist mistrust of republican motives. John Taylor, the deputy leader of the Ulster Unionist party, for instance has claimed that republicans were never sincere about the peace accord. On the other hand Danny Morrison, the former Sinn Féin publicity director, has been effusive in his praise for the 'peacemakers' in the republican leadership.[2]

A more critical appraisal would extend beyond the rival interpretations of Taylor and Morrison and conclude that, not only are the Provisionals earnest about peace, but that such seriousness arises from the defeat of the Provisional IRA—despite the protestations to the contrary from republicans among others.[3] Furthermore, a critical evaluation would locate that defeat in the strategic/political/ideological sphere rather than, as in the work of Holland—who, to his credit, does acknowledge such an outcome—in the military/organizational or structural realm.[4]

If traditional republican ideology is the yardstick for measuring the success or otherwise of the Provisional republican project then it is plausible to contend that the Belfast Agreement of April 1998 was an unmitigated disaster.[5] In the view of P. H. Pearse, a man who accepts:

anything less by one fraction of an iota than separation from England . . . is guilty of so immense an infidelity, so immense a crime against the Irish nation, that one can only say of him that it were better for that man (as it were certainly better for his country) that he had not been born. (Pearse quoted in Smith, M. L. R., *The Role of the Military Instrument in Republican Strategic Thinking An Evolutionary Analysis* (Kings College: University of London, 1991), 78.)

Sinn Féin leaders Mitchel McLaughlin, Martin McGuinness, and Gerry Adams have each attempted to minimize the extent of the shortfall from the 'traditional' interpretation by couching their comments in strategic-transitional terms. Thus, their party:

accepted the responsibility to manage the political transition . . .[a] . . . you could have a situation where Sinn Féin is in government in the North and Sinn Féin in government in the South. The logic is that the division of the country will have to end . . .[b]
. . .we believe the Good Friday agreement is the transitional structure that will allow us to achieve that legitimate objective. . .[c]   [a] Mitchel McLaughlin quoted in Breen, S., *Irish Times*, 21 January 2000; [b] Martin McGuinness quoted in Coulter, C., *Irish Times*, 14 June 1999; [c] Moriarty, G., *Irish Times*, 30 November 1999.)

However, the minimum contents of any such transition, as articulated by Gerry Adams a matter of weeks prior to the Belfast Agreement,[6] were not met by its terms. Notwithstanding the justifiable comparison between 'Pinocchio' and Peter Mandelson drawn by republicans, the British Secretary of State could on this occasion credibly claim that 'as far as we can see, the Good Friday Agreement is the end settlement'.[7] If, however, the shortfall between transition and outcome is regarded as work for another day and if, for now, Provisional republicanism is conceptualized in terms other than those of essentialist reductionism, it becomes possible to view the Agreement as the logical structural culmination of the Provisional campaign:

the principal problem in the North of Ireland has been that there was for fifty years one administration in office . . .[a]
. . . the permanent majority in the North, the Protestants, were at no pains to win the trust of the permanent minority; and in the end they paid dearly for their negligence.[b]
[a] Liam Cosgrave quoted in Walsh, D., *Irish Times*, 6 October 1973; [b] Editorial, *Sunday Times*, 25 March 1973.)

Thus, there always existed the structural potential for an outcome that would constitute the outworking of structural processes of grievance, regardless of how the latter might be rhetorically or ideologically defined. As a *Guardian* correspondent could recently observe: 'All sides know in their hearts, however, that there will only ever be one show in town: power-sharing in Northern Ireland buttressed by cross-border links with the Irish Republic'.[8] Such an outcome would see republican politics pulled back to the structural baseline of a more general northern nationalist politics.

A distinct functional and intellectual space therefore needs to be created between a methodological structural approach of this type and a more ideology focused paradigm that searches for consistency between the outcome of the Provisional campaign and the tenets of traditional republican ideology. That is not to lessen the charge of defeat. Rather, it compels analysts to become more focused in the search for its source. In setting aside the disparity between the ideals of tradition and the reality of outcome, analysts cannot ignore the conscious role of the Provisional republican leadership in promoting the aims of traditionalist republican ideology and expecting to be judged by it. It was never the case that the present republican leadership at all times sought to guide the ship of republicanism through the violently pulsating currents of republican tradition, the most turbulent of which has been physical force.[9]

The leadership which eventually settled for the Belfast Agreement mirrored unionism in so far as it had long acted as a major block to the type of solution that was crafted in that agreement. For instance, it had earlier undermined attempts that it perceived to be some form of *rapprochement* between the British and republicans,[10] pejoratively dismissing as 'Fianna Failers'[11] those who had tried. Similarly, it had castigated those alleged to be prepared to settle for less than the objectives of traditional republicanism,[12] and berated others who judged that the peace process could only lead to a Sunningdale-type outcome.[13] That it did so was a matter of the conscious and openly stated pursuit of goals discursively framed within the ensemble of tradition. As Wright has found, the Provisionals in general actively worked to construct legitimacy around their cause rather than assume it was an immanent part of the overall republican package.[14] They set themselves a 'carefully devised campaign to *take possession* of the entire tradition of Irish republicanism.'[15]

In short, the Provisional republican leadership defined the objective; strategically articulated physical force to it—in the words of Gerry Adams, 'if at any time Sinn Féin decide to disown the armed struggle it won't have me as a member')[16]—and ultimately abandoned it. The IRA leadership has thus found it difficult to avoid the kind of accusation levelled against NATO during its attack on the Serbs: of having been 'stupendously incompetent in matching methods to aims'.[17] And the more it has deviated from the demands of the armed campaign, the more incompetent its management of that campaign may subsequently appear.

Danny Morrison[18] and Eoghan Harris[20] have both argued that while the IRA had not won, neither had it been defeated. Yet it is only possible to draw such a conclusion if the IRA is denuded of a political dynamic and explained instead only in terms of a self-regenerating military machine which, because it remained intact, could not therefore be said to be defeated. Such a line of reasoning is all the more surprising from Morrison rather than Harris who, because of his Workers' party background, was always a self-proclaimed 'implacable enemy of the irredentist ideology of the Provisional IRA'.[20]

But even here the extent to which both men set sails against their own wisdom is evident. Harris, addressing the Unionist party conference in 1999 asserted: 'Look, Sinn Féin fought for 30 years. It's like a kid wanting a bike for Christmas. The bike they wanted was a united Ireland. They didn't get the bike.

Please give them a few stickers'.[21] Morrison, in outlining what the Provisionals had conceded, referred to:

the deletion of Articles 2 and 3 of the Irish constitution; the return of a Northern Assembly; Sinn Féin abandoning its traditional policy of abstentionism; reliance on British-government-appointed commissions on the equality and human rights issues and on the future of policing; and the implicit recognition of the principle of unionist consent on the constitutional question. (Morrison, D., *Guardian*, 13 July 1999.)

There is undoubted merit in maintaining that the IRA was not militarily defeated and in this context to refer to the guerrilla force, as Gerry Adams does, as 'the undefeated army'.[22] But this ignores the possibility that the British State preferred an IRA that was not militarily defeated, if defeat entailed the potential for fissiparous tendencies that would re-engage the British in a military theatre. Successive British governments have acknowledged that the IRA must remain intact for prospects of a lasting peace to endure,[23] while RUC leader Ronnie Flanagan, when head of its Special Branch, spoke of the need to maintain a united IRA.[24]

The purpose and organizational integrity of an offensive military force only has meaning if it has the capacity to effect the type of political change it advocates. O'Muilleoir's contention that the IRA victory lay in avoiding defeat[25] has been described as 'the politics of madness'.[26] Militarily crushing the IRA became a redundant strategic exercise for the British State once the organization had vacated the political battlefield on which it pitted its strength and wits against the British. Again, Mandelson achieved the balance—while noting the difference—when he shrewdly observed in relation to the decommissioning issue that 'surrendering long-fought and hardline political ground is one thing. Appearing to be forced to surrender altogether is quite another'.[27]

In this context it should be remembered that Britain had no quarrel with constitutional nationalism or the gradual and peaceful extension of its hegemony over the thirty-two counties. [28] The political objective of the Provisional IRA was to secure a British declaration of intent to withdraw. It failed. The objective of the British State was to force the Provisional IRA to accept—and subsequently respond with a new strategic logic—that it would not leave Ireland until a majority in the North consented to such a move. It succeeded.[29] For these reasons it comes as little surprise to find British diplomat David Goodall[30] claiming that everything was going almost according to plan, and former MI6 director, Michael Oatley,[31] expressing public admiration for the Sinn Féin leadership.

Insisting on the truism that the IRA emerged from the strategic defeat militarily and organizationally intact may in one sense be largely immaterial to the analysis. In another it can only serve to blur analytical clarity. The *real* defeat of the Provisional IRA is to be found in the almost total thwarting of its own stated political objectives. These were encapsulated in Brian Feeney's observation that republicans have 'unsaid everything they said in the seventies and eighties and ultimately settled for less than the SDLP got in 1973, which republicans regarded then as a sell out'.[32] In fact, for striking the 1973 deal Gerry Adams insisted that the SDLP had become the first Catholic partitionist party.[33] Merlyn Rees, the British Secretary of State at the time of the Sunningdale collapse, observed in 1994 that 'there is nothing that the IRA can get now that they couldn't have had anytime in the last twenty years',[34] a point now seemingly accepted by Gerry Adams.[35] In other words, compromise at the margins but not at the centre of the disputed object.[36]

Consequently, since jettisoning the articulation between the IRA campaign and the demand for a British declaration of intent to withdraw—a position arrived at with the 1994 cease-fire—there emerged a republican strategy of 'never but will'.[37] This witnessed republicanism describing its strategic failures as either 'new phases of struggle'[38] or as 'staging posts'.[39] This process of transformation, which saw Provisional republicanism move away from its impossibilist demands, involved a strategy of deception amusingly alluded to by Paul Bew.[40] But leadership deception, the tendency to become middle-class and middle-aged,[41] or the emergence of a new bureaucratic politics so ably identified by Bean,[42] provide a superficial rather than a structural explanation for the changes. Such accounts help mask the essence of Provisional republicanism: that is, a conjunctural phenomenon of largely urban insurrectionary politics that expresses the marginalization of many nationalists within the North of Ireland. This is distinct from primarily expressing a cultural-cum-political sense of enforced separation from the twenty-six counties not under British administration.

Wrongly Explaining Provisional Republicanism

It is a legitimate exercise for Danny Morrison to argue that the Provisional IRA came from the events of August 1969, but to further claim 'all historians agree on that'[43] is somewhat more contentious. The manner in which Provisional republicanism came to be discussed helped to establish what Foucault would term a 'regime of truth'.[44] A discursive structure, at ease with the republican tradition, was distilled from a much wider and more complex vocabulary. Those analysts who failed to challenge the structure have erroneously accepted the republican movement's 'own pronounced tendency to a monochrome remembrance of itself'.[45]

While today books on the Provisional IRA could stock a small library, in their formative days it was observed of the Provisionals that 'there is universal ignorance of them.'[46] The earliest works providing us with knowledge of IRA history were those of Coogan,[47] and Bowyer Bell.[48] In many respects both authors came to be regarded as authorities in the field of Provisional republicanism. When Bowyer-Bell's book was published in 1970, the chief of staff of the Official IRA described it as 'the most important book of reference . . . on the history of the IRA'.[49] Coogan also came to be regarded as an 'expert' on the IRA, although the Provisional's first chief of staff insisted that Coogan's first IRA book was 'the worst crap ever written'.[50] In fact, neither work examined the Provisionals. This in itself was indicative of a thought process—if you 'knew about' republicanism it automatically followed that you 'knew about' Provisionalism. The process of conferring 'authority' on this basis underlined the extent to which the argument of tradition was already accepted on its own terms.

Joe Lee has contended that 'those whose psyches depend on neat straight lines leading inexorably to the next "stage" should not do history, or attempt historical thought'.[51] Crucial, therefore, to understanding a fundamental weakness in the works of these authors when they eventually did come to deal with Provisionalism, is that they grafted onto the new phenomenon their earlier studies of pre-Provisional Irish republicanism. As historians of the IRA they extended that history to cover the Provisional period. But IRA history was not of primary epistemological significance to the construction of a necessarily specific Provisional historiography. Without ever having a peculiarly 'Provisional' paradigmatic construction, both authors—less true for Bowyer Bell than Coogan—became 'authorities' by default. New findings were allowed to deposit as a form of common-sense sediment on a pre-existing layer of understanding. Indeed these 'new' findings themselves could never have been epistemologically 'uncontaminated' by the 'old' method of understanding.

Critical history is about preventing continuities overriding the discontinuities that become evident during the course of examination[52] and as such Patterson is correct to draw attention to the deficiencies of studies which failed to emphasize the discontinuous.[53] It was not until Burton[54] wrote on republicanism in 1978, followed by Moxon-Browne[55] in 1981, that some epistemological movement toward conjunctural rather than traditionalist methods of conceptualizing republicanism began to emerge.

A More Conjunctural Explanation

The existence of a pervasive and seamless thirty-two county nationalist sentiment, both its substance and sensitivity enhanced by the existence of partition, is a dubious claim. The Southern Irish State experienced no crisis of legitimization spawned by its basis in partition. As early as the 1930s, the postrising generation was 'utterly indifferent to the great story that began in Easter 1916 . . . even bored by it'.[56] For the population of the Irish Republic, territorial unification had no value if measured in material terms such as the removal of British troops from *their* streets or an end to Loyalist domination over *them*.[57] Garret Fitzgerald observes:

despite the persistence of the aspiration to Irish unity in this part of Ireland, and despite the genuine concern that exists here for the plight of the people of Northern Ireland, the fundamental loyalty of most people in this part of Ireland is to our own State—rather than to a notional and abstract united Ireland. (Fitzgerald, G., *Irish Times*, 9 May 1998.)

In other words, the nation-state already existed,[58] rendering the national question 'almost totally irrelevant in the South'.[59]

Gerry Adams has spoken of the depth of insecurity felt by nationalists arising from 'the history of the *six county statelet*',[60] which suggests the existence of exclusively northern factors that feed a particular anti-systemic protest dynamic and which is more nebulous than anti-partitionism *per se*. What in fact constituted systemic protest and, by extension, what was actually being protested against, has remained a contested issue within Northern nationalism.

The partition-spawned political entity of Northern Ireland, like all other institutions, embodied the following characteristics:

a defined *structure* or order which by definition conditions the behaviour of its members. Such structures are not neutral, for they establish patterns of authority and confer the right to take decisions on some individuals and not others; in effect they institutionalise relationships between rulers and ruled, domination and compliance. (McGrew, T., 'Conceputalising Global Politics', in Paper 1, Block 1, *Global Politics: D312*, (Milton Keynes: The Open University, 1988), 18.)

Unlike the South, where economic and political policies could cater for, or at least mollify a diverse range of interests and opinion, and where no processes of structural exclusion along purely sectarian political or religious lines could generate strong nationalist opposition to the partitionist twenty-six county state, the Northern partitionist state 'in its genesis, its operation and the setting of its borders . . . was profoundly undemocratic and discriminatory'.[61] From its inception it was effectively governed without consensus,[62] excluding Catholics from political influence and maintaining widespread economic discrimination against them.[63] In McGrew's terms what Northern Ireland 'institutionalized' was a democratic deficit or structure of domination.[64] Given such domination, if politics can mean initiatives from below 'which seek to alter systematically the dominant form of contemporary democracy',[65] Provisional republicanism—including the IRA's armed struggle—may be viewed as one such political initiative 'the logic of whose development contradicts the institutionally dominant social logic.'[66]

Although a structurally induced complicity rather than ideological approval determined the attitude of the British State to such social logic, that logic was fortified by a combination of that State's repression, its peripheralization of the North as a political entity, and the constitutional guarantee it provided to a majority of people in the North of Ireland. Cecil King's rationale that there was an extreme reluctance to become involved in Irish affairs[67] explains rather than justifies British policy. The consequence of maximum inaction being viewed as preferable to minimum action,[68] was that the worst effects of the conflict were to be displaced by the British State on to those considered to possess minimum ability to do much about adverse matters—the least powerful group in Ireland, northern nationalists.[69] In such circumstances coercion becomes both *determinant and dominant.*[70]

Concerned primarily with protecting its own interests and reputation, the British State—perceiving that nothing much could be done and that the only guide to the future was the past—opted in 1969 for the 'least disturbing option'[71] namely, limiting 'its intervention to measures designed to restore the credibility of Unionist rule in the eyes of the world.'[72] Structurally and strategically, rather than ideologically or through individual minister's appetites, this meant that British force became the guarantor for a sectarian hegemon,[73] 'designed to underpin and secure the unionist position as top dogs in perpetuity.'[74] Consequently, British State strategy rather than republican tradition 'created the best possible conditions for the development of the Provisionals.'[75]

Subsequently, the dynamics of Provisional Irish republicanism are to be *primarily* found in the post-1969 relationship between large elements of the nationalist working class and the British State. The 'structural determination'[76] of this *particular* group lay in the geographically specific institutional dynamics of partition. As a social stratum it cannot be viewed in essentialist terms. That is, as a preconstituted body seamlessly at one with the rest of the island's nationalists, and endowed with those cultural, ideological, and political characteristics which enabled it to be viewed as a continuation of an unbroken tradition dating back to 1916 and beyond, with an ontological vocation to complete unfinished business. Given the disparity in attitudes towards their respective partitionist States by the populations in both parts of the island, partition in itself was insufficient to nourish, let alone sustain, a thirty-two-countywide nationalist ideology articulating the necessity of completing the 'unfinished business' of 1921. Consequently, where tradition played a determining role, northern nationalism impacted more on the development of Provisional republicanism than did the wider traditionalist physical force influence of 1916.[77] In the north it was said that 'the Divis Street riots stimulated interest in republicanism; but if it did it was not to any significant degree'.[78] Traditional republicanism had its own stage two years later in 1966 when, because of the anniversary of the 1916 rising, there was 'a big revival of interest in republicanism' in the North.[79] But the moment was fleeting: the stage, like shadow and penumbra from another age, vaporized.

Sluka's view, therefore, has much relevance. He observed that fear of attacks by Protestant mobs remained an entrenched and historically validated element of Catholic political culture in the North of Ireland.[80] 'Fear of attack by loyalist or British forces'[81] is not merely a useful self-justifying rationale crafted by republican ideologues, as is thematically suggested in O'Doherty's work.[82] In August 1969 the Northern Ireland Civil Rights Association would claim that 'in recent days the CRA has supported people forced to use defensive violence.'[83]

So just how accurate is it to contend, as Guelke does of the Provisionals in the 1980s, that: 'the grounding of the legitimacy of the Provisional IRA's campaign in a traditional republican interpretation of Irish history is now much less emphasised than it was at the start of the campaign'?[84] If, as has been the logic informing this chapter, a dynamic different from that of traditional republicanism was behind the mushrooming of Provisional republicanism, it is inescapable that evidence of this would be most pronounced in the formative stages of Provisionalism—when the dust had yet to settle and more manufactured rationales had yet to be devised.

The contested meaning of the symbolism, however, is never far from the surface. In terms of localized cultural expression, for example, Kenney has argued that the phoenix mural visible in so many nationalist ghettos depicts an arising from 'the defeat suffered by the martyr heroes of the 1916 Easter Rising'.[85] However, the words accompanying the phoenix refer to the Provisionals arising *out of 1969*. Certainly, more traditionalist republicans such as Bernadette Sands McKevitt would see no need to dig deeper into the founds of Provisional republicanism, viewing it as an uncomplicated continuation of all that had gone before.[86] This leads to her to claim with much conviction that her brother, the hunger striker Bobby Sands, 'did not die for cross border bodies with executive powers . . . [nor for] . . . nationalists to be equal British citizens within the Northern Ireland state.'[87] But the fervent nationalism of Bobby Sands was the product of post-1969 events. It was an ideology which 'while rooted in history is *above all* the result of . . . [a] . . . learning process which began with the civil rights campaign'.[88] In his childhood days Sands viewed British soldiers as his heroes. However, because of the actions of British soldiers on Belfast streets:

no longer did I think of them as my childhood 'good guys', for their presence alone caused food for thought. Before I could work out the solution it was answered for me in the form of early morning raids.   (Bobby Sands quoted in Feehan, J. M., *Bobby Sands and the tragedy of Northern Ireland* (Dublin: Mercier, 1983), 66–7.)

Gerry Adams made the point that in embarking on his republican odyssey, part of his pre-Provisional programme was that 'we wanted to be treated the same as citizens in Britain'.[89] This was consistent with even the radical political flavour of the time, as the experience of Ed Moloney would suggest. Rallying to the banner of 'People's Democracy' he recalls that its anti-State activity 'had little to do with nationalism or republicanism. If anything, we were trying to make Northern Ireland more British, not less'.[90] The first Belfast Provisional leadership did not 'seem to have known what they wanted. Only Leo Martin. . . . was really talking about a united Ireland.'[91] The first recorded words spoken by the Provisional IRA were critical of 'the failure to provide the maximum defence possible.'[92] These sentiments were repeated at the 1998 commemoration for those from the Greater Ballymurphy area who had died. The IRA's Belfast brigade statement put it bluntly: 'we *originally came into being* because our community had to defend itself against a regime bent on its destruction'.[93] It is perhaps of little surprise that part of the earlier membership was comprised of 'bigots'.[94]

Even the language of old republicanism was not part of the natural language of the new urban northerners from the disadvantaged working class estates.[95] Where it did exist, traditional republican discourse more often constituted the elocuted voice rather than the raw tone of Provisionalism. If 'sheer common sense' means that 'everybody could identify with the nation in some way'[96] then it made sense for the Provisionals to behave as such. McKinley has argued that the Provisionals, *vis-à-vis* some of their detractors in the nationalist camp, were possessed of 'more foresight, guile and dishonesty.'[97]

While Easter may have been 'the most emotive date in the republican calendar',[98] August 1969 and the perceived threat of 'destruction' had greater meaning for Provisionalism. As Morrison puts it: 'It didn't matter if you had brilliant politics or awful politics. It didn't matter if your politics were progressive or conservative. If you failed to defend the people you deserved to go to the wall'.[99] In March 1999 Gerry Kelly would refer to Bombay Street rather than Easter as necessitating the IRA's retention of its weaponry. His closest discursive allusion to Easter pertained to Belfast 1998—not Dublin 1916—and the 'Good Friday' Agreement.[100] In terms of republican tradition, one former Provisional argued that 'August 1969 added fuel only to a *very, very low* smouldering political fire.'[101]

The Provisional IRA, while certainly 'more closely allied with the physical force tradition,'[102] was not the product of that tradition. While the Belfast founders and leadership may have been steeped in the republican tradition, the post-1969 northern recruits joined in response to State violence.[103]

Giddens has argued that the influence of leaders is crucial in the development of nationalist ideology.[104] But it has been the tunnel vision, focusing on early leaders who were 'born and reared'[105] in the republican tradition, which has led to Provisionalism being so mischaracterized. The post-1969 stratum in fact clashed with the Provisional leaders who, because of their pre-1969 experience, were bemused at 'the influx of incredible numbers of new members which they had never experienced before in their lives.'[106]

If the new stratum is examined it becomes clear that 'their socialisation into republicanism has been formed during the "troubles"'.[107] Andersonstown, one of the areas to mount stiff Provisional resistance—and from which many Provisional IRA volunteers would emerge—'never had a republican tradition and indeed it was against their will that a large section of the population gave their support to the struggle, and the thanks goes to the British army and their brutality'.[108] This new Provisional stratum was increasingly to engage in the republican struggle as a result of British State initiatives such as the Falls curfew and internment. Each acted as a catalyst in creating a nationalist perception of 'rule by terror'[109]—the repetitive repressive acts which Moxon-Browne found so crucial to the durability and resilience of the IRA.[110] Consequently, it is unconvincing to claim that people joining the Provisionals were joining 'a movement with a history' and 'an understanding of Ireland's predicament'.[111] On the contrary, if such a movement ever existed it *became absorbed* into the Provisionals and its history articulated into Provisional discourse as part of a legitimization process precisely because Provisionalism had in fact 'very little in common with its precursor'.[112] In this context it is analytically lazy to claim that the Provisionals in 1969–70 restored the IRA's traditional position of defending the 1916 proclamation.[113] For many, the proclamation of 1916 had as much relevance as the Dead Sea Scrolls.[114]

Despite the claim that there were many nationalists who 'were brought up to venerate Pearse',[115] a certain irreverent attitude towards republican tradition and 1916 was observed by Danny Morrison: 'there was a good cynicism among young people that came into the Republican Movement in 69/70. The type of cynicism that had them saying "fuck those bastards Pearse and Connolly"'.[116]

A brief examination of the less irreverent attitudes of early Provisionals is instructive in this regard. Martin McGuinness, for instance, who claims to be a product solely of the troubles, situates his rite of passage thus:

The Duke Street beatings, the attack on Sammy Devenny, and the killing of Cusack and Beattie were the four incidents why I became a republican.[a] . . . I am a product of British injustice. It was the British and the unionists who made me a republican, not the Christian Brothers.[b] ([a] Martin McGuinness quoted in Toolis, K., *Rebel Hearts: Journeys within the IRA's Soul* (London: Picador, 1995), 304; [b] Martin McGuinness quoted in Moriarty, G., 'SF's chief negotiator hopes for end to conflict', *Irish Times on the Web* 1998.)[117]

In the case of Gerry Kelly: 'It was an issue of protecting our areas'[118] '. . . mostly it was a sense of defending our people. I was only vaguely aware of Irish history, Wolfe Tone and all that.'[119] According to one IRA volunteer of the time, later to command IRA prisoners in Long Kesh, 'neither I nor most others that I knew in Derry joined the IRA because we were republicans. That all came later when we went to jail and the like'.[120]

The difference in perception between those in the new stratum and the 'keepers of the flame'[121] was encapsulated in an encounter in 1969 between two of them. Eighteen-year old Bernard Fox, seeking a gun for the purposes of protecting his family and friends, approached an IRA leader and was asked 'Could you shoot a British soldier?' Fox was shocked: 'At that time I hadn't the idea that it was the British Government's fault'.[122] This type of attitude prevailed strongly until early 1971. Danny Morrison recalls that, on the deaths of three Scottish soldiers in March:

People were appalled at the deaths of the three young Scottish soldiers. In a sense they weren't ready for it. They were out of uniform, unarmed and lured. They weren't shot in a whippet car going down the Falls Road. (Danny Morrison. Interview with Anthony McIntyre, 23 November 1995.)

Yet the physical force tradition could have legitimized the killing of 'foreign soldiers' on Irish soil—'as long as British soldiers remain in Ireland the Irish republican tradition will fight and kill them.'[123] But even here a consciousness of the existence of a further gulf between traditional republicanism and Provisionalism was evident in relation to this very operation. As Martin Meehan commented, 'it was not the type of job Patrick Pearse would have done'.[124]

It is not implausible, therefore, to argue that in northern urban areas, where class was to prove a crucial determinant of political allegiances,[125] that the 'deep atavistic fear in Belfast's working class Catholic population of a Loyalist pogrom',[126] became intermeshed with a strand of conflict which, for most nationalists, was a 'civil rights struggle fought through republican rhetoric'.[127] What leant the rhetoric substance was that British State strategy through initiatives, such as internment and Bloody Sunday, had established 'definitive events from which many people take their understanding of the role of the British state in Northern Ireland'.[128] Despite forays into traditionalist discourse, it was around British army actions that the IRA was able to construct the 'most legitimacy surrounding its violence'.[129] For example, until the British killings of Seamus Cusack and Desmond Beattie 'effectively there was no IRA in Derry.'[130] Until internment and Bloody Sunday: 'republicanism in Derry was the preserve of less than a dozen steadfast and tenacious families who were isolated and out-of-tune with the prevailing nationalistic and conservative political reality in the town'.[131] As Waters contends, essential to the entire process of the development of Provisional republicanism:

was an iconography drawn less from the ancient history of Irish republicanism than from the recent history of the troubles: Bloody Sunday, the hunger strikes of the early 1980s, and occasional outrages against republican activists such as the Gibraltar shootings of 1988. (Waters, J., *Irish Times*, 12 May 1998.)

The urban content of Provisional republicanism can be evidenced from its organizational mushrooming in the cities. The IRA in Belfast and Derry grew to be massive but not so in the rural areas. Whereas over a thousand people from one tiny Belfast estate, Ballymurphy, were imprisoned throughout the conflict, 'there are about 100 ex-IRA prisoners in Fermanagh'.[132] Indeed, without the participation of the big cities, in particular Belfast, it is questionable if the rural areas could have conducted a revolt qualitatively different from the IRA campaign of the 1950s. In a sense, institutional patterns were shaping a mass of urban people 'out of which protest can arise.'[133]

The urban base of republican insurrectionary politics makes the city/rural dichotomy crucial to the understanding of early Provisional republicanism. Being geographically and time specific, it flourished only in the most deprived Catholic areas rather than in all nationalist areas, where, unlike other regions, the unskilled working class was increasing and nurturing a vast reservoir of opposition to unionism and indifference to moderation.[134] City republicanism was specifically conjunctural and therefore *provisional*. Rural republicanism was less conjunctural and was rooted in *traditional* ideology. While organizationally part of the Provisional movement, rural republicanism was much less *provisional* and was 'to some extent a different animal'.[135] Former Tyrone activist Tommy McKearney amplified that areas such as Tyrone—'a crucible of republicanism in the North'[136]—could not be reduced to a Provisional core:

The Provisional movement is only part of the wider republican spectrum. It is not a unique political movement in itself. It developed somewhat differently in Tyrone than in Belfast. In the 1950s Tyrone was very much republican based. Tyrone was electing republican candidates in the 1950s in a way that Belfast was not. As the Provisionals were born in Belfast, that movement was going to have its own unique base in Belfast. Tyrone was and still remains a traditionally republican county. (Tommy McKearney. Interview with Anthony McIntyre, 26 October 1997.)

Provisionalism was republicanism in a mass form, a form not previously achieved by traditional republicanism in the north. In order to sustain that form it had to be fed with material substance rather than vaporous ideology. Provisional republicanism went into serious decline as a result of those material needs being addressed from late 1972 to 1974 rather than as a result of intensified British militarization post-'Motorman'. But those needs were addressed in a manner that neither affected the constitutional *status quo* nor differed greatly from the Belfast Agreement. As the former Prime Minister Edward Heath stated in the wake of the latter, 'We know the people who were working out the new agreement went back over the whole of Sunningdale and more or less copied it.'[137]

Crucially, however, a raw attitudinal nerve was touched upon. And, like protest groups elsewhere, deprived of 'critical attitudinal supports', the Provisionals found it hard to mobilize those sections of society needed to sustain the project.[138] It was only in that crucial period from the autumn of 1972 to the summer of 1973, which witnessed the decline of Provisionalism as hegemon within working class nationalist communities, that the centre of republican gravity shifted towards the more traditionally republican rural areas.[139] Accompanying this was a shift in discourse ably charted by Fisk:

Six months ago the IRA's *modus vivendi* would have been represented as a reaction to the riots of 1969. The Provisionals we would have been told, had been the only army prepared to defend the Roman Catholic community, prepared if necessary to squat in the tower of that Catholic church in Ballymacarret to protect it from the Protestants . . . [now] asked to justify a campaign in which over 800 people had been killed, O'Connell fell back on the precedence of 1916 and at one point Twomey, literally shaking with anger at the attitude of an Irish reporter, retorted that 'the authority of the second Dail' had been passed onto them by Thomas Maguire, its last republican member. (Fisk, R., *The Times*, 16 July 1973.)

All of this lends credence to O'Doherty's view that the IRA's 'application of violence was always a form of political protest'.[140] Such protest is not unusual for a 'dominated group', that is, 'one that is excluded from one or more of the decision-making processes that determine the quantity and quality of social, economic and political rewards that groups receive from a society.'[141] Determining the essence of that political protest by looking at the 'transformations which fail to correspond to the calm, continuist image that is normally accredited'[142] may prove most revealing about the nature of Provisional republicanism. It also allows us to answer affirmatively the question once posed by W. B. Yeats, 'is there logic to outweigh MacDonagh's bony thumb?'[143]

A Structural Overview

The formative years of the Provisionals suggests that they became a structural element rooted in northern nationalists who were themselves compelled by the logic of British State interests to turn decisively *away from* a malevolent state rather than enthusiastically *towards* the ideal of a united country.[144] Living conjunctural parameters were themselves sufficient to shape republican political and strategic formulation. It is hardly necessary, therefore, to ask as Cox does 'what was the justification of an armed struggle designed to force them out' if the British in fact had no overriding strategic interest in remaining?[145] It would have proved more purposeful to have posed the question in the following terms: while the British State had no direct strategic or economic interest in *being in* Northern Ireland, what impact did its activities *while there* have for northern nationalist politics? As Gurr observes, States are more inclined to employ force against the politically marginal than against the more powerful.[146] In other conflict situations 'dominated groups at different times attempt to change their situation of powerlessness by engaging in non-traditional and usually non-legitimised struggles with power holders'.[147] The IRA's campaign helped reduce the 'power disparity' between the structure of domination and those most dominated.[148]

The range of collective actions open to a relatively powerless group is normally very small. Its program, its form of action, its very existence are likely to be illegal, hence subject to violent repression. As a consequence such a group chooses between taking actions which have a high probability of bringing on a violent response (but which have some chance of reaching the group's goals) and taking no action at all (thereby ensuring the defeat of the group's goals). (Tilly, C., Tilly, L., and Tilly, R. quoted in McAdam, D., *Political Process and the Development of Black Insurgency*, 39.)

'Deprived by their institutional location of the opportunity to use other forms of defiance'[149], people were attracted to that rather than *republican* militancy *per se*. For the vast majority of northern nationalists who sought improvement in their lives and who were not beholden to a republican tradition, a satisfactory conclusion was potentially one that remained considerably far removed from any prescription drawn up by republicanism. The British unlocked the structural code in the period from the autumn of 1972 to the summer of 1973 and decimated Provisionalism. Unable to sustain the momentum due to the unionist 'strategy of threat,'[150] the British State reverted to type—repressing those most aggressively opposed to the *status quo*. Such repression produced the hunger strikes. And the subsequent intense alienation kept armed Provisionalism in business. But ultimately the gravitational pull of a Belfast Agreement type framework would always prove stronger than any tangents along the way. The strategic corollary was that the constitutional mountain of northern nationalism did not go to the Provisionals—they went to it. As the most formative years of Provisionalism indicate, it was structurally inscribed—traditional republican ideology simply had not read the script.

Conclusion

There has been so much 'spin' put on the Belfast Agreement that one could almost be forgiven for sharing Conor Cruise O'Brien's view that spin involves 'routine resort to deception.'[151] Terms like 'creative ambiguity'[152] amount to little more than putting spin on spin. Whatever political purpose such terminology may serve, it can have no place in academic investigation: 'If even academics lie there is little hope'.[153]

While there are genuine differences of interpretation these do not always overcome the grip of ambiguity. Jennifer Todd, to cite a case in point, explores the possibility that republicans, rather than rejecting anti-partitionism for partitionism, have merely rejected this organizing ideological dichotomy.[154] Todd, however, fails to distinguish sufficiently persuasively between constitutional nationalism and 'new republicanism'. Her analysis comes unstuck in republican 'linguistic mazes'.[155] There is no effective illustration of the novelty of 'new republicanism' in a manner that would suggest the emergence of a qualitatively new phenomenon. Todd is left to claim that the Belfast Agreement was 'a major turning point' on the basis of minor criteria, having insufficiently demonstrated the non-constitutional nationalist content of 'new republicanism'.

The 'old wine in new bottles' character of the Agreement is readily evident. Apart from the essentially non-constitutional equality agenda, which has been viewed as radical and innovative,[156] the Belfast Agreement 'is testament to what has been central to SDLP thinking for years,'[157] and 'represents the best deal unionists could possibly have won.'[158] In the words of the British Prime Minister:

this offers unionists every key demand they have made since partition 80 years ago . . . The principle of consent, no change to the constitutional status of Northern Ireland without the consent of the majority of people, is enshrined. The Irish constitution has been changed . . . A devolved assembly and government for Northern Ireland is now there for the taking. When I first came to Northern Ireland as prime minister, these demands were pressed on me as what unionists really needed. I have delivered them all. (Tony Blair, quoted in Kearney, V. and McManus, J., *Sunday Times*, 4 July 1999.)

To get a measure of how little has been ceded by unionists—and by implication how much by republicans—we need only view it through the following prism:

If, for example, through the Good Friday Agreement, the unionists had signed up to a British declaration of intent to withdraw from the North and a Dublin declaration of intent to annex the six counties, no amount of wordplay and casuistry would have permitted this outcome to be regarded as anything other than a resounding defeat. Small consolation it would have been to them to have won outright on Strand One matters, such as keeping the RUC intact or the prisoners locked up. Unionism would have lost on the great philosophical question of consent.   (McIntyre, A., 'Britain—The Sovereign Power' on *And None Who Shall Censor Us*, Irish Republican Writers' Group Website, 12 February 2000: http://www.rwg.phoblacht.com)

While Todd claims that it has become even more difficult to assess the direction of 'new republicanism'[159] it is more prudent to feel that 'the future holds years of negotiating, and wheeling and dealing, and peace processing, with an eventual outcome very different from the traditional republican dream'.[160]

The Belfast Agreement was a defining moment in a new political dispensation, the purpose of 'which was to isolate paramilitarism'.[161] This was to be achieved by 'including republicans in the political process but excluding republicanism'.[162] The extent to which such a 'strategy was both necessary and successful'[163] has not gone unnoticed by Tom McGurk: 'It is no exaggeration to say that had the Sinn Féin leadership suggested such things only a decade ago, they might have ended up floating in the Lagan'.[164] Pearse may have been less ruthless—simply wishing that such a leadership had never been born.

ENDNOTES

1. King, S., *Sunday Tribune*, 30 January 2000.
2. Morrison, D., *Guardian*, 13 July 1999.
3. Adams, G., *Irish News*, 8 March 1999; McGuinness, M., *Irish News*, 3 March 1999; *Irish Times*, 28 December 1999; Preston, P., *Guardian*, 14 February 2000.
4. Holland, J., *Hope Against History* (London: Hodder & Stoughton 1999).
5. I have argued this position elsewhere. See McIntyre, A., *Sunday Tribune*, 12 April 1998.
6. Adams, G., *Ireland on Sunday*, 8 March 1998. Amongst the 'minimum' criteria were powerful cross bodies immune from the Northern Assembly; RUC disbandment; no weakening of Dublin's constitutional claim to the North.
7. Peter Mandelson, quoted in Millar, F., *Irish Times*, 21 January 2000.
8. Watt, N., *Guardian*, 4 February 2000.
9. Some writers debate and, in some cases, confuse the nature of my argument in relation to this matter. For instance, the unionist commentators Stephen King and Henry McDonald draw opposing conclusions from what I have written. Neither in fact has examined the

argument in full. See King, S., *Belfast Telegraph*, 11 November 1999 and McDonald, H., *Observer*, 14 November 1999.

10. McGuinness, M., *Magill*, 13 November 1986.
11. Gorman, T., *Feile Radio*, 27 February 2000.
12. Connolly, F., *Sunday Business Post*, 2 January 1994.
13. In one case in early 1995 at a 'republican family' meeting in West Belfast, Sinn Féin *ard comhairle* members stated that it was beyond their comprehension how I or anyone else could envisage the party ever signing up to anything remotely resembling Sunningdale. Austin Currie, a minister in the 1974 power-sharing executive, actually feels the Sunningdale Agreement was a better deal for nationalists than the Belfast Agreement. See *Irish Times*, 2 December 1999.
14. Wright, J., 'PIRA Propaganda: The Construction of Legitimacy', *Conflict Quarterly*, (Summer 1990): 24.
15. D. Donoghue, quoted in Arthur, P., 'Republican Violence in Northern Ireland: The Rationale', in J. Darby, N. Dodge, and A. C. Hepburn (eds.), *Political Violence: Ireland in a Comparative Perspective* (Belfast: Appletree, 1990), 49 (my emphases).
16. Adams, G., *Andersonstown News*, 1986.
17. Johnson, B., *Daily Telegraph*, 2 June 1999.
18. Morrison, D., *Guardian*, 11 May 1998.
19. Harris, E., *Sunday Times*, 19 September 1999.
20. Harris, E., *Irish Times*, 14 October 1999.
21. Eoghan Harris, quoted by Moriarty, G., *Irish Times*, 11 October 1999.
22. Gerry Adams, quoted by Preston, P., *Guardian*, 14 February 2000.
23. O'Dowd, N., *Irish Times* 17 January 2000.
24. Ronnie Flanagan, quoted in *Irish News*, 18 January 1995.
25. O Muilleoir, M., 'Hearts And Minds', BBC TV, 28 October 1999. O Muilleoir is a former Sinn Féin councillor and now editor of the *Andersonstown News* in west Belfast.
26. Tony Catney, conversation with Anthony McIntyre, 29 October 1999. Catney is a former member of the Sinn Féin *ard comhairle* (governing body) and a former long-term sentence prisoner.
27. Peter Mandelson, quoted by Cusack, J. and Breen, S., *Irish Times*, 5 February 2000.
28. Bew, P., 'The Ambiguous Dynamics of the Anglo Irish Agreement', in A. O'Day and Y. Alexander, (eds.), *Ireland's Terrorist Trauma: Interdisciplinary Perspectives* (New York, NY: St Martin's, 1989), 154.
29. McIntyre, A., *Guardian*, 22 May 1998.
30. Goodall, D., 'Actually it's all working out almost exactly to plan', *Parliamentary Brief*, (May/June 1998).
31. Oatley, M., *Sunday Times*, 31 October 1999.
32. Feeney, B., *Irish News*, 31 March. 1999
33. Adams, G., *The Politics of Irish Freedom* (Kerry: Brandon, 1986), 110.
34. Interview with Rogelio Alonso, 4 December 1996. Unpublished: Universidad Complutense de Madrid.
35. Graham, W., *Irish News*, 11 December 1999.
36. Smith, M., *The Role of the Military Instrument*, 375.
37. McIntyre, A., *Sunday Tribune*, 4 July 1999.
38. See for example 'Plotting course for future—Adams', *An Phoblacht/Republican News*, 18 November 1999.
39. Gerry Adams, cited in *News Letter*, 23 February 1999.
40. Bew, P., *Irish Times*, 25 May 1999.
41. Jenkins, S., *The Times*, 17 November 1999.
42. Bean, K., 'Every picture tells a story', *Fourthwrite* (journal of the Irish Republican Writers' Group), 1 (2000).
43. Danny Morrison, cited in *Belfast Telegraph*, 20 October 1999.
44. Foucault, M., 'Truth, Power and Sexuality', in V. Beechey and J. Donald (eds.), *Subjectivity and Social Relations* (Milton Keynes: Open University Press 1985), 93.
45. Patterson, H., *The Politics of Illusion: Republicanism And Socialism In Modern Ireland* (London: Hutchinson Radius, 1989), 3.

46. Pilgrim, J., 'The Provisionals', *Fortnight*, 11, 19 February 1971.
47. Coogan, T. P., *The IRA* (London: Pall Mall, 1970).
48. Bowyer Bell, J., *The Secret Army: A History of the IRA 1916–1970* (London: Blond, 1970).
49. Goulding, C., 'A book for the IRA', *This Week*, 17 December 1970.
50. Interview with Anthony McIntyre, 3 October 1995.
51. Lee, J., *Sunday Tribune*, 14 March 1999.
52. Foucault, M., in J. Lechte, *Fifty Key Contemporary Thinkers: From Structuralism to Postmodernity* (London: Routledge, 1994), 111.
53. Patterson, *The Politics of Illusion*, 6.
54. Burton, F., *The Politics of Legitimacy: Struggles in a Belfast Community* (London: Routledge & Kegan Paul, 1978).
55. Moxon-Browne, E., 'The Water and the Fish: Public Opinion and the IRA in Northern Ireland', in P. Wilkinson (ed.), *British Perspectives on Terrorism* (London: George Allen and Unwin, 1981), 50.
56. O'Connor, F., *The Big Fellow: The Life of Michael Collins* (London: Thomas Nelson, 1937), x.
57. White, R. W., *Provisional Irish Republicans: An Oral and Interpretive History* (Westport, CT: Greenwood, 1993), 122.
58. Cronin, S., *Irish Nationalism: A History of its Roots and Ideology* (Dublin: Academy, 1980), 220.
59. Smyth, J., 'Northern Ireland—Conflict Without Class', in A. Morgan and B. Purdie (eds.), *Ireland: Divided Nation Divided Class* (London: Ink Links, 1980), 47.
60. Adams, G., *Irish Times*, 14 June 1995, my emphases.
61. Harpur, A., *Irish News*, 2 April 1998.
62. Aughey, A., 'Political Violence in Northern Ireland', in H. H. Tucker (ed.), *Combating the Terrorists: Democratic Responses to Political Violence* (New York, NY: Centre for Security Studies, 1988), 79.
63. Rowthorn, B. and Wayne, N., *Northern Ireland: The Political Economy of Conflict* (Cambridge: Polity Press, 1988), 166. See also Maudling, R., *Memoirs* (London: Sidgwick and Jackson 1978), 185; Cormac, R. J. and Osborne, R. D., 'Disadvantage and Discrimination in Northern Ireland', in R. J. Cormac and R. D. Osborne (eds.), *Discrimination And Public Policy In Northern Ireland* (Oxford: Clarendon Press, 1991); Bloomfield, K., *Stormont In Crisis: A Memoir* (Belfast: Blackstaff 1994), 68.
64. This term is borrowed from Roberts, K., 'Democracy and the Dependent Capitalist State in Latin America', *Monthly Review* (October 1985), 24.
65. Held, D., 'Introduction: New Forms of Democracy', in D. Held and C. Pollitt (eds.), *New Forms of Democracy* (London: Sage, 1986), 7.
66. Manuel Castells, quoted in Piven, F. F. and Cloward, R. A., *Poor People's Movements: Why They Succeed, How They Fail* (New York, NY: Vintage Books, 1977), 17.
67. King, C., *On Ireland* (London: Jonathan Cape, 1973), 140.
68. O'Malley, P., *The Uncivil Wars: Ireland Today* (Belfast: Blackstaff, 1983), 206.
69. O'Brien, B., *The Long War: The IRA and Sinn Fein—1985 to Today* (Dublin: O'Brien Press, 1993), 100.
70. Anderson, P., 'The Antinomies of Antonio Gramsci', *New Left Review*, November 1976–January 1977, 21.
71. King, *On Ireland*, 140.
72. Guelke, A. and Smyth, J., 'The Ballot Bomb: Terrorism and the Electoral Process in Northern Ireland', in L. Weinberg (ed.), *Political Parties and Terrorist Groups* (London: Frank Cass, 1992), 104.
73. Moxon-Browne, 'The Water and the Fish', 50.
74. Harpur, A., *Irish News*, 2 April 1998.
75. Henry Patterson, *The Politics of Illusion: A Political History of the IRA* (London: Serif, 1997), 149.
76. This term is borrowed from Poulantzas, N., *Classes In Contemporary Capitalism* (London: New Left Books, 1975), 14.
77. For a useful discussion of post 1969 republicanism *vis à vis* pre-1969 republicanism see White, R. W., *Provisional Irish Republicans*.

78. Hill, P., *Stolen Years: Before and After Guildford* (Toronto: Doubleday, 1990), 34.
79. O'Doherty, M., *The Trouble With Guns: Republican Strategy and the Provisional IRA* (Belfast: Blackstaff, 1998), 23.
80. Sluka, J. A., *Hearts and Minds, Water and Fish: Support for the IRA and INLA in a Northern Irish Ghetto* (Greenwich, CT: JAI Press, 1989), 121.
81. Adams, G., *Belfast Telegraph*, 27 October 1995.
82. O'Doherty, *The Trouble With Guns*.
83. NICRA, *Irish News*, 20 August 1969.
84. Guelke, A., *Northern Ireland: The International Perspective* (Dublin: Gill and MacMillan, 1988), 41.
85. Kenny, M., 'The Phoenix and the Lark: Revolutionary Mythology and Iconographic Creativity in Belfast's Republican Districts', in A. Buckley (ed.), *Symbols in Northern Ireland* (Belfast: The Institute of Irish Studies, Queen's University, 1998), 153.
86. Interview of McKevitt by Anthony McIntyre, *The Sovereign Nation*, October 1998.
87. Bernadette Sands in Breen, S., 'The ideals Bobby died for are ideals I hold dear and which have always motivated me', *Magill*, January 1998.
88. Hartley, T., *Irish News*, 6 January 1994. Elsewhere Hartley is forceful on this point. Interview with Anthony McIntyre, 19 May 1994.
89. Gerry Adams, quoted in Collins, T., *Irish News*, 8 January 1994.
90. Moloney, E., 'The Media: Asking the Right Questions?', in M. Farrell (ed.), *Twenty Years On* (Kerry: Brandon, 1988), 138.
91. The Sunday Times Insight Team, *Ulster* (Harmondsworth: Penguin, 1972), 197.
92. The first statement of the Army Council of the Provisional IRA made on the 28 December 1969. Cited in McStiofain, S., *Memoirs of a Revolutionary* (Edinburgh: Gordon Cremonesi, 1975), 143.
93. Belfast Brigade, IRA, Statement read out to the Ballymurphy commemoration at the Felons Club, west Belfast, 2 October 1998. My emphases. Copy obtained by author.
94. Loughran, S., *Observer*, 6 August 1972.
95. O'Brien, *The Long War*, 105.
96. Smyth, J., 'Dependent Interdependence: Ireland and British Imperialism', 1976, 46. Paper lodged in the Political Collection, Linen Hall Library, Belfast.
97. McKinley, M., 'The Irish Republican Army and Terror International: An Inquiry into the Material Aspects of the First Fifteen Years', in P. Wilkinson and A. M. Stewart (eds.), *Contemporary Research on Terrorism* (Aberdeen: Aberdeen University Press, 1987), 205.
98. Kearney, V. and Ryder, C., *Sunday Times*, 14 March 1999.
99. Danny Morrison, Interview with Anthony McIntyre, 23 November 1995.
100. Kelly, G., *Irish News*, 12 March 1999. On the development of this type of argument see O'Doherty, M., *Belfast Telegraph*, 9 March 1999. The position of Kelly contrasts with the view of Eamonn McCann: 'the defence of specific Catholic areas which have suffered armed assault in the past . . . is a strong practical consideration in any discussion of arms. But it does not have the profound significance of defence of the Republic', *Belfast Telegraph*, 24 March 1999.
101. Seamus Loughran, Interview with Anthony McIntyre, 7 September 1995.
102. Garland, R., *Irish News*, 23 June. 1997.
103. White, *Provisional Irish Republicans*, 11.
104. Giddens, A., *Social Theory and Modern Sociology* (Cambridge: Polity, 1987), 179.
105. Drumm, M., *Daily Express*, 8 January 1973.
106. Danny Morrison, Interview with Anthony McIntyre, 23 November 1995.
107. Taylor, R., 'Running on empty', *Fortnight*, February 1990.
108. *Republican News*, quoted in Walsh, P., *Irish Republicanism And Socialism: The Politics Of The Republican Movement 1905 To 1994* (Belfast: Athol, 1994), 125.
109. Walter, E. V., *Terror and Resistance: A Study of Political Violence* (New York, NY: Oxford University Press, 1969), 3.
110. Moxon-Browne, 'The Water and the Fish', 52
111. Ryan, M., 'From the centre to the margins: the long demise of Irish Republicanism', 1998, 2. Paper lodged in the Political Collection, Linen Hall Library, Belfast.

112. Taylor, M. and Quayle, E., *Terrorist Lives* (London: Brasseys, 1994), 60.
113. Connolly, R. E., *Armalite and Ballot Box: An Irish-American Republican Primer* (Fort Wayne, IN: Cuchullain Publications, 1985) 27.
114. Bernadette Sands McKevitt. Interview with Anthony McIntyre, 2 February 1999.
115. O'Brien, C. C., 'IRA still holds true to theory of blood-sacrifice', *Independent Online*, 23 January 2000.
116. Danny Morrison. Interview with Anthony McIntyre, 23 November 1995.
117. McGuinness's comments are enlightening as they serve as a foil to a strong theme in O'Doherty's work regarding the influential role ascribed there to the Christian Brothers in promulgating republican ideology. See O'Doherty, *The Trouble With Guns*, 20.
118. Gerry Kelly, quoted in Borrill, R., *Ireland on Sunday*, 8 February 1998.
119. Gerry Kelly, quoted in Cadwallader, A., 'Sinn Féin's mystery man', *The Northern Ireland Monitor*, Issue 97/2.
120. Jim Moran. Interview with Anthony McIntyre, 9 January 1999.
121. Kelley, K., *The Longest War: Northern Ireland and the IRA* (London: Zed Books, 1988), 127.
122. Bernard Fox, quoted in Trainor, L., *Irish News*. 24th November. 1998
123. *An Phoblacht*, 30 March 1973.
124. Martin Meehan. Interview with Anthony McIntyre, 14 February 1998.
125. Bean, K., *The New Departure: Recent Developments in Irish Republican Ideology & Strategy*, Occasional Papers in Irish Studies, 6 (The Institute of Irish Studies: The University of Liverpool, 1994), 7.
126. Moloney, E., *Sunday Tribune*, 7 November 1999.
127. Morgan, M., *Andersonstown News*, 21 March 1998.
128. White, R. W. and White, T. F., *Repression And The Liberal State: The Case Of Northern Ireland, 1969–1972* (Undated, Draft Copy, Lodged in the Political Collection, Linen Hall Library, Belfast), 1.
129. Wright, 'PIRA Propaganda', 36.
130. Martin McGuinness, quoted in Moriarty, 'SF's chief negotiator hopes for end to conflict'.
131. McGuinness, M., 'Discarding the fetters of republican myth', *Fortnight*, March 1985.
132. *Irish Times*, 4 December 1998.
133. Piven and Cloward, *Poor People's Movements*, 21
134. Bew, P., Gibbon, P., and Patterson, H., *Northern Ireland 1921–1994: Political Forces and Social Classes* (London: Serif, 1994), 146, 154.
135. O'Connor, F., *In Search of a State: Catholics in Northern Ireland* (Belfast: Blackstaff, 1993), 72.
136. Moloney, E., *Sunday Tribune*, 7 February 1999.
137. Edward Heath, quoted in Millar, F., *Irish Times*, 20 October 1998.
138. McAdam, D., *Political Process and the Development of Black Insurgency: 1930–1970* (Chicago, IL: University of Chicago Press, 1985), 228.
139. See for example, Hildrew, P., *Guardian*, 29 November 1973; *Tyrone Constitution*, 22 August 1973; *Tyrone Constitution*, 17 August 1973; Fisk, R., *The Times*, 18 August 1973; *Newsletter*, 26 September 1973; Barker, G., *Daily Telegraph*, 14 September 1973; Fisk, R., *The Times*, 7 November 1973; South Down IRA, quoted in *Irish News*, 13 October 1973; MacAnthony, J., *Sunday Independent*, 6 January 1974; Hetherington, P., *Guardian*, 18 October 1973.
140. O'Doherty, M., *Belfast Telegraph*, 9 March 1999.
141. Morris, A. D., *The Origins of the Civil Rights Movement: Black Communities Organising for Change* (New York, NY: Free Press. 1984), 282.
142. Foucault, M., in Beechey and Donald (eds.), *Subjectivity and Social Relations*, 89.
143. W. B. Yeats, quoted by de Breadun, D., *Irish Times*, 9 May 1998.
144. O' Dochartaigh, N., *From Civil Rights to Armalites: Derry and the Birth of the Irish Troubles* (Cork: Cork University Press, 1997), 12.
145. Cox, M., 'Bringing in the "international": the IRA ceasefire and the end of the Cold War', *International Affairs*, 73 (1997): 685.
146. Gurr, T. R., 'The political origins of state violence and terror: A theoretical analysis', in M. Stohl and G. A. Lopez (eds.), *Government Violence and Repression: An Agenda for Research* (Westport, CT: Greenwood, 1986), 52–3.

147. Morris, *The Origins of the Civil Rights Movement*, 282.
148. McAdam, *Political Process*, 146.
149. Piven and Cloward, *Poor People's Movements*, 18.
150. Kelly, J., *The Courage of the Brave* (Meath: Kells, 1989), 10.
151. O'Brien, C. C., *Independent Online*, 20 February 2000.
152. *The Times*, 18 February 2000.
153. Smith, N., *Chomsky: Ideas and Ideals* (Cambridge: Cambridge University Press, 1999), 203.
154. Todd, J., 'Nationalism, Republicanism And The Good Friday Agreement', in J. Ruane and J. Todd (eds.), *After the Good Friday Agreement: Analysing Political Change in Northern Ireland* (Dublin: University College, 1999), 57.
155. *Irish Times*, 19 February 2000.
156. Campbell, B., *Guardian*, 24 February 2000.
157. Peter Mandelson, quoted in Haughey, N., Irish *Times*, 8 November 1999.
158. Hardy, J., *Guardian*, 5 February 2000.
159. Todd, After the Good Friday Agreement, 62.
160. McKittrick, D., *The Independent,* 7 February 2000.
161. McGurk, T., *Sunday Business Post*, 7 February 2000.
162. McIntyre, A., *Sunday Tribune*, 14 November 1999.
163. O'Toole, F., *Irish Times*, 5 February 2000.
164. McGurk, *Sunday Business Post*.

12

The Belfast Agreement and the Republic of Ireland

JOHN COAKLEY

Introduction

Electoral and survey data from the Republic of Ireland at the end of the twentieth century suggested the emergence of a remarkable consensus on what was for long known as 'the national question'—the partition of the island and the relationship with Great Britain. A referendum on the Belfast Agreement on 22 May 1998 saw a vote of 94 per cent in favour of a set of constitutional changes designed to permit its implementation. A poll in mid-December 1999 showed that 96 per cent of those expressing a view on the matter would like a united Ireland—though subject to a rather indefinite time limit: 'at some stage in the future'.[1]

The coexistence of this apparently committed support for the Agreement—and for its implications—with apparently strong endorsement of Irish unity, lends some credence to the view that the Agreement was seen in the South as a victory for nationalism—or that it was seen at least as being compatible with the traditional nationalist objective of unity. Since, however, the analysis of public opinion data on matters bearing on national identity presents a notoriously difficult challenge, it is worth exploring what may lie behind these figures. The object of this essay is thus to assess the broad pattern of public and élite opinion in the Republic towards the Agreement and what it represents.

One possible approach to this issue would be to begin with the mass of public opinion data and seek to draw inferences from this regarding underlying principles and, perhaps, values. Alternatively, one may begin by seeking first to identify those principles which appear to be relevant to the Agreement, by exploring relationships between them, and by assessing the extent to which they appear to be compatible with empirical data. We adopt the latter approach here, and begin by isolating two underlying dimensions. The first of these is a normative one: the question whether the island of Ireland should or should not be unified—to oversimplify, we assume that there are only two answers or major sets of answers to this. The second lies in the sphere of empirical analysis: the question whether the Agreement is calculated to hasten or retard the attainment of unity—again, we confine ourselves to two simple answers to this question.

The four following sections of the chapter explore in turn the two positions adopted in response to each of these two questions: the traditional nationalist preoccupation with territorial unity; the more recent development of a form of state-centred patriotism; the interpretation of the Agreement as a half-way house to unity; and the view that the Agreement underwrites partition. In the concluding section, some general observations are made on the interplay between these two dimensions.

Irredentist Nationalism and its Variants

Although the broad outlines of the traditional nationalist perspective are so well known that they scarcely need to be rehearsed, it is worth drawing attention to their central features. At its simplest, traditional Irish nationalism—which we may identify with what became known simply and eccentrically in twentieth century Ireland as 'republicanism'—rests on an organic conception of the nation, an anglophobic interpretation of history, and an expansionist territorial programme.[2]

The idea of the nation as an organic entity with a life of its own is by no means distinctively Irish; indeed, it has old roots in European history. It may be traced back to the eighteenth-century German philosopher, Johann Gottfried Herder (1744–1803). His writings were influential in disseminating the view that a nation or a nationality is more than the sum of the individuals who comprise it: that it is a living organism based on community of language or culture. For Herder, such a grouping has a soul analogous to the individual soul, and this is manifested in various aspects of culture and in particular in language and literature; its life predated the lives of the individuals who composed it and would outlive them.[3]

The centrality of this conception of the nation to the dominant traditional strand in Irish nationalism is clear. While a number of other examples might be cited, the most compelling, arguably, is the perspective articulated by Patrick Pearse, acknowledged by many militant nationalists as their spiritual father. Pearse's arguments, published shortly before his death by firing squad following the Easter 1916 rebellion, may be interpreted as follows. Nations are like persons: each possesses a body, soul, and mind. Just as it is wrong for one human being to enslave another, so too is it wrong for any nation to attempt to enslave another. In the case of human slaves, while the body 'belongs' to another, the soul may remain free. Similarly, while a nation may be physically enslaved, its soul may remain free, this freedom reflected in the maintenance of its own distinct language and culture. Ireland, an enslaved nation, must consequently win back its complete freedom—physical and spiritual—and can only realistically do so by use of force.[4]

The impact of this organic conception of the nation on modern nationalist movements has been diminished hardly at all by the enormous practical dilemmas to which it gives rise. Perhaps the biggest difficulty lies in defining the boundaries of the collectivity that possesses a 'national soul'. The reality is that the boundaries of linguistic communities are typically imprecise, and deciding whether variation in speech patterns is merely dialectal or is sufficient to distinguish separate languages can be problematic. Furthermore, a particular collectivity defined in terms of community of language might, for instance, share cultural values and social and political institutions with other linguistic communities; it might, on the other hand, be fragmented into different cultures with distinct literary traditions and institutions. In such circumstances, determining the boundaries of the entity that corresponds to a national 'soul' may be almost impossible.

For traditional Irish nationalists, however, an unambiguous answer was forthcoming: the soul resided in a clearly defined body, the island of Ireland. The implications of this were, first, that the island itself was the appropriate decision-making unit in matters regarding its own future and, second, that the mind of Ireland had no right to betray the soul of Ireland: the people of Ireland had a right to make collective decisions on the full range of political matters, but had no right to make any decision that would compromise the existence of the nation.

Linked with this conception of the nation has been a distinctive interpretation of history. In a nutshell, this held that the British presence in Ireland was based on conquest, not consent; that it was maintained by coercion, not agreement; that it was economically, socially, culturally, and spiritually damaging; that progress implied an end to this relationship; and that the relationship could be brought to an end only by the same means as that which sustained it, namely violence. In this interpretation, the political changes that resulted in the creation of an independent Irish State had left an important element of 'unfinished business', and the completion of this business through the incorporation of Northern Ireland was defined as a major national task.

There should be no doubt as to the centrality of this perspective in the official life of the new southern Irish State. Particularly in the case of the first generation of political leaders after 1922, the theme of the 'national freedom struggle' was prominently recalled in politicians' speeches, and involvement in this struggle was an electoral asset. The state primary education system was used to drive the nationalist message home. From the early 1930s to the beginning of the 1970s, the trainee schoolteacher was advised by the Department of Education of the importance of 'imbuing the minds of his pupils with the ideals and aspirations of such men as Thomas Davis and Patrick Pearse'.[5] Neither was the teacher left in doubt as to the identity of the bearer of the national soul:

The history of Ireland is the history of the various peoples who inhabited Ireland ever since the first advent of man to our shores, but it is more particularly the study of the Gaelic race and Gaelic civilisation, and of the resistance of that race and civilisation for a thousand years to foreign domination, whether Norse, Norman or English. (Department of Education, *Notes for teachers: history*, 13.)

The implications of this combination of conception of the nation and interpretation of history for the political programme were clear: the central objective was the attainment of Irish unity. The 'national aim' of unifying Ireland was written into the statement of objectives of the major political parties and, more solemnly, the 'national territory' was defined in the constitution in 1937 as including 'the whole island of Ireland, its islands, and the territorial seas'.[6] The illegitimacy of the new State of Northern Ireland formed a major component in the public rhetoric of political leaders, culminating in the late 1940s—following the severing of the remaining constitutional links between the south and the United Kingdom—in a vigorous, all-party campaign to end partition.

The apparently peculiar obsession with the 'national territory' is not unusual from a comparative perspective. As a noted scholar of nationalism put it many years ago:

The idea of the national territory is an important element of every modern national ideology. Every nation regards its country as an inalienable sacred heritage, and its independence, integrity, and homogeneity appear bound up with national security, independence and honour. This territory is often described as the body of the national organism and the language as its soul. In the ideology of almost every nation, therefore, its historical territory is looked upon almost as a living personality which cannot be partitioned without destroying it altogether. (Hertz, F., *Nationality in history and politics: a psychology and sociology of national sentiment and nationalism* (London: Routledge and Kegan Paul, 1944), 150–1.)

An anthropomorphic perception of the fatherland or, rather, motherland has been identified in one psychoanalytical interpretation of Irish nationalism: the island of Ireland has been personified as a maiden, and Irish history could be interpreted in symbolic terms as the rape of this maiden by Britain, which might have expected a different outcome to the Anglo-Irish relationship if it had 'instead of ravishing virgin Ireland as though she were a harlot, wooed her with the offer of an honourable alliance'.[7] Despite its highly speculative nature, this interpretation is plausible in the light of the diet of literary allusions and historical myths on which the Irish nationalist movement has fed.

Political leaders and the public no doubt varied in the strength of their attachment to the components of this rather distinctive nationalist ideology. The idea of the nation as an abstract entity that predated the state was a more reassuring starting point for some than for others. The interpretation of Irish history as a bilateral struggle between this nation and the British provided a more complete and a more convincing account of the past for some than for others. The identification of Irish unity as the ultimate goal was therefore one to which some were more committed than others. But for long there was remarkably little debate as to the legitimacy of the goal itself.

The major division within this perspective hinged on means rather than ends. For the more purist traditionalists, the military route was the appropriate one: the British had a fundamental vested interest in Northern Ireland, and could only be ousted by force. But this perspective was abandoned by the main state-building party—now represented by Fine Gael—in the early 1920s, and by its more nationalist opposition—now Fianna Fáil—in the later 1920s. Since then, it has been associated with the fundamentalist republican tradition, represented until the 1990s by Sinn Féin and the IRA. For more hard-nosed realists to whom the possibility of a military victory over the British appeared remote, or for those with moral objections to the use of force, alternative strategies suggested themselves. One was to persuade the British simply to part with Northern Ireland; an alternative was to persuade Northern Ireland unionists of the value of unity. Whether either of these was a realistic strategy, they remained part of the thinking of the mainstream political parties until the end of the twentieth century.

State Patriotism and its Variants

By contrast with the traditional nationalist perspective, a new form of identity that has begun to challenge it in recent years has attracted rather less analytical attention. Observers who have noted a shift in southern Irish political culture have described this in terms of a toning down of traditional nationalism rather than seeing in the new perspective a radically different phenomenon with a distinct point of departure. This alternative perspective, which may also be labelled 'Twenty-six-county nationalism', rests on a voluntaristic conception of the nation, a 'revisionist' interpretation of history, and a defensive territorial programme.[8]

The idea of the nation as body made up of individuals consenting to their membership of this collectivity has roots in the same era as the organic conception. To the extent that it is associated with a particular parent, this is the eighteenth-century Swiss-French philosopher Jean-Jacques Rousseau (1712–78), for whom a nation was a collection of free individuals consenting to be governed as a unit, as an expression of a general will.[9] In this perspective, the nation is rooted in a sense of shared territoriality, a tradition of life under a common government, and adhesion to agreed symbols.

The literature on nationalism has long recognized the distinction between these two conceptions of the nation. The organic (or deterministic) and the voluntaristic forms have also been labelled, respectively, 'eastern' and 'western' forms, or 'ethnic' and 'demotic' forms.[10] Notwithstanding the implication that each is characteristic of a particular geographical area, the two can co-exist within the same community—or, perhaps, they can even be present within the same individual.

Thus, even if the organic concept were to become dominant in nineteenth-century Ireland, its position was by no means unchallenged. The earliest group to articulate the alternative approach was arguably the United Irishmen. There is a case for seeing their belief system as sharing more with eighteenth-century French rationalists than with contemporary Irish republicans—for seeing it as related to a great European or 'Atlantic' movement of the late eighteenth century rather than as a stage in the evolution of an Irish nationalist tradition.[11] Their primary objective was democratic rather than nationalist, but under the constitutional arrangements of the 1790s, progress towards the principle of parliamentary control of the government would inevitably lead to a weakening of the links between Britain and Ireland. If, furthermore, the form of government were to be changed from monarchical to republican, the last links between the two countries would be severed—on the assumption, that is, that Ireland and Britain would choose separate heads of state.

This inclusive conception of the nation, linking 'Catholic, Protestant, and Dissenter', followed a difficult path in the nineteenth century, especially in the context of the great Catholic nationalist mobilization that began in the time of Daniel O'Connell. One of those who stood against the surge of ethnic nationalism was Thomas Davis, who believed in 'a tolerant and all-embracing nation, not reared upon any exclusive principle of blood, or religion, or culture'.[12] Indeed, the tension between the two forms of nationalism was expressed very clearly by a contemporary, George Gavan Duffy, who thus described Davis's influence on his personal evolution:

When I knew him first . . . I was a strong nationalist, but a nationalist of the school of Roger O'Moore, who burned with desire to set up again the Celtic race and the Catholic church. Davis it was who induced me to aim, ever after, to bring all Irishmen, of whatever stock, into the confederacy to make Ireland a nation. (Duffy, G. G., cited in Edwards, R. D. 'The contribution of Young Ireland to the Irish national idea', in S. Pender (ed.) *Feilscribhinn Torna*, (Cork: Cork University Press, 1947), 125.)

The essence of this form of essentially territorial nationalism is that identity derives from the political system rather than constituting its prerequisite. Up to 1922, the relevant political system was the Kingdom of Ireland—strangely, signs of territorial or civic nationalism corresponding to the United Kingdom are hard to find even in embryonic form. After 1922, this form of nationalism of course survived. It is very difficult to measure its intensity, but there is some evidence that it is rather stronger in Northern Ireland than in the Republic. Inevitably, however, this form of '32-county' civic nationalism was increasingly challenged by two other rather more vigorous forms that corresponded to the two Irish States.

Civic nationalism based on the six counties of Northern Ireland is not our central concern here, but it is not irrelevant to this discussion. It is true that survey evidence suggests that Northern Ireland Protestants now identify themselves as more 'British' than in the late 1960s, when many opted for the label 'Ulster'; and it also suggests that a majority of Catholics continue to see themselves as 'Irish'. It is difficult also to see signs of an emerging Northern Irish identity at the level of symbols. The increased popularity of the Ulster flag, for instance, implies an Ulster Protestant identity that is not compatible with a cross-denominational Northern Irish identity. Nevertheless, it would be surprising if such an identity were not emerging slowly, even if it continues to be overshadowed by more powerful alternatives, and survey evidence offers modest support for this.[13]

In the South, while survey evidence is of little value in tracking the development of civic nationalism, indirect evidence is more abundant, if difficult to interpret. The word 'Ireland' is increasingly used in a narrow sense, to refer to the territory of the State—this is not surprising, though it may be ironic, since this is precisely the name of the State as defined in the 1937 constitution. It seems to be the case that people's identity as 'Irish' is increasingly based on a perception of the community as extending over 26 rather than 32 counties.[14]

This development no doubt reflects the impact of 80 years of partition. The generation that grew to political maturity at a time when Ireland was a single political unit has now almost passed away. The experience of separate—and quite different—patterns of experience in the educational and welfare systems, in political life, and in other aspects of societal infrastructure have contributed to cultural differentiation between those on either side of the border. In many respects, the separate development of southern nationalists has placed them in a relationship to northern nationalists that resembles that between Finns and Karelians, or between Romanians and Moldavians—in each case, the two groups, though sharing a linguistic and cultural heritage with each other, developed a distinct identity—and in the east European cases even elements of a separate language—after a lengthy period of political separation.

This new form of identity was associated also with an alternative interpretation of history. Of course, unionists had always rejected the traditional nationalist interpretation of Irish history, and some had explicitly advanced the idea that the 'Irish nation' was confined essentially to the Catholic population.[15] This view was not without supporters also on the nationalist side, though such voices were rare.[16] Although historical 'revisionism' originally referred to the reinterpretation of specific episodes in the past in the light of new or even existing evidence, it came eventually to refer to the process of offering a new interpretation of the whole path of Irish history in which the unidimensional nationalist interpretation was effectively sidelined.[17]

These changes were reflected most dramatically of all in the primary school curriculum. In part to reflect developments in philosophy of education but also in response to changed political circumstances, the primary school history syllabus was revised radically in the early 1970s. The explicit political goals of the earlier period were replaced by a concern to cultivate personal discovery by the child, and the chronological presentation of Irish history as the story of a long political struggle was replaced by a thematic approach that paid much greater attention to social and economic history, and to developments outside Ireland. Concern with the impact of history teaching on contemporary politics was reflected vividly in the new guidelines for teachers:

Care should also be taken that in the presentation of the facts there is no distortion or suppression of any truth which might seem to hurt national pride. The picture of events which the child carries with him from the classroom should be true to the facts and unspoiled by special pleading of any kind. It should, in particular, represent fairly the contribution of all creeds and classes to the evolution of modern Ireland. . . . The special problem which . . . arises is how to present past ill-doing without so arousing the child's emotion as to prejudice his mind in relation to existing conditions. (Department of Education, *Primary School Curriculum: Teachers' Handbook*, 2 vols (Dublin: Browne and Nolan, 1971) 2: 87–8.)

Official concern with explicit interpretation of the past extended also in the 1970s and the 1980s to the management of public symbolism. There was, for example, a striking contrast between the vigour and enthusiasm with which the State commemorated the 50th anniversary of the 1916 rising at Easter, 1966, and the small-scale commemoration that took place to mark the 75th anniversary in 1991; indeed, the official annual commemorations of the rising were altogether discontinued in the 1970s. In general, official rhetoric moved rapidly and decisively away from the nationalist sloganizing of the past, and the public broadcasting media came under pressure to withhold coverage of the radical nationalist tradition.

When we move to the level of official attitudes towards partition it becomes less easy to identify evidence in favour of the geopolitical *status quo* on the island. For long, Irish Governments continued to call on the British Government to initiate negotiations on the subject of Irish unity. But a critical change took place as the civil unrest in Northern Ireland forced southern politicians to give more careful consideration to the complexity of the problem. The period in which Fianna Fáil's Jack Lynch served as Taoiseach (1966–73) was a watershed. The rapidity of change is illustrated in two quotations from Lynch's collected speeches and statements on the problem at the point where the transition from old to new values was being worked through most painfully (1969–71). It is worth quoting one extract from the first and one from the last speech in the collection. In the first, dating from August 1969, Lynch repeated the traditional nationalist mantra: his Government intended to request the British to enter into early negotiations on the constitutional position of Northern Ireland, in view of the fact that 'the re-unification of the national territory can provide the only permanent solution for the problem.'[18] In the last, dating from October 1971, there was a shift in emphasis. Although the need for unity was hinted at, the Government's immediate priority was quite different: 'There will be no beginning to permanent peace in Ireland . . . until the British Government accept their proper responsibilities and assert in the interim their claimed authority over Northern Ireland'.[19]

From the 1970s onwards, unity was increasingly defined in the Republic as a long-term goal, and political leaders appeared content to leave the problem to the British. Of course, southern politicians were inevitably drawn into the conflict, but the moderation of their position has been notable. There has been little evidence of significant public or élite dissatisfaction with the border, and a good deal of concern to ensure that the problem does not spill over into the South.[20] Indeed, the southern parties have *de facto* adopted a policy of favouring an internal solution to the problem, reinforced by a harmless Irish dimension. This was reflected in a remarkable—but unremarked—shift in policy on unity: the Downing Street Declaration of 1993 made this explicitly dependent on endorsement by referendum not only in the North *but also in the South*—see discussion in 'The Agreement as a Path to Unity' later in this chapter.

We may, of course, find variants on this form of state patriotism in two directions. First, it is clear that many whose primary allegiance is to the twentieth century State rather than to the nineteenth century nation nevertheless hesitate to surrender the territorial claim to Northern Ireland. This perspective has been most pronounced within Fianna Fáil, even under its leader Charles Haughey (1979–92), whose nationalism reflected his family's northern roots. It was largely under Haughey's influence that the inter-party New Ireland Forum recommended in 1984 as a preferred final outcome to the conflict the establishment of 'a unitary state, achieved by agreement and consent, embracing the whole island of Ireland'.[21] Haughey also dismissed the prospects for an internal solution in Northern Ireland, which, in his words, 'as a political entity, has failed'.[22]

Secondly, at the opposite extreme, many from the nationalist tradition accepted the logic of the distinctness of Northern Ireland Protestants, and acknowledged their right to opt out of the Irish state.[23] This position was also adopted increasingly by leading public figures such as Conor Cruise O'Brien.[24] In time, this was extended to become not merely an acceptance of the right of unionists to remain outside the Republic of Ireland but, for some, also a rejection of the right of northern nationalists to join the Republic and an increasingly committed defence of the existing border—a classical statement of State patriotism.

The Agreement as a Path to Unity

It is appropriate now to turn from the domain of values to that of empirical matters. Given the investment of time and effort made in the Belfast Agreement by two governments, several political parties and groups, and external mediators, and interpretations of the agreement as a landmark in relations between the two main traditions in Northern Ireland, between North and South, and between the Republic of Ireland and the United Kingdom, it is worth examining this complex document with a view to assessing its compatibility with the two value systems within the Republic of Ireland that have just been outlined. In this assessment, several of the important features of the Agreement will be ignored with a view to focusing on the question of Irish unity. Thus the issues of devolved power-sharing government, equality between the two traditions within Northern Ireland, human rights, policing, the judicial system, security, decommissioning of weapons, prisoner release, and victim support—though all of them have implications also in an all-Ireland context—are not discussed directly here.

Much political reaction to the Agreement—hostile and sympathetic alike—rested on an interpretation that saw in it a half-way house to Irish unity. Although additional evidence in support of this viewpoint could be and was produced, this perspective rested on what were seen as three central features of the agreement: British benevolence on the issue of unity, the provision of a mechanism for ending partition, and the creation of an embryonic all-island political entity through new North-South institutions.

British commitment to neutrality on the issue of Irish unity and to implementation of the wishes of the Irish people should they opt for a united Ireland was indeed written into the Agreement. Thus the joint intergovernmental statement that formed part of the Agreement provided that the two governments:

recognise that it is for the people of the island of Ireland alone, by agreement between the two parts respectively and without external impediment, to exercise their right of self-determination on the basis of consent, freely and concurrently given, North and South, to bring about a united Ireland. (Annex to the *Agreement*, article 1(ii).)

This was made more concrete by a commitment by the British Government to prepare legislation to give effect to Irish unity in the event of this being agreed, and to repeal the *Government of Ireland Act* of 1920, detested by many nationalists as the 'partition act'.

The Agreement thus carried to its ultimate stage what had been emerging British policy since 1973. Up to that point, the stark language of the *Ireland Act* of 1949 had defined Northern Ireland's constitutional position: 'in no event will Northern Ireland or any part thereof . . . cease to be part of the United Kingdom without the consent of the Parliament of Northern Ireland'. This guarantee to the Northern Irish political establishment was replaced after the fall of Stormont by a guarantee to the Northern Irish majority: the last phrase of the 1949 guarantee was replaced by the expression 'without the consent of the majority of the people of Northern Ireland voting in a poll held for the purposes of this section'.[25] The Sunningdale Agreement of 1973 supplemented this negative provision—specifying circumstances in which Northern Ireland *could not* leave the United Kingdom—by a positive provision—specifying circumstances in which Northern Ireland *could* leave the United Kingdom: 'if in the future a majority of the people of Northern Ireland should indicate a wish to become part of a united Ireland, the British Government would support that wish'.[26] This commitment was repeated with more precise wording in the 1985 Anglo-Irish Agreement, where the British and Irish Governments promised that 'if in the future a majority of the people of Northern Ireland clearly wish for and formally consent to the establishment of a united Ireland, they will introduce and support in the respective parliaments legislation to give effect to that wish'.[27] The commitment was in turn incorporated in the 1993 Downing St Declaration.[28] In a further gesture, it was agreed in 1998 that the *Government of Ireland Act* of 1920—article 75 of which included a declaration that 'the supreme authority of the Parliament of the United Kingdom shall remain unaffected and undiminished over all persons, matters, and things in Ireland and every part thereof'— would be repealed.[29]

There also appeared to be substantial reasons for accepting the validity of the British expression of disinterest in the retention of Northern Ireland within the United Kingdom. In the early and middle years of the twentieth century, there were powerful strategic and emotional reasons behind British support for the union. But as the ideology of imperialism waned, as the end of the cold war undercut Northern Ireland's strategic importance, and as the continuing integration of both the United Kingdom and the Republic of Ireland within the European Union undermined the significance of the border, any cost-benefit analysis based on material considerations would have to conclude that the continuing attractiveness of Northern Ireland to Great Britain could not have rested on concrete or measurable factors. Even at the more elusive political level, the sceptical thrust of international opinion on Britain's involvement in Northern Ireland made the relationship with the province a less than happy one. Although official statements of neutrality on the issue of the British-Northern Irish union—such as the notable one by Secretary of State Brooke in 1990—need to be interpreted in the light of government decisions and actual policy implementation, the existence of a long-term British stake in Northern Ireland was much less obvious at the end of the twentieth century than it had been at its beginning.[30] Such a declaration was incorporated in the 1993 Downing St Declaration, in which the British Prime Minister 'reiterates, on behalf of the British Government, that they have no selfish strategic or economic interest in Northern Ireland. Their primary interest is to see peace, stability and reconciliation among all the people who inhabit the island.'[31]

Secondly, the Agreement also provided a mechanism for bringing about Irish unity. The Secretary of State for Northern Ireland was to be empowered to direct the holding of a poll to ascertain the views of the electorate 'at any time it appears likely to him that a majority of those voting would express a wish that Northern Ireland should cease to be part of the United Kingdom and form part of a united Ireland'. Such polls could take place repeatedly provided they were at least seven years apart, and given the rapid pace at which the Catholic-

Protestant population ratio in Northern Ireland was changing, there were grounds for assuming that in due course one such poll would produce a pro-unity majority.

Thirdly, the Agreement provided for a set of all-Ireland institutions that could be seen as the embryo of a united Irish State. At the head of these was to be a North-South Ministerial Council which would meet regularly and frequently to formulate policy on all-Ireland matters and to oversee the implementation of decisions reached. A permanent secretariat would support the work of the Council, and a minimum of six implementation bodies would assume responsibility for specific policy sectors. In addition, in a further six areas at a minimum, provision was made for institutionalized co-operation through existing bodies in Northern Ireland and the Republic under the aegis of the ministerial council. To emphasize the capacity of these institutions to evolve, provision was also made for a possible parliamentary tier and for a North-South consultative forum comprising the social partners and others.

Indeed, even the change in the Republic's constitution that was included as part of the Agreement could be interpreted in a pro-unity light. Although the expansive definition of the national territory would disappear—a definition that, in any case, was unenforceable—it could be argued that the nationalist thrust of the constitution had been barely altered. The Irish constitution would continue to assume the existence of a distinct people and claim for them a right to self-government, and the goal of unity would remain.[32] But it could be argued that the new wording was helpful to northern nationalists, and that the new article 2, by defining membership of the nation in voluntaristic rather than strictly territorial terms, would make it more difficult for the political institutions of the Republic to exclude from participation members of the 'nation' from Northern Ireland—thus making less likely the kind of incidents that had taken place in the past, when nationalist representatives from Northern Ireland were denied rights of audience in the Dáil.[33]

Overall, then, it is possible to read into the Agreement positive signals that point in the direction of Irish unity in the longer term and that both provide a mechanism for bringing this about and establish an embryonic set of institutions with the capacity to evolve into something much greater. The problem is that it is also possible to arrive at a rather different reading of the document, one that tends instead in the direction of supporting the *status quo*. It is to this interpretation that we now turn.

The Agreement as an Obstacle to Unity

While certain critics and supporters of the Agreement based their positions on interpretations that it was a 'sell-out' of unionism and a 'victory' for nationalism respectively, others, rather less numerous, reversed these positions in their entirety. We thus find another set of opponents of the Agreement who see in it a 'sell-out' of nationalism, while others support it precisely because they see it as bringing the nationalist or republican gallop to a halt. While additional arguments could be raised, the three most important points correspond to those already discussed: the views that the Agreement reinforced partition and British rule in Northern Ireland; that, while it may have created a theoretical channel for bringing Irish unity about, it also erected additional obstacles to the achievement of unity; and that the institutions it created were far removed from those that would be associated with an embryonic Irish State.

There were three obvious respects in which the Agreement could be seen as reinforcing partition. First, although the text declared solemnly, as we have seen, that it was 'for the people of the island of Ireland alone . . . to exercise their right of self-determination', the wording of this section of the agreement made it quite clear that this was not a statement of the right of the people of Ireland, as such, to self-determination. Instead, 'self-determination' was to be exercised 'by agreement between the two parts' of the island, an unambiguous, small-print contradiction of the headline principle of self-determination of the people of Ireland. To hammer this point home, the Agreement also stipulated that the two governments accepted that the right to self-determination 'must be achieved and exercised with and subject to the agreement and consent of a majority of the people of Northern Ireland', and that 'it would be wrong to make any change in the status of Northern Ireland save with the consent of a majority of its people'. Intergovernmental consensus on this position, though achieving its most solemn status in the Agreement, had been evolving since 1973.

The second obvious respect in which the Agreement could be seen as reinforcing partition was, however, quite new: for the first time, the Irish Government agreed to an amendment of the Irish constitution that would remove any sense that it implied a territorial claim to Northern Ireland. The two articles that were at the centre of debate read as follows:

Article 2. The national territory consists of the whole island of Ireland, its islands and the territorial seas.

Article 3. Pending the re-integration of the national territory, and without prejudice to the right of the Parliament and Government established by this Constitution to exercise jurisdiction over the whole of that territory, the laws enacted by that Parliament shall have the like area and extent of application as the laws of Ireland and the like extraterritorial effect.

It had been commonly held among constitutional lawyers up to 1990 that these articles constituted a political statement that was aspirational in form, an interpretation that depended on a conventional distinction between the sociologically imprecise concept 'nation' and the juridically exact concept 'State'.[34] In 1990, however, the Supreme Court ruled in favour of an alternative interpretation—that the articles amounted to a claim of legal right.[35] The proposed new wording of these articles was radically different from the original wording, and went considerably further than the wording proposed by the committee on the constitution in 1967.[36] The agreed wording was as follows:

Article 2. It is the entitlement and birthright of every person born in the island of Ireland, which includes its islands and seas, to be part of the Irish nation. That is also the entitlement of all persons otherwise qualified in accordance with law to be citizens of Ireland. Furthermore, the Irish nation cherishes its special affinity with people of Irish ancestry living abroad who share its cultural identity and heritage.

Article 3.1. It is the firm will of the Irish nation, in harmony and friendship, to unite all the people who share the territory of the island of Ireland, in all the diversity of their identities and traditions, recognising that a united Ireland shall be brought about only by peaceful means with the consent of a majority of the people, democratically expressed, in both jurisdictions in the island. Until then, the laws enacted by the Parliament established by this Constitution shall have the like area and extent of application as the laws enacted by the Parliament that existed immediately before the coming into operation of this Constitution.

Article 3.2. Institutions with executive powers and functions that are shared between those jurisdictions may be established by their respective responsible authorities for stated purposes and may exercise powers and functions in respect of all or any part of the island.

Quite apart from such implications as this change might have for citizenship, the new wording gave explicit constitutional recognition to the right of Northern Ireland to opt out of a united Ireland. The change, in other words, went further than mere deletion of the articles: it extended a powerful constitutional weapon to supporters of partition by specifying new constitutional conditions required for unity. It could, indeed, be argued that since the status of Northern Ireland was defined in the Belfast Agreement much more explicitly than in 1985, amendment of articles 2 and 3 was a necessary rather than an optional part of the Good Friday package. In any case, the new articles will now have a life of their own; the view has been expressed that they were apparently not drafted principally by lawyers, that their primary initial role was at the level of political rhetoric, but that they are now subject to pragmatic legal interpretation.[38]

The third respect in which the Agreement could be seen as reinforcing partition was the termination of the Anglo-Irish Agreement of 1985. This had given the Irish Government a consultative role in the internal affairs of Northern Ireland—in sensitive political, security and legal matters including the administration of justice, as well as in other areas—and had made provision for additional cross-border co-operation. A standing Anglo-Irish Intergovernmental Conference, serviced by a permanent secretariat located within Northern Ireland, was established to implement this. Although the Irish Government's role was to be consultative, provision was made for 'determined efforts' to resolve any differences between the two governments. It has been argued that the fact that it did not specify the status of Northern Ireland—which, however, was recognized without being defined—permitted the 1985 Agreement to be interpreted as compatible with articles 2 and 3 of the constitution.[39]

Under the 1998 Agreement, this framework was replaced by a system of Co-operation that was different in two main respects. First, although it was to deal with 'the totality of relationships', the emphasis was on bilateral co-operation rather than on domestic Northern Ireland or all-Irish matters. Secondly, its membership was expanded beyond the two governments to 'relevant executive members' of the new Northern Ireland administration. Although the practical significance of the new system is unclear, it seems designed to dilute that voice of the southern government on northern and all-Ireland matters. Since even the 1985 Agreement had been dismissed by nationalist critics as 'inherently deficient and defective', the corresponding arrangements 13 years later are unlikely to have been much more attractive to this strand of opinion.[40]

A further feature of the Agreement, part of the package of nationalist demands, could be seen as having little significance for the ending of partition. This was the repeal of the *Government of Ireland Act* of 1920. Though denounced by its opponents in the south as the measure that implemented par-tition, the act in reality provided a tangible expression of Irish unity that its nationalists critics, ironically, were not prepared to tolerate. Thus, under pres-sure from a secession-bent southern political élite, the British agreed in the *Irish Free State (Consequential Provisions) Act*, 1922, to the abolition of the all-Irish offices that had survived partition: those of Lord Lieutenant and Lord Chancellor, and the Irish Privy Council, a body whose members would have included both the northern and southern governments. The Council of Ireland—explicitly intended to be an embryonic all-Irish parliament—for which the Government of Ireland Act made provision suffered a similar fate: although the Northern Ireland House of Commons selected its representatives to the Council at its first meeting and the Senate followed suit, this institution attracted little support in the south. Finally, it was abolished by Irish and British legislation in 1925, with few expressions of regret to be heard in the Dáil.[41] The surviving claim to British sovereignty over Northern Ireland that was removed in 1998 was of little significance—especially since the *Act of Union* of 1800, which declared that Great Britain and Ireland shall 'for ever, be united into one Kingdom', remains on the statute books.

The second broad area was that of mechanisms for bringing about Irish unity. It is true that the provision for polls on this issue within Northern Ireland and the growing size of the Catholic minority there pointed to the possibility of a pro-unity majority at some time in the future. Indeed, on the basis of popula-tion projections, one demographic analyst suggested that Catholics might con-stitute a majority of the population by the early 2030s, though alternative projections suggested a much later date.[42] But a demographic majority is not necessarily an electoral majority, and an electoral majority is not necessarily a pro-unity majority. A favourable reading of the 1991 census suggests that Catholics amounted to approximately 42 per cent of the population. But if we narrow our analysis to people of voting age, the Catholic proportion drops to 38 per cent.[43] Furthermore, survey evidence consistently suggests that a considerable proportion of Catholics favour maintenance of the union, or some other outcome short of Irish unity, and that only something in the region of 50–60 per cent support a united Ireland—at least at present; further changes in political, economic, and demographic relationships may cause this figure to alter.[44] Even when allowance is made for the small number of Protestants who support Irish unity—in typical polls, about 5 per cent—the present trend suggests that notwithstanding demographic change opponents of Irish unity are likely to outnumber its supporters by at least two to one well into the future.[45]

Furthermore, the mechanism for unifying Ireland introduces a new hurdle that must be overcome by opponents of partition: the southern veto. This appeared already in the Downing Street Declaration of 1993,[46] and was written into the 1998 Agreement as part of the requirement for 'free and concurrent' assent to unity by the people of the south. But opinion poll evidence from the south consistently shows that support for unity would depend critically on the nature of the package, and that an 'expensive' package entailing economic, political, or symbolic costs would be rejected.[47] Of course, potentially unpleasant packages can be presented in attractive ways, and political élites would have little difficulty in dressing up a unity package in pleasant garb—if they wished to do so. Even if it is to be supposed that a referendum on Irish unity would be carried in the south, though, the very fact that a southern consensus on the issue can no longer be taken for granted makes the southern veto a political reality and not merely a theoretically interesting footnote.

The third area in which the persistence of partition was arguably clear was that of all-island institutions. There was to be a North-South Ministerial Council 'to develop consultation, co-operation and action within the island of Ireland', but its decisions were to be by agreement between the two sides, thus giving each side a veto. So-called 'implementation bodies' were to be established in a minimum of six areas, but some of the areas given as examples were ones where cross-border EU programmes were already well established, and others could be dismissed as embracing very narrowly defined policy sectors—for example, animal and plant health, teacher qualifications and exchanges, inland waterways, entitlements of cross-border workers and fraud control, inland fisheries, and accident and emergency services. Although the bodies whose establishment was in fact agreed in December 1998 covered areas of significance, the Agreement itself gave no guarantee that any major sector would be covered.

Viewed from the perspective of the Sunningdale Agreement of 1973, the Irish dimension in the 1998 Agreement indeed appeared to have been watered down. Although the areas listed as examples for practical north-south co-operation in 1973 were not obviously more significant than those of 1998, there was provision in 1973 for all-Ireland security arrangements with potentially far-reaching consequences. Furthermore, the executive role of the 1973 council was more clearly spelled out, and provision was made for a symbolically important consultative assembly, comprising sixty members drawn equally from the Dáil and the northern Assembly.

Conclusion

It is appropriate in conclusion to draw together the threads from these conflicting perspectives on Irish unity and the Belfast Agreement. Since we have been considering two responses to each of two questions, it is clear that we can get four combinations of answers, corresponding to four notionally distinct strands of opinion:

(1) supporters of Irish unity who see in the Agreement movement in the direction of their desired objective;
(2) supporters of Irish unity who see the Agreement as making realization of their desired objective more difficult;
(3) opponents of Irish unity who see the Agreement as an alarming concession that may undermine partition; and
(4) opponents of Irish unity who see the Agreement as securing a desirable geopolitical *status quo*.

It is worth considering these perspectives in turn.

For optimistic nationalists, the Agreement constitutes a flexible framework within which a range of exciting possibilities may be realized. A clearly defined mechanism for ending partition has been put in place, and the growing demographic strength of the northern Catholic community suggests that this need not be of merely notional significance. The cross-border institutions provided for initially may be restricted in scope, but they have the capacity to grow. The change in the Irish constitution leaves the aim of unity intact, and arguably permits northern participation in the State's political institutions in a way not previously thought possible. This is the interpretation most prominently associated with Sinn Féin, but it is close also to the formal position of the main southern parties and to the stated position of the Taoiseach, Bertie Ahern.

For the more pessimistic supporters of unity, the Agreement is a 'sell-out'. The cross-border bodies are of paltry significance. Constitutional change has recognized partition more solemnly than ever before. The evolutionary potential of the new institutions and the mechanism for bringing unity about are illusory, since the agreement formalizes a northern veto. Most critically, the Agreement has abandoned the long-standing nationalist argument that the people of the island of Ireland are the appropriate decision-making unit by conceding Northern Ireland's right to self-determination—a fundamental violation of the organic conception of the nation. This is the perspective of Republican Sinn Féin and of the Thirty-two County Sovereignty Committee, both based on factions that broke away from Sinn Féin.

But opponents of the Agreement are to be found also in a second camp: those who accept partition as the most satisfactory outcome for the future, but who fear that it may have undermined this. This group broadly accepts the analysis presented by its nationalist supporters, but come to the opposite political conclusion: the Agreement is politically destabilizing, a threat alike to southern institutions and to the rights of northern unionists. It is difficult to find significant political groups in the south who articulate this perspective—in the north, this is the position of the Democratic Unionist party, of the United Kingdom Unionist party and of many within the Ulster Unionist party—but prominent individuals such as Conor Cruise O'Brien have expressed views compatible with this position.[48]

Finally, there are those who support the Agreement precisely because it appears to them to guarantee the *status quo*. This group shares the analysis of Republican Sinn Féin, but reverses its political conclusion: the Agreement reinforces partition, and is therefore to be welcomed. For a number of reasons, elaborations of this perspective are often confined to the private domain; but it is to be found within all of the southern political parties, and may even be the dominant view in some of them. Indeed, the shift to this position had been detected by one observer even before the peace process had culminated in the signing of the Agreement. Noting the changes in southern political perspectives especially within Fianna Fáil by the mid-1990s, he suggested that 'the Treaty settlement of 1922, much fought over at the time, is now complete, and Ireland can finally move on.'[49]

Opinion polls offer little help in dividing the southern population into these four categories. But the results of the 1998 referendum do tell us that the combined voting strength of the first and last groups at that time was 94 per cent, leaving only 6 per cent to be divided between the second and third groups, the pro-unity and pro-partition opponents of the Agreement. However, any attempt to provide too clearly defined a set of categories in this respect is likely to be both empirically frustrating because of the difficulties of measuring the size of each, and theoretically misleading because of the complexities involved. The categorization around which this chapter is based has been adopted only to facilitate discussion. In reality, the two dimensions considered above are far too deeply embedded in complex political realities for any dichotomous judgements to be altogether satisfactory. The Belfast Agreement is an extraordinarily elaborate document that seeks to respond to a set of political needs so complex that many have despaired of ever understanding them.[50] The real as opposed to the stated positions of the main actors are not only difficult to infer, but are not necessarily stable—in particular, the republican movement has undergone a profound ideological transformation.[51] Nevertheless, it seems clear that southern opinion is, for whatever reason, close to a consensus—even if this is permissive rather than exclusive—on the model for the future government of the island, and that this consensus is likely to outlive whatever fate political developments in Northern Ireland may have for the institutions of government themselves.

ENDNOTES

1. *Irish Independent*, 21 December 1999.
2. For a general introduction to Irish nationalism, see Boyce, D. G., *Nationalism in Ireland* (London: Croom Helm, 1982) and, for a more specific analysis, Hutchinson, J., *The dynamics of cultural nationalism: the Gaelic revival and the creation of the Irish nation state* (London: Allen and Unwin, 1987).
3. Ergang, R., *Herder and the foundations of German nationalism* (New York, NY: Columbia University, 1931), 82–112; for a warning about the risks of projecting more modern concepts of 'nation' back to Herder's time see Spencer, V., 'Herder and nationalism: reclaiming the principle of cultural respect', *Australian Journal of Politics and History*, 43 (1997): 1–13.
4. See *Collected works of Padraig H. Pearse: political writings and speeches* (Dublin: Phoenix Publishing Company, 1924), and especially the essay 'Ghosts', 219–55, first published in December 1915. For analyses of Pearse's thought, see Shaw, F., 'The canon of Irish history: a challenge', *Studies*, 61 (1972): 113–53; Edwards, R. D., *Patrick Pearse: the triumph of failure* (London: Victor Gollancz, 1977); Coakley, J., 'Patrick Pearse and the 'noble lie' of Irish nationalism', *Studies*, 72 (1983): 119–36; and Moran, S. F., *Patrick Pearse and the politics of redemption: the mind of the Easter Rising, 1916* (Washington, DC: Catholic University of America Press, 1994).
5. Department of Education, *Notes for teachers: history* (Dublin: Stationery Office, 1933), 26. This publication remained the standard set of guidelines for history teaching for almost 40 years. See Coakley, J., 'The Northern conflict in Southern Irish school textbooks', in A. Guelke (ed.) *New perspectives on the Northern Ireland conflict* (Aldershot: Avebury, 1994), 119–41.
6. For the traditional formal statements of the parties as expressed in their constitutions, see Chubb, B. (ed.), *A source book of Irish government* (Dublin: Institute of Public Administration, 1964); the most irredentist party was Labour which endorsed the constitutional reference to the territory of the nation, followed by Fianna Fáil, with Fine Gael making only incidental reference to the irredentist argument.
7. Jones, E., 'The island of Ireland: a psycho-analytical contribution to political psychology' (1922), in *Essays in applied psycho-analysis* 2 vols. (London: Hogarth, 1964), 1, 95–112.
8. Among observers who have commented extensively on this trend and traced it back to the early years of the state, see O'Halloran, C., *Partition and the limits of Irish nationalism: an ideology under stress* (Dublin: Gill and Macmillan, 1987); and Bowman, J., *De Valera and the Ulster question 1917–1973* (Oxford: Oxford University Press, 1989), especially 331–8. For sustained discussion of the further evolution of state-centred or 'revisionist' nationalism in more recent years, see Power, P. F., 'Revisionist 'consent', Hillsborough, and the decline of constitutional republicanism', *Eire-Ireland*, 25 (1990): 20–39, and 'Revisionist nationalism's consolidation, republicanism's marginalisation, and the peace process', *Eire-Ireland*, 31 (1996): 89–122.
9. Cobban, A., *Rousseau and the modern state*, 2nd ed. (London: George Allen & Unwin, 1964), 107–16.
10. Among early works, see Kohn, H., *The idea of nationalism: a study in its origins and background* (New York, NY: Macmillan, 1946) on 'eastern' and 'western' forms: and Francis, E. K., *Interethnic relations: an essay in sociological theory* (New York, NY: Elsevier, 1976) on 'ethnic' and 'demotic' forms.
11. See Palmer, R. R., *The age of democratic revolution: a political history of Europe and America, 1760–1800*, 2 vols. (Princeton, NJ: Princeton University Press, 1959 and 1964). Palmer suggests a parallel between the Irish and Dutch cases: Dutch revolutionaries believed that the

kingpin of conservatism, the orange regime, was maintained by English support (vol. 2, 496–7). The struggle for democracy consequently entailed a nationalist struggle, though the formal context of the latter was quite different in the two cases. On the primarily democratic goals of the early United Irishmen and on the contrast between their views on nationalism and those that were to develop in the nineteenth century, see McDowell, R. B., *Ireland in the age of imperialism and revolution 1760–1801* (Oxford: Clarendon Press, 1979), 363–73.

12. Moody, T. W. *Thomas Davis 1814–45* (Dublin: Hodges, Figgis and Co., 1945), 56.

13. In four surveys between 1989 and 1994 the proportion of Protestants describing their identity as 'Northern Irish' ranged from 11 per cent to 16 per cent; the corresponding proportion of Catholics ranged from 25 per cent to 28 per cent—most Protestants described themselves as British, and most Catholics as Irish; Trew, K., 'National identity', in R. Breen, P. Devine, and L. Dowds, (eds.), *Social attitudes in Northern Ireland* (Belfast: Blacktree Press, 1996), 140–52, here 142.

14. Already in 1983, 34 per cent of respondents in the Republic saw the Irish nation as constituting 26 counties—63 per cent saw it as comprising 32; and only 41 per cent saw the people of Northern Ireland as 'Irish'; Cox, W. H., 'Who wants a united Ireland?', *Government and Opposition*, 20/1 (1985): 29–47.

15. For an early expression, see Monypenny, W. F., *The two Irish nations* (London: Murray, 1913).

16. Among exceptions, one of the earliest nationalist figures to concede explicitly the fact that Ulster Protestants are not 'Irish' was Arthur Clery, a columnist in the *Leader*; see Chanel, pseud. [Arthur Clery], *The idea of a nation* (Dublin: James Duffy, 1907), 62–5.

17. Brady, C., '"Constructive and instrumental": the dilemma of Ireland's first "new historians"', in C. Brady, (ed.), *Interpreting Irish history: the debate on historical revisionism 1938–94* (Dublin: Irish Academic Press, 1994), 3–31.

18. Lynch, J., *Speeches and statements: Irish unity, Northern Ireland, Anglo-Irish relations August 1969–October 1971* (Dublin: Government Information Bureau, 1971), 3.

19. Ibid., 95–6.

20. For example, in the course of an election campaign in late 1982 Garret FitzGerald's support for an all-Ireland police force was used vigorously against him by a Fianna Fáil opposition that sought to play on southern fears of police from the north exercising authority in the south; see FitzGerald, G., *All in a life: Garret FitzGerald: an autobiography* (Dublin: Gill and Macmillan, 1991), 419–20.

21. New Ireland Forum, *Report* (Dublin: Stationery Office, 1984), section 5.7.

22. Speech to Fianna Fáil *ard-fheis*, 16 February 1980, in Mansergh, M. (ed.), *The spirit of the nation: the speeches and statements of Charles J. Haughey (1957–1986)* (Cork, Dublin: Mercier, 1986), 335.

23. For an early expression, see Chanel, *Idea of the nation* (1907); in the late 1960s this idea was taken up by a small group known as the Irish Communist Organization—later renamed the British and Irish Communist Organization—which explored the question in a number of highly original but rarely cited studies: *The economics of partition* (1969), *The birth of Ulster unionism* (1970), and *The home rule crisis* (1972), which together document the development of Ulster's distinctiveness, and *Against Ulster nationalism* (2nd ed., 1977).

24. See O'Brien, C. C., *States of Ireland* (London: Hutchinson, 1972).

25. *Northern Ireland Constitution Act* 1973 (c. 36), section 1. Provision was made for polls on this issue; they were to be separated by a period of at least 10 years.

26. *Northern Ireland: agreed communiqué issued following the conference between the Irish and British Governments and the parties involved in the Northern Ireland Executive (designate) on 6th, 7th, 8th and 9th December 1973* [Sunningdale Agreement, 1973], section 5.

27. *Agreement between the Government of Ireland and the Government of the United Kingdom* [Anglo-Irish Agreement, 1985], section 1 (c).

28. *Joint declaration by an Taoiseach, Mr Albert Reynolds, TD, and the British Prime Minister, the Right Hon John Major, MP, 15 December 1993* [Downing St Declaration], sections 4, 7.

29. *The Irish Free State (Consequential Provisions) Act* 1922, had restricted this provision to Northern Ireland.

30. See McGarry, J. and O'Leary, B., *Explaining Northern Ireland: broken images* (Oxford: Blackwell, 1996), 46–7, 56–7.

31. *Downing St Declaration*, section 4.
32. Clarke, D. M., 'Nationalism, the Irish constitution, and multicultural citizenship', *Northern Ireland Legal Quarterly*, 51 (2000): 100–19.
33. O'Donnell, D., 'Constitutional background to aspects of the Good Friday Agreement: a Republic of Ireland perspective', *Northern Ireland Legal Quarterly*, 50 (1999): 76–89. In 1925 a deputation of Northern nationalists had been refused permission to address the Dáil in the course of the debate on the boundary commission report, and in 1951, notwithstanding the new constitution, a group of nationalist parliamentarians was again refused the right to speak in the Dáil.
34. See, for example, Forde, M., *Constitutional law of Ireland* (Cork, Dublin: Mercier, 1987), 36–7, 50–3. The Irish Government's recognition in the 1973 Sunningdale Agreement and the 1985 Anglo-Irish Agreement of the 'status' of Northern Ireland could be seen as *de facto* recognition only, since this 'status' was not defined. However, it has been argued that the latter agreement amounted to a *de facto* abandonment of the perspective of the 1937 constitution; see Carty, A., 'The Irish constitution, international law and the northern question—the need for radical thinking', in T. Murphy and P. Twomey (eds.), *Ireland's evolving constitution, 1937–97: collected essays* (Oxford: Hart, 1998), 97–105.
35. Kelly, J. M., *The Irish constitution*, 3rd ed., by G. Hogan and G. Whyte (Dublin: Butterworth, 1994), 12–14.
36. The committee had proposed in 1967 that article 3 be replaced by the following:

    1. The Irish nation hereby proclaimes its firm will that its territory be re-united in harmony and brotherly affection between all Irishmen.
    2. The laws enacted by the Parliament established by this constitution shall, until the achievement of the nation's unity shall otherwise require, have the like area and extent of application as the laws of the Parliament which existed prior to the adoption of this Constitution. Provision shall be made by law to give extra-territorial effect to such laws.

    Report of the Committee on the Constitution, December 1967 (Dublin: Stationery Office, 1967), 6–7.
38. O'Donnell, 'Constitutional background', 88.
39. Forde, *Constitutional law*, 52–3.
40. See Murphy, B. P., *Patrick Pearse and the republican ideal* (Dublin: James Duffy, 1991), 193–4.
41. Even those speakers most intimately involved in the state-building process—William Cosgrave, Kevin O'Higgins, and Desmond FitzGerald—were dismissive of the Council; Ernest Blythe, notwithstanding his northern roots, described it as 'an artificial method of imposing certain political machinery on the country'; and, from the government side, only Richard Mulcahy hinted at momentary misgivings—which he managed to overcome. Expressions of support for the Council of Ireland were few and brief, and were confined to the opposition benches; see *Dáil debates*, vol. 13, 7–10 Dec 1925, cols. 1313–673.
42. Compton, P., *Demographic review of Northern Ireland 1995* (Belfast: Northern Ireland Economic Development Office, 1995), 222–6. This projection was based on the assumption that age-specific birth and mortality rates for the two main denominational groups would continue to be the same as in 1988–91; but if it were to be assumed that the drop in the Catholic birth rate would continue to the point of equalization with the other group by 2011, substantial equality between the two groups would be reached by 2071. These projections do not take account of migration differentials, and the substantial group claiming not to have any religion are grouped with the non-Roman Catholics. See also Doherty, P., 'The numbers game: the demographic context of politics', in A. Aughey and D. Morrow (eds.), *Northern Ireland politics* (London: Longman, 1996), 199–209.
43. These calculations are based on the—unsafe, but interesting—assumption that those refusing to indicate their religious affiliation and those indicating that they have no religious belief may be omitted from the picture, or be allocated proportionally to the two main cultural groups.
44. See Breen, R. and Devine, P., 'Segmentation and the social structure', in P. Mitchell and R. Wilford (eds.), *Politics in Northern Ireland* (Boulder, CO: Westview, 1999), 52–65.
45. This is compatible with the results of the 'border poll' in 1973, when, in a turnout of 58.7 per cent, 98.9 per cent voted that Northern Ireland should remain within the United Kingdom—

the main nationalist groups urged abstention from the poll. Since the pro-union vote amounted to 57.5 per cent of the total electorate, a sizeable number of Catholics appear to have voted in favour of the union—the only alternative to this interpretation is that Protestant turnout broke all records: an implausible hypothesis in a poll whose outcome was a foregone conclusion.

46. *Downing St Declaration*, section 4.

47. In the December 1999 poll quoted at the beginning of this chapter, for instance, the proportions prepared to pay specific political and economic costs varied widely: of those expressing an opinion, 71 per cent were prepared to see northern Unionists participating in an Irish government, but only 45 per cent were prepared to abandon the traditional policy of military neutrality by joining NATO, 30 per cent would be prepared to see Ireland rejoin the Commonwealth and a mere 10 per cent would be prepared to pay higher taxation—*Irish Independent*, 21 December 1999. This is compatible with earlier data; in 1993, for instance, which showed that, in return for a closer relationship with Northern Ireland, 57 per cent would be prepared to amend the law to meet the demands of minorities and 52 per cent would be prepared to share power with unionists, but only 19 per cent would be prepared to pay higher taxes; see Marsh and Wilford, 'Irish political data 1993'. These findings coexist with the large majorities that endorse unity as an aspiration; see Ruane, J. and Todd, J., *The dynamics of conflict in Northern Ireland: power, conflict and emancipation* (Cambridge: Cambridge University Press, 1996), 250. Because of remarkable variation in question wording, it is almost impossible to track support for Irish unity as a preferred option over time, but the following general points apply in the case of surveys where respondents were asked to choose from a range of options: in the 1970s, clear majorities generally favoured Irish unity; in the 1980s support appeared to have fallen off; and by the 1990s combined support for other options normally eclipsed support for unity; see Rose, R., McAllister, I., and Mair, P., *Is there a concurring majority about Northern Ireland* (Strathclyde: Centre for the Study of Public Policy, Studies in Public Policy 22, 1978); Cox, 'Who wants a united Ireland?'; Marsh, M. and Wilford, R., 'Irish political data 1993', *Irish political studies*, 9 (1994), 189–245.

48. O'Brien, C. C., *Memoir: my life and themes* (Dublin: Poolbeg Press, 1998).

49. Garvin, T., *1922: the birth of Irish democracy* (Dublin: Gill and Macmillan, 1996), 207. But another analyst who extrapolated from the period of the founding of the State to the end of the century concluded that the partition issue had not been finally settled: 'the two Irelands, for all their cosmopolitan millennial glitter, have yet to escape the shadow of their revolutions'; Fitzpatrick, D., *The two Irelands 1912–1939* (Oxford: Oxford University Press, 1998), 243.

50. For an illustration of a range of interpretations of the agreement in the context of the conflict, see Ruane, J., 'The end of (Irish) history? Three readings of the current conjuncture', in J. Ruane and J. Todd (eds.), *After the Good Friday agreement: analysing political change in Northern Ireland* (Dublin: UCD Press, 1999), 145–69.

51. Todd, J., 'Nationalism, republicanism and the Good Friday agreement', in Ruane and Todd, *After the Good Friday agreement*, 49–70; Munck, R., 'Irish radical nationalism: from irredentism to democratic compromise', *Canadian Review of Studies in Nationalism*, 26 (1999): 107–21.

13

International Dimensions of the Belfast Agreement

ADRIAN GUELKE

Introduction

The external factors that contributed to the political settlement of the 'Irish Question' embodied in the Belfast Agreement are perhaps best conceived of as a series of threads woven into a pattern of influence on a conflict which had been sustained largely by its own internal dynamics. At least five significant dimensions of external influence on the peace process can be identified:

(1) change in the strategic environment;
(2) the impact of South Africa's example;
(3) the role of the American connection;
(4) European integration; and
(5) human rights norms.

All of these 'threads' became intertwined during the peace process. However, it remains possible to separate them and this chapter will examine each of these influences in turn, pointing out, when appropriate, connections among the various dimensions. This list is not exhaustive and, in passing, the chapter will refer to other factors that deserve mention. In the course of the analysis it will also become apparent that the contribution external factors have made to the peace process, while generally positive, have not been entirely unambiguous in their implications. Indeed, they are also bound up with some of the difficulties that have been encountered in the implementation of the Belfast Agreement.

The Strategic Dimension

On 9 November 1990, the Secretary of State for Northern Ireland, Peter Brooke, delivered a major speech in his Westminster constituency in which he set out Britain's stance on the Northern Irish problem. In the course of his speech he said that Britain would accept the unification of Ireland if that was the wish of a majority of people in Northern Ireland, but much more significantly he put the following gloss on British policy:

The British government has no selfish strategic or economic interest in Northern Ireland: our role is to help, enable and encourage. Britain's purpose, as I have sought to describe it, is not to occupy or exploit, but to ensure democratic debate and free democratic choice. (Mallie, E. and McKittrick, D., *The Fight for Peace: The Secret Story behind the Irish Peace Process* (London: Heinemann, 1996), 107.)

In particular, in denying a strategic motive for maintaining the link between Great Britain and Northern Ireland, Brooke was addressing what had been a central assumption of the republican movement since the mid-1970s. Namely, that strategic considerations were a major part of the explanation why British Governments had failed to be moved by majority public support in Britain for a policy of withdrawal from Northern Ireland.

Unusually for British Ministers in Northern Ireland, Brooke closely followed republican thinking. This had been shown the previous year when he had given an interview marking his first hundred days as Secretary of State. In contrast to his predecessors, Brooke made no claim that the security forces could defeat the Provisional Irish Republican Army (IRA). Instead, he acknowledged the IRA's capacity to sustain its campaign, while also stressing its futility. In this context he declared that the Government would be generous in its response if the campaign of violence ended. Both these comments, and his comparison of Northern Ireland with the case of colonial Cyprus, provoked a storm of criticism. Brooke's readiness to run the risk of criticism inside and outside his own party stemmed from his recognition that republican assumptions about the nature of the conflict had been shaken to a degree by the Anglo-Irish Agreement of 15 November 1985. He sought to capitalize on that and was encouraged to do so by the leader of the Social Democratic and Labour Party (SDLP), John Hume.

Hume's first draft of a proposed joint declaration by the British and Irish Governments intended to form the core of a peace initiative contained the words: 'The British Government reiterate yet again that they no longer have any selfish political or strategic interest in remaining in Ireland'. This draft was written in October 1991. A second draft composed with the assistance of the Irish Government modified these words as follows:

The British Prime Minister reiterates on behalf of the British Government that they have no selfish, strategic, political or economic interest in Northern Ireland, and that their sole wish is to see peace, stability and reconciliation established by agreement among the people who inhabit the island. (Mallie, E. and McKittrick, D., *The Fight for Peace: The Secret Story behind the Irish Peace Process* (London: Heinemann, 1996), 372.)

These words remained unchanged in a February 1992 draft of the joint declaration proposed by Sinn Féin, an indication of their acceptability to the republican movement. Thereafter, they are reiterated unchanged in subsequent drafts of the joint declaration emanating out of the talks involving Hume, Adams, and the Irish Government. However, as it stood, this wording was not acceptable to the British Government. The formulation which finally appeared in the 1993 'Joint Declaration' by the British and Irish governments which launched the Irish peace process returned to Brooke's words of November 1990. The relevant section of the Joint Declaration reads as follows:

The Prime Minister, on behalf of the British Government, reaffirms that they will uphold the democratic wish of a greater number of the people of Northern Ireland on the issue of whether they prefer to support the Union or a sovereign independent Ireland. On this basis, he reiterates, on behalf of the British Government, that they have no selfish strategic or economic interest in Northern Ireland. Their primary interest is to see peace, stability and reconciliation established by agreement among all the people who inhabit the island, and they will work together with the Irish Government to achieve such an agreement, which will embrace the totality of relationships. (Joint Declaration: Downing Street, 15 December 1993.)

While the Joint Declaration as a whole was rejected by Sinn Féin in July 1994, there was sufficient in the declaration to the liking of the republican movement to help to bring about the IRA cease-fire of August 1994.

It is difficult to assess precisely how important Brooke's words of November 1990 were for this outcome, since it was one of a number of factors that helped to change the republican movement's assessment of British policy. But that they influenced republican thinking in a positive direction is unquestionable. It may be objected that Brooke's words were no more than a statement of the obvious, and that any intelligent analyst of British policy in the 1980s would have concluded that strategic factors were not a significant influence on the Government's approach to the conflict. For example, the Deputy Director of the Institute of Strategic Studies in London stated in the context of debate on the Anglo-Irish Agreement that technology had greatly reduced the strategic significance of Northern Ireland, describing it as a 'non-issue'.[1] However, there were instances in which British Ministers had spoken of Northern Ireland in terms that reinforced the republican movement's assumption that British strategic interests were at stake in the conflict. A notable example was a warning by the Secretary of State for Northern Ireland, James Prior, in 1983 to a meeting of Conservative MPs, that Ireland could become another Cuba if Sinn Féin came to power.[2] The purpose of Prior's remarks was to persuade sceptical unionist die-hards in the Conservative party of the need to shore up the position of constitutional nationalism in the face of the revivified electoral challenge it was facing from Sinn Féin. The unintended outcome of Prior's remarks was confirmation of the republican movement's analysis of the conflict and the reinforcement of its belief that British policy was designed to prevent the emergence of a united Ireland which would be neutral and thus could refuse facilities to NATO forces.

It is also clear that, before the end of the Cold War, any statement to the effect that Britain had no strategic interest in Northern Ireland would have excited staunch opposition within the Government. In particular, a residual strategic importance was assigned by some defence specialists to Northern Ireland as, unlike the rest of the island, part of NATO by virtue of its membership of the UK. Thus, it has subsequently been reported that Margaret Thatcher had delayed Brooke's declaration because of her concern over the implications for the nuclear submarines, which passed close to Northern Ireland when patrolling the Atlantic.[3] Thus, while the republican movement's assumption of a strategic dimension to British policy in Northern Ireland never enjoyed much support among academic studies of British policy, in practice, an official denial that such an interest existed had to await the end of the Cold War, with the collapse of the Berlin Wall in 1989.

What is more, for such a declaration to have an impact on the perceptions of the republican movement, it was necessary not merely that it should be *made* but that it would be *believed*. Numerous British declarations in the 1970s and 1980s to the effect that the Government would not stand in the way of a united Ireland if it was the wish of a majority in Northern Ireland had been greeted with scepticism by the republican movement—which justified its campaign of violence partly on the basis that no constitutional route to unification existed. The end of the Cold War was also an important factor in persuading the republican movement to treat Brooke's declaration as a credible statement of British interest, notwithstanding the qualification of 'strategic or economic interest' by the term 'selfish'. It was evident from the response of leading figures in Sinn Féin to Brooke's declaration in November 1990 that the republican movement regarded it as a significant development. However, that it might open the way to the abandonment of the IRA's campaign of violence was far from apparent, although such a possibility was mooted by Father Alec Reid, whose contacts with Sinn Féin leaders provided him with a profound insight into their thinking.[4]

While the retention of Brooke's words in the Downing Street Declaration of December 1993 underlines its importance within the context of the development of the peace process, the limit of its influence on republican thinking also needs to be acknowledged. Thus the 'TUAS' (Tactical Use of the Armed Struggle) document circulated within the republican movement before the Provisional IRA cease-fire in August 1994 would only conclude that 'present British intentions are the subject of much debate and varied opinion'.[5] The issue of British strategic interest played no discernible part in the negotiations leading up to the Belfast Agreement and there is no reference in the Agreement to a strategic dimension to its objectives of 'the development of a peaceful environment' and 'a normalisation of security arrangements and practices' (paragraph 1 of section on Security).

The South African Example

During the 1980s, the comparison of the Provisional IRA's campaign of violence with the 'armed struggle' of the African National Congress (ANC) in South Africa, and that of the Palestine Liberation Organisation (PLO) against the state of Israel and its continuing occupation of territories captured in 1967, became an important part of the rhetoric of the republican movement. It was reflected both in murals in west Belfast highlighting connections among the different campaigns[6] and in the writings of Gerry Adams.[7] The need for the republican movement to find external reference points to legitimize IRA violence was related to the abandonment of the notion that victory was in reach and the adoption of the long war strategy, which presupposed that it would need to sustain its campaign well into the twenty-first century to achieve its objectives. In these circumstances, lending meaning to acts of violence that had no immediate reward presented a large problem for the republican movement, especially in the context of Sinn Féin's entry into electoral politics as a byproduct of political mobilization during the 1981 hunger-strike crisis.

The illegitimacy of Northern Ireland was crucial to the republican movement's justification of the long war, as was the associated proposition that Northern Ireland as a political entity was beyond reform. The context that best supported such propositions was the representation of British rule in Northern Ireland as a species of colonialism. Direct rule from London tended to lend verisimilitude to this view of the situation. A book putting a republican perspective on the conflict in Northern Ireland, Kevin Kelley's *The Longest War: Northern Ireland and the IRA*,[8] which was published in 1982, contained an epilogue that set out in some depth the analogy between South Africa and Northern Ireland. To sustain the comparison, Kelley imagined that South Africa had been partitioned and that part of the country was still a colony, while the rest was a neo-colony. Despite its contrived basis, Kelley's analogy achieved considerable popularity among republicans: its welcome reception reflected how much they felt they needed to find a basis for legitimizing a long war strategy that simply could not be justified on the premise that victory lay within reach.

The emphasis placed by republicans on the analogy between apartheid in South Africa and sectarianism in Northern Ireland inevitably meant that President de Klerk's liberalization of the South African political system in February 1990 posed a considerable challenge to their view of the conflict in Northern Ireland. If fundamental change could occur in apartheid South Africa, of all places, through negotiation and without revolution, how could republicans sustain the argument that it was impossible in Northern Ireland? Further pressure was placed on republicans by the agreement between Israel and the PLO in 1993.

A more immediate and significant challenge to republican assumptions had occurred before these developments: the Anglo-Irish Agreement (AIA) of

November 1985. The republican movement's response to the AIA oscillated between, on the one hand, the accusation that it copper-fastened partition and, on the other, attempts to claim part of the credit for the benefits that accrued to nationalists under its terms. At the same time, the favourable international reaction to the Agreement undercut the republican movement's continuing presentation of the IRA's campaign of violence as a national liberation struggle against British colonialism.

In May 1987 Sinn Féin published a document restating the basic position of the republican movement, in particular, its demand for a declaration of intent to withdraw from Northern Ireland by the British Government. However, the language of the document was intended to put the most reasonable gloss possible on the stance of the movement, as was reflected in its title, *A Scenario for Peace*.[9] In January 1988 the leader of the SDLP, John Hume, met Gerry Adams, the Sinn Féin President, thereby inaugurating a series of exchanges between the parties that lasted until the following September. Much of the argument between the parties revolved round the issue of the meaning of self-determination. Sinn Féin asserted that the self-determination of the Irish people required a British declaration of intent to withdraw, whereas the SDLP vainly attempted to persuade the republican movement that the Anglo–Irish Agreement amounted to a British declaration of neutrality on the constitutional status of Northern Ireland.

In February 1992 Sinn Féin launched a fresh peace initiative with the publication of *Towards a lasting peace in Ireland*,[10] which represented a considerable advance on the stance taken in *A Scenario for Peace*. It described the armed struggle as 'an option of last resort' and put the onus on 'those who proclaim that the armed struggle is counter-productive to advance a credible alternative'. It even went so far as to state: 'The development of such an alternative would be welcomed by Sinn Féin.' But what undercut the impact of the implication that the republican movement might be ready to abandon the campaign of violence against British rule was the document's assessment that armed struggle 'is likely to be sustained for the foreseeable future'. In analysing the two documents, Ronnie Munck contrasted the 'theological' and 'absolutist' nature of *A Scenario for Peace* with what he characterized as the 'new realism' of *Towards a lasting peace in Ireland*—a shift in thinking he likened to similar changes in South Africa in the early 1990s.[11]

When it was published, *Towards a lasting peace in Ireland* attracted relatively little attention and the evidence it presented of a greater pragmatism on the part of Sinn Féin failed to prevent the defeat of Gerry Adams in west Belfast in the British general election of April 1992. This was in large part because hopes for political progress in Northern Ireland were then seen as depending upon the talks among the constitutional parties that had been initiated in 1991. It was only after the failure of a further round of negotiations among the constitutional parties through the summer of 1992 that an opening was created for Sinn Féin's peace initiative to be put to the test. In April 1993 it became public knowledge that a series of meeting had begun between John Hume and Gerry Adams and in September they announced that they had reached agreement on a joint proposal to put to the Irish and British Governments. The British Government responded somewhat guardedly to this initiative because it complicated efforts designed to bring the constitutional parties closer together. However, the Irish Government was more supportive. In a speech at Bodenstown on 17 October the *Taoiseach*, Albert Reynolds, declared that the Hume-Adams proposal could 'supply an important part of the basis for peace', urging the parties to take their cue from the progress made in South Africa and Israel/Palestine 'between people who had far stronger objective and emotional reasons for remaining forever irreconcilable'.[12]

Reynolds's invocation of the South African transition and the Middle East peace process echoed similar statements by leading republicans. In an interview with Paul Johnson, Martin McGuinness declared: 'If the British Government was prepared to learn from South Africa and Israel, then we could see a solution within six to 12 months'.[13] In a similar vein Gerry Adams asserted in an interview with Owen Boycott:

If someone hadn't grasped the nettle in South Africa or in Palestine . . . Mandela would still be slopping out his cell rather than preparing to be president. The Government is part of the problem and it has to be part of the solution. (*Guardian*, 2 October 1993.)

Ironically, when the two governments launched their own peace initiative with the Joint Declaration of 15 December 1993, the republican movement found itself placed under pressure to respond positively to the initiative in terms of the same analogies. When Adams was interviewed by a leading American magazine in the summer of 1994, the first question put to him was 'Over the past year, once bitter enemies in South Africa and the Middle East have made tremendous progress in working together. Why haven't you tried to seize the moment here with the British?'[14] When the IRA cease-fire came at the end of August, so strongly did the case of South Africa feature in republican explanations of the movement's peace strategy that it prompted James Fenton, to dub it 'the Mandela Manoeuvre'.[15]

Powerful reinforcement was given to the South African comparison by the enthusiasm with which the comparison was treated in South Africa itself where the cease-fire was reported under the banner headline: 'IRA takes "SA option"'.[16] Far from repudiating comparison with the IRA, as the PLO had done in the 1980s, the ANC willingly did all it could to assist Sinn Féin in its peace strategy. This extended from aiding the leadership in persuading the grass roots of the republican movement that the right course was being followed, to using its good offices to help Sinn Féin in its negotiations with other parties. For example, before the IRA renewed its cease-fire in July 1997, all the parties that won seats in the elections to the Northern Ireland Forum in 1996 were invited to a seminar in South Africa on the lessons of the transition. At the Sinn

Féin annual conference immediately following the Belfast Agreement, the Deputy Secretary-General of the ANC, Thenjiwe Mtintso, spoke on the importance of trusting the leadership. A senior ANC delegation also came to Belfast and spoke at a number of meetings organized by Sinn Féin, as well as visiting IRA prisoners in the Maze.

Republicans were not alone in viewing the success of the South Africa's transition as helpful to the Northern Irish peace process. For example, the non-party 'Yes' campaign sought to involve Nelson Mandela in its efforts during the referendum on the Belfast Agreement.[17] The favourable impression made by the transition in South Africa prompted the borrowing of both expert opinion and of ideas from that case. Most notable in this respect was the use of 'the principle of sufficient consensus' as a basis for decision-making during the multiparty negotiations that led to the Belfast Agreement. This was interpreted as the requirement that substantive decisions should have the support of majorities of both unionists and nationalists. Admittedly, use of this principle is not new in Northern Ireland. Previously it went under the different label of parallel consent. However, the association of the principle with South Africa's successful transition gave it much wider legitimacy during Northern Ireland's negotiations on a political settlement. The importance of the principle is reflected in its incorporation in the Agreement as one of the rules governing decision-making by the Assembly, though in the Agreement it is referred to by its old label of parallel consent.

But the use made of the South African case by other parties has tended to mask the special significance that the analogy has had for the republican movement, which has been to underpin its anti-colonial analysis of the conflict in Northern Ireland, thereby legitimizing the objective of a united Ireland. That perspective is further reflected in the republican movement's insistence that the Belfast Agreement is merely transitional, in effect a stepping stone to its ultimate aim. This has had both positive and negative implications for the peace process. South Africa's example has been used by the leaders of Sinn Féin to persuade the rank and file of the republican movement of what it is possible to achieve through the route of constitutional negotiations. Yet there remains considerable ambiguity as to whether the movement has accepted that it may only legitimately pursue the aspiration of a united Ireland through the constitutional mechanisms provided for under the Agreement. This is related to the issue of whether the Belfast Agreement is a final settlement of the Irish Question or not. Comparison of the Belfast Agreement with the liberalization of the South African political system in 1990, rather than with Mandela's inauguration as President in 1994, may be taken as underlining the republican movement's view of the Agreement as only a starting point.

The American Connection

Almost from the start of 'the troubles' in 1968, nationalists in Northern Ireland have sought support for their cause from the Irish diaspora in the United States, although, in practice, only a very small number of the country's 40 million Irish-Americans has taken an active interest in events in Northern Ireland. Irish Northern Aid, or NORAID, was formed in 1970 shortly after the formation of the Provisional IRA. It raised funds in the United States to send to Ireland for the purpose of assisting the families of republican prisoners. NORAID's founder, Michael Flannery, held the view that the IRA border campaign of 1956 to 1962 had failed in part for the want of support for the prisoners. In short, the motive for helping the families of prisoners was not simply charitable. Further, NORAID was strongly suspected by the authorities of siphoning funds for the purchase of weaponry in the United States for the Provisional IRA, as well as of sending undeclared money to Ireland that the republican movement was free to spend as it wished.

The other main Irish-American organization concerned with conflict in Northern Ireland was the Irish National Caucus (INC), founded in 1974. Although originally linked to NORAID, under Father Sean McManus the INC developed its own distinct identity and approach to the conflict. With offices in Washington it became the main organization lobbying for American intervention in the conflict. In this principal endeavour it was relatively unsuccessful. The State Department strongly opposed the taking of any action in relation to the issue of Northern Ireland that might damage American relations with Britain, the country's most important ally in Europe in the context of the Cold War. However, the INC did achieve considerable success in the campaign it launched over the issue of discrimination in employment. It formulated a set of principles, named the MacBride principles after the Republic's former Minister of External Affairs, Sean MacBride, as a code of conduct for American firms operating in Northern Ireland and lobbied at state and city level for action to enforce compliance with the principles. Local politicians, less concerned with the possible damage to American foreign policy, proved more amenable to the case put forward by the INC.

A group of senior Irish-American politicians, known as the 'Four Horsemen'—after the famous backs of Notre Dame's football team—had greater success than the INC in securing a modification of the State Department's non-interventionist stance on the conflict. The four Democrats—Senator Edward Kennedy, Senator Patrick Moynihan, Speaker 'Tip' O'Neill, and Governor Hugh Carey—persuaded President Carter to issue a statement on Northern Ireland at the end of August 1977. While it did not challenge the fundamental basis of British policy in urging that there should be a settlement involving the Irish Republic, the simple fact that it treated the conflict as a legitimate concern of American foreign policy disturbed the British Government. Even more disturbingly for the British Government, in 1979 the State Department suspended the sale of handguns to the Royal Ulster Constabulary (RUC) as a result of a scandal over the RUC's interrogation methods. Furthermore, not merely did President Reagan fail to lift the suspension, but he also put pressure on the British Government to acknowledge the legitimacy of the Irish Republic's concern over the situation in Northern Ireland. These acts contributed to the pressure that persuaded Margaret Thatcher to sign the Anglo-Irish Agreement in November 1985.

Nevertheless, it remains largely true that prior to the Clinton Presidency, American involvement in the conflict was largely reactive. Influential in changing the basis of American engagement with the problem was a new organization, 'Americans for a New Irish Agenda' (ANIA). As with many previous Irish-American organizations concerned with the conflict in Northern Ireland, it was sympathetic to the republican movement's interpretation of the conflict. However, it reflected a shift in the attitudes of Irish-Americans away from the assumption that Britain was the cause of the conflict—and Irish unity the answer—to a more subtle appreciation of the political forces in Ireland, coupled to the wish to contribute to an end to the conflict without prejudging the shape of a settlement. It canvassed support during 1992 for a set of proposals on Northern Ireland, which included that the next President of the United States should appoint a peace envoy to the province, grant a visa to Gerry Adams, and exert diplomatic pressure on Britain over the issue. As a candidate for the nomination of the Democratic Party, Bill Clinton gave qualified support to the proposals and was rewarded by the formation of 'Irish-Americans for Clinton/Gore'. However, after his election Clinton disappointed the Irish-American lobby. On the advice of the Irish Government he declined to appoint a peace envoy. Further, the Clinton Administration continued the policy of refusing visas to leading figures in Sinn Féin. Nevertheless, ANIA persisted in its efforts to bring about change both in American policy and in the stance of the republican movement in Northern Ireland. Eventually it was to succeed.

At the beginning of 1994 Clinton granted Gerry Adams a 48-hour visa to attend a one-day conference on Northern Ireland. The conference, which took place in New York at the beginning of February, was organized by the National Committee on American Foreign Policy, and chaired by a prominent Irish-American, Bill Flynn, closely associated with ANIA. The decision was a highly controversial one *within* the Clinton Administration, the White House overruling the advice of other agencies of the Government. And, despite the launch of an Anglo-Irish peace initiative a month earlier, the decision provoked a furious reaction from the British Government. However, it is arguable that British fury had as much to do with disquiet over the implication that in the new post-Cold War world the United States no longer needed to give such a high priority to British wishes as it did for the decision's actual impact on Northern Ireland. Niall O'Dowd, the founder of *The Irish Voice* and a leading figure in ANIA, noted that the grant of the visa 'overturned a 50-year hegemony over Irish policy that the British government had exercised through the State Department'.[18] The fact that the IRA eventually declared a cease-fire on 31 August 1994 was widely seen as a vindication of Clinton's judgement on the visa. That was underscored by the prominent role attributed to Irish-American groups in the decision, both because of documentation circulated within the republican movement ahead of the decision and because of a meeting between Sinn Féin leaders and an Irish-American delegation shortly before the announcement of the cease-fire.

The terms of the cease-fire declared by the IRA fell short of British demands for a statement that there would be a permanent end to political violence. In March 1995 in a speech in Washington, the Secretary of State for Northern Ireland, Sir Patrick Mayhew, laid down conditions for Sinn Féin's participation in negotiations on a political settlement. The most important of these, designed to justify dropping insistence on a commitment to the permanence of the cease-fire, was that there should be a start made to the process of the decommissioning of arms by the IRA. The condition became known as 'Washington Three' and was reportedly supported by President Clinton.[19] The result was a political impasse: the IRA was as unwilling to embark upon the decommissioning of its arsenal of weapons as it had been to declare the cease-fire permanent. The issue cast a shadow over President Clinton's impending visit to Northern Ireland in November 1995. At American prompting, the British and Irish Governments on the eve of the visit agreed to refer the issue to an International Body which was given the task of arriving at a formula to enable political progress to be made. This decision lifted the gloom that had settled over the peace process and contributed to the enthusiastic welcome Clinton received throughout his visit.

The former Democratic party Senator, George Mitchell, was appointed to chair the International Body. Thereafter, Mitchell became the key figure in America's prolonged engagement with the peace process, in many respects fulfilling the role of a peace envoy. Mitchell's accommodationist approach to political differences in Northern Ireland, and his acceptance that these differences stemmed from genuinely held political convictions about the nature of the society, made him a very successful mediator. When Mitchell, the Clinton Administration, and the Irish-American lobby have been of one accord in coaxing the republican movement towards the need to accept a political settlement, they have been able to exert a measure of influence on Sinn Féin. However, when difficulties have arisen in the peace process, the Irish-American lobby's disposition to accept the republican interpretation of the conflict has tended to limit America's influence in this context. Similarly, rewards for positive actions by the republican movement have formed a more important element of American engagement in the peace process than the imposition of penalties for negative ones. This has fuelled criticism of American involvement as little short of the appeasement of terrorism, by figures such as the former American ambassador to the United Kingdom, Raymond Seitz.[20] It also explains the sharp

divide in attitudes towards American involvement between unionist supporters
and opponents of the Belfast Agreement.

The compromise proposed by the International Body in January 1996 was that
decommissioning should take place alongside negotiations on a settlement—in
effect, jettisoning the notion that decommissioning should be a precondition for
Sinn Féin's participation in all-party negotiations. However, it also proposed
that all parties to the negotiations should commit themselves to a stringent set
of principles forswearing the use of violence for any purpose, going well beyond
the terms of existing paramilitary cease-fires.[21] Disagreement over whether these
principles could be accepted was a factor in the abandonment of the IRA cease-
fire in February 1996. However, this was masked by the British Prime Minister's
introduction of a new element into the equation: his insistence on elections to a
Northern Ireland Forum ahead of all-party negotiations. Admittedly, elections
were mentioned as a possible confidence-building measure in the Report of the
International Body, but without being recommended, with the result that outside of the Ulster Unionist party, which had advocated the holding of elections,
Major's proposal had caused consternation. The consequence was that much of
the blame for the breakdown was laid at the door of Major and the Conservative
government—see Patterson, in Chapter 9 of this volume—particularly within
Irish-America. A further period of prolonged stalemate in the peace process followed. Sinn Féin protested that it should be entitled to participate fully in any
political process on the basis of its electoral mandate, regardless of the pursuit
of a limited campaign of violence by the IRA, but failed to secure support for
this proposition from any significant source. The stalemate was finally broken
after the election of new governments in Britain and the Republic of Ireland in,
respectively, May and June 1997. The IRA resumed its cease-fire on 20 July on
the same basis as in 1994.

The renewal of the IRA cease-fire, strongly urged on the republican movement by both the Clinton Administration and the principal Irish-American organizations, opened the way to Sinn Féin's participation in what turned out to be
multi-party talks since the DUP and UKUP left the negotiations on Sinn Féin's
entry. Despite moments when the process appeared to be on the point of collapse, the talks were brought to a successful conclusion under the chairmanship
of George Mitchell. In retrospect, it appears that key junctures in the path to a
settlement were the two governments' publication of the outline of the broad
shape of a settlement in January 1998, which enhanced unionist confidence in
the process, and Mitchell's setting of the deadline of midnight 9 April for agreement—although the latter slipped until the late afternoon of the following day.
Each forced the parties to judge the terms of any settlement in the light of what
the two governments were likely to impose on Northern Ireland should the
process fail.

The implementation of the Agreement proved problematic from the outset
with the Ulster Unionists insisting that a start to decommissioning of paramil-

itary arsenals should precede the formation of the Executive. As a consequence, President Clinton's second visit to Northern Ireland in September 1998 was far from simply being the victory lap and a distraction from his domestic troubles that his critics in the American media presented. The combination of the Omagh outrage and Clinton's visit elicited verbal concessions from the Sinn Féin President, Gerry Adams, that enabled progress to be made on the shape of devolved government and the responsibilities of cross-border bodies, without solving the central issue of the formation of the Executive. Two further efforts were made to solve this problem by the British and Irish Governments in the spring and summer of 1999. Their failure forced a review of the implementation of the Agreement chaired by George Mitchell. In contrast to the period leading up to the Belfast Agreement, Mitchell received little assistance from the two governments in handling the lengthy and difficult review, which he brought to a successful conclusion after 11 weeks in November 1999. The deal achieved in the review allowed the Executive to be set up and the other institutions under the Agreement to come into operation. However, when the Provisional IRA failed to deliver on a start to decommissioning by the end of January 2000, suspension of the Agreement followed, with Mitchell declining involvement in any subsequent review.

The Impact of European Integration

There are relatively few references in the Belfast Agreement to the European Union. In discussing the functioning of the devolved institutions in Northern Ireland, the Agreement provides as follows:

Terms will be agreed between the appropriate Assembly representatives and the Government of the United Kingdom to ensure effective co-ordination and input by Ministers to national policy-making, including on EU issues. (The *Agreement*,, Strand One section, paragraph 31.)

The section of the Agreement detailing the functioning of the North-South Ministerial Council provides for the Council 'to consider the European Union dimension of relevant matters, including the implementation of EU policies and programmes and proposals in the EU framework' (paragraph 17 of section on Strand Two). At the same time, the annex to this section outlining possible areas for north-south co-operation and implementation includes in its list relevant EU programmes. In Strand Three, detailing the establishment and role of the British-Irish Council (BIC)—see Walker, G. in Chapter 7 of this volume—'approaches to EU issues' is listed among suitable issues for early discussion in the BIC (paragraph 5).

Differences among the parties in Northern Ireland over the relevance of the European dimension to settling the issue of Northern Ireland's place in the world explain the relative paucity of the references to European integration. In particular, the wording of the Agreement reflects unionist objections to according a role to the European Union in the definition of Northern Ireland's constitutional position. From a unionist perspective, an unacceptable implication of redefining Northern Ireland as a region of the European Union was the weakening of the province's position as part of the United Kingdom. This carried more weight than the argument that the province's sectarian divisions might be transcended in the embrace of a European identity. The accommodation of unionist objections on this point meant that the significant role that the European dimension played in the approach of nationalists to the Agreement was not fully reflected in the final text. However, it is worth mentioning in this context the provision in the Agreement that the d'Hondt rule should be used for the purpose of allocating Executive posts to members of the different parties, as well as for the election of the Chairs and Deputy Chairs of Assembly Committees. Familiarity with the d'Hondt rule—and hence acceptance of its legitimacy—comes from its use in the European Parliament.

For unionists it was important that the Agreement should be seen as confirming that Northern Ireland was part of the United Kingdom. Equally significant for them was that the provisions for cross-border bodies should be seen in the context of relations with a neighbouring State—and of accommodating the wishes of the nationalist minority for such links—rather than as indicating any measure of ambiguity as to Northern Ireland's status as a political entity. One reason for nationalist distress at the suspension of the devolved institutions on 11 February 2000 was precisely the implication that British sovereignty over Northern Ireland remained undiluted by the Agreement.

The European dimension loomed much larger in the peace process leading up to the Belfast Agreement than it did in the actual Agreement itself. In particular, the SDLP had based its proposals to the Brooke/Mayhew talks among the constitutional parties in 1992/93 on a model it derived from the functioning of the European Commission. It suggested that Northern Ireland should be governed by a six-person commission, comprising three members directly elected by the people of Northern Ireland, two members appointed by the British and Irish Governments respectively and the last appointed by the European Commission. None of the other parties in Northern Ireland regarded the proposals as a sensible starting point for discussion of a new constitutional dispensation. A somewhat less ambitious employment of the European dimension was put forward by the British and Irish Governments in their joint framework document of February 1995. In discussing the powers of cross-border institutions the two Governments suggested:

Any EU matter relevant to the competence of either administration could be raised for consideration in the North/South body. Across all designated matters and in accordance with the delegated functions, both Governments agree that the body will have an important role, with their support and co-operation and in consultation with them, in developing on a continuing basis an agreed approach for the whole island in respect of the challenges and opportunities of the European Union. (*A New Framework for Agreement: A shared understanding between the British and Irish Governments to assist discussion and negotiation involving the Northern Ireland parties* (Belfast: HMSO, 1995))

In short, the dynamic of cross-border co-operation was in part linked to the progress of European integration. The hostile reaction of the unionists to the document underscored their fear that what was being suggested was a mechanism that would facilitate the growth of the powers of cross-border institutions that would ultimately bring about a united Ireland.

The European dimension also played a significant role in the evolution of republican thinking during the 1990s away from the objective of a sovereign, united Ireland free of external encumbrances of any kind. In particular, although Sinn Féin supported a 'no' vote in the referendum in the Republic of Ireland on the Maastricht treaty, the party's 1992 document, *Towards a lasting peace in Ireland*, hinted at a new approach to the European dimension in the context of the changes taking place on the continent after the fall of the Berlin Wall. It noted:

Irish republicanism has its roots in the crucible of Europe during the great French Revolution. The current and profound changes demand an equivalent breadth of vision and willingness to innovate. Irish republicans will not be found wanting. (Sinn Féin, *Towards a lasting peace in Ireland* (1992), 14)

In an interview with Michael Cox, Mitchel McLaughlin, a leading figure in Sinn Féin, was more explicit, arguing that one of the factors that had made the peace process possible was 'the Single European Act and the dominance of the EU on the island of Ireland'.[22] From this post-Cold War perspective, the progress of European integration becomes a factor facilitating the objective of a united Ireland rather than an additional obstacle, alongside partition, to the achievement of a fully independent Ireland. At a practical level, the European Commission established the 'Special Support Programme for Peace and Reconciliation' to assist the peace process in the wake of the 1994 paramilitary cease-fires. Part of the rationale for a package that focused on the alleviation of social exclusion was that it would 'provide an incentive for paramilitary leaders and their supporters to maintain the cease-fires'.[23]

Human Rights

Commitments to the maintenance of human rights form an important and extensive part of the Belfast Agreement. In a section of the Agreement headed 'Rights, Safeguards and Equality of Opportunity', the parties affirm their commitment to a whole series of rights. These are detailed in paragraph 1 of the

Agreement as follows:

(1) the right of free political thought;
(2) the right to freedom and expression of religion;
(3) the right to pursue democratically national and political aspirations;
(4) the right to seek constitutional change by peaceful and legitimate means;
(5) the right to freely choose one's place of residence;
(6) the right to equal opportunity in all social and economic activity, regardless of class, creed, disability, gender or ethnicity;
(7) the right to freedom from sectarian harassment; and
(8) the right of women to full and equal political participation.

The Agreement also contains a commitment by the British government to:

complete incorporation into Northern Ireland law of the European Convention on Human Rights (ECHR), with direct access to the courts, and remedies for breaches of the Convention, including power for the courts to overrule Assembly legislation on grounds of inconsistency. (the *Agreement*, paragraph 2)

There is a further commitment in paragraph 5 that a new Northern Ireland Human Rights Commission would be established under Westminster legislation to monitor observance of human rights. For its part, the Irish Government undertook to strengthen the protection of human rights in the Republic and in this context agreed both to establish a Human Rights Commission with a remit similar to the body set up in Northern Ireland and to ratify the Council of Europe Framework Convention on National Minorities (paragraph 9).

While the promotion of human rights had been a feature of the United Nations in its first years of existence, the issue became a significant element affecting the conduct of British policy in Northern Ireland as a result of two developments. The first was the Irish Republic's referral of interrogation techniques employed by the British army after the introduction of internment in August 1971 to the European Commission of Human Rights. This eventually resulted in a judgement of the European Court of Human Rights in January 1978 that the army's interrogation methods had subjected internees to inhuman and degrading treatment in violation of Article 3 of the European Convention on Human Rights. The second was America's adoption of a human rights standard in the conduct of its foreign policy as a means of limiting its commitments to non-Communist States in the wake of its defeat in Vietnam. Under the rubric that the United States would not supply arms to countries or institutions which had violated basic human rights, Irish-American groups were able to persuade the American State Department to suspend the sale of handguns to the RUC in August 1979. This followed an Amnesty International report strongly alleging official connivance at the serious maltreatment of suspects at police holding centres in Northern Ireland.

Through the 1980s the British Government continued to face embarrassment internationally over persistent allegations of human rights violations by the security forces in Northern Ireland. The government sought to minimize such criticism through such strategies as 'criminalization', that stressed the containment of political violence through the ordinary processes of law, although jury-less courts made it difficult for the Government to present the administration of justice in Northern Ireland as other than extraordinary, as did the reliance of the security forces on emergency powers. From a unionist perspective the British Government paid too much attention to outside opinion on this issue, thereby undermining the efforts of the security forces to combat terrorism. By contrast, to nationalists the seeming incapacity of the British Government to maintain its rule over Northern Ireland without violating human rights was proof of the illegitimacy of direct rule, if not that of partition itself. However, by the 1990s the significant evolution in approaches to the monitoring of the observance of human rights that had occurred undercut this polarization of opinion.

Concern over the violation of human rights by non-State actors led to a change in the practices of organizations such as Amnesty International with the consequence that criticism for violations of human rights was no longer solely directed at governments or State agencies. In the context of Northern Ireland, it exposed the paramilitary organizations on both sides of the sectarian divide to strong criticism. This entailed that human rights monitoring was no longer perceived by moderate unionists as tantamount to undermining the security forces. At the same time, the paramilitary cease-fires reduced the apparent necessity for the security forces to be equipped with wide-ranging emergency powers. In this context, the inclusive nature of the Agreement was important, since without the participation of parties linked to the paramilitaries, confidence that cease-fires would continue during implementation of the Agreement might have been diminished. Furthermore, a greater emphasis in the 1990s on minority rights meant that both communities could look to international conventions in this area as offering a measure of protection for cultural and other group rights under the general rubric of human rights. A final element promoting convergence in the positions of unionists and nationalists on the inclusion of the protection of human rights in the Belfast Agreement was the recognition that such provisions would considerably enhance the international legitimacy of the Agreement. The Agreement's favourable reception by international opinion[24] remained very clearly in the interest of both pro-Agreement unionists and pro-Agreement nationalists.

Conclusion

The role of internationalization in making possible a political settlement in Northern Ireland, albeit one that has encountered obstacles in its implementation, has tended to be underestimated for two very good reasons. The first is

the dominance of what John Whyte has called the 'internal-conflict' interpretation of the conflict, in his meticulous survey of the literature of the troubles.[25]
That is to say, most scholars have accepted that sectarian antagonisms within
Northern Ireland have constituted the primary dynamic behind the conflict. The
second is the assumption that the internationalization of the problem has tended
to compound sectarian divisions by both reinforcing the siege mentality of
Protestants, and in persuading the republican movement that the goal of a
united Ireland is achievable—in the context of the polarization of the two communities as a result of violence. That was a credible view of the role of internationalization during the early years of the conflict. Thus, at the start of the
troubles, the republican view that Britain held onto Northern Ireland to secure
strategic interests in the six counties and to maintain the Republic as a neo-
colony enjoyed a measure of support, particularly among former British
colonies. The economic success of the Republic in the era of globalization has
made such opinions seem archaic.

As the anti-colonial model of the conflict has lost influence in the outside
world—though it has by no means disappeared altogether, as ANC pronounce-
ments on the issue have underlined—and the view has grown that the conflict
is an ethnic one, comparable to countless such conflicts in formerly Communist
states, the impact of internationalization has changed. One consequence has been
that moderate unionism has become far more comfortable with the role of external actors, though the change has been a gradual one and remains confined to
pro-Agreement unionists. It has contributed to the shift in the position of pro-
Agreement unionists, from initially grudging and qualified acceptance of the
Agreement, to a more whole-hearted embrace of the accommodationist spirit
underpinning the Agreement. This has occurred despite continuing unionist
disquiet over some aspects of the implementation of the Agreement, such as the
reform of policing.

However, while international trends in the post-Cold war world have facilitated the credibility of an internal settlement qualified by 'soft' sovereignty and
external linkages, there are some aspects of current trends that run counter to
the approach taken in the Belfast Agreement. The most obvious of these is the
evolution of a consensus that the perpetrators of serious human rights violations—whether acting as agents of the state or not—should in no circumstances
enjoy impunity. The release of members of paramilitary organizations, including individuals with convictions for more than one murder, clearly runs counter
to the spirit of the times. The current concern that the victims of conflicts
should not be forgotten by the general public also militates against closing the
chapter of the troubles and the very necessary process of forging a new
relationship between the communities that is not constantly undermined by differing interpretations of the past. That said, the overall impact of internationalization in helping Northern Ireland to move towards a prospectively better
future has been positive. Of the factors discussed in this chapter, the American

and the South African dimensions have proved the most influential through the whole course of the peace process, with the former perhaps the more enduring and crucial of the two.

ENDNOTES

1. Alford, J., 'North's strategic value is a non-issue', *Irish Times*, 31 January 1986.
2. *Irish Times*, 11 November 1983.
3. Gillespie, P., 'NI accord is EU-style sovereignty pooling to optimise influence', *Irish Times*, 4 December 1999.
4. Mallie and McKittrick, *The Fight for Peace*, 109.
5. Ibid., 382.
6. Rolston, B., *Drawing Support: Murals in Northern Ireland* (Belfast: Beyond the Pale Publications, 1992).
7. Adams, G., *The Politics of Irish Freedom* (Dingle: Brandon, 1986).
8. Kelley, K., *The Longest War: Northern Ireland and the IRA* (Dingle: Brandon, 1982).
9. Sinn Féin, *A Scenario for Peace* (Dublin, 1987).
10. Sinn Féin, *Towards a lasting peace in Ireland* (Dublin, 1992).
11. Munck, R. 'Irish Republicanism: Containment or New Departure' in A. O'Day (ed.), *Terrorism's Laboratory: The Case of Northern Ireland* (Aldershot: Dartmouth, 1995).
12. *The Citizen*, 18 October 1993.
13. *Guardian*, 18 September 1993.
14. *Time*, 1 August 1994.
15. *Independent*, 5 September 1994.
16. *Star*, 1 September 1994.
17. Oliver, Q., *Working for 'YES' The story of the May 1998 referendum in Northern Ireland* (Belfast: The 'Yes' Campaign, 1998).
18. Coogan, T. P., *The troubles: Ireland's ordeal 1966–1995 and the search for peace* (London: Hutchinson, 1995).
19. *The Times*, 13 March 1999.
20. Seitz, R., *Over Here* (London: Weidenfeld and Nicolson, 1998).
21. The International Body recommended that the parties should 'affirm their total and absolute commitment: a. To democratic and exclusively peaceful means of resolving issues; b. To the total disarmament of all paramilitary organisations; c. To agree that such disarmament must be verifiable to the satisfaction of an independent commission; d. To renounce for themselves, and to oppose any effort by others, to use force, or threaten to use force, to influence the outcome of all-party negotiations; e. To agree to abide by the terms of any agreement reached in all-party negotiations and to resort to democratic and exclusively peaceful means in trying to alter any aspect of that outcome with which they may disagree; and f. To urge that "punishment" killings and beatings stop and to take effective steps to prevent such actions'.
22. Cox, M., 'Northern Ireland: the war that came in from the cold', *Irish Studies in International Affairs*, 9 (1998): 73–84.
23. Tuam, E., 'The European Commission and the Conflict in Northern Ireland: A Supranational Role?', *Cambridge Review of International Affairs*, 11/1 (1997): 8–27.
24. An example of the favourable reception accorded to the Agreement was the issuing of a special statement by the G8 summit in Birmingham on 16 May 1998.
25. Whyte, J., *Interpreting Northern Ireland* (Oxford: Clarendon Press, 1990).

Index